The Politics of Wilderness Preservation

The Politics of Wilderness Preservation

Craig W. Allin

University of Alaska Press
Fairbanks

University of Alaska Press
P.O. Box 756240
Fairbanks, AK 99775-6240

ISBN 978-1-889963-025-5

Library of Congress Cataloging-in-Publication Data
Allin, Craig W. (Craig Willard)
    The politics of wilderness preservation / Craig W. Allin.
        p. cm.
    Originally published: Westport, Conn. : Greenwood Press, 1982.
    Includes bibliographical references.
    ISBN 978-1-60223-025-5 (pbk. : alk. paper)
    1. Nature conservation—Political aspects—United States. 2. Wilderness areas—Political aspects—United States. I. Title.
    QH76.A44 2008
    333.78'2160973—dc22

                                                    2008010054

Cover design by Dixon Jones, UAF Rasmuson Library Graphics

This publication was printed on acid-free paper that meets the minimum requirements for ANSI / NISO Z39.48–1992 (R2002) (Permanence of Paper for Printed Library Materials).

CONTENTS

for my parents

ILLUSTRATIONS

TABLES

PREFACE TO THE 2008 EDITION

The United States has led the world in wilderness preservation. The story of preservation politics in America is one of the seminal stories of American history, charting our evolution as a people and a culture. Public policy is a measure of what we value as a society. Originally regarded as a powerful enemy, wilderness was the target of countless land laws aimed at its destruction. Once it had been largely defeated, wilderness came to be seen as a vanishing and valuable resource and an essential contributor to the American character. New policies reflected the new thinking, and the interval from the Wilderness Act to the Alaska Lands law (chapters 4 through 7) remains the defining period of modern environmental policy. Lord James Bryce, British ambassador to Washington, is generally credited for the claim that "the national park is the best idea America ever had."[1] But that remark was directed at national parks before the admission of automobiles, which Bryce vigorously opposed.[2] Today wilderness areas are a better approximation of Bryce's ideal.

Three decades can be an eternity in terms of public policy, so books about public policy tend to have short shelf lives. It comes as something of a surprise to find myself writing a new introduction to a volume that has aged better than I could reasonably have hoped. Aside from a few typographical errors and one reference to an erroneous source,[3] I feel comfortable with the facts I presented and the conclusions I drew almost thirty years ago. What then seemed a first draft of history now seems increasingly historic. In the post-Kyoto climate with "earth in the balance"[4] and environmental policy apparently paralyzed, it seems appropriate to celebrate an era when government policy makers were able—if only for a brief moment—to elbow aside vested economic interests and embrace the preservation of nature for its own sake.

The story of America's slow march toward the Wilderness Act and the crescendo of preservation policy in the interval from 1964 through 1980 remains timely and important despite a host of more recent books that have added new depth and detail to the people and events discussed here. There are new biographies of John Muir by Michael Cohen[5] and Thurman Wilkins[6] and of Gifford Pinchot by Char Miller.[7] Aldo Leopold is the subject of new scholarship, including books written by Curt Meine,[8] Marybeth Lorbiecki,[9] and Julianne Lutz Newton[10] and one edited by Tom Tanner[11] to which I contributed. Colorado's Congressman Wayne Aspinall, who was a major obstacle to passage of the Wilderness Act, has been the subject of biographies by Steven C. Schulte[12] and Steven C. Sturgeon.[13] Mark Harvey has penned a biography of Howard Zahniser, father of the Wilderness Act.[14] Nathaniel P. Reed and Dennis Drabelle[15] and Robert L. Fischman[16] have written what amounts to biographies of the Fish and Wildlife Service, and Ronald A. Foresta[17] and Alfred Runte[18] have each penned accounts of the Park Service. James G. Lewis has written a centennial history of the U.S. Forest Service.[19]

Critical events chronicled in these pages continue to fascinate scholars. The impact of the automobile on the thinking of wilderness luminaries like Aldo Leopold and Robert Marshall is explored in *Driven Wild: How the Fight against Automobiles Launched the Modern Wilderness Movement* by Paul S. Sutter.[20] The controversy over dams in Dinosaur National Monument (pp. 89–95) is the subject of *A Symbol of Wilderness: Echo Park and the American Conservation Movement* by Zahniser's biographer, Mark W. T. Harvey.[21] It took more than two decades, but there is now a book length treatment of the Alaska lands controversy (pp. 207–261): Daniel Nelson's *Northern Landscapes: the Struggle for Wilderness Alaska.*[22] The story of the California Desert Protection Act (discussed in the new epilogue) is recounted by political insider Frank Wheat in *California Desert Miracle.*[23]

A great deal has been written about the management of critical wilderness landscapes. Alston Chase wrote a blockbuster critique of national park management in Yellowstone.[24] Robert B. Keiter and Mark N. Boyce presented a broad spectrum of views in *The Greater Yellowstone Ecosystem,*[25] and Robert McNamee chronicled *The Return of the Wolf to Yellowstone.*[26] Alfred Runte has written a history of Yosemite,[27] and Stephen J. Pyne, America's preeminent historian of fire, has devoted a volume to the Grand Canyon.[28] James N. Gladden[29] and Kevin Proescholdt et al.[30] have interpreted events in the Boundary Waters Canoe Area Wilderness.

The competition between the Park Service and the Forest Service has been the subject of a book by Ben Twight,[31] and a dozen or more volumes deal with the tension between pleasure and preservation in the management of the national parks: Alfred Runte,[32] John C. Freemuth,[33] R. Gerald Wright,[34] Frederic H. Wagner et al.,[35] Richard West Sellars,[36] Linda Flint McClelland,[37] Bob R. O'Brien,[38] James A. Pritchard,[39] Mark David Spence,[40] and David Louter.[41]

Even the politics of wilderness preservation has gotten some attention since 1980. William D. Doron has explored the RARE II process in California.[42] Dennis M. Roth has penned a history of wilderness in the national forests.[43] William L. Graf has captured the wilderness counterattack by "sagebrush rebels."[44] Doug Goodman and Daniel McCool have edited a volume on wilderness conflicts in Utah.[45] Michael Frome's *Battle for the Wilderness* has been released in a revised edition[46] as has the best selling of all wilderness books, Roderick Nash's *Wilderness and the American Mind*.[47] J. Baird Callicott and Michael P. Nelson have edited a definitive anthology of conceptual wilderness writing,[48] and Dave Foreman has proffered an aggressive agenda for the next century of wilderness preservation.[49]

This volume contains a new epilogue that brings *The Politics of Wilderness Preservation* up to date, but the history of wilderness politics since 1980 is mostly a story of gridlock. The status of wilderness preservation in America has not changed dramatically since the Alaska lands legislation was passed. What has changed—and changed dramatically—is how we think about wilderness. First, we think about wilderness increasingly in terms of ecological preservation rather than recreational space. Second, we are coming to understand that the preservation of untrammeled nature is a far more difficult task than it once appeared.

In 1964 both advocates and detractors imagined the purpose of wilderness largely in terms of conserving a few relatively pristine natural areas, primarily for recreational purposes. To be eligible for wilderness preservation, areas had to be both available and attractive. Outside of Alaska, most of the commercially exploitable federal land had already been developed, so areas available for wilderness preservation were generally of little economic value. Where these leftover lands showed promise for primitive recreation, they became obvious candidates for inclusion in the National Wilderness Preservation System.

Four decades later, we no longer think about wilderness primarily in terms of preserving recreational space. Especially within the scientific community, there is a growing appreciation that the greatest contribution of wilderness may be in preserving ecosystems and biological diversity. Typical of this approach, C. R. Margules and R. L. Pressey write: "Reserves have two main roles. They should sample or represent the biodiversity of each region and they should separate this biodiversity from processes that threaten its persistence."[50] Unfortunately, the National Wilderness Preservation System (NWPS), which has been modestly successful in preserving recreational space, makes a less impressive contribution to preserving the diversity of American ecosystems. In 1999, Barbara L. Dugelby and Dave Foreman reported that 157 of 261 ecosystems were represented in the NWPS, but only 50 of them were in wilderness areas greater than 250,000 acres.[51] In this the NWPS is typical. Again quoting Margules and Pressey: "Existing reserve systems throughout the world contain a biased sample of biodiversity, usually that of remote places and other areas that are unsuitable for commercial activities."[52] Here in the United States, J. Michael Scott et al. conclude, "The small area dedicated to nature reserves on more productive soils at lower elevations suggests that the existing network of nature reserves is inefficient in terms of its ability to protect a representative sample of the nation's biodiversity."[53]

Second, in 1964 most everyone assumed that "untrammeled" wilderness could be effectively preserved by establishing legal boundaries and placing reasonable restrictions on human activities within those boundaries. In the 1960s and 1970s, external threats to wilderness appeared relatively inconsequential. Educated observers understood that atmospheric nuclear testing had resulted in trace amounts of radiation worldwide and that transboundary air pollution could damage certain terrestrial and aquatic ecosystems. Nevertheless, the resulting threats to naturalness appeared negligible or at worst, manageable.

Today we have reason to worry that we have intentionally modified landscape and unintentionally modified climate to the point where the Wilderness Act's characterization of wilderness as an area "where the Earth and its community of life are untrammeled by man" describes a historical ideal that is no longer attainable. In the words of Peter Kareiva, chief scientist at the Nature Conservancy, et al., "there really is no such thing as nature untainted by people.... The reality of the human footprint renders discussions about what areas of the world to set aside as wild and protected areas as somewhat irrelevant.... In the modern world, wilderness is more commonly a management and regulatory designation than truly a system without human imprint."[54]

Increasingly we appreciate how vulnerable wilderness areas are to all sorts of external threats and how little protection is actually afforded by mere legal designation. In wilderness areas across the country, climate change now threatens the very features that have made them popular recreational destinations and attractive candidates for preservation in the first place. These concerns are no longer exclusive to wilderness managers and scientists. In 2007, *Backpacker* magazine devoted an entire issue to the future of wilderness under the onslaught of global warming. Among the dire predictions for various wilderness areas across the country were melting permafrost; extirpation of charismatic megafauna including grizzly bears, big horn sheep, wolves, and moose; wholesale losses of iconic boreal forest in places like the Boundary Waters Wilderness; a Glacier National Park without glaciers; a Joshua Tree Wilderness without Joshua trees; and an Everglades wilderness submerged.[55] At about the same time the National Parks Conservation Association published *Unnatural Disaster: Global Warming and Our National Parks*, supported by scores of academic studies and drawing similarly pessimistic conclusions about the peril to parks.[56]

Although many mourn what they see as inevitable loss, America is not bereft of dreamers and visionaries, people with big ideas who imagine a more sustainable future with more wilderness—not less. In 1987, Deborah Epstein

Popper and Frank J. Popper noted shrinking populations in the relatively arid regions of the Great Plains, argued that current agricultural uses of this area were ecologically unsustainable, and proposed an enormous "Buffalo Commons...the world's largest historic preservation project, the ultimate national park."[57]

In 1991, a group of wilderness activists and conservation biologists led by Dave Foreman and Michael Soulé formed the Wildlands Project. Recognizing that traditional conservation was insufficient to prevent wholesale extinction, they proposed development of interconnected wild areas on a continental scale. Projects to date include regional conservation plans for the Sky Islands of Arizona and New Mexico, the New Mexico Highlands, the central Rockies, the southern Rockies, and the northern Appalachians.[58] The Wildlands Project promotes "rewilding," which "emphasizes large core wild areas, functional connectivity across the landscape, and the vital role of keystone species and processes, especially large carnivores."[59] The related Rewilding Institute, established in 2003, emphasizes restoration of the key wildlife species throughout their natural ranges and encourages the use of ecological, rather than recreational, criteria in the selection and design of wilderness areas.[60] The shared vision of the Wildland Project and the Rewilding Institute are elaborated in Dave Foreman's book, *Rewilding North America: A Vision for Conservation in the Twenty-first Century.*[61]

Established in 1993, and loosely affiliated with the Wildland Project, the Yellowstone to Yukon Conservation Initiative (Y2Y) is an attempt to apply the principles of conservation biology to the vast and relatively intact northern Rocky Mountain ecoregion. This area—nearly half a million square miles generally above 3,500 feet of elevation—already boasts the largest concentration of national parks and wilderness areas in the contiguous United States and Canada. Y2Y seeks to expand these core protected areas, to provide connective corridors for wildlife movement, and to facilitate the development of environmentally sustainable human communities.[62]

Our grandchildren and great-grandchildren will not enjoy the same wilderness that we enjoy today. Nor is the wilderness we enjoy early in the 21st century the same one enjoyed by Arthur Carhart, Aldo Leopold, and Bob Marshall in the early twentieth century. Nor was their wilderness the same one experienced by Henry David Thoreau and George Catlin, or by the members of the Lewis and Clark expedition, in the early nineteenth century. Thoreau advocated preservation because he saw wilderness retreating around him; Catlin because he imagined that European civilization would transform the West as it had the East. Carhart, Leopold, and Marshall required less imagination, because the frontier was closed and wilderness was in full retreat across the West.

Wilderness changes, and so does our understanding of wilderness. Some wilderness advocates have seen their mission as a kind of historical preservation, but the possibility of preserving a particular biological moment in time and space for decades or centuries has always been an illusion. Other wilderness advocates have seen the mission in terms of preserving space where nature can find its own way without domestication and remain, at least relatively speaking, "untrammeled by man." As Roderick Nash observed in 1978, wilderness is a cultural concept. "The road to the appreciation and protection of nature leads inevitably to and through a highly sophisticated, technological, urbanized civilization."[63] What seemed a wild and untamed wilderness to the first European settlers was the known world and home to millions of Native Americans. Wilderness takes on much of its meaning not because of what it is in some objective biological sense, but because of how it differs from the thoroughly domesticated environments in which we humans increasingly live.

So the wilderness of generations yet unborn will be an objectively different wilderness. Perhaps more important, it will be a subjectively different wilderness, viewed through different eyes and seen in contradistinction to a different and ever-changing culture. We cannot be certain how future generations will regard the scattered tracts of wilderness we leave behind, but it is hard to imagine that they will think we did too much to preserve the biological diversity and recreational opportunity associated with wilderness areas. If wilderness preservation is not the best idea America ever had, it must be high on the list.

Craig Allin, Mount Vernon, Iowa
August 2007

NOTES

1 James Bryce, "Quotes on National Parks," Wilderness Society, http://www.wilderness.org/Library/Documents/NationalParks_Quotes.cfm (accessed August 14, 2007).

2 James Bryce, "National Parks: The Need of the Future," *Outlook* 102 (December 14, 1912): 813.

3 These known errors have been corrected for this edition.

4 Al Gore, *Earth in the Balance: Ecology and the Human Spirit* (Boston: Houghton Mifflin, 2000).

5 Michael Cohen, *The Pathless Way: John Muir and the American Wilderness* (Madison: University of Wisconsin Press, 1984).

6 Thurman Wilkins, *John Muir: Apostle of Nature* (Norman: University of Oklahoma Press, 2000).

7 Char Miller, *Gifford Pinchot and the Making of Modern Environmentalism* (Washington, DC: Island Press, 2004).

8 Curt Meine, *Aldo Leopold: His Life and Work* (Madison: University of Wisconsin Press, 1987).

9 Marybeth Lorbiecki, *Aldo Leopold: A Fierce Green Fire* (New York: Oxford University Press, 1999).

10 Julianne Lutz Newton, *Aldo Leopold's Odyssey: Rediscovering the Author of* A Sand County Almanac (Washington, DC: Island Press, 2006).

11 Thomas Tanner, ed., *Aldo Leopold: The Man and His Legacy* (Ankeny, IA: Soil Conservation Society of America, 1987).

12 Steven C. Schulte, *Wayne Aspinall and the Shaping of the American West* (Boulder: University Press of Colorado, 2002).

13 Stephen C. Sturgeon, *The Politics of Western Water: The Congressional Career of Wayne Aspinall* (Tucson: University of Arizona Press, 2002).

14 Mark W. T. Harvey, *Wilderness Forever: Howard Zahniser and the Path to the Wilderness Act* (Seattle: University of Washington Press, 2005).

15 Nathaniel P. Reed and Dennis Drabelle, *The United States Fish and Wildlife Service* (Boulder: Westview Press, 1984).

16 Robert L. Fischman, *The National Wildlife Refuges: Coordinating a Conservation System Through Law* (Washington, DC: Island Press, 2003).

17 Ronald A. Foresta, *America's National Parks and Their Keepers* (Washington: Resources for the Future, 1984).

18 Alfred Runte, *National Parks: The American Experience* (Lincoln: University of Nebraska Press, 1987).

19 James G. Lewis, *The Forest Service and the Greatest Good: A Centennial History* (Washington: USDA Forest Service, 2005).

20 Paul S. Sutter, *Driven Wild: How the Fight against Automobiles Launched the Modern Wilderness Movement* (Seattle: University of Washington Press, 2002).

21 Mark W. T. Harvey, *A Symbol of Wilderness: Echo Park and the American Conservation Movement* (Albuquerque: University of New Mexico Press, 1994).

22 Daniel Nelson, *Northern Landscapes: The Struggle for Wilderness Alaska* (Washington: Resources for the Future, 2004).

23 Frank Wheat, *California Desert Miracle* (San Diego: Sunbelt Publications, 1999).

24 Alston Chase, *Playing God in Yellowstone: The Destruction of America's First National Park* (San Diego: Harcourt Brace Jovanovich, 1987).

25 Robert B. Keiter and Mark S. Boyce, *The Greater Yellowstone Ecosystem: Redefining America's Wilderness Heritage* (New Haven: Yale University Press, 1991).

26 Thomas McNamee, *The Return of the Wolf to Yellowstone* (New York: Henry Holt and Company, 1997).

27 Alfred Runte, *Yosemite: The Embattled Wilderness* (Lincoln: University of Nebraska Press, 1990).

28 Stephen J. Pyne, *How the Canyon Became Grand: A Short History* (New York: Viking Adult, 1998).

29 James N. Gladden, *The Boundary Waters Canoe Area: Wilderness Values and Motorized Recreation* (Ames: Iowa State University Press, 1990).

30 Kevin Proescholdt, Rip Rapson, and Miron L. Heinselman, *Troubled Waters: The Fight for the Boundary Waters Canoe Area Wilderness* (St. Cloud, MN: North Star Press of St. Cloud, 1995).

31 Ben W. Twight, *Organizational Values and Political Power: The Forest Service Versus Olympic National Park* (University Park: Pennsylvania State University Press, 1983).

32 Runte, *National Parks: The American Experience.*

33 John C. Freemuth, *Islands Under Siege: National Parks and the Politics of External Threats* (Lawrence: University of Kansas Press, 1991).

34 R. Gerald Wright, *Wildlife Research and Management in the National Parks* (Urbana: University of Illinois Press, 1992).

35 Frederic H. Wagner, Ronald Foresta, Richard Bruce Gill, Dale Richard McCullough, Michael R. Pelton, William F. Porter, Hal Salwasser, and Joseph L. Sax, *Wildlife Policies in the U.S. National Parks* (Washington, DC: Island Press, 1995).

36 Richard West Sellars, *Preserving Nature in the National Parks: A History* (New Haven: Yale University Press, 1997).

37 Linda Flint McClelland, *Building the National Parks* (Baltimore: Johns Hopkins University Press, 1998).

38 Bob R. O'Brien, *Our National Parks and the Search for Sustainability* (Austin: University of Texas Press, 1999).

39 James A. Pritchard, *Preserving Yellowstone's Natural Conditions: Science and the Perception of Nature* (Lincoln: University of Nebraska Press, 1999).

40 Mark David Spence, *Dispossessing the Wilderness: Indian Removal and the Making of the National Parks* (New York: Oxford University Press, 1999).

41 David Louter, *Windshield Wilderness: Cars, Roads, and Nature in Washington's National Parks* (Seattle: University of Washington Press, 2006).

42 William D. Doron, *Legislating for the Wilderness: RARE II and the California National Forests* (Millwood, NY: Associated Faculty Press, 1986).

43 Dennis M. Roth, *The Wilderness Movement and the National Forests* (College Station, TX: Intaglio Press, 1988).

44 William L. Graf, *Wilderness Preservation and the Sagebrush Rebellions* (Savage, MD: Roman and Littlefield, 1990).

45 Doug Goodman and Daniel McCool, *Contested Landscape: The Politics of Wilderness in Utah and the West* (Salt Lake City: University of Utah Press, 1999).

46 Michael Frome, *Battle for the Wilderness,* revised edition (Salt Lake City: University of Utah Press, 1997).

47 Roderick Nash, *Wilderness and the American Mind*, 4th Edition (New Haven: Yale University Press, 2001).

48 J. Baird Callicott and Michael P. Nelson, eds., *The Great New Wilderness Debate* (Athens: University of Georgia Press, 1998).

49 Dave Foreman, *Rewilding North America: A Vision for Conservation in the Twenty-first Century* (Washington, DC: Island Press, 2004).

50 C. R. Margules and R. L. Pressey, "Systematic Conservation Planning," *Nature* 405 (May 11, 2000): 243.

51 Craig W. Allin, "The Triumph of Politics Over Wilderness Science," in *Wilderness Science in a Time of Change Conference*, ed. Stephen F. McCool, David N. Cole, William T. Borrie, and Jennifer O'Loughlin, vol. 2, *Wilderness Within the Context of Larger Systems* (Ogden, UT: USDA Forest Service Rocky Mountain Research Station, 2000), 180.

52 Margules and Pressey, "Systematic Conservation Planning," 243.

53 J. Michael Scott, Frank W. Davis, R. Gavin McGhie, R. Gerald Wright, Craig Groves, and John Estes, "Nature Reserves: Do They Capture the Full Range of America's Biological Diversity?" *Ecological Applications* 114, 4 (August 2001): 999–1007.

54 Peter Kareiva, Sean Watts, Robert McDonald, and Tim Boucher, "Domesticated Nature: Shaping Landscapes and Ecosystems for Human Welfare," *Science* 316 (June 29, 2007): 1866, 1869.

55 Jonathan Dorn, "All Over the Map: Global Warming is Coming to a Wilderness Near You," *Backpacker* 353, no. 7 (September 2007): 9.

56 Jennie Hoffman and Eric Mielbrecht, *Unnatural Disaster: Global Warming and Our National Parks.* July 11 2007, National Parks Conservation Association, http://www.npca.org/globalwarming/ (accessed August 9, 2007).

57 Deborah Epstein Popper and Frank J. Popper, "The Great Plains: From Dust to Dust—A Daring Proposal for Dealing with an Inevitable Disaster," *Planning* (December 1987), http://www.planning.org/25anniversary/planning/1987dec.htm (accessed August 5, 2007).

58 "Our History," Wildlands Project, http://www.twp.org/cms/page1127.cfm (accessed August 5, 2007).

59 "Southern Rockies," Wildlands Project, http://www.twp.org/cms/page1114.cfm (accessed August 5, 2007).

60 "The Rewilding Institute," the Rewilding Institute, http://rewilding.org/index.htm (accessed August 5, 2007).

61 Foreman, *Rewilding North America: A Vision for Conservation in the Twenty-first Century.*

62 "People Working Together to Maintain and Restore the Unique Natural Heritage of the Yellowstone to Yukon Region," Yellowstone to Yukon Conservation Initiative, http://www.y2y.net/ (accessed August 5, 2007).

63 Roderick Nash, "The Exporting and Importing of Nature," in *Earthcare: Global Protection of Natural Areas*, ed. Edmund A. Schofield (Boulder: Westview Press, 1978), 600.

PREFACE

Like winds and sunsets, wild things were taken for
granted until progress began to do away with them.
Now we face the question whether a still higher "standard of living" is worth its cost in things natural, wild,
and free.   —Aldo Leopold
                                    A Sand County Almanac

I discovered the Boundary Waters wilderness of Minnesota at age 13. That
visit whetted an appetite for wild country that persistently beckons me to
experience the American wilderness. That desire bore no relationship to my
professional training in political science and public policy until my
discovery, in 1970, that the world lacked any scholarly survey of American
wilderness policy. That discovery set in motion a chain of events that eventually produced this volume.

Preservation politics has run nearly full circle in the United States. Early
Americans confronted a continental wilderness and set about taming it.
With the birth of the nation, the federal government became a partner in the
conquest, squandering its birthright to further industrial development and
economic expansion. Today wilderness has become a scarce commodity
outside of Alaska, and policymakers have responded with legislation to
preserve portions of what little remains.

This volume traces the genesis and development of the wilderness issue in
American politics from a period of resource abundance to the present age of
scarcity. Wilderness is a natural resource like coal, oil, fertile soil, pure
water, and clean air. Economic growth depletes all these resources, but
wilderness is the first to go. The growing appreciation of wilderness scarcity, among policymakers and the public, has forced the nation to come to
grips with Aldo Leopold's question, "whether a still higher 'standard of living' is worth its cost in things natural, wild, and free." This is the story of
how our policymakers have answered that question so far.

                                                Craig W. Allin

ACKNOWLEDGMENTS

As what has sometimes seemed an impossible task comes to an end, it is fitting to acknowledge the assistance provided by others. Without their help, the task might well have proven impossible.

For financial support I am indebted to Princeton University and Cornell College. Particular thanks go to Dean Robert Lewis of Cornell for twice dipping into his limited budget on behalf of this project.

For research support I am grateful to the professional staffs of the Firestone Library at Princeton University, the Cole Library at Cornell College, the Perkins Library at Duke University, and the University of Iowa Libraries. Scott Letts and Catherine Mode also assisted in the research.

A host of busy people have made themselves available to answer my questions: Brock Evans, Molly Harris, William Magie, and Joe Penfold from the preservation community; Susan Brannigan, Ken Cunningham, Ned Leonard, Rob McKim, Pat Pourchot, John Seiberling, Steve Silver, Stan Sloss, Tom Tauke, and Rebecca Wodder on Capitol Hill; and Jim Bradley, Donald Girton, James Howe, Owen Jamison, Dick Joy, Gil Knight, Michael Lamb, John Leasure, Bob Potter, Mark Reimers, Cynthia Wilson, and Joe Zylinski in the Agriculture and Interior departments.

For professional advice and moral support I am indebted to Kathleen Armstrong, Nick Berry, Gerald Garvey, Duane Lockard, Elizabeth Sparks, and Robert Sutherland. Virginia Davis and Shelley Wagener typed various editions of the manuscript; Beverly Allin and Phylis Judge provided editorial assistance.

Finally, my thanks to James Sabin of Greenwood Press. His decision to publish this volume provided substantial incentive to complete it.

The Politics of
Wilderness
Preservation

INEXHAUSTIBILITY: THE POLITICS OF EXPLOITATION TO 1862

1

O beautiful for pilgrim feet,
Whose stern, impassioned stress
A thoroughfare for freedom beat
Across the wilderness!
—from "America the Beautiful"
by Katharine Lee Bates

The story of the "march of civilization" from the Atlantic to the Pacific has been told and retold, usually with a considerable sense of accomplishment. It remains a great American success—an achievement of nothing less than continental proportions. In 1890, only 400 years after Columbus first saw the New World and a mere 100 years after the nation received its Constitution, the Census Bureau declared that the frontier had come to a close. In the 90 years since that time, the United States has become the greatest economic force the world has ever known. Its population has become largely urban, and its economic apparatus has engulfed nearly every acre of its land space. Americans paid the price for this incredible economic success through an erosion of environmental quality. Inevitably, the first victim was American wilderness.

In 1962 a report of the Outdoor Recreation Resources Review Commission identified only sixty-four wilderness tracts in the lower forty-eight states. Those tracts comprised a total of twenty-eight million acres in nineteen states.[1] Thus, just over 1 percent of the nation's land received this classification, and portions of that had been logged and grazed.

This chapter and the two that follow describe the forces that have created and shaped the wilderness issue in American politics from the time of the first settlements on the Atlantic coast to the midpoint of the twentieth century. The central theme is that the economic and intellectual development of the United States altered the environment of politics so as to make an issue of wilderness preservation. This thesis is summarized in figure 1.

The first European settlers faced a world of wilderness. Natural resources were available in superabundance, but the labor and capital necessary for

FIGURE 1   THE DEVELOPMENT OF RESOURCE ISSUES IN AMERICAN POLITICS:
THE CASE OF WILDERNESS

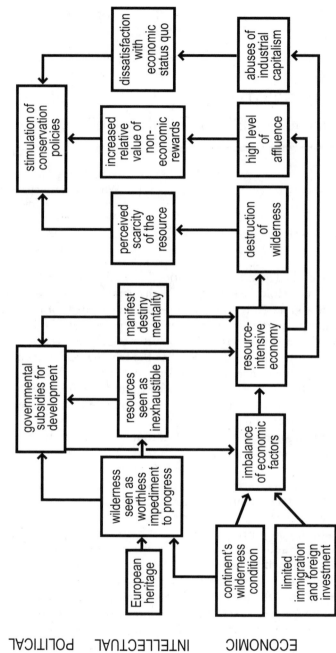

their development were in short supply. The predictable result was a resource-intensive economy. The abundance of natural resources also permitted Americans to believe in resource inexhaustibility, and this perception reinforced European attitudes of hostility to wilderness. This combination of economic and intellectual trends prior to the industrial revolution produced a national policy geared to subsidize development rather than to promote conservation.

Clearly, such a policy could not be permanent. In a world of finite resources a resource-intensive economic system must ultimately be self-limiting. The existence of such a system over a prolonged period of time must inevitably produce major changes in the society of which it is a part. Three such changes are apparent in the American experience. Destruction of wilderness conditions by development has created the perception of wilderness as a scarce resource. High levels of affluence have encouraged Americans to endorse the noneconomic values of wilderness. The abuses of industrial capitalism have produced popular dissatisfaction with the economic status quo, generally, and with resource extractive industries, specifically. The ultimate result of these developments has been to create a favorable climate for public policies that emphasize conservation and, particularly, wilderness preservation.

WESTERN CIVILIZATION CONFRONTS THE AMERICAN WILDERNESS

Consider two interrelated matters: the physical environment of the North American continent and the intellectual and cultural heritage of the early Europeans who confronted it.

The physical circumstances of North America at the time of the first colonization were quite unlike anything to be found in Europe. Its very size put it in a class apart. Exclusive of Russia, all of Europe covered less than two million square miles. The North American continent, though the early settlers obviously could not have guessed the fact, covered well over nine million square miles—all of it, by our standards or theirs, a wilderness. The entirety of the continent was unsurveyed, unfenced, and unfarmed—in a word, uncivilized in the most convincing way. The negative reaction of most early settlers was not surprising. In the words of Roderick Nash, "When William Bradford stepped off the *Mayflower* into a 'hideous and desolate wilderness' he started a tradition of repugnance."[2] Wilderness was a threat to the very survival of the colonizers, the force against which they were compelled to struggle for their existence.

This alone might have been enough to create an attitude of fear and hatred, but the European colonists had another problem. Although the

North American wilderness was most different from anything in their experience, the concept of wilderness was not unknown to them. By the turn
of the seventeenth century, the wilderness concept had acquired substantial
symbolic meaning.

Western civilization had traditionally gloried in the pastoral, not the
wild. Indeed, our word *paradise* in its original Persian meant "luxurious
garden" the very antithesis of wilderness. The Greeks and Romans believed
wild places to be inhabited by assorted monsters and demons, and this
belief was not limited to the Mediterranean civilizations. Northern Europe
had its fiends and wild men always lurking in the deepest corner of the
darkest forest, and biblical tradition fostered the notion that paradise and
wilderness were antipodes.[3]

It is reasonable that the inhabitants of the early religious colonies looked
to the Scriptures for guidance in meeting the adversity thrust upon them by
the wildness of the lands they settled. They had come looking for a new
Canaan, anxious to establish a new civilization in the promised land. They
found, instead, in the words of Francis Higginson, a "Countrey being verie
full of Woods and Wilderness, [which] doth also much abound with Snakes
and Serpents of strange colours and huge greatnesse."[4] Clearly, such a place
must either be made habitable or deserted, and in Genesis 1:28 the early colonists found sufficient formal justification for their course. "The whole
earth is the lords Garden," wrote John Winthrop justifying settlement of a
plantation in New England,

& he hath given it to the sonnes of men, wth a generall Condition, Gen: 1:28. Increase & multiply, replenish the earth & subdue it.

In a true developer's spirit, he added:

Why then should we stand hear striving for places of habitation, (many men spend-
ing as much labor & cost to recover or keep sometymes a Acre or two of land as would
pcure many hundred as good or better in an other country) and in ye mean tyme suffer
a whole Continent, as fruitful and convenient for the use of man to lie waste wth out
any improvement.[5]

Thus Winthrop, and, no doubt, many of his contemporaries, joined the
desires of a developer with the commandment of their God. Conquering the
wilderness became a national goal long before there was a nation.

As time passed, life in America was secularized, the Puritan gave way to
the frontiersman, but the struggle to subdue the wilderness continued.
Many a man on the frontiers of civilization looked upon a vast and magnificent wilderness and could see only its potential for development.

ADMINISTRATION OF THE ORIGINAL PUBLIC DOMAIN

Land policy had been critical to the political and economic development of the original colonies. Various measures had to be devised to deprive the Indian inhabitants of their lands without provoking widespread warfare. Once this was accomplished, and sometimes before it was, there was the problem of distributing land to settlers. Numerous practices were used, influenced by geography, climate, and the varied legal traditions brought from Europe, but most colonial proprietors were eager to get land into the hands of those who would work it.[6]

During the Revolutionary War, a question arose about the disposition of the "western" land claims of some of the thirteen colonies. These claims were the result of the vague language in most of the original colonial land grants. Grants to seven of the thirteen colonies ceded all lands between certain parallels of latitude from the Atlantic to the Pacific, though in practice even these claims were terminated at the Mississippi River after 1763. This termination resulted from English acceptance of the Spanish claim to the territory west of the river. The Quebec Act of 1774 made most western land claims of Massachusetts, Connecticut, New York, and Virginia a part of Quebec, but this Northwest Territory was returned in the peace settlement after the war.[7]

These state claims were vast and many overlapped; but some states had none at all. Led by Maryland, states without western land claims pressed for common ownership of all western lands by the federal government. Such demands were given substance after the war by the fact that the Northwest Territory had, in effect, been won by the Continental army. Commonly owned lands also would solve a major crisis for the Continental Congress, which had promised a military land bounty for those who deserted the enemy ranks or who served the Continental army for the duration. The advocates of national ownership were eventually victorious. Between 1781 and 1802 a public domain of 237 million acres was ceded to the federal government by the states.[8]

Governance for the public domain was an early problem for the new nation. Thomas Jefferson is often quoted as favoring free distribution of the lands to actual settlers,[9] but his idea was not to be officially recognized as national policy for nearly 100 years. The majority opinion seemed to be that the sale of the public lands offered the surest remedy for the outstanding war debt. This desire to raise revenue prompted passage of the Land Ordinance of 1785, but market conditions ensured that land would be cheap. States were selling land for a few cents an acre, and while the federal land was presumably to be sold for no less than one dollar an acre, payment in depreciated government securities made federal land competitive.[10] This act was not much help to the small settler, who generally had to buy from speculators, but many ignored technicalities of ownership and just settled where they wished. This illegal settlement, or "squatting," had become well established before the Revolution, especially in the South, and the government apparently lacked either the will or the resources to prevent it.

Federal land management in the early years of the Republic was a virtual merry-go-round of acquisition and disposal. The Land Ordinance of 1785 and wholesale squatting set the tone for early dispositions. All the while, the federal government was receiving land ceded by the states and "extinguishing" Indian occupancy in the West.

EXPANSION OF THE PUBLIC DOMAIN

Only one year after the last state land cession, the United States made its first major acquisition from a foreign power. Jefferson's purchase of the Louisiana Territory in 1803 nearly doubled the area of the nation. About 560 million acres were added to the public domain at a cost of about three cents an acre.[11] This was but the beginning. By midcentury the United States had consolidated a continent. Five more additions had been made to the public domain by 1853. The Florida Purchase of 1819 added 46 million acres; the Oregon Compromise of 1846 added 183 million. The rest of the contiguous United States came from Mexico directly or indirectly. The Mexican Treaty of 1848 added 339 million acres, and the subsequent Gadsden Purchase of 1853 expanded that area by an additional 19 million acres. Texas had been annexed in 1845, but this added no land to the public domain until 79 million acres were purchased from the state in 1850.[12] The nation's final major land acquisition came in 1867 when Secretary of State William Henry Seward negotiated the purchase of Alaska from Russia for seven million dollars.

Altogether, between Independence and 1867, the nation grew by about 325 percent to near its present size. During the same period, the public domain was created and grew to 1.84 billion acres, at a cost to the federal government of about sixty-nine million dollars, less than four cents per acre.

It should be noted that these purchase prices are far from the real costs involved. The Mexican Cession had cost a war, as well as sixteen million dollars, and most of the lands acquired were held by Indians as well as claimed by Mexico or one of the European powers. According to Marion Clawson, "It is impossible to estimate the total sum paid to the Indians for their interests in the land. It certainly exceeds many times the amounts paid to foreign powers."[13] In addition, some of the lands acquired were already in private ownership, and where this was the case, the United States recognized the private titles. Thus, the territories actually acquired by the federal government are not quite as vast, and the costs are not quite as low, as frequently reported. Nevertheless, the acquisitions taken as a group may represent the greatest territorial windfall ever to a developing country. The cost can hardly be considered significant for a nation which, by the mid-1830s, was plagued by the problem of what to do with its treasury surplus.[14] Clearly, the federal lands were acquired "dirt cheap."

TOWARD AN EXPANSIONIST LAND POLICY

With land being acquired at such a rate, and in such quantity, it is not surprising that by the time of the Civil War the federal government had begun to give land away to settlers. The continent was so vast that the supply of land, like the supply of other raw materials, must have seemed nearly inexhaustible in the early years.

The Ordinance of 1785 had been designed to raise revenue, but the land sales could never be a major source of revenue as long as citizens continued to appropriate government real estate for their own use without payment. This squatting was widely approved in the West, where it was seen as the most efficient way to get land into the hands of actual settlers who would make it economically productive. To legalize squatting many westerners argued for a policy of "preemption," which would authorize the settlement of federal lands prior to their being offered for sale. Once surveyed, the land would be offered to the settlers at the minimum price even if other purchasers were willing to pay more.

It had been agreed in principle, at the time of the state land cessions, that the public domain was communal property. If the westerners had their way about preemption, clearly the bulk of the benefits from these communal lands would flow to the West where settlement and economic development would be encouraged. The rest of the nation, and particularly the industrial Northeast, tended to oppose preemption because it diminished the government's revenue from land sales. Substantial revenue from land sales was seen as an alternative to taxation and thus a particular blessing to those who paid the bulk of the nation's taxes.

Taxpayers had their way and land sales for revenue were continued in the land laws of 1796, 1800, and 1804, but not without concessions to the West. These laws all allowed credit sales, and were regularly accompanied by measures to extend the credit of those actual settlers who could not meet payments. By 1820, however, westerners and southerners were in debt to their government to the extent of twenty-four million dollars, far more than could ever be repaid. In response to this situation, Congress returned to a cash sale system at a price of $1.25 per acre. Like the previous acts, this law was followed by a series of relief measures that mitigated the hardship to actual settlers. There were altogether eleven relief measures between 1821 and 1832.[15] Still, there was no recognition of a right to preemption.

Between 1820 and 1841 only cash sales were made. But for the development of claim clubs, this practice might have been disastrous for squatters. The clubs acted as local governments for the settlers, and sometimes used threats and violence to prevent the acquisition of squatters' land by speculators.[16] In Illinois, squatters agreed that to

sustain each other against the speculator, no settler should bid on another's land. If a speculator should bid on a settler's farm, he was knocked down and dragged out of the office, & if the striker was prosecuted and fined, the settlers paid the expense by common consent among ourselves.[17]

This recourse was rarely necessary, however, because juries were composed of settlers.

Squatting itself was generally illegal. An 1807 act forbade the settlement of public lands prior to legal authorization.[18] By 1837, however, thirty-seven preemption acts had been passed applying to special situations. Two others were of a general, but temporary, nature. This type of legislation encouraged settlers to believe that they had a general right to preempt the public lands, even if that right had to be maintained extralegally. Squatting was sufficiently widespread to lead Paul W. Gates to declare that "the aims of general prospective pre-emption had already been achieved before 1841 by settler action."[19]

Land was not sold exclusively to settlers by any means. During periods of economic prosperity in the first half of the nineteenth century, speculation on western lands became a national pastime. Speculators were not well liked by many citizens, and their excesses contributed to a policy shift toward the western position on land policy. The West demanded cheap land for settlers only and encouragement for "internal improvements," what we would today call public works.

As early as 1811 Louisiana had been given rights to 5 percent of revenue from future land sales for the purpose of building roads, and by 1823 Congress was making direct grants of free land to states to finance internal improvements.[20] Unimproved land was seen as worthless and a hindrance to economic development. Land was given value only by virtue of improvements made upon it that would bring it into the economic system. In this regard the squatter performed the same function as did the railroad builder: the furtherance of economic growth. To many in the West it was apparent that the squatter should be rewarded for his efforts with free land as the railroads had been.[21]

GENERAL PROSPECTIVE PREEMPTION

By degrees, the western position on cheap land and internal improvements was accepted by Congress, and a general preemption act was passed in 1841.[22] This act was prospective in that it not only decriminalized squatting where it had already taken place, but also legalized it for the future. It allowed preemption by any head of a family on unreserved public domain and granted each of the public land states one-half million acres to be sold to finance internal improvements.[23]

The Preemption Act of 1841 was, in part, a response to the panic of 1837. Throughout this period of boom and bust in the economy, the West pressed for preemption, credit, or free land. The pressures were especially great when money was short and settlers were threatened by predatory speculators.

The 1841 act was still not all the West would have desired. It was not free land; it was not universally applicable; and because it was less than everything, it was widely abused. Its major significance is that it marked a decisive step in the movement away from the revenue-raising mentality of the old Northeast and toward a national commitment to the notion that the land belonged to anyone who could work it for a profit.

OTHER LAND DISPOSAL MEASURES

A number of other developments during the pre-Civil War period strengthen the impression that the federal government had embarked on a program of wholesale disposal of the public domain. While the general land laws made land available to settlers and speculators, other statutes provided for military land bounties, grants to states, and grants to private corporations, especially railroads.

The practice of granting land scrip for military service was well established by the end of the Revolutionary War. Succeeding wars—the War of 1812 and the Mexican War—resulted in issuance of new batches of military land warrants. Before the Civil War, more than fifty million acres of federal lands had been disposed of in this manner.[24]

States were given federal lands upon their entry into the union and for internal improvements. Grants to states upon admission were dependent on the specific laws authorizing statehood. Grants for internal improvements were more general, though the actual acreage acquired by different states varied widely. The 500,000 acres granted to each public land state by the 1841 Preemption Act were part of a larger pattern. Close on its heels was a series of swamp reclamation acts. The most significant, the Swamp Land Act of 1850,[25] granted "the whole of those swamps and overflowed lands, made unfit thereby for cultivation" to the respective states. Within ten years, 57 million acres had been selected by the states under this act, though only 44 million had been processed by the General Land Office.[26] States received public land for other purposes as well, including public buildings, education and penal institutions, and grants for wagon roads, canals, and railroads. By 1860 the federal government had parted with 132 million acres for these purposes,[27] including direct grants to private companies.

Between 1840 and 1860 federal policy clearly shifted to the advantage of western interests. Laws providing free lands for states and private companies brought the government closer to embracing the western demand of free land for settlers. As the federal government came around to the western position, the vast resources of the continent were made available for rapid and exploitive economic development. The result was tremendous economic growth and a national attitude of certainty in endless progress.

THE ECONOMICS OF SUPERABUNDANCE

Americans failed to treasure their natural resources because they perceived perpetual surpluses. Labor and capital, on the other hand, were very scarce. What is more, "the early stages of colonization, clearing and settlement, are very highly labor intensive."[28] Early Americans were not only in a position to exploit their resource wealth, but actually found it in such a preponderance as to be a hindrance to development. The wilderness condition was favorable to widespread property ownership, but not to the "population density, factor mobility, and . . . ease of communications . . . upon which the development of a complex economy depends."[29] As a consequence, the colonial economies were resource-intensive, depending on timber and fish in the North and soil-depletion farming in the South.

In the normal course of events, as resources are used, capital is created, population increases, and after a time the factors of production, namely, land, labor, and capital, achieve a different balance. The economy diversifies and prospers; exploitive use of natural resources slows. The United States did not follow the normal course. Instead, the nation quadrupled in size, assuring that land would remain abundant and the capital and labor necessary to work it, scarce. Thus, while the population did grow rapidly, and while capital was created, rapid expansion kept the factors of production out of balance until well after the Civil War. The nation grew at a rapid pace, but its economy remained resource-intensive. There were always more resources; there was never enough labor. It is only logical that families moved on to greener pastures after a few years of farming depleted the soil. New land remained cheaper than more intensive management. Similarly, loggers burned or left to rot many times the value of lumber that they actually marketed. With such abundance it was unprofitable to utilize any but the best trees; the rest were simply impediments to progress.[30]

WILDERNESS APPRECIATION: AN IDEA WHOSE TIME WAS COMING

There was little concern for preservation or conservation of resources before the Civil War. It was, after all, "the taming of the wilderness [which] gave meaning and purpose to the frontiersman's life."[31] The first buds of wilderness appreciation to appear in America were transplanted from abroad. Enthusiasm for the primitive developed in Europe long before it was accepted in America. Tastes that had once appreciated only the pastoral now grew to encompass the rough, wild, and irregular nature of "unimproved" lands. This "primitivism" was part of what literary scholars call romanticism. It glorified uncontrolled nature and believed in the "noble savage." Naturally, America was a great inspiration for this sort of thinking, at least at a distance.[32]

When this new view of nature came to the United States, it was embraced by men not unlike its European advocates—men of letters and urbane tastes. These men were a distinct minority in America. Only occasionally did they face the wilderness firsthand more than a few miles from civilization. When they did, it was by choice, not economic necessity. One early writer who did make a concerted effort to see the wilderness for himself was Estwick Evans. In 1818 he set out on an adventure, which he described in a romantic account entitled *A Pedestrious Tour of Four Thousand Miles Through the Western States and Territories.* He wrote, "There is something in the very name of wilderness, which charms the ear, and soothes the spirit of man."[33] More commonly, those in regular contact with the wilderness had a more pragmatic view. Alexis de Tocqueville made the point most cogently in discussing his 1831 trip to the Michigan wilderness:

To break through almost impenetrable forests, to cross deep rivers, to brave pestilential marshes, to sleep out in the damp woods, those are exertions that the American readily contemplates, if it is a question of earning a guinea; for that is the point. But that one should do such things from curiosity is more than his mind can take in. Besides, living in the wilds, he only prizes the works of man. He will gladly send you off to see a road, a bridge or a fine village. But that one should appreciate great trees and the beauties of solitude, that possibility completely passes him by.[34]

Appreciation of nature proved to be something more than a transient fad among eastern literati. It took on a central importance for American transcendentalists. The transcendentalists, like the Puritans before them, saw religious significance in wilderness. But while the Puritans, believing man inherently evil, saw wilderness as a place where a man risked the falling away of Christian civilization, the transcendentalists, believing in man's goodness, saw wilderness as a force for the liberation of the best in the human spirit.

Henry David Thoreau, best known among early American advocates of wilderness preservation, combined the transcendentalist view of nature with a growing disenchantment with the fast-paced, materialistic civilization that had grown up in America. Thoreau believed wilderness was a necessity for its beneficial effects on mankind, but he was not anticivilization. Indeed, he believed that only a cultivated mind could truly appreciate the totally uncultivated in nature. For Thoreau the only answer was a balance; man must draw strength from wilderness and support from civilization.[35] Thus, Thoreau set forth a view of the need for wilderness that was thoroughly compatible with an increasingly affluent and urban civilization.

Thoreau's belief in the importance of wild nature and his vision of an ever-expanding materialistic society led him not only to retreat to primitive places for occasional contemplation, but also to call for steps to preserve these places for their contribution to man. "I would not have . . . every part of a man cultivated, any more than I would have every acre of earth."[36] To Thoreau it was clear that a man who would have both civilization and wilderness must take conscious steps to set aside and protect the latter.

Why should not we . . . have our national preserves . . . in which the bear and panther, and even some of the hunter race, may still exist, and not be "civilized off the face of the earth"—our forests . . . not for idle sport or food, but for inspiration and our own true recreation?[37]

But if Thoreau was the most eloquent of early preservationists, he was not the first. In 1832 George Catlin wrote of his "contemplations on the probable extinction of buffaloes and Indians."[38]

Many are the rudenesses and wilds in Nature's works, which are destined to fall before the deadly axe and desolating hands of cultivating man. . . . Such of Nature's works are always worthy of our preservation and protection; and the further we become separated (and the face of the country) from that pristine wildness and beauty, the more pleasure does the mind of enlightened man feel in recurring to those scenes, when he can have them preserved for his eyes and his mind to dwell upon.[39]

To Catlin's mind, prevention of the catastrophe lay in creation of a park.

What a splendid contemplation . . . [that] they *might* in future be seen (by some great protecting policy of government) preserved in their pristine beauty and wildness, in a *magnificent park*. . . . *A nation's Park*, containing man and beast.[40]

Thus, in one letter out of the West, Catlin embodied three ideas crucial to wilderness preservation. First, he recognized, unlike most of his contemporaries, that inexhaustibility was a myth, and that American civilization, unless restrained, was destined to cover the continent. Second, he foresaw that as civilization expanded over the land, future generations would have an increased appreciation for wild scenes, if they could find them. Finally, he suggested a "nation's Park," the result of "some great protecting policy of government." His is probably the first public suggestion of the national park concept in America, forty years before the establishment of our first national park.[41]

It is interesting to note that Catlin's remarks corresponded in time with the nation's first natural reservation, the Arkansas Hot Springs. This reservation, however, was not much of a precedent for government wilderness preservation. The belief that the springs had medicinal value led to their appropriation for public purposes.[42]

SUMMARY

The entire pre-Civil War period was characterized by territorial expansion, rapid economic growth, and westward migration; all encouraged by a superabundance of natural resources, an expansionist land policy, and an exploiting, profit-minded populace. The postwar period was to witness the culmination of these trends in an American industrial revolution.

The prewar period contained only the foreshadowings of a movement to preserve the American wilderness. Few Americans had the preservationist foresight of Catlin or the poetic force of Thoreau. The birth of a substantial sentiment for wilderness preservation awaited the industrial revolution.

NOTES

1. Outdoor Recreation Resources Review Commission, *Study Report 3: Wilderness Recreation—A Report on Resources, Values, and Problems* (Washington, D.C.: Government Printing Office, 1962), pp. 43-50.

2. Roderick Nash, *Wilderness and the American Mind* (New Haven: Yale University Press, 1967), pp. 23-24. Nash's quotation is from William Bradford, *Of Plymouth Plantation* (New York: Alfred A. Knopf, 1952), p. 62.

3. Quite the opposite is true of the Eastern religions. Nash, *Wilderness and the American Mind*, pp. 8-21.

4. Francis Higginson, "New-Englands Plantation" (1630), in Peter Force, *Tracts and Other Papers*, 4 vols. (New York: Peter Smith, 1947), vol. 1, no. 12, pp. 11-12.

5. John Winthrop, "Conclusions for the Plantations in New England" (1629), *Old South Leaflets* 2 (1896): 5.

6. Paul W. Gates, *History of Public Land Law Development* (Washington, D.C.: Government Printing Office, 1968), chap. 2; Herman E. Krooss, *American Economic Development*, 2d ed. (Englewood Cliffs, N.J.: Prentice-Hall, 1966), p. 73.

7. Gates, *History of Public Land Law Development*, pp. 49-50.

8. Ibid., pp. 50-57.

9. Thomas Jefferson to Edmund Pendleton, August 3, 1776, in Julian P. Boyd, ed., *The Papers of Thomas Jefferson*, 19 vols. to date (Princeton, N.J.: Princeton University Press, 1950-), 1: 492, 7: 141.

10. Gates, *History of Public Land Law Development*, chapter 4.

11. The area of the Louisiana Purchase is given as 523 million acres by Gates, *History of Public Land Law Development*, p. 77. The exact size of many of these acquisitions is difficult to establish. For the sake of consistency I have relied on data from Marion Clawson and Bernell Held, *The Federal Lands: Their Use and Management* (Baltimore: Johns Hopkins Press, 1957).

12. Entering the Union as an independent republic, Texas was able to make retention of her public lands a condition of her entry.

13. Clawson and Held, *The Federal Lands*, p. 21. White Americans have typically shown little concern over the costs of territorial expansion borne by the Indian population.

14. Gates, *History of Public Land Law Development*, pp. 12-14.

15. Ibid., pp. 121-43.

16. Ibid., pp. 145-61.

17. Alfred Brunson, "A Methodist Circuit Rider's Horseback Tour from Pennsylvania to Wisconsin, 1835," *Collections of the State Historical Society of Wisconsin* 15 (1900): 277, quoted in Gates, *History of Public Land Law Development*, p. 154.

18. *United States Statutes at Large* (Washington, D.C.: Government Printing Office), vol. 12, p. 445. Hereafter U.S. Statutes will be cited in abbreviated form: 12 Stat. 445. Samuel Trask Dana, *Forest and Range Policy* (New York: McGraw-Hill Book Co., 1956), p. 375.

19. Gates, *History of Public Land Law Development*, pp. 162-64.

20. Dana, *Forest and Range Policy*, pp. 375-76.

21. Until 1850 land grants to the railroads were technically made to the states to avoid constitutional issues. When Congress began to make direct grants to private railroad corporations in 1850, the logic of the settlers' position was strengthened accordingly. Dana, *Forest and Range Policy*, pp. 375-76.

22. 5 Stat. 453.

23. Preemption is prospective when it grants a future right to preempt the land. The 1841 act provided that actual settlers would be allowed to buy up to 160 acres at the established price of $1.25 per acre without competition from other buyers. Many earlier preemption acts had been retrospective in that they decriminalized squatting where it had already occurred but made no provision for future rights.

24. Gates, *History of Public Land Law Development*, chap. 11.

25. 9 Stat. 519.

26. Gates, *History of Public Land Law Development*, p. 329.

27. United States Department of Commerce, Bureau of the Census, *Historical Statistics of the United States, Colonial Times to 1957* (Washington, D.C.: Government Printing Office, 1960), pp. 236-39. All figures of this sort should be considered rough approximations regardless of source. The 132 million acres cited in the text is a comprehensive figure including the 44 million acres of swamplands. It does not include land sold, however, whether to settlers or speculators.

28. Peter Jones, *America's Wealth* (New York: Macmillan Co., 1963), p. 6.

29. Ibid., pp. 8-12, 34.

30. The particular destructiveness toward trees in the very early period may have been partly a function of the mistaken belief that land without trees was infertile. It followed that clearing land of trees was a prerequisite to agriculture.

31. Nash, *Wilderness and the American Mind*, p. 40.

32. Nash is the definitive source on wilderness aesthetics.

33. Estwick Evans, *A Pedestrious Tour of Four Thousand Miles* (Concord, N.H.: Joseph C. Spear, 1819), p. 102.

34. Alexis de Tocqueville, *Journey to America* (New Haven: Yale University Press, 1960), p. 335.

35. Nash, *Wilderness and the American Mind*, chap. 5.

36. Henry David Thoreau, "Walking," in Henry David Thoreau, *Excursions* (Boston: Houghton, Mifflin and Company, 1894), p. 292.

37. Henry David Thoreau, "Chesuncook," *Atlantic Monthly* 2 (August, 1858): 317.

38. George Catlin, *North American Indians*, 2 vols. (Philadelphia: Leary, Stewart, and Co., 1913), 1:ix.

39. Ibid., 1:292-93.

40. Ibid., 1:294-95. Emphasis added.

41. John Ise mentions no one prior to Catlin in his definitive history of the national parks. Ise, *Our National Park Policy: A Critical History* (Baltimore: Johns Hopkins Press, 1961), p. 461. James P. Gilligan calls Catlin "the first to make a definitive suggestion that the federal government should preserve [wilderness] lands." Gilligan, *The Development of Policy and Administration of Forest Service Primitive and Wilderness Areas in the Western United States*, 2 vols. (Ph.D. diss., University of Michigan, 1954), 1:10. Catlin's statement is a public one because his letter is, in effect, a correspondent's report published by the *New York Daily Commercial Advertiser* in 1833.

42. Ise, *Our National Park Policy*, p. 13.

> "And God blessed them, and God said to them, 'Be
> fruitful and multiply, and fill the earth and subdue it;
> and have dominion over the fish of the sea and over
> the birds of the air and over every living thing that
> moves upon the earth.' "
>
> —Genesis I: 28 [R.S.V.]

Although the Civil War was not particularly important in the history of wilderness preservation,[1] the political situation which resulted was. Prewar history had been characterized by the gradual development of a political alliance between the Northeast and the West. One of the consequences had been the increasing dominance of the western point of view on the questions of land dispositions and internal improvements.

The election of 1860 was the culmination of this alliance. It brought to power a new Republican party very much oriented to the industrial economy of the Northeast, and a Republican president from Illinois, Abraham Lincoln. With the South's secession from the Union, most of the opposition to the policies advocated by North and West disappeared from Congress. The result was a rapid stream of major legislation with obvious sectional implications. Even before Lincoln's inauguration, the Republican Congress had passed the Morrill Act, the nation's first comprehensive protective tariff. The National Bank Act was passed in 1863 to provide the banking stability an industrial economy needed. A contract labor law, passed in 1864 to encourage immigration and mitigate the labor shortage, also served the interests of the business community. Other legislation more clearly served the interests of the West. Two legislative landmarks were passed in 1862. The Homestead Act culminated the long movement toward a policy of free land for settlers, and the Pacific Railway Act ushered in America's Gilded Age, the railroad era.

The Homestead Act of 1862[2] was not the first act to provide free land to settlers,[3] but it was the first general statute to do so, and, consequently, the most significant.[4] The act allowed any man over the age of twenty-one to enter 160 acres of surveyed land subject to preemption and, after a period of five years' residency, obtain title to it, paying only a filing fee.[5]

GRANTS TO RAILROADS: WHOLESALE ALIENATION OF THE PUBLIC DOMAIN[6]

The passage of the Pacific Railway Act of 1862[7] showed the continuing coincidence of liberal land policies and internal improvements—the major planks in the western economic platform. Under this act, as modified on July 2, 1864,[8] the Union Pacific and Central Pacific railroads were authorized to build a transcontinental railroad, for which they were to receive a 400-foot right of way and 20 odd-numbered sections, a total of 12,800 acres, for every mile of track built, free use of timber and stone from the public domain, and federal loans of up to forty-eight thousand dollars per mile to cover construction costs.[9] This act set the precedent for direct federal grants to railroad companies. It was probably not considered a major change of policy, since the grantee, whether state or corporation, was expected to sell the land to individuals. In any case, the government's decision was forced by the absence of any states through which to channel the funds.[10]

This was but the first of the major railroad grants. By far the largest was made to the Northern Pacific Railroad Company in 1864. The total area granted is estimated to be 45 million acres, or more than 21,000 acres for each of the 2,128 miles of track from Duluth to Tacoma and Portland. The grant amounted to more than 33 square miles of land for every mile of track, but the construction was so arduous that the Northern Pacific bankrupted itself once prior to eventual completion of the project in 1883.[11] While the Northern Pacific grant was the greatest ever conferred by Congress, it was not unusually generous. Other railroads received substantially the same terms, but for shorter constructions.

Altogether, Congress granted more than 94 million acres to various railroads, mostly in the space of a few years during and immediately after the Civil War. An additional 37 million acres were granted to the states for railroad construction. Generally, this land was transferred to corporate hands with no attempt on the part of the states to profit from the transaction. Finally, about 16 million acres, granted to states for internal improvements generally, were channeled into railroad projects. The sum of these grants—182 million acres, including 35 million granted by the state of Texas—is some measure of the price that was paid for the rapid development of the West between 1850 and 1870.[12]

The West's desires for free land and internal improvements proved to be not altogether reconcilable. Historian Paul Gates writes:

The West wanted internal improvements almost as much as it wanted free land and was nearly unanimous in supporting land grants for roads, canals, and railroads. Yet it had a phobia against "land monopoly." When it saw evidence that railroads were not prompt in bringing their lands on the market and putting them into the hands of farm makers, the West turned from warm friendship to outright hostility to the railroads.[13]

Although the railroads had been considered a blessing in the West, the huge railroad holdings presented the same problem to the settler as the vast and hated holdings of eastern speculators. In addition, the railroads' monopolistic control of western trade routes seriously affected the agrarian population and contributed to such antirailroad movements as the Patrons of Husbandry (1867), commonly called "Grangers"; the National Farmers' Alliance (1880); the Farmers' Alliance and Industrial Union (1888); and the Populist movement. The antirailroad sentiment is apparent in the 1892 platform of the Populist party, which called for government ownership of the railroads and government confiscation of railroad lands for distribution to actual settlers.

The western dissatisfaction with the railroads was symptomatic of a growing public displeasure with the abuses of laissez-faire industrialism in the second half of the nineteenth century. This dissatisfaction was to be an important ingredient in the coming of age of the conservation movement between 1872 and 1916.

GRANTS TO INDIVIDUALS: RETAIL ALIENATION OF THE PUBLIC DOMAIN

The Homestead Act opened the floodgate to other free-land bills in much the same manner that the Pacific Railway Act had paved the way for further railroad grants. The Homestead Act had not repealed the Preemption Act, so many settlers were able to occupy two quarter sections, one under the provisions of each law.

Passage of the Timber Culture Act of 1873 allowed entry of a third quarter section if the entryman planted and cultivated forty acres of trees.[14] The Timber Culture Act did not have the desired consequences.[15] Most westerners entered land under the act only for the purpose of selling their rights to it later. This is an interesting example of the abuses to which federal land law was easily subjected. Entry under the Timber Culture Act gave control of the land to the entryman for thirteen years. During this time land became more scarce and prices rose, but without actual title there were no taxes to be paid. Latecomers were sometimes willing to pay a settler to relinquish his claim so they could preempt or homestead the land. This method was one by which westerners could engage in minor land speculation without capital. It was illegal, but there was no real threat of prosecution.[16]

By 1877 it was widely recognized in Washington that in arid and semiarid regions more land was required to sustain a family farm. The Desert Land Act passed in that year authorized the entry of a full section, 640 acres, at twenty-five cents per acre. If irrigation proved successful, full title could be obtained by the payment of an additional dollar per acre.[17] The act's major use was as a tool for the fraudulent acquisition of water rights by stockmen and others.[18]

T. H. Watkins and Charles Watson provide a vision of the possibilities that emerge from the application of multiple federal land disposal statutes. They suggest a "relatively modest cattle outfit" run by a family of four adults with twelve hired hands.

If each member of the family and each cowboy filed under [the Homestead, Timber Culture, and Desert Land] laws, that outfit could accumulate no less than 15,360 acres of public lands. It is of such stuff that empires are made, and it should come as no surprise to learn that dozens of cattle operations were not "outfits," but baronies comprising hundreds of thousands of acres.[19]

THE USE AND ABUSE OF TIMBER

In June of 1878 two more significant acts designed to dispose of federal assets were passed. The Free Timber Act[20] allowed residents of the Rocky Mountain states to cut timber on government mineral lands for nearly any purpose except resale. The Timber and Stone Act[21] offered for sale nonagricultural lands chiefly valuable for timber or stone in Nevada and the three Pacific Coast states. The price was to be $2.50 per acre, and buyers were to be limited to a single quarter section. The Timber and Stone Act was pushed through Congress by representatives from the West Coast, and it provided a convenient way for speculators and lumbermen to amass large tracts of valuable timber for a pittance, using fraudulent entries. According to Gates, the $2.50-per-acre price represented less than 10 percent of the value of the timber alone, for the act was used primarily in the forests of giant redwood on the Pacific Coast where as much as 200,000 board feet of lumber could be harvested per acre.[22]

The timber industry was of great importance to the national economy during this period. At its zenith, employment in timber production exceeded that in all industries but farming, mining, and railroading.[23] Timber harvest flourished because farming, mining, and railroading demanded vast quantities of wood for fencing, construction, and fuel. Despite its importance, all was not well with the timber industry. No national timber policy existed and the level of waste was phenomenal.

When settlers moved into the old Northwest, the loggers moved with them. Where wood was sparse, whatever was found was cut. Timber on public lands was considered common property by most settlers, and private property was often considered public. In areas where wood was plentiful like Michigan, Wisconsin, and Minnesota, enterprising lumbermen went to work to supply the needs of the area's growing population.

The first feeble attempts to prosecute timber trespass had been made in the 1850s, but this sort of law enforcement was considered an outrage in most of the West, where the needs of settlers had an understandably high priority. Territorial Delegate Henry Hastings Sibley of Minnesota, reflecting the common view, called efforts to uphold the law "a disgrace to the country and to the Nineteenth Century."[24] Early timber agents had to make their money from the fines they levied, a situation which led to many abuses and made these early forest rangers even less welcome in areas where they were already considered something of a plague.

The tenure of Carl Schurz as interior secretary, beginning in 1877, was a marked exception to the general rule of lax enforcement of the timber laws. Schurz was familiar with the forest practices of Europe and echoed the early preservationists in his desire to preserve a portion of America's finest forest land from development.[25] It was to blunt the efforts of Schurz and others of like mind that Congress passed the Free Timber and Timber and Stone acts. Still, there were indications that to an increasing degree, those in positions of public trust were aware that timber depredations were an important matter requiring governmental action of some kind.

MINING AND MINERALS

The history of federal control of mining parallels the history of the general land laws. After an early experiment with the leasing of land for the production of lead, Congress entered a period of wholesale cash disposal of mineral lands. Generally, the minimum price was higher than that set for agricultural lands, but procedures were similar, including frequent acknowledgment of a preemptory right for those working the lands prior to sale.[26]

In 1849 and 1850 events occurred that were to set the tone for mineral law in the latter half of the nineteenth century. The onslaught of the California gold rush dates from 1849. Most of the forty-niners committed mineral trespass in illegally prospecting and mining public lands. For sixteen years Congress did nothing about these violations, thus acquiescing in, and establishing a major precedent for, free and unregulated mining on the public domain. When major mining laws were enacted in 1866, 1870, and 1872, it was too late to do more than legitimize the prevailing practice and impose minimal regulations.

In 1850 the United States Attorney General J. J. Crittenden offered the opinion that lands "merely" containing iron ore were not mineral lands according to prevailing federal law. As a consequence of this opinion, the Department of the Interior proceeded to dispose of the nation's greatest iron ore deposits under the terms of the Cash Sale, Preemption, and Homestead acts, with a large proportion of the entries being made fraudulently by agents for land speculators.[27]

CONSEQUENCES OF A RESOURCE-INTENSIVE ECONOMY

Although farmers, loggers, miners, and railroad workers engaged regularly in various frauds and violations of federal law, their industries were contributing to a massive economic growth. Farming productivity increased enormously between 1860 and 1920. This agricultural revolution was based on two trends: increasing mechanization and land reclamation. The aggregate value of farm machinery during this period increased fourteen-fold. Food surpluses and low prices for agricultural commodities resulted.[28]

Mining developed quickly under minimal government controls, just as agriculture and timber harvest had. While most forty-niners never struck it rich, California gold production for a time constituted nearly half of the world's total. The mining of iron ore, which amounted to about 3 million long tons in 1860, had reached 70 million by 1920. The production of bituminous coal rose from 20 million to 658 million short tons in the same period. Previously unknown or largely unused minerals made their way into the economy including aluminum, copper, zinc, lead, and sulphur.[29]

American railroads increased their trackage from 30,000 to 400,000 miles, allowing farmers in the Midwest and South to supply distant population centers with their produce. The railroads were also responsible for the shift of the cattle industry to the Great Plains states where its growth was phenomenal.[30]

All this expansion, aided and abetted at every turn by the policies of the federal government, had three crucial effects. First, it made the United States the world's wealthiest nation. The population more than tripled from 1860 to 1920, increasing from 31 million to 106 million, but the economy grew even faster. Productivity increased dramatically as capitalization per worker grew. Technology created more and more specialization, and by 1920 the United States was an urban nation.[31]

The second crucial effect of unrestrained growth was the destruction of wilderness on a very large proportion of the nation's land surface. Vacant public lands were estimated at 200 million acres in 1920, less than half the figure for 1907.[32]

Third, unrestrained growth provided the setting for substantially unrestrained business practices in the nation's dominant industries. Business abuses were widespread in timber harvest, mining, and railroading. Among the inevitable consequences were a degree of dissatisfaction with big business and an erosion of the "growth and progress" mentality which had so captivated the previous generations of Americans.

THE IMPETUS FOR PRESERVATION

Unprecedented wealth, wholesale destruction of wilderness, and the abuses of industrial capitalism created conditions conducive to wilderness preservation.

Nothing in the early history of the preservation movement contradicts this hypothesis. The early preservationists, like Thoreau and Catlin, were ahead of their time precisely because they were not typical Americans. They were men of letters, and in the 1830s and 1840s that meant that they were in close contact with the intellectual climate of the Old World. In England and on the continent of Europe, where civilization had conquered all but a few traces of wilderness, an interest in preservation had already taken root. Thoreau and Catlin were also men of comparative wealth. What is significant is not that they possessed fabled riches, for they did not; but that their economic situation freed them for substantial periods of time from the mundane considerations that must preoccupy anyone in a subsistence economy. Preservation, like fine art, is a luxury. Neither is possible unless the economy generates surpluses.

In the process of taming the continent, economic surpluses were generated which made a modicum of education and leisure available to a greater number of Americans. These men and women were sufficiently freed of the oppressions of a subsistence economy to value wilderness in its own right and to concern themselves over its diminution.

The logical result was an increased interest in wilderness preservation. The preservation movement gained strength between 1860 and 1916, but was challenged by the emergence of a competitor, the "wise-use" conservation movement spearheaded by professional forestry. These movements existed in some harmony and to mutual advantage for a time, but the alliance was fragile, and as the conservation movement in general gained strength, it was inevitable that its two components would split.

YOSEMITE: THE POLITICAL DEBUT OF PRESERVATION

The first significant act of preservation by the United States Congress was to cede the Yosemite Valley and the Mariposa Big Tree Grove to the state of California "upon the express conditions that the premises shall be held for public use, resort and recreation; [and] shall be held inalienable for all time."[33] This act followed more than a decade of increasing interest in the area.

The valley had been seen by white men as early as 1833, but attracted no particular attention until after the gold rush had brought large numbers of people to California in 1849. In 1851 Major James Savage led a military contingent into the area to punish the Yosemite Indians who had not proven totally submissive when miners had expropriated their land.[34] One member of Savage's party, L. H. Bunnell, was overwhelmed by the sight of the valley. He wrote, "As I looked, a peculiar exalted sensation seemed to fill my whole being, and I found myself in tears with emotion."[35] Major Savage, however, probably expressed the majority view. "It's a hell of a place!" he is reported to have told Bunnell.[36]

The Mariposa Big Tree Grove was discovered one year later, as was the North Calaveras Grove, a similarly superlative group of giant sequoia trees. In 1853 the latter grove, now protected in California's Calaveras Big Tree State Park, was vandalized. George Gale and an associate removed the entire bark up to a height of 116 feet from a tree they billed as the "Mother of the Forest," and took it on tour as a curiosity in the East and in London. As a promotion, however, the project was a failure, for "owing to the immensity of the circumference, nobody would believe that the bark had come from one tree."[37] Those who did believe in what they saw were dismayed that anyone would skin the "Mother of the Forest," and as a consequence, the perpetrators of this feat were discredited. This "Calaveras tree murder" aroused a great deal of sentiment in the East, and, according to Hans Huth, "caused people to ponder their duty of protecting nature against the vandalism of enterprising businessmen."[38]

Between the Calaveras tree murder and the Yosemite cession, the valley was frequently hailed in the eastern elite press, and by 1859 the articles contained pictures.[39]

Frederick Law Olmsted arrived in California in 1863 and immediately became interested in preserving the Yosemite area as a public park. Olmsted's collaborator, I. W. Raymond, evidently had the political standing to attract the attention of Senator John Conness. Early in 1864 he wrote Conness suggesting language for a bill to reserve the area and appoint commissioners to supervise it. The letter was forwarded to the commissioner of the General Land Office who drafted the bill incorporating most of the language of the Conness letter.

When the bill was debated, Senator Conness cited the Calaveras tree murder, but he was also quick to allay the fears of development-minded colleagues. He described Yosemite as composed of "lands that are for all public purposes worthless, but which constitute perhaps some of the greatest wonders of the world."[40] The curious contradiction embodied in his statement serves as a reminder that in the 1860s the notion of worth remained the exclusive property of economics. It is ironic that Conness would argue that strictly economic notion of worth in support of a bill which made a substantial deviation from that narrow view. Federal land grants to states were nothing new, but a grant that forever bound a state to a nonutilitarian undertaking was a major precedent for wilderness preservation.

Congress passed the bill with little fuss, and President Abraham Lincoln signed it on June 29, 1864. Both Olmsted and Raymond were among the original commissioners. Also appointed was Galen Clark, an early settler who was to become the park's first official guardian.[41] Olmsted set about making plans for the park that was now under state control. In 1865 he dispatched a preliminary report to the California State Legislature,[42] but he was hired away to design New York City's Central Park before he could implement his proposals. Although he left Yosemite to accept another challenge, Olmsted wrote that it was "far the noblest park or pleasure ground in the world."[43]

Before he departed, Olmsted was host to several visitors from the East. Among them was the publisher, Samuel Bowles. Bowles was so taken with the idea of preserving the area that he suggested a system of such areas "all over the Union." Thinking more specifically about the areas he knew best, he added:

New York should preserve for popular use both Niagara Falls and its neighborhood and a generous section of her famous Adirondacks, and Maine, one of her lakes and surrounding woods.[44]

This is probably the first published suggestion of a system of parks for the protection of sites of national interest, though Bowles, following the example of Yosemite, foresaw state control of these areas.

George P. Marsh published *Man and Nature* in 1864, the year of the Yosemite Grant. This treatise, clearly ecological in orientation, recommended preservation of a portion of New York's Adirondacks, arguing that considerations of climate, watershed, and sound economics all pointed in that direction. He also recognized what he called "poetical" motives for preservation. He summarized:

Both these classes of consideration have a real worth. It is desirable that some large and reasonably accessible region of American soil should remain, as far as possible, in its primitive condition.[45]

Marsh's book placed science on the side of forest preservation and was very influential. Hans Huth suggests that even prior to their publication, Marsh's ideas were known to those responsible for the Yosemite cession.[46] In any case, the book was reprinted several times during the next three decades. The Adirondacks, Niagara Falls, and a lake in Maine with the surrounding woods were all eventually preserved by action of the respective states, but not until a number of years had passed.

YELLOWSTONE: THE FIRST NATIONAL PARK

In the meantime the impact of the gold rush had spread back to the Rocky Mountain area, precipitating the exploration of what was to become Yellowstone National Park. Yellowstone was first visited by white men in the early part of the century, but the "mountain men" who may have frequented the area were too far removed from the mainstream of American thought or life for their observations to become generally known. John Colter is frequently credited with the first visit to the area after he left the Lewis and Clark expedition in 1806.[47] Through Colter the world first heard of the area's thermal wonders. His reports were greeted with widespread disbelief, and for years the area was derisively called "Colter's Hell."[48]

Several persons are known to have traveled the area before the first major expedition in 1869, and while their reports were generally not believed, the accumulation of strange tales influenced the organization of the Folsom-Cook expedition.[49] This expedition was apparently the first organized for the purpose of seeing the natural wonders. Its leader, David E. Folsom, is regarded as the first to suggest that the area be reserved as a park. This suggestion notwithstanding, Folsom and his colleagues did not want to strain their credibility with too much loose talk about what they had seen.[50] Folsom's suggestion might have died an early death, but his reports were sufficient to spark interest in a second major expedition to the area by General H. D. Washburn, Lieutenant Gustavous Doane, Nathaniel Pitt (N.P.) Langford, and Samuel T. Hauser. The latter two, prominent citizens of Montana, were the chief sponsors. Their standing was sufficient to assure a military escort to protect against possible unpleasantness with the Crow Indians. Lieutenant Doane was the head of the military escort, and his inspired report of the expedition to the secretary of war did a great deal to publicize the area's magnificence.[51] Newspaper accounts by the various members of the expedition were also widely reprinted and received favorable comment in the eastern press. Finally, N. P. Langford traveled the lecture circuit recounting the adventure. By all accounts, his talks were enthusiastically received. Some listeners jokingly claimed his initials stood for National Park.[52]

All this attention produced yet a third expedition headed by Professor F. V. Hayden of the Department of the Interior. In 1871 the Hayden expedition brought back the first photographs and interest in the area peaked. Bills to create a national park were introduced in Congress, and in the space of ten weeks one of them had been signed into law. President Ulysses S. Grant signed this preservation landmark on March 1, 1872.

Since many other bills calling for various land reservations were never passed, it is difficult to explain the ease with which this bill passed. A number of people connected with the project have claimed primary responsibility, but the facts seem to suggest a fortuitous combination of circumstances. First, the various reports had elicited widespread interest in Yellowstone. Second, Langford and several other expedition members were present in Washington and active in lobbying for the bill. Third, the Interior Department's report on the bill was written by Professor Hayden, who was probably involved in drafting the bill as well. Fourth, the Montana Legislative Council had petitioned Congress to support the park, and the bill was endorsed by the territory's newly elected delegate. Fifth, several of Congress's most prestigious members had taken an interest in the area and supported the bill. Finally, since the area was considered useless for most economic enterprises, developers and preservationists could agree on the bill, the former because it would arouse interest in the area and bring tourists, and the latter because they feared private exploitation and excessive admission fees would prevent access to the area's wonders.[53] It is generally thought, for example, that Jay Cooke of the Northern Pacific Railroad financed some of Langford's lectures and may even have greased the wheels a bit for legislative approval. The Northern Pacific would, of course, have been the chief beneficiary of the forthcoming tourist dollars.

With Yellowstone, as with Yosemite, wilderness preservation was an incidental by-product of the desire to reserve scenic curiosities of a rather specific sort. The enormous size of the Yellowstone reservation had been suggested by Hayden largely to avoid missing any wonders not yet discovered which might exist in the same general area.[54]

GROUP INTEREST IN PRESERVATION POLITICS

The Yosemite cession and the Yellowstone reservation began a long history of interest-group involvement in the formation of federal policy concerning the preservation of wilderness areas. Jay Cooke of the Northern Pacific Railroad clearly attempted to aid the establishment of Yellowstone, though it is difficult to assess his influence on the bill's passage. I. W. Raymond, who wrote the crucial letter to Senator Conness which led to the Yosemite cession, was an executive of the Central American Steamship Transit Company of New York. Although Huth argues that Raymond "certainly did not take this step to further any of his business interests,"[55] one can assume that increased interest in California would not damage the prospects for a firm engaged in transportation to that area. Yet, aside from transportation companies, the only substantial institutional interest came from newspapers.

The age of associations had not yet arrived in the United States, and would not until the Progressive era, when economic issues became politicized on other than a sectional basis. The lack of organizations is probably indicative of a general consensus that government should stay out of business and vice versa. There were only a few exceptions to the general rule. The National Wool Growers Association had been organized in 1865, but would not play a role in wilderness politics for many years. Some logging and mining organizations also formed quite early, notably the American Forestry Association (1875), the American Paper and Pulp Association (1878), and the Colorado Mining Association (1876). There were also a number of outdoor or mountain clubs: the Little Alpine Club of Williamstown, Massachusetts (1863); the White Mountain Club of Portland, Maine (1873); the Rocky Mountain Club of Denver (1875); and the Appalachian Mountain Club of Boston (1876).[56] Outdoor clubs did not constitute a significant political force until after the formation of the Sierra Club in 1892.

One early association that did have some political influence was the American Association for the Advancement of Science (AAAS), founded in 1848. In 1873 at the association's twenty-second meeting Franklin B. Hough presented a paper, "On the Duty of Governments in the Preservation of Forests," which prompted the association to make recommendations to Congress and the state legislatures.

The AAAS's recommendation provoked a bill in Congress to establish a commissioner of forestry. The bill was reported favorably by the House Committee on Public Lands, but there was no further action. When prospects for a similar bill looked bad in 1876, Congressman Mark H. Dunnell of Minnesota, the bill's sponsor, attempted to attach his proposal to a pending appropriations bill. This tactic proved successful, and when the bill became law the Department of Agriculture found itself charged with the study of forest conditions.[57] Franklin B. Hough himself was appointed the nation's first commissioner of forestry.[58] Hough served until 1883 and his successor until 1886. In that year Congress extended statutory recognition to the Division of Forestry in the Department of Agriculture, and Bernhard E. Fernow, an immigrant and the nation's only professional forester, succeeded to the position of commissioner.[59]

In 1873, the same year that Hough presented his AAAS paper, John A. Warder, an American in Vienna, became interested in studying European forestry practices. Upon his return to the United States he organized the American Forestry Association (AFA), the nation's first forestry organization. The AFA was later absorbed by the American Forestry Congress, and in 1889 the combined group resumed use of the American Forestry Association name. These groups probably had little political influence in their early years, but their formation marks the emergence of conservation-minded interest groups. Bernhard Fernow had held several posts in the AFA, and his appointment to the Department of Agriculture must have been an asset to the group's campaign to interest legislators in forestry.[60]

THE ADIRONDACKS: PRESERVATION FOR THE SAKE OF BUSINESS

Forestry and preservation interests found themselves allied as early as 1872, when New York State established a State Park Commission to investigate the possibility of preserving a part of the Adirondacks area, as Marsh had suggested eight years earlier. This idea was not completely new, even with Marsh. Samuel Hammond had called for a "100 mile circle" of wilderness in the Adirondacks in 1857, and the *New York Times* had advocated preservation in 1864.[61] The new State Park Commission was less a result of interest in preservation or sound forestry, however, than it was a reaction to widespread scandal and waste in the state's administration of the area. The state had sold vast acreages for trivial sums, and there was little doubt that payoffs were made to those charged with the sales.[62]

The commission, of which Hough was a member, reported in 1873, calling for a moratorium on sales and illegal cutting until the question of a park or preserve could be decided and suggesting that some efforts must be expended "to assure a steady, constant supply of water from [the] streams of the wilderness."[63]

A committee headed by Professor Charles S. Sargent of Harvard University also recommended a forest preserve, stressing commercial benefits. Hough drafted a number of bills for a preserve based on these reports, but Bernhard Fernow wrote the bill that the legislature passed in 1885. The bill's passage was aided by the efforts of the New York Board of Trade and Transportation, representing New York City businessmen. Their interest arose, at least in part, from the belief that further timber harvest in the Adirondacks could lower the water level on the Erie Canal-Hudson River route sufficiently to make it unnavigable, thus giving the railroads a monopoly on transport to the detriment of all who depended on trade for a livelihood. The Adirondack wilderness was preserved primarily out of business necessity.[64]

The 1885 act set aside 715,000 acres of land to be "forever kept as wild forest lands."[65] It is surprising that a bill composed by Hough and Fernow, two men deeply imbued with the ideals of professional forestry, would contain such a distinctly preservationist phrase. Reality was more in keeping with forestry principles. In 1892 the area was made a state park, and the legislation opened the area to timber sales once again. Still, the Adirondacks were poorly administered. The new timber sales and the continuing problem of poaching caused widespread discontent with the state's policy.[66]

An officer of the New York Board of Trade was the first to suggest a constitutional bar to development of the Adirondack wilderness as a method of dealing with the continuing problems. In 1894 the "forever wild" clause of the 1885 act was made Article VII, Section 7, of the New York State Constitution. It has since withstood many challenges, both in the courts and at the polls.[67]

The Adirondacks had been set aside as a wilderness, but for economic and commercial reasons. The area's designation as a "park" in 1892 evidenced growing awareness of the Adirondacks as valuable for recreation. Finally, at the Constitutional Convention of 1894, David McClure, who had drafted Article VII, Section 7, declared that the area's value "as a great resort for the people of this state" was the first consideration in its preservation.[68] There was no dissent. Apparently by 1894 the Adirondack wilderness was recognized primarily for its recreational and aesthetic values, a clear shift from the early American view of wilderness as wasteland.

YELLOWSTONE PARK: EVOLUTION OF AN IDEA

A similar trend can be seen in the case of Yellowstone National Park. At the time of its creation wilderness preservation was not the primary concern of Congress. Yellowstone Park had included a vast wilderness largely to avoid excluding unknown curiosities, and development was the order of the day. *Scribner's Magazine* exemplified the development mentality, predicting gleefully that "Yankee enterprise will dot the new Park with hostelries and furrow it with lines of travel."[69]

By 1883, however, when the park was under attack in Congress, Senator George G. Vest defended it, saying:

money, money, l'argent, l'argent, is the cry everywhere, until our people are held up already to the world as noted for nothing except the acquisition of money at the expense of all esthetic taste and of all love of nature and its great mysteries and wonders. . . . This Park . . . answers a great purpose in our national life.[70]

Yet, at the same time, he felt called upon to give lip service to the economic argument: "This mountain wilderness is absolutely without value unless it be for mineral purposes, and the minerals have not yet been discovered."[71]

Three years later the minerals had been discovered. They were not in the park, but they were so situated as to prompt a move for a railroad right of way which would dip across the park's northern boundary at some distance from any of the curiosities. If the park's sole purpose had been to protect these natural wonders, there could hardly have been any objection to the proposal. Yet, Congressman Isaac Newton Cox of New York rose to call the right of way bill, "a bill for the spoliation of this Yellowstone Park," a measure "inspired by corporate greed and natural selfishness against national pride and natural beauty."[72] The bill's sponsor seemed not to comprehend the growing strength of the view that the park should be preserved as a single wilderness sanctuary. "I confess," he told the House, "that I cannot understand the sentiment which favors the retention of a few buffaloes to the development of mining interests."[73] The preservationists were accused of arguing on "purely sentimental and visionary grounds," but mention of the buffalo seemed to touch a raw nerve, and preservation carried the day by a vote of 107 to 65.[74] In the words of Roderick Nash, "Never before had wilderness values withstood such a direct confrontation with civilization."[75]

THE MOUNTAIN PARKS OF CALIFORNIA

Times were clearly changing. In 1890 Congress created three major national forest reserves in California: Yosemite, Sequoia, and General Grant. These areas were generally considered to be national parks like Yellowstone. The language of the laws creating them was very similar to the language in the Yellowstone Act, but the term *national park* was never used. They are parks today because the secretary of the interior and other interested parties persisted in calling them national parks.

Yosemite Park is a memorial to the efforts of John Muir, America's foremost man of the wilderness, and the founder of the Sierra Club. He arrived in California in 1868 and devoted the next twenty-two years to enjoying the Sierra wilderness and enticing others to do likewise through numerous and widely read articles in eastern magazines. Muir was a transcendentalist in his soul and was capable of the most excellent prose. As early as 1876 he was an outspoken advocate of government reservations of large forest areas in the high Sierras.

In 1899 Muir was visited by Robert Underwood Johnson, an editor of *Century Magazine*. Muir and Johnson agreed that the area surrounding Yosemite Valley should be made a national park, and at Johnson's suggestion, Muir set out to write two articles on the subject for *Century*.[76]

For some time there had been activity by the state commissioners charged with the administration of Yosemite Valley to have the state grant enlarged. Since the 1864 grant, however, Olmsted had returned to New York, and the commission had fallen into considerable disrepute with preservationists like Muir for allowing farming in the valley and other abuses of the wilderness. Rather than extend the state's jurisdiction, Muir suggested a national park of 1,500 square miles. Unlike the early advocates of Yellowstone, Muir made it perfectly clear that the issue was wilderness preservation.

Although the articles did not appear until late summer, the Muir proposal was contained in letters to Johnson early in the spring. In March when a bill was introduced in the House calling for a Yosemite National Park of only 288 square miles, Johnson lobbied the House Public Lands Committee on behalf of Muir's proposal. Muir himself urged Johnson to support the bill as introduced, arguing that federal management was more important than the size of the park.[77]

A unique chain of events followed. A second bill very similar to the Muir proposal, but creating a "forest reservation" instead of a national park, was substituted for the original bill. The substitute was reported and passed in both houses on September 30, 1890, the last day of the legislative session. Historians have been unable to unearth the moving force behind this rapid passage without apparent opposition.[78] It seems probable that events outdistanced the opposition to the reservation and that many legislators were unaware of what they were actually doing. Some evidence also suggests that preservationists and their allies may have deliberately misled the Congress about the nature of the bill by using the "forest reservation" designation and engaging in nongermane debate. Many historians, and Muir himself, seem to believe that the Southern Pacific Railroad, eager to build its tourist business, was a major force behind the scenes.[79]

Although confusion may have existed over the size of the reservation, there can be little doubt that Congress was inching toward a policy that was willing to tolerate exceptions to the rule of unrestrained economic development everywhere. Progressive thought, unlike the expansionist sentiment of the earlier part of the century, was able to perceive the dark side of the system of free—or at least cheap—enterprise on the public lands.

There is ample evidence for this proposition in the creation, also in 1890, of the General Grant and Sequoia reservations. Sequoia was created just five days before the passage of the substitute Yosemite bill.[80] It was clearly to be a park similar to Yellowstone. In fact, the language of the act was nearly identical to that of the Yellowstone Act.[81] Sequoia was enlarged, and General Grant created by the Yosemite Act which declared them both to be "forest reservations."[82] These "forest reservations," Yosemite, General Grant, and the Sequoia addition, were to be administered in precisely the same way as Sequoia and Yellowstone national parks. Thus, while it seems likely that the Yosemite Act was more generous than it might have been had all interested parties been consulted, when taken together with the Sequoia Act, there can be little doubt that Congress was fully aware that it was making "scenic reservations" with strong protective clauses, whether called forest reservations or national parks.[83]

THE FIRST NATIONAL FORESTS

The 1890s were a historic period for American forestry as well, as advocates of preservation and forestry joined together to create the National Forest System.

The first bills for the creation of forest reserves had been introduced in Congress in 1876, several years after the Yosemite and Yellowstone scenic reservations. These early bills were inspired, for the most part, by a few conservation-minded individuals like Interior Secretary Schurz. Nothing came of these early attempts, and the same fate befell a major effort in 1889—a bill which had the endorsement of Forestry Division Chief Fernow and the American Forestry Congress (AFC). Pressure continued to mount, however. The AFC petitioned President Benjamin Harrison in 1899, and, together with the American Association for the Advancement of Science, sent a delegation to lobby for forest reserves with Interior Secretary John W. Noble.[84]

This pressure bore fruit with the passage of the so-called Forest Reserve Act of 1891.[85] In truth, the Forest Reserve Act was merely Section 24 of a general land law revision that repealed the Preemption and Timber Culture acts among other things. Neither the House nor Senate version of the bill had included any forest reserve provision, but strong enough sentiment for such a provision was felt at the White House and in the Interior Department that Secretary Noble was able to threaten a presidential veto if the bill emerged from the conference committee without a forest reserve provision. The provision was added, and the bill passed both houses without fanfare in the closing days of the legislative session.

John Ise argues that only a chain of unusual circumstances allowed the bill to pass in 1891. It seems probable that the most important factors were an unusually hospitable conference committee, the rush of end-of-the-session measures, and the fact that Section 24 could not have been removed from the conference report without killing the whole bill. Since it was a major piece of legislation, and one that had been fully debated and carefully compromised among various factions, members of Congress were probably willing to risk the consequences of Section 24 to secure the remainder of the bill.[86] Perhaps the best evidence for the proposition that this major conservation measure was forced on an unwilling Congress is the other acts that passed at about the same time, which further encouraged the desolation of forests on the public domain[87] and the Forest Reserve Act itself, which contained no provisions for the protection or administration of the reserves that might be created. Ise concluded:

The laws for the disposal of timber on the public domain were worse in 1891 than they had been in 1878, just as they had been worse in 1878 than ever before.[88]

The absence of a statutory management scheme did not deter President Harrison who proclaimed the Yellowstone Forest Reserve almost immediately. By the end of 1893 he and his successor, President Grover Cleveland, had "reserved" well over seventeen million acres. These forest reserves pleased preservation interests but infuriated most development-minded westerners. Leaders of the forestry movement were also displeased. They favored management plans that would allow the practice of scientific forestry, not mere reservations. Beset by these conflicting interests, Congress was unable to act. The designated forests remained simply "reserved."

In 1896, after five years of deadlock in Congress, the National Academy of Science was asked to prepare a report on the forest reserves in hopes that the organization's recommendation would stimulate Congress to act. The academy appointed a commission to prepare the report, but the commission divided over the question of whether a plan of management for the reserves, or the creation of new reserves, was the first priority. Gifford Pinchot, the commission's consulting forester, favored a management plan, but the majority, including Harvard's Charles Sargent, commission chairman, recommended creating new reserves. President Cleveland had supported the development of a management plan, but he followed the academy's recommendation and created thirteen new forest reserves totaling more than twenty-one million acres.[89]

By following the recommendation of the academy, President Cleveland had raised the stakes without resolving the basic issue. The forests were reserved, but for what purpose? Many westerners concluded that the reserves, like the national parks, might be permanently closed to resource use and moved to have the reservations canceled by Congress. A bill was passed by the House and Senate, but it gave western interests less than they had hoped for. It canceled no reservations, but it did authorize the president to disestablish them at his discretion. This compromise language was attached to an important appropriations measure, but President Cleveland was committed to his reservation policy and pocket-vetoed the legislation which would have allowed a new president to undo his work. The veto left a large portion of the government without funds.[90]

In 1897 President William McKinley came to the White House, and Congress returned to Washington for a special session to rectify the appropriations problem. Senator Richard F. Pettigrew of South Dakota offered a management plan for the forest reserves as an amendment to the new appropriations bill. The amendment had much to recommend it to the West. It suspended the Cleveland reservations for a year, limited the purposes for which reserves could be created, allowed free timber and stone to settlers, and approved prospecting and mining. It also provided new lands to settlers whose holdings were preempted by the reservations. The amendment also gave to the forestry movement what it most needed, authority for the secretary of the interior to establish rules and regulations for the forest reserves and to sell timber without giving up federal title to the land. The Pettigrew amendment out-polled its preservationist opposition by more than two to one in the Senate.[91] The House agreed to a nearly identical amendment, and on June 4, 1897, the United States had its first real policy of forest management, a policy largely created by westerners over the resistance of the more preservation-minded East.[92]

Nothing in this legislation suggested the preservation of wilderness areas or even allowed recreational use of the reserves. Yet, it was under the authority of this statute that the Forest Service would designate wilderness areas by administrative action in the twentieth century.

PRESERVATION AND WISE USE: AN UNSTABLE ALLIANCE

The sequence of events between 1890 and 1897 marked the rise and fall of a unified conservation movement in the United States. In 1891 Muir had supported the first forest reserves as indistinguishable from national parks. The merely "reserved" status which so dismayed developer and forester alike was, but for the lack of protection, perfectly acceptable to Muir. When the sustained yield theory of forestry advocated by Fernow and the American Forestry Association came to Muir's attention, it seemed such a vast improvement over the predatory practices of lumbermen on the reserves that he embraced it in spite of its basic incompatibility with wilderness preservation.

In 1895 Muir, Fernow, and Gifford Pinchot each contributed to a *Century Magazine* symposium on forest management. Pinchot had only recently returned to the United States from Europe, where he had studied forestry. He was destined to become one of the major figures in the conservation movement and the nation's foremost forester. For the moment, however, all were in agreement. Muir's contribution to the symposium espoused the forestry ideal.

The Forests must be, and will be, not only preserved, but used. . . . under trained officers, the forests like perennial fountains, may be made to yield a sure harvest of timber, while at the same time all their far-reaching beneficent uses may be maintained unimpaired.[93]

The "far-reaching and beneficent uses" presumably referred to the spiritual and aesthetic values which Muir had consistently proclaimed for the Sierra region.

The forest commission established by the National Academy of Science toured the West the next year, and Pinchot and Muir met and became close friends. When the commission divided, however, Muir favored the majority position that called for new reserves, and Pinchot encouraged the commission to recommend a plan for scientific forestry in the national woodlands.[94]

When Cleveland aroused the wrath of developers and foresters alike by proclaiming new forest reserves, it was Muir who was called upon to defend the action. He did so in the *Atlantic Monthly* and *Harper's Weekly*,[95] still preaching the benefits of scientific forestry on the European model. Evidently the vast outcry against any reserves drove Muir to compromise with forestry. After all, both preservation and forestry required reserves. It was, however, a coalition of "use," of forestry and development interests, rather than a coalition in favor of reserves, that passed the 1897 Forest Management Act. As the ultimate aim of forestry became more apparent, it proved to be impossible for Muir to continue his support and remain true to preservation principles.

The final break came in Seattle in 1897 where Muir and Pinchot met once again. Pinchot had been quoted in Seattle newspapers as approving the grazing of sheep on the forest reserves. To Muir, sheep were a plague on the wilderness. "As sheep advance," he wrote, "flowers, vegetation, grass, soil, plenty, and poetry vanish."[96] The previous year Muir had personally shown Pinchot areas badly damaged by sheep, and he undoubtedly took the Pinchot remarks as a personal affront. When Muir confronted him over the question, Pinchot stood by his remarks, and Muir reportedly retorted, "I don't want anything more to do with you."[97] Within a few weeks Muir had written "Wild Parks and Forest Reservations of the West" for the *Atlantic Monthly*.[98] The article made it clear that John Muir no longer approved of the forestry movement. Muir's change of mind did nothing to injure his reputation as a writer. The magazine's editor reported that the Muir article had increased circulation enormously.[99] Once it was clear that national parks and forest reserves were to be managed for very different purposes, Muir devoted himself to parks. He did not oppose further reserves, but he never again devoted his energies to their creation.

GIFFORD PINCHOT: BUREAUCRATIC IMPERIALIST

In 1898 Fernow resigned and Pinchot became head of the Agriculture Department's Bureau of Forestry. He immediately set out to relieve the Interior Department of the forest reserves. There was a certain logic in this plan, for the government's only trained foresters were in Pinchot's bureau, and administration of the reserves was very awkward. Pinchot wrote directives for Interior Secretary Ethan A. Hitchcock, who then passed them to his subordinates in the General Land Office for implementation. The situation was so cumbersome that even Hitchcock endorsed Pinchot's proposal to transfer the forest reserves to the Department of Agriculture.[100]

Pinchot's plan was facilitated by two events. The first was the elevation of Theodore Roosevelt to the presidency. Roosevelt was an ardent conservationist, and Pinchot quickly became a most trusted advisor. As long as Roosevelt held office, Pinchot could count on presidential backing for his projects. The second event is less specific. It is the emergence of a dominant point of view about forests that rejected the exploitive use of the past. This movement coincides with, and may well be part of, the Progressive rejection of monopoly capitalism. Massive land frauds in Oregon at about this time served to attract a great deal of public attention to the abuses being perpetrated by many large lumber companies and the occasional complicity of employees of the Interior Department.[101]

Forest management legislation had been passed in 1897 by a coalition of user and forestry interests. That legislation could never be fully functional, however, as long as the reserves remained in the Department of the Interior and the Bureau of Forestry in the Department of Agriculture. The Interior Department was really only capable of protection, a function it was trying hard to fulfill, by restricting grazing, among other things. Meanwhile, under Pinchot, the Bureau of Forestry was more sympathetic to stockmen. These circumstances allowed western interests to swing the balance in favor of Pinchot's proposal.[102] The result was transfer in 1905 of all the nation's forest reserves to the Bureau of Forestry, thereafter known as the Forest Service.[103]

There can be little doubt that Pinchot wanted the national parks for his bureaucratic empire, as well. Pinchot was forever suggesting commissions and conferences on conservation matters, and President Roosevelt frequently acquiesced. Pinchot was invariably a participant, and he used these vehicles to further his own conservation goals. The Committee on the Organization of Government Scientific Work (1903) is an early example. The committee dutifully reported:

The custody and care of the National Forest Reserves and of the National Parks, now in the Department of Interior, should be transferred to the Department of Agriculture. . . . The care and administration of the National Parks is work so closely allied to that of the care of the Forest Reserves as to make it evident that they should be subjected to the same control.[104]

Samuel Trask Dana sums the matter up neatly.

The recommendation [he writes] is not surprising in view of the fact that the Committee was suggested by Pinchot, included him as one of its members, and held most of its meetings at his house.[105]

Gifford Pinchot's influence on the president was demonstrated in Roosevelt's keynote speech to the Society of American Foresters, meeting in 1903 in Pinchot's home. The president told the foresters that the object of United States forest policy was not primarily

to preserve the forests because they are beautiful, though that is good in itself; but the primary object . . . is the making of prosperous homes. . . . Your attention must be directed not to the preservation of the forests as an end in itself, but as a means for preserving and increasing the prosperity of the nation. "Forestry is the preservation of the forests by wise use."[106]

THE RECESSION OF YOSEMITE VALLEY

If President Roosevelt was well attuned to the appeals of Pinchot, he was not entirely deaf to the voices of preservation. The president visited Yosemite in May of 1903 and spent four days with John Muir. Muir evidently charmed his visitor, for Roosevelt emerged in Yosemite Valley, after a night which had deposited four inches of snow on the president, proclaiming it "the grandest day of my life!" Muir confessed to having taken the opportunity to lobby the president, and the result seems to have been a firm commitment on the part of Roosevelt to support the recession to the United States of California's Yosemite grant.[107]

The dissatisfaction of preservationists with state control of the valley had resulted in the creation of a doughnut-shaped Yosemite National Park in 1890. But the valley had continued to be badly administered from the preservationist point of view, and by 1904 there was some momentum toward receding the valley to the federal government. The Roosevelt administration was eager to cooperate; Governor George Pardee of California had promised to sign a recession bill if the legislature passed one; and, for the first time, Muir was able to get unanimous support from the board of directors of the Sierra Club for a strong statement on recession.[108] The California Water and Forest Association, the Sons of the Golden West, and the State Board of Trade also favored recession.[109] In the face of incensed opposition by the San Francisco Examiner, however, even this diverse coalition could not expect success in the state legislature. Transportation interests held the balance of power.

One such interest was the Southern Pacific Railroad. When the Sierra Club learned of its interest in recession for the improvement of the tourist trade, an immediate alliance was formed. The actual recession bill was drafted by William E. Colby of the Sierra Club and William H. Mills of the Southern Pacific Railroad. The bill passed the Assembly handily,[110] but appeared headed for defeat in the Senate. The president of the Southern Pacific Railroad, Edward Harriman, was one of those people Muir had taken on the tour of Yosemite, and when Muir asked for his help, Harriman replied that he would do what he could. His powers were apparently considerable, for nine senators "who were notoriously controlled by the railroad company" and who had been "loud in their opposition to recession," voted in favor of recession on the roll call.[111] The required federal acceptance statute was not passed until June 11, 1906,[112] but recession was won; and the Sierra Club had been weaned from a band of weekend adventurers to a sophisticated political organization worthy of some respect.

A CONSERVATION-MINDED CONGRESS GREETS THE TWENTIETH CENTURY

Two new types of reservation joined national parks and national forests in the first decade of the twentieth century: national monuments and national wildlife refuges.

A bill had been introduced in Congress in 1902 to abolish hunting in the national forests, thus making them sanctuaries for wildlife as well as forest reserves. The bill failed to be enacted, but the idea interested President Roosevelt. The next year he created the first national wildlife refuge on Pelican Island in Florida. Having no statutory authority, Roosevelt set the area aside by executive order. This caused some dissension in Congress, but the area involved was of no obvious economic value, and no interest felt sufficiently inconvenienced to make a major protest. On the other hand, a number of organized interests actively supported the creation of refuges, among them the Boone and Crockett Club (1885), the National Audubon Society (1886), the New York Zoological Society (1895), and the Campfire Club of America (1897). Theodore Roosevelt himself had been active in founding the Boone and Crockett Club.[113]

Americans were particularly aware of the need for wildlife conservation. With the possible exception of forest destruction, the wholesale destruction of wildlife presented the nation's most obvious preservation problem. Several species had been extinguished altogether. The most glaring example of the need for wildlife preservation was the slaughter of the buffalo. This distinctly American beast had once roamed the continent in vast numbers. Before white men entered the Great Plains, the buffalo probably numbered at least twelve million, but the white man and the Indian decimated their ranks rapidly. George Catlin feared their extermination as early as 1832, and by 1903, the year Roosevelt proclaimed the first national wildlife refuge, the national buffalo population stood at thirty-four.[114] Public awareness of wildlife destruction may account for Congress's reluctance to overrule Roosevelt's usurpation of power. The Roosevelt policy received its final vindication when legislative sanction was given to executive withdrawals of land for any public purpose by the Pickett Act of 1910.[115]

NATIONAL MONUMENTS AND NEW NATIONAL PARKS

Authority for the creation of national monuments was vested in the president by the American Antiquities Act of 1906.[116] These reservations probably proved acceptable to Congress for much the same reasons that the early wildlife refuges had; they were generaly small in area and occupied land thought useless for commercial development. Primary support for the act came from scientists interested in protecting early Indian pueblos and cliff dwellings, but its grant of power was broad enough to enable President Roosevelt to set aside the Grand Canyon in Arizona and Lassen Peak in California.[117] Thus, the Antiquities Act became an important tool that conservation-minded presidents might use in the service of wilderness preservation.[118]

Other important acts demonstrate a growing conservation consciousness in the pre-World War I period. In 1899 Congress established Mount Rainier National Park.[119] The National Geographic Society, the Geographic Society of America, the Sierra Club, and the Appalachian Mountain Club all lobbied for the bill in alliance with the Northern Pacific Railroad. "The fact that the Northern Pacific had a large area of rocks in the proposed park which it wanted to trade for good lands elsewhere put financial power behind the movement for a park."[120] The Northern Pacific was particularly successful, being allowed to select replacement lands anywhere in any state where it had tracks. It was thus able to trade many acres of granite and snow for an equal number covered with prime timber in western Oregon.[121]

Crater Lake National Park followed three years after Rainier, with Wind Cave, Sully's Hill, and Platt national parks all created by 1906. Mesa Verde also became a national park in 1906. Glacier National Park was created in 1910. The circumstances of its creation were similar to those of Mount Rainier National Park in that a transportation-preservation coalition was instrumental in passage of the legislation. The Great Northern Railroad had no land grant, but it was in a position to profit by any increase of tourism in the Glacier area, which it served exclusively.[122]

Additional parks were not the only significant conservation measures. The Newlands Act of 1902 created a national reclamation policy.[123] Beginning in 1906, a charge was levied for grazing on the national forests. A joint Congressional Resolution started proceedings to reacquire forfeited land grants, a National Conservation Commission was appointed, and the first federal forest experiment station was established—all in 1908.[124]

The Weeks Act of 1911[125] marks a symbolic turning point in federal reservation policy. It established the machinery for federal acquisition of land to be administered as national forests. Land acquisition entails a good deal of expense. Thus, the Weeks Act demonstrated that Congress was vacating two long-held policies. The policy that called for the public domain to be converted into private ownership as rapidly as possible, already seriously weakened by various reservation policies, was further deemphasized. The policy of making no appropriations for federal lands (a policy which had condoned massive vandalism and timber trespass both in reservations like the national parks and on unreserved public domain) was significantly modified by the adoption of a program that committed Congress to considerable expense.[126]

While many preservationists had been disappointed to find that the national forests were not to be preserves in the sense that the national parks were, most supported further forest reservations including acquisition of land in the East under the Weeks Act. There was a growing awareness among preservationists that productive national forests provided some measure of protection for the national parks. If the forests should cease to produce the necessary timber, they reasoned, it would be only a matter of time before the parks were invaded. A sound forest policy could prevent that day from ever arriving.

PUBLIC POLICY REFLECTS THE NATIONAL MOOD

Preservationists had plenty of reason to rejoice in the century's first decade. There were new national parks and national forests, national monuments, and national wildlife refuges, a conservationist president, and, apparently, a new attitude in Congress. Most of all, however, a new attitude was at large in the nation. All the early preservation accomplishments had been through the dedication of a few activists, occasionally in league with transportation or other development interests. Now, at the beginning of the twentieth century, for the first time interest in preservation was widespread.

The new appreciation for wilderness was probably the reverse side of the same Progressive coin that saw evil in overcivilization. The idea had germinated in the 1870s and 1880s and had first manifested itself in the outcry against monopoly—especially railroad monopoly—by the agrarian sector. A scorn that had once been applied to the wilderness that blocked the road to progress was now directed against the consequences of progress: industrialization and urbanization. Robert A. Woods called the slums of Boston "the city wilderness," and Upton Sinclair entitled his book on the Chicago stockyards *The Jungle*.[127] Lincoln Steffens's exposés on corruption and bossism in the cities were widely read. Clearly, civilization had lost some of its luster. Americans had discovered all that glitters is not gold. They promptly dubbed the so-called Golden Age of Industrial Capitalism through which they had just come, the "Gilded Age." The new perspective made "robber barons" of men previously viewed as "captains of industry."

A second factor in the new appreciation of nature was that wilderness was no longer a significant physical menace. By the turn of the century most

Americans were largely shielded from the elements. For them wilderness was associated with vacations rather than survival. The 1890 census had noted the closing of the frontier; its demise presaged new meanings for wilderness. The transcendentalists, literati, and other early appreciators of nature had not been men who were forced to struggle with nature for their existence. Rather, they were men of education, urbane and literate, men with a modicum of leisure time and security in the necessities of life. By the turn of the century, with the industrial and urban revolutions in full tilt, many more Americans found themselves possessed of significant economic security and free time. They responded, as had Thoreau and Catlin before them, with a sense of appreciation for the American wilderness—a wilderness which the same industrializing and urbanizing forces had reduced from superabundance to a condition of scarcity.

These factors joined to provoke what Roderick Nash has called "the wilderness cult."

The cult had several facets. In the first place there was a growing tendency to associate wilderness with America's frontier and pioneer past that was believed responsible for many unique and desirable national characteristics. Wilderness also acquired importance as a source of virility, toughness, and savagery—qualities that defined fitness in Darwinian terms. Finally, an increasing number of Americans invested wild places with aesthetic and ethical values, emphasizing the opportunity they afforded for contemplation and worship.[128]

While earlier Americans had seen the frontiersman as good, and thus wilderness—his antagonist—as bad, under new conditions, more modern Americans recognized that without wilderness there could have been no able, individualistic frontiersman at all. For twentieth-century Americans wilderness acquired new value. This reassessment of wilderness was at the heart of Frederick Jackson Turner's "frontier thesis." In 1896 Turner had written that "out of his wilderness experience, out of the freedom of his opportunities, he fashioned a formula for social regeneration—the freedom of the individual to seek his own."[129] Thus, Turner linked wilderness to that which is good in the American character, and contributed to the growing dismay at its passing.

The will to recapture what had been lost is evident in the instant success of the Boy Scout movement, in the popularity of the "strenuous life" advocated by President Roosevelt, in the growth of sport hunting, in the movement to create city parks and wooded areas, and in the literary success of Jack London's *The Call of the Wild* (1903) and Edgar Rice Burroughs's *Tarzan of the Apes* (1914).[130]

Perhaps the most dramatic evidence of the degree to which aesthetic appreciation for nature had grown by the turn of the century is to be found in the comparison of Muir's popularity with that of Thoreau. Both were essentially transcendentalists, and Muir the disciple at that. Yet Muir was incredibly successful in his publishing ventures and was widely read in popular magazines, while Thoreau just forty years earlier had been appreciated by only a small circle of intellectuals. Clearly, the difference lay not in their talents or in their philosophical approach to wilderness, but simply in the increased receptivity of the American public.[131]

It was indeed fortunate for preservation that its popularity was on the ascent, for the struggle over the use of Hetch Hetchy Valley in Yosemite National Park would require all the support that preservation could muster in the century's second decade.

HETCH HETCHY: TEMPORARY SUCCESSES

The Hetch Hetchy controversy began in 1900, though few people knew it.[132] On May 29 Congressman Marion DeVries of Stockton, near San Francisco, introduced a bill that was to become the Right-of-Way Act of 1901.[133] Its ostensible purpose was to clear up the confusion that Interior Secretary Hitchcock had noted with respect to rights of way in national parks. There was nothing unusual in such an effort except that the act only dealt with the California parks. It authorized the secretary of interior to

permit the use of rights-of-way through the public lands, forests and other reservations of the United States, and the Yosemite, Sequoia, and General Grant national parks, California, for electrical plants, poles, and lines for the generation and distribution of electrical power . . . and canals, ditches, pipes and pipelines, flumes, tunnels, or other water conduits, and for water plants, dams, and reservoirs.[134]

It is unclear whether DeVries had the Hetch Hetchy Valley in mind when he introduced this legislation, but circumstantial evidence suggests that he did. John Ise has noted that "the act was in most respects perfectly tailored for looters of the parks."[135]

The bill passed without much fuss in Congress and did not attract the notice of groups like the Sierra Club, which could have been expected to oppose it. William Colby, the club's secretary, has been quoted to the effect that the club had no knowledge of the bill until it had become law.[136]

By 1901 the city of San Francisco had plans for Yosemite's Hetch Hetchy Valley. But from the point of view of the city, the Right-of-Way Act of 1901 had a defect. The last sentence specified that "any permission given by the Secretary of Interior under the provisions of this Act may be revoked by him or his successor in his discretion."[137] This defect notwithstanding, the city made three attempts between 1901 and 1905 to convince Secretary Hitchcock to issue a permit for a reservoir and hydroelectric project. Hitchcock rebuffed each attempt.

Roosevelt and Pinchot were less charitable to the park. Both supported the city's request, though Roosevelt was not vocal in his support, and Pinchot assured the Sierra Club that he favored the development of an alternative site first and Hetch Hetchy only if the other eventually proved insufficient.[138] The situation was deadlocked so long as Hitchcock remained in office, though deadlock meant continued preservation, for a change, rather than continued exploitation.

In 1907 Hitchcock resigned to be replaced by James R. Garfield, who issued the permit in 1908. Still developers were haunted by the last sentence of the 1901 act: the permit was valid only so long as Garfield or his successors thought it should be. The city went to Congress for legislation making the grant permanent. A number of resolutions were submitted, but this time the opposition was ready. Hearings were held in 1908 and 1909, and the Sierra Club was joined by the American Civic Association, the American Forestry Association, and the Appalachian Mountain Club in voicing oppositon to the project.

Once again preservationists found themselves in something of an unholy alliance. They were joined by private utility interests to preserve the park just as they had been joined by railroad interests to create it. The utility interests were uninterested in preservation, but because they favored power generation by private enterprise, they joined with preservation forces to forestall public power development. Preservationists also engaged in a campaign to arouse the public by the distribution of an illustrated brochure calling attention to the beauty of the Hetch Hetchy Valley and the alternatives available to the city of San Francisco.[139]

Though Muir could not attend the congressional hearings in person, he was represented by spokesmen from eastern mountain clubs and he wrote prolifically denouncing the development.

These temple destroyers, devotees of ravaging commercialism, seem to have a perfect contempt for Nature, and, instead of lifting their eyes to the God of the Mountains, lift them to the almighty dollar. Dam Hetch Hetchy! As well dam for water-tanks the people's cathedrals and churches, for no holier temple has ever been consecrated by the heart of man.[140]

The numerous appeals apparently divided the congressional committee considering the proposal and the measure was defeated. Even President Roosevelt backed away from his earlier approval of the project. In his eighth annual message, late in 1908, he argued that Yosemite's scenery should be kept "wholly unmarred."[141]

Preservation programs suffer a particular disadvantage as compared with the programs of developers: all victories are temporary, while every defeat is final. So it was with Hetch Hetchy. The reservoir plan had been defeated four times, yet the issue remained alive. The Garfield permit remained in force, and while it required that an alternative site be utilized first, the city was still able to build roads and cut timber at the Hetch Hetchy site.[142]

In 1909 William H. Taft became president and Seattle attorney, Richard Ballinger, secretary of interior. Many preservationists felt that the time was ripe to lobby for a revocation of the permit by the new secretary. Plans were laid for a letter-writing campaign, and a central office was established for the effort on the premises of the American Civic Association (ACA) in Washington, D.C. Ballinger declined to take action, however, because bills were being considered in Congress. Rebuffed by the secretary, preservationists again turned their attention to Capitol Hill.

By late in the year the General Federation of Women's Clubs had joined in support of the park, but the Sierra Club, with its headquarters in San Francisco, was torn by dissension. The dissidents were vocal and heavily reported by the San Francisco press which favored the city's position. The result was considerable embarrassment for the club's directors. The issue was finally resolved early in 1910 by a poll of the entire membership. The directors triumphed, receiving 589 votes to 161 for the dissidents.[143]

In the meantime, Muir had had an opportunity to take Ballinger into the Hetch Hetchy Valley, and Horace McFarland of the American Civic Association had lobbied the secretary in Washington. Both urged a new inquiry into alternative sites. In February 1910 the lobbying paid off, as Ballinger ordered the city to show cause as to why the permit to develop Hetch Hetchy Valley should not be revoked. Hearings on the show-cause order did not resolve the issue, but produced a decision to order an independent investigation by the Army Corps of Engineers. The investigation produced more delay—more than enough to place the matter once more in the hands of Congress.[144]

There was an additional complication. Delay produced a new secretary of interior, Walter Fisher, friendly to both commodity and preservation-oriented conservationists. Fisher was an activist and decided to see the valley for himself. McFarland was able to arrange to be with the party and was very pleased with Fisher's response to the preservationist position.[145]

Fisher reopened the hearings on Ballinger's show-cause order in 1912. The city had produced a massive engineering report reiterating its need of the Hetch Hetchy Valley, and the cooperating preservation organizations had produced a systematic response to it. The hearings lasted six days and resulted in the city's being given more time to remove the inadequacies that had been found in its report. In the meantime the Army Corps of Engineers completed its report, concluding that Hetch Hetchy was the best site for San Francisco's reservoir, but only because it was somewhat less expensive to develop.[146] During his last days in office Fisher refused San Francisco the permit it had labored so hard to get. Although this was the sixth rejection of the reservoir site, prospects looked very bright for the developers.

HETCH HETCHY: EVENTUAL DEFEAT

In 1913 Woodrow Wilson took office. With the change in administration came the usual second—in this case, seventh—chance for development projects previously rejected. There was a special bonus for San Francisco. Wilson's new secretary of interior was Franklin K. Lane, previously San Francisco City Attorney, and a partisan of the Hetch Hetchy project. Wilson had, in effect, appointed one of the contestants as referee.

Lane was most favorable to the city and agreed to support legislation for a permanent grant of the valley to the city for a reservoir site. Representative John E. Raker of California introduced such a bill, and in June and July hearings were held at which Gifford Pinchot supported San Francisco.[147] The bill was reported unanimously by the House committee and passed the full House September 3, 1913, on a vote of 183 to 43.[148]

Preservationists made a last-ditch effort to defeat the bill in the Senate using tactics that had succeeded in 1909. Massive mailings were made to members of preservation organizations and to private citizens listed in Who's Who. To expedite the battle a new organization, the National Committee for the Preservation of Yosemite National Park, was formed under the leadership of Robert Underwood Johnson.[149] Johnson succeeded in enlisting a good many prominent people in the new organization, but there is no clear indication that the effort was to any avail. After considerable debate the Senate passed the bill by a vote of 43 to 25. President Wilson signed it December 19, 1913.[150] After many temporary victories, the first loss was fatal.

HETCH HETCHY: AFTERMATH

Preservationists had done a great deal. They had made Hetch Hetchy a household word and attracted substantial newspaper and public support. In the end they were simply unable to overcome the advantages that had accrued to the developers when Wilson took office. Franklin Lane was a devotee of the project which had administration support.[151] These circumstances did not bode well for preserving the park, and the open hostility of wise-use conservationists led by Pinchot only made the matter worse.

It was a great defeat for preservation. It was hard to believe that so much work could end in nothing. "Some sort of compensation must surely come out of this dark damn-dam-damnation," wrote Muir late in 1913.[152] Writing to Robert Underwood Johnson a few days later, Muir was clearly aware of at least one compensation. "The conscience of the whole country has been aroused from sleep."[153] That in itself was enough to astonish men who failed to keep pace with the growth of American preservationist opinion. Senator James A. Reed of Missouri offered a case in point during the Senate debate.

The Senate of the United States has devoted a full week of time to discussing the disposition of about 2 square miles of land, located at a point remote from civilization. . . . It is merely proposed to put water on these 2 square miles. Over that trivial matter the business of the country is halted, the Senate goes into profound debate, the country is thrown into a condition of hysteria, and one would imagine that chaos and old night were about to descend on the land. . . . The degree of opposition increases in direct proportion with the distance the objector lives from the ground to be taken. When we get as far east as New England the opposition has become a frenzy.[154]

Senator Reed's incredulity is eloquent testimony to the real importance of Hetch Hetchy as a gauge of the intensity and scope of preservationist sentiment. On this point Reed and Muir were in complete agreement. While Reed's politics called upon him to characterize the situation as a "condition of hysteria," Muir referred to the awakening of the nation's conscience. Both were aware that the nation had been aroused to a degree heretofore almost unimaginable in defense of a bit of American wilderness. The developers won Hetch Hetchy but not without a major battle and twelve years of delay. Witnessing the growth of preservation sentiment in one generation, one is tempted to share Senator Reed's disbelief. Preservation had proven itself a force to be reckoned with. Even proponents of the development had prefaced their remarks with professions of love for the wilderness. Roderick Nash sums up the state of affairs after Hetch Hetchy.

Even the partisans of San Francisco phrased the issue as not between a good (civilization) and an evil (wilderness) but between two goods. While placing material needs first, they still proclaimed their love for unspoiled nature. Previously most Americans had not felt compelled to rationalize the conquest of wild country in this manner. For three centuries they had chosen civilization without any hesitation. By 1913 they were no longer so sure.[155]

CREATION OF THE NATIONAL PARK SERVICE

One of the problems that plagued the effort to preserve Hetch Hetchy had been the major commitment of resources on the part of the American Civic Association to the creation of a central bureau to administer the national parks.[156] Horace McFarland of the ACA was the nation's leading advocate of a unified park service. His efforts are generally credited with having greatly influenced the creation of the National Park Service in 1916.

The concept of an agency for the parks was not new. Bills for that purpose had been introduced in Congress at least as early as 1900,[157] but it was not until 1910 that the ACA's prodding resulted in some discernible movement. The 1910 *Report* of Interior Secretary Ballinger called for the creation of a park bureau. Ballinger had been approached by McFarland on the park bureau idea, and he allowed McFarland to confer in drafting the bill. McFarland called in Frederick Law Olmsted, Jr., and the two preservationists rewrote the Ballinger draft. Ballinger's bill had lacked any mention of the purpose of the parks or of the manner in which they might be developed. The McFarland-Olmsted draft stated that the national parks

shall not at any time be used in a way contrary to the purpose thereof as agencies for promoting public recreaton and public health through the use and enjoyment by the people of the same parks, monuments and reservations, and of the natural scenery and objects of interest therein, or in any way detrimental to the value thereof for such purpose.[158]

This passage was to survive all the drafts of the bill and become a part of the legislation passed in 1916. Remarkably, Ballinger accepted all the preservationist revisions, and the bill was introduced early in 1911.[159]

No bill was passed that year, but administrative rearrangements did give the parks more attention in the Interior Department than they had previously received. Secretary Fisher, who succeeded Ballinger, supported a park bureau and authorized several National Park Conferences in 1911 to help sell the idea. During this same time McFarland had been actively lobbying President Taft. Taft agreed to address the ACA Convention in 1911 on the subject of an agency for the parks, and on February 2, 1912, he sent a special message to Congress on the subject.

Congress was slow to respond as a body, but interested members kept the issue alive by repeatedly introducing legislation for the establishment of a park bureau or service. Finally, Congressman William Kent of California, a man with good credentials among both wise-use conservationists and preservationists,[160] introduced a fresh bill with Olmsted's advice and assistance. Senator Reed Smoot introduced a companion measure in the Senate. Although Pinchot and his successor as chief forester, Henry S. Graves, opposed the creation of a National Park Service as uneconomic,[161] preservation had its day. The bill, supported by McFarland's American Civic Association and largely written by Olmsted, was passed by Congress and signed by President Wilson on August 25, 1916.[162] In its final form, the legislation provided that the

service thus established shall promote and regulate the use of the Federal areas known as national parks, monuments and reservations hereinafter specified by such means and measures as to conform to the fundamental purpose of said parks, monuments and reservations, *which purpose is to conserve the scenery and the natural and historic objects and the wild life therein*, and to provide for the enjoyment of the same *in such a manner and by such means as will leave them unimpaired for the enjoyment of future generations*.[163]

The National Park Service Act was a major preservationist document, for which the American Civic Association and its allies deserve much of the credit. "It is not too much to say," wrote Jenks Cameron in 1922, "that the untiring zeal of the organization [the ACA] . . . had more to do with the final successful issue of the movement than any other one factor."[164]

Thus, although the decade of the First World War witnessed the greatest single destruction of national park wilderness, it also witnessed in the passage of the National Park Service Act, what is perhaps the greatest single victory for the parks, a bureau in the federal government dedicated to their administration and charged with their preservation "unimpaired for future generations."

SUMMARY

The period between 1860 and 1920 produced profound changes in American society. The early part of the period was dominated by a western view of progress that stressed free lands and internal improvements as the two-edged sword that would vanquish a wilderness—a wilderness that stood in the path of civilization. Nothing was allowed to slow the pace of economic expansion, least of all a sentimental attitude toward the nation's material resources.

The resulting policy produced the growth that was intended, but that very growth led to the erosion of the beliefs that had dominated the early period. Growth produced wealth. A rising standard of living for most Americans meant more leisure and a diminished preoccupation with the material necessities that could be taken for granted by increasing numbers of Americans. Growth also meant specialization and division of labor, and their concomitant urbanization. Urban Americans were removed from the necessity of struggle against the natural forces that their ancestors had fought. The city brought its own problems and made those of the frontier seem more distant. Growth produced monopoly, and Americans lost their wholesale enchantment with industrial capitalism. Finally, growth was naturally at the expense of wilderness. A continent once entirely wild was largely subjugated by 1920. Wilderness, once a commodity characterized by superabundance, suffered relative scarcity by the end of the period.

Not least among the changes wrought in this period was the growth of the conservation movement. In the post-Civil War decades it was a conservation ethic which, by degrees, replaced the western notion of progress. Preservation, only an idea in the minds of romantics and transcendentalists before the Civil War, saw its first official expression in the Yosemite grant of 1864. Shortly thereafter wise-use conservation was introduced to the United States by the forestry movement. Preservation and forestry grew and prospered together for a time, but their prosperity spelled schism in the ranks, for it was only a common enemy in unregulated development that held the conservation movement together. The coalition of developers and wise-use men, that passed the 1897 Forest Reserve Management Act over the protests of preservationists, marked the beginning of the end for a unified conservation movement. The schism the same year between Pinchot and Muir, the respective cult leaders of forestry and preservation, formalized the break. The schism failed to produce a clear victory, however, for each branch of the movement continued to prosper and grow. Each suffered occasional setbacks, sometimes at the hands of the other, but by 1920 both had recorded major victories, and each had established itself in its own federal bureau.

The proliferation of governmental bureaus that allowed the creation of the Forest Service and the National Park Service had its parallel in the increasing growth and specialization of national organizations in the private sector. The immediate post-Civil War period had seen no organizational interest in wilderness preservation. By the end of World War I, however, organizations had sprung up in both branches of the conservation movement and in those sectors of the economy dependent on resource utilization.

By the end of the nineteenth century some of these organizations were thoroughly politicized and were taking an active part in the formation of government policy. Preservationist organizations, like the Sierra Club and the American Civic Association, had made an exceptionally powerful showing in the battle over the Hetch Hetchy Valley and had won the fight for a unified administration for the National Park System, even over the opposition of wise-use conservationists.

By 1920 the movement for wilderness preservation had clearly emerged from its infancy as a significant political force. Many battles still lay ahead, however, for wilderness victories are only holding actions. There is never any guarantee that wilderness now preserved will not at some future date be sacrificed, while the very nature of physical reality determines that wilderness, once destroyed, can never be regained.

NOTES

1. A major battle of 1864 is generally referred to as the "Battle of the Wilderness." A preservation-minded colleague has remarked that it could hardly have been a wilderness when the battle was over. Most nineteenth-century Americans, equating wilderness with "wasted" land, would probably have reached the opposite conclusion.

2. 12 Stat. 398.

3. A series of acts had granted land to people who had settled or would settle in certain areas. As a rule these were areas where there was a serious Indian menace.

Southerners who were generally opposed to free land were evidently willing to make exceptions if they were portrayed as Indian control measures. Paul W. Gates, *History of Public Land Law Development* (Washington, D.C.: Government Printing Office, 1968), pp. 387-90.

4. Detailed discussion of this act can be found in George M. Stephenson, *The Political History of the Public Lands from 1840 to 1862* (New York: Russell and Russell, 1967); Benjamin H. Hibbard, *History of the Public Land Policies* (New York: Macmillan Co., 1924); and Roy M. Robbins, *Our Landed Heritage: The Public Domain 1776-1936* (Princeton, N.J.: Princeton University Press, 1942).

5. Most land subject to preemption was selling for $1.25 per acre. Some land, however, especially alternate ungranted sections within the limits of railroad grants, had had its price doubled to $2.50 per acre. On these more expensive lands entry was limited to eighty acres.

6. "Alienation" is a legal term denoting the voluntary and absolute transfer of title and possession of land.

7. 12 Stat. 489.

8. 13 Stat. 356.

9. Gates, *History of Public Land Law Development*, p. 364. A section of land is one square mile (640 acres) and also one mile square. Sections are organized into townships consisting of six rows with six sections in each row. Sections within a township are numbered from one to thirty-six beginning in the northeast corner. The northernmost row is numbered right to left from one to six, the second row left to right from seven to twelve, and so forth with rows alternating between right to left and left to right numbering. Under this enumeration selecting odd-numbered sections creates a checkerboard pattern whether one or many sections are involved.

10. Similar circumstances were important in the creation of Yellowstone National Park in 1872.

11. Gates, *History of Public Land Law Development*, pp. 374-75.

12. Ibid., pp. 379, 384-85.

13. Ibid., p. 380.

14. 17 Stat. 605; Samuel Trask Dana, *Forest and Range Policy* (New York: McGraw-Hill Book Co., 1956), p. 383.

15. At the time it was widely believed that planting trees would change the climate.

16. Gates, *History of Public Land Law Development*, pp. 399-400.

17. 19 Stat. 377.

18. Gates, *History of Public Land Law Development*, p. 401.

19. T. H. Watkins and Charles S. Watson, Jr., *The Lands No One Knows* (San Francisco: Sierra Club Books, 1975), p. 226.

20. 20 Stat. 88.

21. 20 Stat. 89.

22. Gates, *History of Public Land Law Development*, pp. 550-52.

23. William B. Greeley, *Forests and Man* (Garden City, N.Y.: Doubleday and Co., 1951), p. 47.

24. United States Congress, *The Congressional Globe* (April 24, 1852): appendix, p. 486. Quoted in Dana, *Forest and Range Policy*, p. 55.

25. Gates, *History of Public Land Law Development*, p. 546.

26. The best source on the history of minerals policy is Robert W. Swenson, "Legal Aspects of Mineral Resources Exploration," in Gates, *History of Public Land Law Development.*

27. Swenson, "Legal Aspects of Mineral Resources Exploration," pp. 707-23.

28. Peter Jones, *America's Wealth* (New York: Macmillan Co., 1963), p. 173.

29. Ibid., pp. 188, 194-95.

30. Ibid., pp. 138, 156-57.

31. United States Department of Commerce, Bureau of the Census, *Historical Statistics of the United States from Colonial Times to 1957* (Washington, D.C.: Government Printing Office, 1960), p. 14; and Jones, *America's Wealth*, pp. 144-45. The 1920 census was the first to show more than one-half of all Americans living in cities and towns of over twenty-five hundred population.

32. "Vacant lands" are not necessarily wilderness, but that is the best measure available. The remaining wilderness is considerably greater if one includes Alaska's 375 million acres. Marion Clawson and Bernell R. Held, *The Federal Lands: Their Use and Management* (Baltimore: Johns Hopkins Press, 1957), p. 21; and Department of Commerce, *Historical Statistics*, p. 237.

33. 13 Stat. 325.

34. John Ise, *Our National Park Policy: A Critical History* (Baltimore: Johns Hopkins Press, 1961), p. 51.

35. Lafayette H. Bunnell, *Discovery of the Yosemite* (Los Angeles: Gerlicher, 1911), p. 63.

36. Freeman Tilden, *The National Parks*, rev. ed. (New York: Alfred A. Knopf, 1968), p. 302. This quotation reported by Tilden does not seem to be from Bunnell. According to Bunnell's own account, Savage told him to quit dreaming or he would lose his hair. Bunnell, *Discovery of the Yosemite*, p. 64.

37. The tree's circumference was sixty-one feet. *Gleason's Pictorial* 5 (1853): 216, quoted in Hans Huth, "Yosemite: the Story of an Idea," *Sierra Club Bulletin* 33 (1948): 63.

38. Huth, "Yosemite: the Story of an Idea," p. 64.

39. Among the journals publishing accounts of the area were *Country Gentleman, Crayon, Ballou's Pictorial Drawing Room, Harper's Weekly*, and, in the West, *California Magazine*. Huth, "Yosemite: the Story of an Idea," pp. 63-65.

40. United States Congress, *The Congressional Globe* (May 17, 1864): 2300.

41. A biography of Galen Clark has been published under Sierra Club auspices. Shirley Sargent, *Galen Clark: Yosemite Guardian* (San Francisco: Sierra Club Books, 1964).

42. Frederick Law Olmsted, "The Yosemite Valley and the Mariposa Big Trees: A Preliminary Report (1865)," reprinted in *Landscape Architecture* 43 (October 1952): 12-25.

43. From Olmsted's unpublished papers, quoted in Huth, "Yosemite: the Story of an Idea," p. 69.

44. Samuel Bowles, *Across the Continent* (Springfield, Mass.: Samuel Bowles and Co., 1865), p. 231.

45. George P. Marsh, *Man and Nature: or, Physical Geography as Modified by Human Action* (New York: Charles Scribner, 1864), p. 235.

46. Huth, "Yosemite: the Story of an Idea," p. 75.

47. Louis C. Cramton, *Early History of Yellowstone National Park and Its Relation to National Park Policies* (Washington, D.C.: Government Printing Office, 1932), p. 5. Of the various early works on Yellowstone, Cramton's is most useful. Cramton was a congressman, and he is thoroughly aware of the political aspects of the park's early history. I have also referred to various editions of Nathaniel Pitt Langford, *The Discovery of Yellowstone Park, 1870; or, Diary of the Washburn Expedition to the Yellowstone and Firehole Rivers in the Year 1870* (N.P. Langford, 1905; 2d ed. approved by the National Park Service, St. Paul: J. E. Haynes, 1923); and Hiram Chittenden, *Yellowstone National Park* (Cincinnati, Ohio: Robert Clarke Co., 1895; 5th ed., Stanford, Calif.: Stanford University Press, 1940). Although both Langford and Chittenden were principals in the park's early history, Chittenden is generally cited as the definitive work.

48. Chittenden, *Yellowstone National Park*, 5th ed., p. 30.

49. Cramton, *Early History of Yellowstone National Park*, pp. 5-10.

50. Folsom did write an article on the subject, but it was rejected by *Lippincott's Magazine*, where it was assumed to be fiction. Later it was published in the *Western Monthly* with Cook listed as the author. Parts of this narrative are historically controversial. I have generally followed Cramton whose evidence is most impressive and whose viewpont is endorsed by Huth, "Yosemite: the Story of an Idea."

51. This report is published as United States Senate, Executive Document No. 51 (41st Cong., 3d sess., March 3, 1871).

52. Cramton, *Early History of Yellowstone National Park*, pp. 12-18.

53. This analysis is based on information scattered throughout Cramton, *Early History of Yellowstone National Park*.

54. Roderick Nash, *Wilderness and the American Mind* (New Haven: Yale University Press, 1967), pp. 111-12.

55. Huth, "Yosemite: the Story of an Idea," p. 66.

56. James P. Gilligan, *The Development of Policy and Administration of Forest Service Primitive and Wilderness Areas in the Western United States*, 2 vols. (Ph.D. diss., University of Michigan, 1954), 1: 55.

57. 19 Stat. 143, 167.

58. Dana, *Forest and Range Policy*, pp. 80-81, 384.

59. Ibid., pp. 82-85. Had he not fallen in love with an American tourist, he would probably have stayed in Germany.

60. Ibid., pp. 87-89.

61. Nash, *Wilderness and the American Mind*, p. 117.

62. Gilligan, *The Development of Policy and Administration of Forest Service Primitive and Wilderness Areas*, 1: 25-26.

63. Commissoners of State Parks of the State of New York, *First Annual Report*, New York Senate Document 102 (May 15, 1873), p. 10.

64. *New York Laws* (1885), chap. 283, p. 482; Gilligan, *The Development of Policy and Administration of Forest Service Primitive and Wilderness Areas*, 1: 25-28; Nash, *Wilderness and the American Mind*, pp. 116-19.

65. *New York Laws* (1885), Chapter 283, p. 482.

66. *New York Laws* (1892), Chapter 709, p. 1459; Gilligan, *The Development of Policy and Administration of Forest Service Primitive and Wilderness Areas*, 1: 29-30.

67. Gilligan, *The Development of Policy and Administration of Forest Service Primitive and Wilderness Areas*, 1: 30-31.

68. William H. Steele, ed., *Revised Record of the Constitution of the State of New York*, 5 vols. (Albany: State of New York, 1900), 4: 132-33; Nash, *Wilderness and the American Mind*, pp. 120-21; Gilligan, *The Development of Policy and Administration of Forest Service Primitive and Wilderness Areas*, 1: 35.

69. "The Yellowstone National Park," *Scribner's Monthly* 4 (1872): 121.

70. United States Congress, *The Congressional Record* 14 (March 1, 1883): 3488.

71. Ibid.

72. United States Congress, *The Congressional Record* 18 (December 14, 1886): 150-51.

73. Ibid., p. 153.

74. Ibid., pp. 153-54. The slaughter of the buffalo had been on such a magnificent scale that it must surely have been recognized as a conservation crisis before the exhaustibility of most other resources was apparent.

75. Nash, *Wilderness and the American Mind*, p. 115.

76. Holoway R. Jones, *John Muir and the Sierra Club* (San Francisco: Sierra Club Books, 1965), p. 43. The articles were: John Muir, "Treasures of the Yosemite," *Century Magazine* 40 (August 1890): 483-500; and John Muir, "Features of the Proposed Yosemite National Park," *Century Magazine* 40 (September 1890): 656-67.

77. Jones, *John Muir and the Sierra Club*, pp. 42-44; William E. Colby, ed., "The Creation of Yosemite National Park, Letters of John Muir to Robert Underwood Johnson," *Sierra Club Bulletin* 29 (October 1944): 49-60; Nash, *Wilderness and the American Mind*, pp. 130-32; Ise, *Our National Park Policy*, pp. 56-59.

78. This act did not abolish the state grant of 1864, but enclosed it with a doughnut-shaped national park.

79. Jones, *John Muir and the Sierra Club*, pp. 45-47. Ise, *Our National Park Policy*, pp. 57-58.

80. 26 Stat. 478.

81. 17 Stat. 32.

82. 26 Stat. 650.

83. I have gone to rather unusual lengths to spell out this complex situation because other authors have frequently added to the genuine confusion over the political forces involved a needless confusion as to what acts created what reservations, and whether they were parks or forest reserves.

84. Dana, *Forest and Range Policy*, pp. 98-100.

85. 26 Stat. 1095.

86. Dana, *Forest and Range Policy*, pp. 100-102; John Ise, *United States Forest Policy* (New Haven: Yale University Press, 1920), pp. 114-18.

87. 26 Stat. 1093; 27 Stat. 348.

88. Ise, *United States Forest Policy*, p. 119.

89. Ibid., pp. 122-30; Dana, *Forest and Range Policy*, pp. 101-7.

90. Dana, *Forest and Range Policy*, pp. 106-7; Ise, *United States Forest Policy*, pp. 128-33.

91. Dana, *Forest and Range Policy*, pp. 106-9; Ise, *United States Forest Policy*, pp. 133-37.

92. 30 Stat. 11, 34; Dana, *Forest and Range Policy*, pp. 107-9; Ise, *United States Forest Policy*, pp. 137-42.

93. "A Plan to Save the Forests," *Century Magazine* 49 (1895): 631.

94. Gifford Pinchot, *Breaking New Ground* (New York: Harcourt, Brace, and Co., 1947), pp. 94, 100, 103; Nash, *Wilderness and the American Mind*, pp. 133-36.

95. John Muir, "The American Forests," *Atlantic Monthly* 80 (1897): 146; John Muir, "The National Parks and Forest Reservations," *Harper's Weekly* 41 (1897): 563-67.

96. Linnie Marsh Wolfe, ed., *John of the Mountains: the Unpublished Journals of John Muir* (Boston: Houghton Mifflin Co., 1938), p. 351.

97. Linnie Marsh Wolfe, *Son of the Wilderness: The Life of John Muir* (New York: Alfred A. Knopf, 1945), pp. 275-76.

98. John Muir, "Wild Parks and Forest Reservations of the West," *Atlantic Monthly* 81 (1898): 15-28.

99. Wolfe, *Son of the Wilderness*, p. 277.

100. Gilligan, *The Development of Policy and Administration of Forest Service Primitive and Wilderness Areas*, 1: 46.

101. A classic story of a major theft is recounted in S. A. D. Puter, *Looters of the Public Domain* (Portland, Ore.: Portland Printing House, 1908).

102. Ise, *United States Forest Policy*, pp. 155-58; Gilligan, *The Development of Policy and Administration of Forest Service Primitive and Wilderness Areas*, 1: 46-47.

103. 33 Stat. 628; 33 Stat. 681.

104. Quoted in Dana, *Forest and Range Policy*, pp. 123-24.

105. Dana, *Forest and Range Policy*, p. 124.

106. Theodore Roosevelt, "The Importance of Practical Forestry," (Address before the Society of American Foresters, Washington, D.C., March 26, 1903), reprinted in *Forestry and Irrigation* 9: 169-72.

107. Quoted in Wolfe, *Son of the Wilderness*, pp. 289-94.

108. The Sierra Club had been formed in 1892, and Muir had been its first and (in 1904) only president. Yet throughout the 1890s many members of the club had cooperated with the state commissioners and had not shared Muir's desire with respect to recession.

109. Jones, *John Muir and the Sierra Club*, pp. 55-64.

110. The vote was 46 in favor, 19 opposed.

111. William E. Colby, "The Recession of Yosemite Valley," *Sierra Club Bulletin* 47 (December 1962): 62; Jones, *John Muir and the Sierra Club*, pp. 65-73.

112. 34 Stat. 831. The delay was the result of wrangling over railroad rights of way and park boundary changes. The issues were not really of a preservation versus development nature, so I have not dwelt on them.

113. Gilligan, *The Development of Policy and Administration of Forest Service Primitive and Wilderness Areas*, 1: 70. While Tocqueville had expounded upon the organizing tendencies of Americans in the 1830s, only with the advent of a truly national culture and economy late in the century did organizations of national significance begin to appear on the scene: the National Wool Growers Association (1865), the American Forestry Association (1875), the American Paper and Pulp Association (1870), the Colorado Mining Association (1876), the Sierra Club (1892), and

the Society of American Foresters (1900). Other groups with a significant stake in federal wilderness policy had organized before 1920. User groups included the National
Association of Manufacturers (1895), the Northwest Mining Association (1895), the
American Mining Congress (1898), the American National Cattlemen's Association
(1902), the Pacific Logging Congress (1909), and the Western Forestry and Conservation Association (1909). Additions to the list of organizations interested in preservation included the American Alpine Club (1902), the Mountaineers of Seattle (1906),
and the American Civic Association (1904). Additional organizations were dedicated
to wildlife preservation.

114. Jones, *America's Wealth*, p. 153. Some estimates of the original herd exceed
fifty million animals. Whatever the number, the extent of their destruction is difficult
to overestimate.

115. 36 Stat. 847.

116. 34 Stat. 255.

117. Both reservations later became national parks by act of Congress.

118. Gilligan, *The Development of Policy and Administration of Forest Service
Primitive and Wilderness Areas*, 1: 65; Ise, *Our National Park Policy*, pp. 143-60.
The ultimate use of the Antiquities Act on behalf of wilderness preservation is
discussed in chap. 7.

119. 30 Stat. 908.

120. Ise, *Our National Park Policy*, pp. 120-21.

121. Ise, *Our National Park Policy*, p. 122; Ise, *United States Forest Policy*, pp.
184-85.

122. Ise, *Our National Park Policy*, pp. 128-42, 163-76.

123. 32 Stat. 388.

124. Dana, *Forest and Range Policy*, pp. 389-94.

125. 36 Stat. 56.

126. The early national parks had been starved for funds on the theory that
revenue from concessions should be sufficient to pay for park administration and
development.

127. Robert A. Woods, *The City Wilderness* (Boston: Houghton, Mifflin, and
Co., 1898); Upton Sinclair, *The Jungle* (New York: Doubleday, Paye, 1906).

128. Nash, *Wilderness and the American Mind*, p. 145.

129. Frederick Jackson Turner, "The Problem of the West," *Atlantic Monthly* 78
(September 1896): 293.

130. Nash, *Wilderness and the American Mind*, pp. 147-56.

131. Ibid., p. 160; Carl Bode, *The Anatomy of American Popular Culture,
1840-1861* (Berkeley: University of California Press, 1959), p. x.

132. The Hetch Hetchy controversy has been studied by a number of scholars.
The best accounts are Jones, *John Muir and the Sierra Club*; and Elmo R. Richardson, "The Struggle for the Valley: California's Hetch Hetchy Controversy
1905-1913," *California Historical Society Quarterly* 38: 249-58. Considerable attention is also devoted to Hetch Hechy in Ise, *Our National Park Policy*; and Nash,
Wilderness and the American Mind.

133. 31 Stat. 790.

134. 31 Stat. 790-91.

135. Ise, *Our National Park Policy*, p. 86.

136. Jones, *John Muir and the Sierra Club*,p. 90.

137. 33 Stat. 791.

138. Jones, *John Muir and the Sierra Club*, pp. 91-92. Lake Eleanor, outside the park, was suitable for water supply but less useful for the generation of electricity.

139. Ise, *Our National Park Policy*, pp. 87-90; Jones, *John Muir and the Sierra Club*, pp. 99-104.

140. The quoted passage does not appear in Muir's published works until 1912, but Heald implies that it was written in 1908 or 1909. See Welden F. Heald, "Sierra Panorama," in Roderick Peattie, ed., *The Sierra Nevada: The Range of Light* (New York: Vanguard Press,1947), chap. 1, p. 35. This exact quotation appears in John Muir, *The Yosemite* (New York: The Century Co., 1912), pp. 261-62; and a very similar one in John Muir, "The Hetch-Hetchy Valley," *Sierra Club Bulletin* 6 (January 1908): 220.

141. Theodore Roosevelt, "Eighth Annual Message to the Senate and House of Representatives" (December 8, 1908), in *The Works of Theodore Roosevelt*, 20 vols., memorial edition (New York: Charles Scribner's Sons, 1925-26), 17: 618. Roosevelt has been described as always eager to keep preservation and wise-use factions of the conservation movement together. Nash, *Wilderness and the American Mind*, p. 163. This passage is an interesting example. The same paragraph of his address contains a call for the transfer of the national parks to the Department of Agriculture.

142. Jones, *John Muir and the Sierra Club*, p. 104.

143. Ibid., pp. 105-17.

144. Ibid., pp. 117-27.

145. Ibid., pp. 127-30.

146. The report indicated that San Francisco's proposal would be twenty million dollars cheaper than the alternatives. United States Advisory Board of Army Engineers, *Hetch Hetchy Valley: Report . . . to the Secretary of the Interior on Investigations Relative to Sources of Water Supply for San Francisco and Bay Communities* (Washington, D.C.: Government Printing Office, 1913), p. 50.

147. United States Congress, House of Representatives, Committee on Public Lands, *Hetch Hetchy Dam Site*, Hearings on June 25-28 and July 7, 1913 (Washington, D.C.: Government Printing Office, 1913), pp. 25-26. It is possible that Pinchot was more interested in seeing the development of public as opposed to private power than he was in the use versus preservation issue, though he is known to have been quite uninterested in the aesthetic value of public lands. Ise, *Our National Park Policy*, p. 87.

148. United States Congress, House of Representatives, *Hetch Hetchy Grant to San Francisco*, Report No. 41 (63rd Cong. 1st sess., August 5, 1913). United States Congress, *The Congressional Record* 50 (September 3, 1913): 4151.

149. Earlier in the battle the inner circle of the Sierra Club had formed the Society for the Preservation of National Parks, California Branch, to avoid problems caused by the lack of unanimity within the club. A short time later members dissatisfied with the Appalachian Mountain Club's stand on the issue formed the Society for the Preservation of National Parks, New England Branch. The new national committee was officially responsible for most of the fliers and pamphlets produced by preservationists.

150. Jones, *John Muir and the Sierra Club*, pp. 159-67.

151. Indeed, the voting revealed few Democratic defections in either house of Congress.

152. John Muir to Vernon Kellogg, Palo Alto, December 27, 1913, Colby Papers, Bancroft Library, University of California-Berkeley. Quoted in Jones, *John Muir and the Sierra Club*, p. 168.

153. Muir to Robert Underwood Johnson, January 1, 1914, Johnson Papers, University of California-Berkeley. Quoted in Nash, *Wilderness and the American Mind*, p. 180.

154. United States Congress, *The Congressional Record* 51 (December 6, 1913): 362.

155. Nash, *Wilderness and the American Mind*, p. 181.

156. Jones, *John Muir and the Sierra Club*, p. 131. The Sierra Club appointed a committee to promote the idea in 1910, but the major organizational force remained the American Civic Association. Ise, *Our National Park Policy*, p. 188.

157. Congressman John F. Lacey of Iowa introduced H.R. 11021 (56th Cong. 1st sess.) on April 26, 1900.

158. Quoted in Hans Huth, *Nature and the American* (Berkeley: University of California Press, 1957), p. 191.

159. Huth, *Nature and the American*, pp. 190-91.

160. His support of the Hetch Hetchy reservoir project earned him the blessing of wise-use conservationists, while his donation of the Muir Woods National Monument a few years earlier is indicative of his relationship with preservation interests. Kent himself chose the monument's name. Until the establishment of Redwood National Park in 1968, the Muir Woods was the only stand of coastal redwood trees under federal protection.

161. Pinchot's desire to transfer the national parks to the Department of Agriculture has been noted earlier.

162. 39 Stat. 535; Ise, *Our National Park Policy*, pp. 185-90.

163. 39 Stat. 535. Emphasis added.

164. Jenks Cameron, *The National Park Service* (New York: D. Appleton and Co., 1922), p. 11.

THE POLITICS OF WILDERNESS PRESERVATION, 1916–1955 3

> Why, did you know that if a beaver two feet long with
> a tail a foot and a half long can build a dam twelve feet
> high and six feet wide in two days, all you would need
> to build Boulder Dam is a beaver sixty-eight feet long
> with a fifty-one foot tail?
> —The Dodecahedron
> Norton Juster
> *The Phantom Tollbooth*

The philosophy of preservation grew from virtual nonexistence to a significant political force between 1860 and 1916, but preservation was only one
force among many in 1916. Although the belief in unregulated growth suffered in competition with the rising conservation ethic, America's yearning
for progress was hardly extinct. Rather, those with instincts for development were coming to realize that some accommodation with conservation
would be required.

CONTINUED ECONOMIC PRESSURES ON WILDERNESS

From 1916 to 1955 continued rapid economic growth placed ever greater
demands on resources. The popularity of conservation generally led both
developer and preservationist to moderate the rhetoric of their struggle. Increasingly, developers learned to justify their projects on the basis of wise-
use conservation; preservationists followed suit, attempting to expose
unwise use disguised as wise use and attempting to appropriate a greater
share of the middle ground in the American conservation movement. A
Sierra Club slogan put the preservationist approach succinctly: "Not blind
opposition to progress, but opposition to blind progress."

Between 1920 and 1955 the American population increased by 60 million,
from 106 million to 166 million.[1] Sheer numbers were not the only changes
in the American population. The economic development that accompanied
population growth altered and increased the demands placed upon land and

resources. The simultaneous growth of affluence and diminution of wilderness, which had given rise to the preservation movement continued into the post-1916 period, but there were important changes in the direction of economic growth.

In the pre-Civil War period the major thrust of development, and the major threat to wilderness, came from the advance of the agricultural frontier and the growth of exploitive timber harvest and mining techniques. The post-Civil War period was characterized by further agricultural advance accelerated by various free-land acts, expansion of the timber and mining industries, and especially by the revolution in transportation resulting from the rapid development of railroads. In the period between 1916 and 1955 some of these crucial economic trends continued; others were altered.

The advance of the plow continued, but at a more moderate pace than in the earlier periods. The number of acres in farms more than doubled between 1860 and 1920, from 407 million acres to 956 million, an increase of more than 9 million acres per year. By 1955 the land area in farms had grown to 1,202 million acres, but the annual increase between 1920 and 1955 had dropped to 7 million acres.[2] Farm acreage has consistently grown less rapidly than the nation's population.[3] As table 1 indicates, the acreage in farm land per capita has declined steadily since the Civil War.

The reasons for the decline in per capita farm acreage are complex, but improved farm technology, based on the development of chemical fertilizers and the replacement of work animals with tractors, is the root cause. The widespread introduction of tractors, for example, freed 120 million acres of pasture and cropland previously used to feed horses and mules.[4] As a result, this land became available for the production of human consumables without any net increase in the area devoted to farms. Technology decreased the relative acreage demands of agriculture, but population pressure still forced the total farm acreage upward by more than 200 million acres between 1920 and 1955.

Timber harvest, a second major threat to wilderness in previous periods, continued to increase between 1920 and 1955. Several factors worked to mitigate the threat to wilderness. More efficient utilization of the timber cut, increased growth, and better management of commercial forests, both public and private, allowed a greater wood harvest per acre. At the same time, technological change led to the general replacement of wood by petroleum products as the nation's primary fuel source. There was a similar, but less profound, decline in the per capita use of wood for construction and other purposes. Only the per capita consumption of pulpwood for paper increased substantially between 1916 and 1955. Domestic production of pulpwood increased 602 percent during that period from 4.4 million to 30.9 million cords.[5] In spite of this growth, pulpwood still constituted only 22 percent of the total timber harvest in 1952. The general result of all these trends was little absolute change in the quantity of standing timber between 1916 and 1955.

The substitution of mineral-based products for wood accounts for much of the decline in per capita wood use. The most obvious examples are the substitution of mineral fuels, like oil, gas, and coal, for fuelwood and the substitution of metals, glass, plastics, stone, and concrete for lumber in construction. Figure 2 portrays graphically the change in the proportion of total energy consumed from oil and gas, coal, and fuelwood. This picture would be far more dramatic if it adequately portrayed the increase in total energy consumption. For example, while fuelwood made up nearly one-half of the total energy consumption in 1900, the actual volume of wood burned was less than twice the amount consumed in 1952, when wood constituted only 4 percent of total energy consumption.[6]

Of course, the substitution of mineral for wood products increased the demand on the nation's mineral resources between 1916 and 1955. The total value of mineral production increased 145 percent in constant dollars while the value of mineral fuels increased 173 percent.[7]

The Mineral Leasing Act was passed in 1920, and by 1955 the number of acres of public domain under lease for the production of oil and gas had risen to more than seventy-three million.[8] The creation of the Federal Power Commission (FPC), also in 1920, signaled a growing awareness of the importance of electrical power to the nation's expanding economy. After 1920 pressure to lease government lands for petroleum production or hydroelectric generation was an increasing menace to wilderness areas in the West. Table 2 demonstrates the changing pattern of energy consumption by fuel source from 1860 to 1977. As the table indicates, total energy consumption more than doubled from 1916 to 1955.

The era following World War I was marked by a revolution in the field of transportation, as the post-Civil War period had been. In both cases technological change was aided by massive governmental subsidy. In 1862 the Pacific Railway Act had provided the vehicle for the subsidy.[9] It and its successors fostered the rapid expansion of the nation's railroads. The American railroad network reached its maximum physical size in 1916 when 254,000 miles of track were in use.[10] The United States had paid a high price for that expansion, handing over 182 million acres—more than 9 percent of the land surface of the continental United States exclusive of Alaska— directly or indirectly, to railroads in the twenty years between 1850 and 1870.

While 1916 marked the full maturity of the railroad industry, it was only the coming of age for automobile transportation. The Federal Aid Road Act of 1916[11] ushered in the era of federal assistance for road construction. Yet,

Table 1   FARM ACREAGE, 1860–1955

	1860	1920	1955
Acres (millions)	407	956	1202
Population (millions)	31.5	106.5	165.9
Per Capita Acres	12.9	9.0	7.2

SOURCES: United States Department of Commerce, Bureau of the Census, *Statistical Abstract of the United States* (Washington, D.C.: Government Printing Office, 1979), pp. 6, 686; United States Department of Agriculture, Bureau of Agricultural Economics, *Supplement to Major Uses of Land in the United States*, U.S.D.A. Technical Bulletin 1082 (Washington, D.C.: Government Printing Office, 1953), pp. 61-62; United States Department of Commerce, Bureau of the Census, *Historical Statistics of the United States, Colonial Times to 1957* (Washington, D.C.: Government Printing Office, 1960), pp. A1-16, 239.

Table 2   UNITED STATES ENERGY CONSUMPTION IN 1860, 1915, 1955, AND 1977

	1860		1915		1955		1977	
Source	energy	%	energy	%	energy	%	energy	%
Fuelwood	2.6	84	1.7	10	1.1	3	—	—
Coal	0.5	16	13.3	78	11.7	29	14.1	19
Oil			1.4	8	16.3	41	34.6	46
Gas			0.7	4	10.4	26	22.0	29
Hydroelectric					0.4	1	2.4	3
Nuclear							2.7	3
Geothermal							0.1	—
Total	3.1	100	17.1	100	39.9	100	75.8	100

SOURCES: United States Department of Commerce, Bureau of the Census, *Historical Statistics of the United States, Colonial Times to 1957* (Washington, D.C.: Government Printing Office, 1960), pp. 354-55; United States Department of Commerce, Bureau of the Census, *Statistical Abstract of the United States* (Washington, D.C.: Government Printing Office, 1979), p. 606.

NOTE: Energy is presented in Quads. 1 Quad = 10^{12} British Thermal Units. Rounding may prevent totals from corresponding to the exact sum of the component figures.

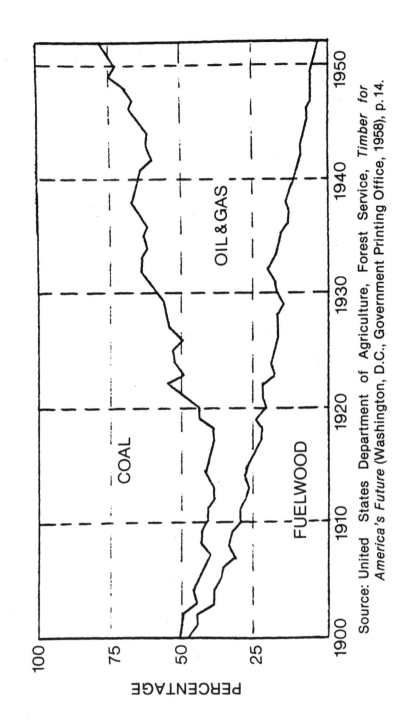

FIGURE 2 RELATIVE ENERGY CONSUMPTION BY FUEL SOURCE

1900–1952

COAL

OIL & GAS

FUELWOOD

100

75

50

25

PERCENTAGE

1900   1910   1920   1930   1940   1950

Source: United States Department of Agriculture, Forest Service, *Timber for America's Future* (Washington, D.C., Government Printing Office, 1958), p. 14.

it was not so much road building that threatened wilderness preservation after 1916 as it was the automobile itself. Road mileage did increase 27 percent between 1914 and 1955,[12] but during that same period vehicle registrations increased by more than 3,400 percent to over 60 million, and vehicle miles driven increased by more than 9,000 percent to over 600 billion.[13]

The great bulk of road construction since 1916 has been for replacement or renovation of existing routes. Most of this work has been done by the state and local governments, and consequently there has been no major transfer of lands out of the public sector as there was for railroad construction. The actual acreage covered by roadways seems small compared to the place that automobile and truck traffic have come to have in our national life. As late as 1959, according to one estimate, only 20.4 million acres were devoted to roads exclusive of city streets—just over 1 percent of the nation's land area.[14]

The specter that was to haunt advocates of wilderness preservation between 1916 and 1955 was not so much the devouring road builder as it was the new mobile Americans, 160 million strong, each trying to escape the others, fanning out across the nation in 50 million family cars, and threatening the last remnants of uncivilized America. Increasingly after 1916, the major threat to wilderness came not from the enterprising developer, for most of the remaining wilderness was of marginal economic value, but rather from the multitudes of tourists and solitude seekers who desired easy access to the remaining wilderness. For the first time in American history, the wilderness was endangered by overappreciation.

STEVE MATHER: WILDERNESS ENTREPRENEUR

The National Park Service had been created in the nick of time, for with the automobile came the first great rush of tourists to the nation's parks. The automobile became the vehicle for the expression of vacation fever, a national mood which showed no signs of diminishing in 1916. Both the Park Service and the Congress were eager to accommodate the American motorist. Steven T. Mather, the first director of the National Park Service, saw in the automobile the mechanism that would populate his parks. Exposure would increase public interest and probably congressional appropriations as well. If the auto tourist should threaten the parks with overcrowding, the solution was simply to create more parks. Congress, previously stingy about appropriating money for the parks, seemed attuned to the new national mood. Under the pressure of Mather's promotional activities and the geometric increase in auto travel, congressional appropriations for the parks and for park roads began to increase dramatically.

Steven Mather had come to Washington in 1915 to run the national parks

under Interior Secretary Franklin K. Lane. Mather was a wealthy in-
dustrialist with an abiding interest in the parks, as his Sierra Club and
American Civic Association memberships testify. In 1914 he wrote Lane, an
old college friend, to complain about the administration of the parks. Lane
replied, "Dear Steve, If you don't like the way the National Parks are being
run, come on down to Washington and run them yourself."[15] Mather did.
Assisted by Horace Albright, he set out to build the park system. Both
worked tirelessly for the creation of a unified park service. When that goal
was achieved in 1916, Mather and Albright became director and assistant
director respectively. The Park Service was to continue under their leadership until 1933.

Mather, a self-made millionaire, proved to be a bold progressive. He
entered into this work with a dedication and promotional fervor similar to
that Pinchot had displayed in the Forest Service a decade earlier. He was
able to enlist the aid of the General Federation of Women's Clubs, travel
and tourist organizations, and numerous writers, artists, and
newspapermen. Railroads, a well-established source of aid for the preservation cause, were used more effectively than ever before. Many contributors
to Mather's efforts were in a position to profit from increased tourism, and
Mather mercilessly used their self-interest to the benefit of the parks.

Out of this diffuse set of organizations and interests Mather forged a great
machine for publicizing the wonders of the parks at little or no cost to the
government. When additional funds were needed, Mather often supplied
them himself. And when Congress forbade private funding of governmental
programs, Mather was influential in the creation of the National Parks
Association to carry on the private promotional work.[16] Since its foundation, the National Parks Association has been a staunch defender of what
have come to be called "pure national park principles," a stance which has
sometimes brought the organization into conflict with more compromising
spokesmen in the Park Service itself.

Mather's promotional work was rewarded almost immediately. The auto
tourists came in increasing numbers. They were followed in short order by a
virtual flood of appropriations for park roads. By 1920 major development
was under way in parks that had been under military administration until
recently for lack of funds in the Interior Department.

Congressional generosity extended to the creation of new parks as well.
Rocky Mountain had been established in 1915, and Hawaii and Lassen
Volcanic were added in 1916.[17] In 1917, with active lobby support from the
Boone and Crockett Club and the Campfire Club of America, Mount
McKinley, the highest peak in North America, was added to the park
system.[18] Under the leadership of its aggressive director the Park Service ac-
quired Grand Canyon, Lafayette (now Acadia), and Zion in 1919.[19]

PARK SERVICE EXPANSION THREATENS THE NATIONAL FORESTS

The creation of new national parks was perceived as a threat in the Forest Service. Nearly all the potential park areas already had national forest status. Each new park meant a loss of Forest Service domain. Early in the century Pinchot had coveted the national parks and argued that they should be entrusted to the Forest Service. Not only had he failed in this attempt, but now the domain he had established was being plundered by the newly created National Park Service.

All of this was possible, not because the Forest Service was in any particular disfavor with Congress, but because preservationist sentiment was very strong, and the National Park Service was seen as the most logical agency to administer a preservation policy. The National Park Service was charged to preserve by law, while the Forest Service was thoroughly imbued with the principles of scientific forestry and committed to "wise use" of all the nation's resources. The Forest Service concept of usefulness stressed economic values. In 1920 it lagged far behind the Park Service and the rest of the nation in realizing the economic potential of tourism.

The Forest Service's tree farm mentality was threatened from several sides, however. In addition to the deletions of Forest Service domain threatened by national park expansion, effectively organized efforts to save primeval forests were developing both inside and outside the Forest Service. The new mobile American was descending on national forest areas for recreation, whether invited or not. This twentieth century squatter had no permanent designs on the land, but he had every intention of utilizing its recreational potential.

Recreational use that did not involve wilderness preservation was not difficult to square with Forest Service tradition and philosophy, though recreation had not been recognized as legitimate so long as Pinchot headed the service. As early as 1910, when Henry Graves replaced Pinchot as forester, the situation changed. In that year the American Academy of Political and Social Sciences held a symposium on public recreation facilities. The paper presented by Treadwell Cleveland, Jr., on behalf of the Forest Service made recognition of recreation by the Forest Service explicit and predicted that the recreational value of the national forests would increase.[20]

By 1917 recreational visits to the national forests had increased to three million, and Frank A. Waugh was commissioned by Forester Graves to conduct a study of recreational use of the forests. The Waugh report recommended that recreational use be governed by the wholesale application of the service's multiple-use doctrine. He cited four main uses of national forests: timber production, grazing, watershed protection, and recreation. He concluded:

where two or more of these main uses can be served at the same time on the same area they are carried forward side by side. . . . Whenever two of these uses come into conflict, some authority determines which is likely to render the greater public service. . . . On principle areas of the national forests recreation is an incidental use; on some it is a paramount use; on a few it becomes the exclusive use.[21]

Although the Waugh report stressed the commercial value of recreation, many foresters in the decentralized Forest Service were reluctant to endorse any recreational use. But in spite of foot-dragging in the field, the 1921 Forest Service manual of administrative practice stated that forest plans should recognize and coordinate recreational uses.[22] The Washington headquarters of the Forest Service was well ahead of most of its field offices in recognizing the importance of recreational use.

THE FOREST SERVICE RESISTS WILDERNESS PRESERVATION

Although recreation of a general sort could be fitted into the multiple-use concept with little difficulty, wilderness preservation was more resistant. A Forest Service commitment to wilderness preservation came later than its commitment to general recreation, and only under considerable pressure.

Writing in *Forestry and Irrigation*, G. Frederick Schwarz had advocated wilderness preservation in the national forests as early as 1905, the year the Forest Service was created. He cited the "uplifting influence" of wilderness preserves as well as their "general scientific and historic interest."[23] Still, there was no widespread interest in such a program until massive road building began in the forests around 1916.[24] Between 1916 and 1921 Congress appropriated thirty-three million dollars for roads in and around national forests, and large roadless tracts began to disappear quickly.[25] Road building proceeded at a rapid rate in both national forests and national parks. Foresters favored road building because it improved timber access and fire protection, even though it also provided access to tourists. Park Service staff favored road construction precisely because it aided tourist travel. With road construction blessed by the guardians of each system, destruction of the nation's remaining public wilderness became a distinct possibility.[26]

Organizations, old and new, acted to forestall the complete loss of wilderness in America. Among the new organizations interested in wilderness was the Ecological Society of America (ESA), founded in 1918. The ESA advocated wilderness reserves for the sake of science and feared that neither the Forest Service nor the National Park Service was capable of administering such areas.[27] Francis B. Sumner, speaking in 1919, described the ESA's goal as "nature conservation," as opposed to resource conservation, and called for the setting aside of areas of every ecological description "as a source of scientific knowledge and of the highest esthetic enjoyment of mankind."[28] The American Association for the Advancement of Science endorsed a similar position in 1921.[29]

CARHART AND LEOPOLD: WILDERNESS ADVOCATES IN THE FOREST SERVICE

Pressures on the Forest Service by groups like the ESA and the AAAS were supplemented by preservation sentiment from a dedicated minority within the service itself. The earliest internal activist was probably Arthur H. Carhart, a landscape architect serving as recreation engineer. In 1919 Carhart was assigned to survey the Trapper's Lake area of the White River National Forest, Colorado, to establish homesites and the route for a proposed road. Carhart did so, but he also informed his immediate superior that acting on the survey would be a mistake. He believed that any development in the area was inappropriate. Carhart's superior agreed to keep the Trapper's Lake area roadless and arranged for Carhart to meet Aldo Leopold. Leopold was assistant district forester in Albuquerque, New Mexico, and he shared Carhart's interest in preservation. Following the meeting Carhart wrote to Leopold suggesting the rudiments of the modern concept of wilderness preservation. Carhart outlined four types of areas that should be kept free of development, and he predicted that the "time will come when these scenic spots, where nature has been allowed to remain unmarred, will be some of the most highly prized scenic features of the country."[30] This memorandum was the first Forest Service document to argue for wilderness preservation; it would not be the last. Carhart's proposals were incorporated in the District Recreation Plan and forwarded to Washington.

In January 1921 Carhart attended a National Parks Conference sponsored by the National Park Service in Des Moines, Iowa. He seized the opportunity to tell the conference that the national forests could also serve important recreational needs. Park Service Director Mather took exception to Carhart's remarks, arguing that the national forests should not try to imitate the national parks. In his agitation Mather went so far as to admit that he had personally intervened with the chairman of the House Appropriations Committee to see that the Forest Service received no funds for recreational development. Sierra Club President W. F. Bade endorsed the National Park Service view. The Sierra Club and National Park Service alliance in this matter is natural, for the Forest Service had been out of favor with the club since Muir's break with Pinchot in 1897. In 1921 club members failed to appreciate the opportunities for preservation presented by the new Forest Service interest in recreation. In spite of the opposition of the Sierra Club and of the host National Park Service, the National Parks Conference adopted a resolution, drafted in part by Carhart, endorsing recreational use of the national forests.[31]

Carhart's final contribution to saving the American wilderness was probably his greatest. Carhart proposed a roadless area in the Superior National Forest of Minnesota. Carhart's proposal was round one in the fight to preserve the area known today as the Boundary Waters Canoe Area (BWCA). The Carhart plan was approved by the district forester, but others within the service favored continuing road construction. The dispute over Carhart's roadless area was finally resolved in favor of preservation by Secretary of Agriculture Henry Wallace in April 1923. It was the first cabinet-level decision ever in favor of explicit wilderness preservation in the national forests.[32]

Arthur Carhart retired from the Forest Service at the end of 1922 but remained influential for several years, working behind the scenes and writing for *American Forestry* magazine. In spite of its importance, Carhart's influence on Forest Service policy is less widely appreciated than that of his early collaborator, Aldo Leopold. It is Leopold who has been characterized as the "Father of the National Forest Wilderness system."[33]

Leopold's interest in wilderness preservation was a by-product of his concern for wildlife. He believed that to preserve fish and game habitat effectively, one must ultimately preserve wilderness.[34] To Leopold, wilderness meant nothing less than an area large enough to contain a two-week pack trip without the participants' ever having to backtrack or cross their own trail. He set out his own plan for such a reservation in 1921, in what was to be the first of many articles on the subject.[35] His concluding recommendation called for the creation of a wilderness preserve in New Mexico's Gila National Forest. The next year District 3 forester, Frank Pooler, acted on Leopold's recommendation and set aside an area of 574,000 acres for wilderness recreation.[36]

Like Carhart's plan for Trapper's Lake, the Gila reservation was set aside as a part of a district recreation plan. Such reservations might eventually be overruled at a higher administrative level, but the affected lands were at least temporarily protected from development.

At least one preservation proposal received some attention outside the Forest Service during this period. A 1922 proposal by Emerson Hough in the *Saturday Evening Post* to set aside the Kaibab National Forest on the north rim of the Grand Canyon as a so-called President's Forest devoted to wilderness recreation received considerable reader support.[37] In spite of the interest generated by the Hough article, wilderness preservation was not yet on the national agenda.

The first National Conference on Outdoor Recreation, chaired by Theodore Roosevelt, convened in May 1924. If there was a logical forum for the discussion of wilderness preservation, surely this was it. Nevertheless, in three days of discussion the conference never touched on the subject of wilderness recreation. The failure to deal with the wilderness question distressed Leopold who continued to try to mobilize the public with magazine articles like "The Last Stand of the Wilderness."[38] Leopold was indefatigable in his cause, but he had neither the position nor the resources to carry the campaign further without the support of his superiors. Most professional foresters were not yet ready to accept recreation in the national forests, much less wilderness preservation. Leopold was ahead of his time, and, like Carhart, he eventually resigned from the Forest Service in the belief that he could be more effective on the outside.

THE FOREST SERVICE MOVES TOWARD PRESERVATION

The Washington staff of the Forest Service, headed since 1920 by William B. Greeley, faced a different set of realities than did foresters in the field. To Greeley and some of his colleagues, the Carhart and Leopold proposals provided a possible means of rechanneling the widespread interest in preservation that threatened to perpetually build the National Park System at the expense of the national forests. The National Park System under Mather had become very development minded, albeit development for the sake of recreation rather than resource exploitation. A policy of wilderness preservation in the Forest Service might rescue the Agriculture Department's image with preservationists and prevent further transfer of Forest Service lands to the national parks. Between 1923 and 1926 Greeley embraced this kind of thinking and moved slowly toward a policy of limited wilderness preservation in the national forests.

In order to resolve the interagency wrangling over possible national park sites, the 1924 National Conference on Outdoor Recreation had established a committee to adjudicate the territorial disputes between the Forest Service and the Park Service. Greeley and Mather personally represented their respective agencies on the committee. In 1926 the committee visited all the disputed areas to determine their best use.

A particularly interesting incident occurred while the group was traveling in the vicinity of the Upper Yellowstone River, an area proposed for addition to Yellowstone National Park. The Park Service had already published a plan to build a road through the area. "While the group was assembled on a high bluff overlooking a splendid view, one member of the party declared, 'What a beautiful scene—it should be preserved forever in this condition.' Greeley promptly drew Mather's plan from his pocket, saying, 'Of course, I agree—but look what Steve Mather wants to do to it.'"[39] This criticism of Park Service development plans is a clear indication that Greeley was on his way to endorsing a Forest Service wilderness system.[40]

Another product of the 1924 National Conference on Outdoor Recreation was the establishment of a Joint Committee of the American Forestry Association and the National Parks Association. The joint committee was charged to study the use and potential use of the federal lands for recreation.[41] While the National Conference on Outdoor Recreation had not discussed it, the joint committee was interested in wilderness preservation and in what the Forest Service intended to do about it. The Sierra Club and the Izaak Walton League (IWL) were also pressing for wilderness preservation in the national forests by 1926.[42]

In December 1926, having tested the idea and found support for it, Greeley enunciated a general Forest Service policy on wilderness preservation. In a letter to all western district foresters Greeley called for:

a. A review of our Forest Road Development plans, to make sure that they do not contemplate a needless invasion of areas adapted to wilderness forms of use. . . .

b. A review of the special use . . . policies . . . to make sure that they safeguard areas adapted to wilderness . . . against summer homes, hotels, and other structures. . . .

If proper safeguards against these two possibilities are established, I believe that reasonable provision for the wilderness idea will have been made.[43]

This policy was sufficiently vague to allow the district forester for Colorado and Wyoming to create forty-two wilderness areas totaling 2.5 million acres by 1928, while the district forester in neighboring Montana created none.[44]

Greeley's conversion to the utility of preservation was not yet complete. A year after his first policy directive on wilderness, Greeley was edging closer to a firm commitment to preservation. In the December 1927 issue of *Sunset Magazine* he described three proposals to develop Forest Service lands that were still wild. One proposal involved a cable car to the summit of Mount Hood in Oregon and the other two mountain highways in California. In every case Greeley opposed the projected developments and argued that the wilderness character of these tracts should be preserved. He also hinted that the Park Service might not be so preservation minded. He recalled his trip to the Yellowstone with Mather and concluded:

Let us add it [the Upper Yellowstone area] to the national park if that is where it belongs; but curses on the man who bisects it with roads, plants it with hotels, and sends yellow busses streaking through it with sirens shrieking like souls in torment.[45]

Greeley argued that national forests should "provide some sizeable areas of real wilderness. . . . These mountain wildernesses," he added, "may not be used by numbers of people in any wise commensurate with those who will throng the highways, but their individual service will be immeasurably greater."[46] He concluded that without active planning and protection civilization would obliterate the wilderness completely at a great cost to the nation.

Greeley's article in a popular western magazine was an appeal for public support on behalf of a significant change in Forest Service policy. Greeley needed allies for his growing commitment to wilderness preservation, for many in the ranks of the Forest Service remained opposed.

New support for Greeley's emerging preservation policy came in 1928. The 1928 National Conference on Outdoor Recreation received the report of the joint committee, which had been created by the 1924 conference. The report, *Recreation Resources of Federal Lands*, devoted its longest chapter to the national forests, and fully half of that chapter to the values of wilderness recreation. It cited Emerson Hough's proposal for a "President's Forest," quoted extensively and approvingly from Aldo Leopold's "Last Stand of the Wilderness," and described twenty-one areas of de facto wilderness in the national forests comprising a total of 12.5 million acres. The report's conclusions stressed the importance of wilderness.

It is then the great responsibility of the federal government to provide those forms of outdoor life and recreation which it alone can give and which are associated only with the wilderness.[47]

To this end specific policy recommendations included:

a clear definition by law of the status of recreation on the national forests as a coordinated use . . . [and a] formal delimitation by proclamation of the Secretary of Agriculture of wilderness areas within the national forests and suppression of . . . uses inimical to the enjoyment of simple wilderness sports.[48]

The report did not recommend wilderness designations in the national forests far out of line with the service's new policy, for by 1928 Greeley's directive to district foresters had resulted in the designation of over five million acres of wilderness.[49] It did go beyond the existing policy in calling for the designation of wilderness areas at the highest administrative level by the secretary of agriculture. Within the year L. F. Kneipp had drawn up regulations to accomplish the task.

Kneipp had been head of National Forest Recreation Planning under Greeley, where his presence had undoubtedly been one factor contributing to Greeley's cautious movement toward wilderness advocacy. When Greeley resigned in May 1928, Kneipp stayed on under the new chief forester, R. Y. Stuart. Other important personnel changes took place at about the same time. Ill health forced the retirement of Steven Mather, National Park Service director and Greeley's chief rival, in January 1929.

Mather was replaced by Horace Albright who had been second in command at the Park Service throughout Mather's administration. Aldo Leopold resigned from the Forest Service in July 1928. Thus, in the space of eight months, the cast of characters that had dominated the wilderness issue for more than a decade was removed from the scene. The next years belonged to Kneipp and Albright and others yet to be recognized.

REGULATION L-20: PRIMITIVE AREAS IN THE NATIONAL FORESTS

Kneipp's draft of new wilderness regulations was circulated within the Forest Service late in 1928. The apparent permanence of the areas to be created under the proposed regulation aroused a good deal of opposition within the Forest Service, and by the time the new regulation, L-20, was officially promulgated by Forester Stuart in 1929, the strength of the commitment to Forest Service wilderness areas had been significantly weakened.[50] Regulation L-20 stated:

The Chief of the Forest Service shall . . . [establish] . . . a series of areas to be known as primitive areas, and within which will be maintained primitive conditions . . . with a view to conserving the values of such areas for purposes of public education and recreation.[51]

The supplement that accompanied the new regulation cast further doubt on the magnitude of the service's commitment to wilderness. It stated that, "establishment of a primitive area ordinarily will not operate to withdraw timber, forage or water resources from industrial use."[52] To put it simply, the instructions for the implementation of L-20 were much less restrictive than a casual reading of the regulation would suggest. It is probable that L-20 was deliberately worded to please a concerned, but naive, public without significantly straining relations with the usual Forest Service clientele of lumber, stock, and mineral interests.

While the provisions of Regulation L-20 were designed to appeal primarily to wilderness recreation enthusiasts, primitive areas were not the only type of reservation created. In deference to groups like the Ecological Society of America and the American Association for the Advancement of Science, the authority to create "research reserves" was also established.[53] The Park Service had attempted to gain the support of the scientific community with a similar program two years earlier. Beginning in February 1927 the Park Service created scientific reserves called "primitive areas" in some national parks. These were real ecological control areas for scientific study by permit only.[54] These reservations brought the Park Service no particular support from the scientific community, and they were eventually abolished.

INTERAGENCY RIVALRY: CONSEQUENCES FOR WILDERNESS

The National Park Service had also been active in the defense of its interests. The Park Service's efforts to boost tourist development and the Forest Service's move to usurp the preservationist mantle left each service in the position of trying to please both development and preservation-minded constituencies. Thus, at the same time that Mather was widely promoting national park development, he reiterated his commitment to wilderness.

It is not the plan [he reported in 1924] to have the parks gridironed by roads, but in each it is desired to make a good sensible road system so that the visitors may have a chance to enjoy them. At the same time large sections of each park will be kept in a natural wilderness state without piercing feeder roads and will be accessible only by trails to the horseback rider and the hiker.[55]

It is difficult to assess the effects of this period of interagency rivalry either for the agencies involved or for wilderness preservation generally. Several facts do, however, stand out.

1. The early parks were created with the aid of development as well as preservation interests. Transportation interests were instrumental in the creation of Yosemite and Yellowstone national parks, as well as in several other cases not covered in detail here. Even after the creation of the National Park Service, the expansion of the National Park System, widely supported by preservationists, rested largely on the efforts of a tourist-minded transportation lobby. Thus, preservation ideals never monopolized park policies in any period of park history. The swing of preservationist sentiment away from the parks in the Mather administration was simply the disillusionment brought about by a more realistic appraisal on the part of preservationists of their influence on park policy. Preservationists were not losing ground with the Park Service, but they had overestimated the ground they controlled.

2. Preservation interests had generally supported the creation of the national forests in the 1890s. The coalition of users that came to dominate forest policy—industrial users and professional foresters—quickly subordinated preservation interests, and preservationists like Muir turned their attention to creating parks. Preservationist disenchantment with the Park Service provided an opportunity for forestry officials to regain preservationist backing with a system of national forest "primitive areas." This was a decided gain for preservation, for it signaled the willingness of the Forest Service to attempt to compromise its longstanding quarrel with preservationists over forest use. Increased preservationist influence with the Forest Service was achieved without any loss of influence with the National Park Service.

3. The desire of both services to please the preservation constituency, whenever possible, is indicative of the relative position of preservation vis-a-vis other interests. Preservation was strong, but not dominant within the constituency of either service. Being courted from both sides probably enhanced preservationist influence. Preservation interests were in a position to play one service off against the other. Some other interests, for example, logging and mining concerns, were too wedded to the Forest Service to be able to gain much influence by a threat to withdraw support.

Any further assessment of the impact of this period of interservice rivalry on the state of wilderness preservation resolves itself into two questions: Did the creation of national forest primitive areas stem the tide of national park expansion? And if so, did the areas preserved by the Forest Service outweigh the gain for preservation which would have occurred if the National Park System had been allowed to expand unchecked by Forest Service competition? Neither question can be answered definitively. The pace of park expansion did slow, but it might well have done so regardless of Forest Service activity in the area of wilderness preservation. After all, the areas with the most obvious national park potential were the first to be encompassed by the National Park System. As time went on, the proposed additions were significantly less outstanding than the areas already included. Where areas of truly exceptional beauty remained outside the National Park System, Mather rarely came away empty-handed, though he never fulfilled his highest hopes either.

In a compilation of National Park Service expansion projects between 1920 and 1928, Gilligan lists nine major projects totaling in excess of 2.3 million acres. In that same period, Mather was successful in adding only 592,000 acres to the park system, about one-fourth of what he wanted. Even if Mather had been successful in completing his entire 2.3-million-acre expansion program, the greatest possible addition to preserved wilderness would have been less than half the five million acres of wilderness created by the Forest Service between 1920 and 1928.[56] Wilderness preservation gained significantly from this period of interbureau rivalry spearheaded by Mather and Greeley.

CONGRESS MOVES TO PROTECT WILDERNESS

The wilderness issue was introduced to the legislative arena during this period. The threat of roads in the Superior National Forest, which had so concerned Arthur Carhart, had proved to be but the first of many threats to this unique lakeland wilderness. Preservation of the area had quickly become the foremost task of the Izaak Walton League.[57] By 1928 the League's battle to save the northern Minnesota canoe country had reached the halls of Congress. In April of that year Senator Henrik Shipstead and Congressman Walter H. Newton, both from Minnesota, introduced identical bills embodying the IWL's proposals for the canoe country.[58] The bills prohibited any artificial change in the water levels of lakes over a three-million-acre area between the north shore of Lake Superior and the Canadian border. Timber harvest within four hundred feet of shorelines was also prohibited. Since travel by canoe is the dominant form of recreation in the area, timber harvest away from the shoreline was not considered detrimental to recreational use.

The Shipstead and Newton bills were introduced just in time to head off the possible destruction of the canoe country by power developments. Two separate power schemes threatened the area. Each, in its own way, demonstrates the utter feebleness of legal protection for the area in the 1920s.

On August 25, 1920, E. W. Backus, acting as president of the Fort Frances Pulp and Paper Company, made application to the Canadian government

for the right to construct [twelve] dams at the outlets of the several lakes along the international waters above Rainy Lake for the control of the waters flowing into Namakan Lake, as well as, in cases where power is available, the right to develop such power and erect power plants.[59]

Such a project would have flooded a minimum of 40 thousand acres in the United States and Canada.[60] The area in question contained many lakes, some dotted with islands, and all connected by streams, narrows, or waterfalls. Such extensive flooding would have obliterated the area, drowning natural shorelines and islands and covering the connecting waterways. The overall result would have been the substitution of a chain of reservoirs 160 miles long for the present natural lake chain.

Since the proposal concerned the waters of the international boundary, the application was referred to the International Joint Commission (IJC). The IJC had been created by treaty with Great Britain to regulate water levels in Lake of the Woods.[61] When the accord was signed in 1909, it not only gave the IJC jurisdiction over the Lake of the Woods dispute, but also over the probable eventual development of power on all the boundary lakes. The IJC undertook a study of the proposed project in 1925, but its decision was delayed while it waited for the army engineers and the Canadian engineers to study the project. Public hearings held by the IJC also disclosed that there was substantial public opposition to the proposed project[62]

The second power scheme involved the Minnesota Power and Light Company, a public utility of the city of Duluth. In 1924 the company built dams and created water impoundments in Gabbro and Bald Eagle lakes in the

Superior National Forest. Only after the actual construction had taken place and the dams were in operation, did the Minnesota Power and Light Company make application to the Forest Service and the Federal Power Commission for the appropriate licenses. In fact, the Federal Power Commission application was not made until 1926, when the utility contemplated enlarging its reservoirs. The FPC dutifully notified the state of Minnesota of the application which, if granted, would lead to the flooding of state-owned lands reserved as a state forest.

Incredibly, this was apparently the state's first indication that the original dams had been built. Perhaps even more incredible was the state's apparent impotence to prevent the new dams from being built. The FPC expressed dismay over the state's lack of "authority to determine the disposition of its own property."[63]

While inexplicable, the state's powerlessness was evidently quite real. The state administration was adamant against construction of the dams, and the FPC was willing to hold up the license almost indefinitely if it had some indication that the state would act to pass water power legislation. The greatest response the legislature could muster, however, was a memorial to Congress to pass the Shipstead-Newton-Nolan bills and thus save it from embarrassment.[64]

The threat posed by these two separate power proposals, and the inability of any lesser governmental agency to dispose of the threat in a manner satisfactory to the preservation and recreation interests headed by the Izaak Walton League, pointed to the need for congressional action. It was to meet that need that the Shipstead and Newton bills were introduced. The bills were supported by the Coolidge administration, and were aided by an executive order withdrawing all of the lands in question for entry under the federal land laws.[65] The order came in May 1928, a month after the bills were introduced. Both bills were reported out by their respective committees, but neither house passed the legislation during the Seventieth Congress.[66]

The bills were reintroduced in the Seventy-first Congress, with Congressman William I. Nolan of Minnesota replacing Congressman Newton as chief sponsor in the House. By the time they were reintroduced, the bills had gained support from some additional outside sources. The memorial from the state of Minnesota has already been mentioned. The American Legion also endorsed the plan, arguing that the canoe country should be preserved as an international monument to those who fought in the Great War. The equivalent Canadian organization, the Canadian Legion of the British Empire Service League, supported the idea as well.[67] As a consequence, the Legion's resources were marshaled for a measure that, under normal circumstances, would have been of no particular concern to servicemen.

Both the Shipstead and Nolan bills were reported out in the spring of 1930. The Senate bill was passed by a voice vote on May 7, 1930,[68] and sent to the House for consideration. In the House the major obstacle seemed to be the oppositon of Congressman William A. Pittenger, whose district encompassed the canoe country. In order to avoid any economic damage to his tourist and timber-dependent constituents, Pittenger introduced a substitute which protected less than half the three million acres covered by the Shipstead-Nolan proposal. The latter bills he denounced as the work of "the Minneapolis propagandists."[69] Pittenger's allies on the Rules Committee were able to prevent House consideration of the bill. When the proponents agreed to compromise on the question of area, Pittenger's support in the Rules Committee dissolved.[70] The Shipstead bill, amended to embrace just over two million acres, was granted a rule, and passed by the House on July 3, 1930.[71]

Preservationist ardor was obvious in the floor debate. Several congressmen expressed the view that Congress should "go all the way" and make the area a national park. Others were reminded of Hetch Hetchy. Among them was Congressman William Stafford of Wisconsin, who called his vote for the Hetch Hetchy reservoir "the one vote I regret more than any other."[72] The bill as amended was accepted by the Senate the same day—the last day of the Seventy-first Congress—and signed by President Herbert Hoover on July 10.[73]

In the Shipstead-Newton-Nolan Act Congress had, for the first time, created by statute what amounted to a national forest wilderness area, and a large one at that. Covering 1,269,000 acres of federal lands, the Superior Roadless Area, as it came to be called, was larger than any primitive area established by the Forest Service.[74]

The protestations of some members of Congress that the area should be a national park, notwithstanding, the Superior Roadless Area had important protection that no national park shared. It was protected from recreational development and road building. By 1933 the Minnesota State legislature was sufficiently recovered from its bout of impotence to pass a law, very similar to Shipstead-Nolan, protecting the state lands in the boundary area.[75] With unprecedented legislative protecton this "wilderness sanctuary" seemed safe, but not for long.[76]

A new conservation organization, the Quetico-Superior Council, had been created to fight the water power reservations of the 1920s. It had proposed a program of balanced management for the area. After interest in a memorial park was expressed by veterans' organizations, the council adopted the proposal as its own. The work of the council was endorsed by President Franklin D. Roosevelt in 1934, when he created the President's Quetico-Superior Committee by executive order.[77] Ernest C. Oberholtzer, a guiding light on the council, was made executive secretary of the committee.[78] The same year, the International Joint Commission denied all applications for development of the boundary chain, and its secretary endorsed the program of the Quetico-Superior Council.[79]

The Quetico-Superior Committee reported its recommendations in 1938.[80] After informal consultations in the two nations, the committee concluded that the memorial park ought to be created by treaty with the Dominion of Canada, and to that end, the United States government should place all land within the proposed park under federal control. Roosevelt endorsed the report and forwarded it to the secretary of state for formal proposal to the Canadian government. The Second World War intervened, however, and the project was set aside indefinitely.[81]

While the negotiations with Canada have never been completed, the federal government has proceeded to acquire private inholdings. The Thye-Blatnik Act of 1948 authorized one-half million dollars to acquire private lands within the area's boundaries, and the Izaak Walton League has contributed money to speed public acquisition.[82] The unprecedented use of an executive order in 1949 to preserve the wilderness character of the boundary waters is testimony to continuing interest in the area.[83]

The decade following the passage of the Shipstead-Newton-Nolan Act was a period of relative quietude in the politics of preservation, and of profound disquiet in the nation at large. It was a decade of depression which ended in war. There was little thought of preservation, for the minds of most Americans were diverted by more pressing events. This is entirely consistent with the thesis that economic surpluses and the concomitant leisure are prerequisites for wilderness preservation. The preservation movement was not altogether dormant, but compared to that bustle of activity that had characterized the first thirty years of the century, the next two decades seemed slow-paced.

ROBERT MARSHALL: NEW WILDERNESS CHAMPION

The publication in 1930 of Robert Marshall's "The Problem of Wilderness"[84] marked the emergence of a new champion of the wilderness movement. Marshall's life was to be very short, but he managed to fill it with a succession of impressive accomplishments. By 1930 he had earned his doctorate at Johns Hopkins University and had developed a thorough philosophy of wilderness preservation.[85] Marshall argued for the physical, mental, and aesthetic benefits that accrue to those who seek out the remaining wilderness. Furthermore, he argued, enthusiasts have a right to those benefits. Citing the "philosophers of democracy"—John Stuart Mill, Thomas Paine, and Thomas Jefferson—he wrote:

this prerogative is valid even though its exercise may encroach slightly on the fun of the majority, for there is a point where an increase in the joy of the many causes a decrease in the joy of the few out of all proportion to the gain of the former.[86]

For the next ten years, Marshall carried on a one-man battle for wilderness preservation. His first opportunity to proselytize within the system came with his selection to write the forest recreation chapters of the Copeland Report,[87] the nation's first comprehensive appraisal of its forest policy. He seized upon the opportunity to recommend protected status for nearly every substantial area of de facto wilderness in the nation, regardless of whether or not it was publicly owned. Wherever the Forest Service had jurisdiction, he lobbied strenuously for new or expanded primitive areas. Most Forest Service field personnel, however, were unwilling to go further than they already had in making concessions to preservation.[88]

In 1933 Marshall became director of forestry in the Office of Indian Affairs, Department of Interior. This appointment was probably fortunate for the cause of preservation. A major threat to the wilderness in the decade of depression came from government programs designed to increase employment and revitalize the nation's economy. One such program called for massive road construction in the national forests by the Public Works Administration (PWA). No roads were planned in designated Forest Service primitive areas, but Marshall discovered that many were planned for areas of de facto wilderness, which he had argued should be preserved. Interior Secretary Harold L. Ickes administered the funds, and Marshall's position and personal acquaintance with Ickes provided the access necessary to argue that funds for wilderness construction ought to be withheld. After consultaton with the Forest Service, some of the proposed roads were eliminated in 1935.[89]

Forest Service concurrence in these eliminations demonstrates its continuing awareness of preservationist sentiment, and its continuing fear of a land grab by the National Park Service. Less than one year earlier, Chief Forester F. A. Silcox had written to his regional officers:

The Forest Service cannot ignore this [preservationist] sentiment. To do so would probably cause it to seek other and less desirable means by which to attain the same ends. . . . If the Forest Service cannot fully realize the potentialities of the [primitive] areas it will have little valid grounds for objection to a change in their administrative supervision.[90]

Marshall's position in the Office of Indian Affairs gave him many opportunities to visit the West, and he never missed a chance to examine Forest Service territory and badger Silcox about the necessity of more wilderness preserves. By late in 1936 Marshall had completed his own analysis of all the nation's wilderness areas, more than 300 million acres. Thirty-two areas, totaling more than 30 million acres, were within the limits of western national forests. The Forest Service national office circulated the Marshall proposals, but little action was taken on the regional or local levels, in spite of the fact that official primitive areas amounted to only 10.5 million acres.[91]

While he expended great efforts trying to influence Forest Service policy, Marshall did not ignore the possibilities inherent in his own office. He was successful in enlisting the support of his immediate superior in the Office of Indian Affairs, John Collier. Collier, in turn, created a number[92] of wilderness areas on Indian reservations. While this accomplishment was undoubtedly rewarding, the preservation potential of Indian Office lands was small. When Marshall was offered an opportunity to become chief of the Recreation and Lands Division of the Forest Service, he could hardly refuse. He made the transfer in May 1937.

The Marshall appointment probably distressed some members of the Forest Service who considered him an enemy of the multiple-use policy. Yet, the appointment is quite explicable. On a personal level, Marshall and Silcox were quite friendly; on an institutional level, it was reasonable to give Marshall a stake in Forest Service prosperity. Certainly, it would make him less vocal about the national-park-like qualities of the national forest back country. Even in his new position, however, Marshall served the wilderness first and the service second. When Olympic National Park was enlarged at the expense of national forest lands, he expressed his approval, feeling that the National Park Service would better safeguard the area's virgin timber than would his own Forest Service.[93]

Although Marshall enjoyed some success as champion of wilderness preservation within the government, his accomplishments never totally satisfied him. In 1935 he turned outside the government for support. In the company of half a dozen wilderness proponents, including Aldo Leopold, Robert Sterling Yard, and Ernest Oberholtzer, he formed the Wilderness Society.[94]

NEW REGULATIONS FOR NATIONAL FOREST WILDERNESS AREAS

Marshall and his allies in private organizations pressed for major revisions in Regulation L-20 governing primitive areas, as well as for additional primitive area designations. In 1929 Regulation L-20 had been a great advance from the preservationist viewpoint, but it was far from ideal. The instructions sent to district foresters regarding the implementation of L-20 had said, in part:

The establishment of a primitive area ordinarily will not operate to withdraw timber, forage or water resources from industrial use, since the utilization of such resources, if properly regulated, will not be incompatible with the purposes for which the area is designated.[95]

The regulation allowed uses incompatible with modern standards of wilderness preservation. These incompatibilities were not merely theoretical, for James P. Gilligan reports that in 1937:

There were seventy-two primitive areas with a gross of 13,482,421 acres in ten western states. The management plans under L-20 Regulation allowed road construction in fifteen areas, grazing in sixty-two areas, and logging in fifty-nine areas. Only four primitive areas totaling 297,221 acres absolutely excluded logging, grazing and roads.[96]

In 1937, aided by the expansionist pressure of the Park Service, Marshall and his allies were able to initiate discussions aimed at strengthening the regulations. The U Regulations were designed to supersede Regulation L-20, but only after each primitive area was reexamined on its merits, and any necessary boundary changes made.

Regulations U-1, U-2, and U-3(a) were to govern wilderness, wild, and roadless areas, respectively. From the standpoint of wilderness preservation, these regulations made several advances over L-20. Roads and commercial timber harvest were forbidden in wilderness and wild areas.[97] These new restrictions demonstrated a growing seriousness about preserving national forest wilderness. The service was forgoing what might be characterized as its two most basic functions: timber harvest and fire protection. This restriction does not mean that the Forest Service would fail to combat fires in the new wilderness areas, but only that wilderness preservation was given a higher priority than the added fire-fighting efficiency gained by building fire roads.

While some uses that purists disliked were still allowed—grazing, mining, and hunting—the Forest Service had really done about all it could do with the U Regulations. Mining is not within the jurisdiction of the Forest Service but is governed by the mineral laws, even where Forest Service land is concerned. Thus, the Forest Service has no authority to forbid mining and prospecting, no matter how much such a policy might be desired by Forest Service officials. Hunters and dude ranchers (whose businesses require at least limited grazing) were a part of the coalition of forces sure to praise the new restrictions. These groups had a financial as well as an aesthetic stake in wilderness preservation. Wilderness purists, always short on economic arguments to support their position, could hardly afford to alienate these important allies.

The U Regulations differed from L-20 in other ways. The U-1 Regulation placed the authority to make wilderness designations at the highest administrative level, with the secretary of the United States Department of Agriculture. Everyone interpreted the U Regulations to be permanent. Many had considered the L-20 primitive areas to be temporary, subject to change when the economy demanded utilization of the resources they held.

Resistance to this sort of change could be expected from many Forest Service field personnel who had resisted previous "locking up" of timber resources. Surprisingly, this resistance was manifested in two contradictory strategies.

First, the National Park Service had requested maps of all national forests that contained primitive areas. To many in the Forest Service, this was new evidence that the National Park Service was after their land. Under the circumstances, certain foresters saw the reclassification demanded by the new regulations as an opportunity to strip the primitive areas of any territory with any economic potential, before the Park Service could make national parks of them.[98] This is ironic, because a decade earlier National Park Service pressure had been a primary consideration in the creation and protection of national forest wilderness areas. Apparently, while the Washington office saw wilderness preservation as a prime strategy for halting National Park Service raids on national forest lands, some regional and local officers saw preserved wilderness as territory conveniently prepackaged for Park Service expansion. These field officers reasoned that if the Park Service was going to get the primitive areas for parks, the best strategy was immediate review and reclassification under the U Regulations. During the review process they would see to it that the primitive areas were reduced in size and stripped of any lands suitable to commercial exploitation for lumber or minerals.

A second and more common form of resistance was delay on the part of local and regional foresters. Field officers who adopted this strategy believed that, as time progressed, demand for the use of the resources in primitive areas would increase. It followed that fewer acres would be dedicated to permanent wilderness status, if the reviews could be put off while the demand for resources increased. In 1964, the year that Congress created a statutory wilderness system and twenty-five years after the adoption of the U Regulations, over 5.5 million acres of national forest land remained under the L-20 Regulation in the "primitive" classification.[99] This residuum of L-20 lands was to be a significant point of dispute in the battle for statutory recognition of wilderness in the early 1960s.

Robert Marshall died of heart failure in November 1939, only two months after approval of the U Regulations by the secretary of agriculture.[100] He had been described by his friend Robert Sterling Yard in

1937 as the "most efficient weapon of preservation in existence."[101] Yet, for all his valiant efforts on behalf of national forest wilderness, ultimately, it was probably the threat of national park expansion that provided the real driving force for the creation of primitive areas between 1933 and 1940. The system of primitive areas in the West was increased by more than five million acres in this period, and the increases correspond far more closely to areas of interest to the National Park Service than they do to areas of interest to Marshall.[102] This should serve to reemphasize the great importance of the 1916 National Park Service Act. Not only did it give the national parks, which were largely wilderness, an official guardian, but it also indirectly provided the impetus for creation and maintenance of a national forest wilderness system.

PRACTICAL POLITICS AT THE PARK SERVICE

The period of Robert Marshall's efforts at the Forest Service, 1933-40, corresponded closely with the administration of Arno B. Cammerer as director of the National Park Service.[103] While Forest Service policy did not often pose a direct threat to the National Park System during this period, the parks were not unthreatened. Park defenders were called upon to repulse several advances by developers eager to dig up park land. Efforts were made in 1933 and 1934 to open all the parks to prospecting,[104] but they were defeated. Other defense efforts were less successful. Glacier Bay National Monument in Alaska was opened to mining in 1936 in spite of opposition from preservationists.[105] The Colorado Big Thompson Tunnel through Rocky Mountain National Park was authorized the next year, over strenuous opposition led by the National Parks Association. Proponents of the tunnel were able to convince Secretary of Interior Ickes and Congress that this water diversion development would not substantially harm the park, and it was approved after considerable debate.[106]

The National Park Service came under fire from purists for failure to fight to the last man over these invasions of the parks by developers. Director Cammerer and his associates responded that practical politics necessitated concessions, and that a purist approach might well forestall the establishment of new, sorely needed parks. Major new parks, even if less than pristine, were a net gain for preservation. Park Service officials also cited the fact that, frequently, commercial uses permitted in a park's early existence were eliminated at a later date.[107]

The Park Service policy seems to have been an effective one, for several major additions were made to the system despite hard times and economic development's having made obvious new park sites increasingly rare. Preservation purists should have been pleased, as well, for every new park added under Cammerer's administration was a wilderness park. Florida's Everglades, Big Bend on the Rio Grande River in Texas, Olympic in Washington, and Kings Canyon in California constituted the major additions to the National Park System wilderness.,

Everglades National Park was authorized in 1934 after thirty-two years of interest in the area by the National Audubon Society. This interest was sparked by threats to the area's diverse population of rare birds. Early in the century, the birds were threatened with wholesale extermination for their plumage, which brought a fancy price on the fashion market. In addition, their habitat was being systematically destroyed by drainage and development projects. Everglades Park bills, supported by Audubon Societies, Crockett Clubs, the National Parks Association, and the National Park Service, were perennial in Congress from the early 1920s. When a bill was finally passed in 1934, it was with the condition that no appropriations could be made for five years. This restriction was lifted in 1937, demonstrating the wisdom of the National Park Service's pragmatic policy concerning acquisitions.[108]

Yellowstone probably owed its enormity to a desire to encompass any "wonders" not yet discovered in 1872. The creation of Olympic and Kings Canyon national parks demonstrates clearly the entirely changed circumstances that confronted park proposals only two generations later. The wonders of Kings Canyon and the Olympic peninsula were no mystery, and development interests fought to have those which were capable of economic exploitation eliminated from park proposals. Kings Canyon boasted a great potential for water power and reclamation development, while Olympic contained great riches in virgin forest and fabled mineral wealth. No significant mineral deposits were ever located in Olympic, but their presumed presence played an important part in the history of the area.

Portions of the Olympic area were designated as a forest reserve as early as 1897. The area of the reserve was decreased in 1900, increased in 1907, and decreased in 1909, amid clamor for mineral development. In the meantime, it had been transferred from the interior to the agriculture department with the creation of the Forest Service. President Theodore Roosevelt made the central portion a national monument in 1909, but it remained under the Agriculture Department until 1933 when all national monuments were transferred to the Interior Department. President Wilson eliminated half of the monument's area in 1915 to allow mineral development as a war measure. While the invasions of 1909 and 1915 were sanctioned for mineral development, it was inevitably timber that disappeared.[109]

Efforts to make the area a national park date from 1904, but always faced determined opposition from the lumber industry which dominated the area's economy. A major push for the park began in 1935, shortly after the national monument had been transferred to the National Park Service from the Forest Service. In 1936, the Forest Service designated lands adjacent to the monument as a primitive area, demonstrating the major role primitive areas played in Forest Service efforts to avoid encroachment by the National Park Service.[110]

The Forest Service was successful in delaying the final passage of a park bill until 1938, when the direct intervention of President Franklin D. Roosevelt obliged it to accept a compromise giving up much more than it got. In 1935 the Forest Service had defeated a bill for a 624,000-acre park. The 1938 bill called for inclusion of 910,000 acres. The Roosevelt compromise meant a reduction of the park's original size to 680,000 acres with a provision that the president, upon consultation[111] with the governor and appropriate cabinet secretaries, could expand the area up to 892,000 acres. Over a five-year period, Roosevelt took full advantage of his authority to expand the park, although the necessity of acquiring private lands delayed the actual completion of a 892,000-acre park until 1953.[112]

Interest in national park status for the Kings Canyon area dates well back into the nineteenth century, but because the area is adjacent to Sequoia National Park, some people advocated expanding Sequoia rather than creating a new one.[113] Among early sponsors of park status were the California Academy of Sciences, the Sierra Club, and the Interior Department.[114] The effort to establish Kings Canyon National Park paralleled closely the effort made on behalf of Olympic, with opposition coming from the Forest Service, lumber and livestock interests, and parties interested in the area's potential for power and reclamation development. After years of effort by supporters and antagonists, Kings Canyon Park was established in 1940.[115]

THE WILDERNESS IN WARTIME

With the nation engaged in a major war during the 1940s, one would expect little attention would be given to further wilderness protection. Policies are accepted in wartime that might face serious challenge in times of peace. Wilderness policies are no exception. Indeed, "total" war greatly reduces two requisites for wilderness appreciation: economic surpluses and adequate leisure. With a sudden surge in the demand for resources, postures intended to protect wilderness areas from exploitation might easily be interpreted as unpatriotic and selfish. The war effort made it quite unfashionable to question the motives of American free enterprise in developing the nation's resources regardless of social costs or profit margins.

Secretaries of interior must always have divided loyalties where wilderness preservation is concerned, since they are responsible for both preservation and production. Wartime economics increases the stakes, but does nothing to resolve the conflict. Secretary Ickes's policy pronouncement of December 16, 1941 embodies the dilemma clearly. He called upon his subordinates for a

full mobilization of the Nation's natural resources for war . . . upon a basis best suited to serve our military and naval forces without waste, and with a view to saving all that we can of such resources for future generations.[116]

In practice, this meant that compromises would be made with the economic inviolability of the parks, though, in so far as possible, such compromises were to be avoided except in cases of "critical necessity."[117] Critical necessity proved to be a high hurdle for developers, and only a few significant violations of "national park principles" took place. Some Sitka spruce, critical to airplane production, was harvested from land that had been acquired for addition to Olympic National Park, and limited mining was carried on in Yosemite, Death Valley, Olympic, and Mount McKinley, but grazing was kept to prewar levels in all the parks. Military use of the parks was extensive, but most of it did little or no permanent damage.[118] The congressional withdrawal of 6,400 acres of Hawaii National Park for a bombing test range was perhaps the most serious exception.[119]

The wartime situation in national forest wilderness and primitive areas was similar to that in the parks. Limited development of primitive areas took place during the war, contrary to the U Regulations. The Washington office did not move to correct this situation, however, until 1947 when the war effort was over.[120] No major additions to the Forest Service wilderness system were made, but neither were there wholesale declassifications of wilderness areas. All things considered, the war effort did little lasting damage to what was left of the American wilderness.

AUTOMATED TOURISM: AN INCREASING THREAT TO WILDERNESS

By midcentury, the very popularity of wilderness threatened its survival. Overcrowding had been common in some back-country recreation areas in the prewar era, but the depressed economy had kept many people home. As early as 1945, however, national park attendance had boomed to twenty-two million. Visitors in such numbers meant either serious overcrowding in developed areas of parks or gradual encroachment on the parks' remaining wilderness.

In 1949 National Park Service Director Newton B. Drury indirectly pointed up the threat posed by the tourist invitation when he wrote that the park system needed $140 million for physical improvements and $175 million for roads and trails.[121] While some forms of recreation are reasonably compatible with wilderness preservation, automobile camping requiring roads and other "recreational development" is not.

The national parks bore the brunt of the postwar tourist invasion, but the national forests were not immune from damage by hordes of recreationists.

The tourist boom had unique implications for the Superior Roadless Area, the nation's only congressionally protected wilderness.[122] Technology and tourist dollars had made possible a significant challenge to the wilderness nature of the area unanticipated before the war. A number of flying services had been established for the purposes of flying fishermen to interior lakes and tourists to resorts located on private property which still remained within the roadless area. Air service constituted a threat to the wilderness, and was surely contrary to the spirit of a "roadless area."

Concern was expressed by the Forest Service, some local residents and state officials, and by conservation groups led by the Izaak Walton League. As a result, the secretary of agriculture proposed an executive order creating an airspace reservation over the roadless area. He submitted the proposal to the secretary of commerce who advised against the reservation on the basis of a negative decision by the Airspace Subcommittee of the Air Coordinating Committee.

The internal workings of this group show all the classic symptoms of clientele capture. In this case, the clientele was quite uninterested in wilderness preservation. The Department of Agriculture, Department of Interior, and the Quetico-Superior Committee were denied their right to vote and were not informed of the subcommittee's meeting. Preservation groups were similarly uninformed, though the Air Transport Association and the Aircraft Owners and Pilots Association did have representation at the meeting. The subcommittee's recommendation took no cognizance of the special nature of the area:

The national policy calls for the fostering and encouragement of civil aviation and air commerce . . . [T]he proposed airspace reservation would be inconsistent with this national policy.[123]

President Harry S. Truman overruled his commerce secretary and issued the order on December 17, 1949. Its validity was subsequently challenged in federal court, but the judge noted that preservation of the area's wilderness nature was a well-established governmental purpose, and recognized the president's authority to issue the order. It was upheld on appeal.

THE EFFORT TO DAM DINOSAUR

The battle for Hetch Hetchy Valley had been lost to development interests in 1913, but not without a national outcry that surprised preservationists and dumbfounded their critics. That display of preservation sentiment was the result of an economy that had produced a shortage of wilderness, a high level of affluence, and a degree of disillusionment with industrial capitalism. Depression and war diminished the importance of these conditions in the 1930s and 1940s, but in the postwar period the booming economy produced both increased preservation sentiment and new threats to the wilderness.

Perhaps the greatest threats came from the Bureau of Reclamation and the Army Corps of Engineers, both big-budget government bureaus with cohesive and influential backing in Congress and among interest groups. Both agencies had designs on areas of wilderness in the National Park System. Glacier, Mammoth Cave, Kings Canyon, Big Bend, and Grand Canyon national parks were threatened by government dam builders. So were Dinosaur National Monument and the Cloud Peak Primitive Area of Bighorn National Forest.[124]

Dams are generally allowed in national forests but prohibited in national parks. In national monuments dams are permitted if they do not interfere with the purpose for which the monument was created. In the world of practical politics these differences in the level of protection are of small consequence. If Congress should choose to authorize a dam in Grand Canyon National Park, the specific law authorizing construction would supersede the general policy against dams, and the project could be built. The practical situation in national forests is much the same. Dams are permitted as a matter of general policy, but no government agency could build one without asking Congress to appropriate the money required. In short, congressional approval is necessary for any major dam construction project. Once given, that approval overrides any previous legislative or administrative protection. Congress can always revoke protections it has seen fit to grant on some earlier occasion.

Preservationists would have to be alert to meet the challenge of development proposals wherever they occurred. With so many projects planned, there was a danger that any battle lost might serve to open the flood gates to reclamation and power developments throughout the park system.

As it happened, the first major threat was to Dinosaur National Monument. Here developers hoped for a precedent, and here preservationists would have to make a stand. It was far from an ideal location from which to defend the park system. As late as 1946 the area was almost unknown even among park enthusiasts.

The National Park Service, itself, was less than enthusiastic about the area. When Ansel Adams, well-known photographer and Sierra Club notable, asked the Park Service whether Dinosaur ought to be included in his photographic essay on the National Park System, the service reportedly responded, "No, there is nothing there."[125]

Indeed, very few people had ever seen the place. Only the original eighty-acre fossil area was readily accessible by road. It attracted only 22,000 visitors in 1953, although that was double the previous annual attendance record. Fewer still had ever seen the endangered canyon, which had been added by President Roosevelt in 1938 for its spectacular rock formations. About 500 ran the river in boats in 1953, but fewer than that had made the trip in all the years from 1943 to 1952.[126]

Preservationists might have wished that the challenge had come at the Grand Canyon or some other widely appreciated unit of the National Park System. Arousing the nation to defend this spectacular, but little known, area would certainly be more difficult. Still, for wilderness enthusiasts, "unused" is a far cry from "useless." Certain psychic benefits accrue merely from the knowledge that the area remains unspoiled. Furthermore, the potential precedent was critical. The battle would simply have to be fought here.

What theatened Dinosaur National Monument was the planned construction of Echo Park and Split Mountain dams. These structures, a part of the Upper Colorado River Storage Project, would raise water levels 500 feet and flood the canyon's most spectacular formations.[127] The proposed project was to be undertaken by the Bureau of Reclamation, the Interior Department's largest constituent agency.

The proposed development pitted two coalitions of forces against each other. Proponents included a large federal agency and a host of local and regional interests. Officials and staff of the Bureau of Reclamation were eager to carry out their legal mission and thus increase the Bureau's appropriations. In the forefront of regional interests was the Upper Colorado River Commission, representing the economic interests of the four affected states.[128] The commissioners viewed the dams as part of a master plan for regional economic development based on federal tax dollars and the waters of the Colorado River. During the construction phase the project would bring jobs; once completed it would provide water for irrigation and cheap hydroelectric power. Flooding a valley few Americans had ever seen seemed a small price to pay. Senators, congressmen, state and local officials, area businessmen, and an assortment of water-users organizatons shared the views of the river commission.

Taken together, these interests represented a substantial coalition, but hardly a majority in Congress or the executive branch. Nevertheless, the proponents were strategically placed, and under normal circumstances they could count on substantial allied support. Colorado, New Mexico, Utah, and Wyoming together elected only nine congressmen, slightly more than 2 percent of the total House delegation; but they controlled three seats on the crucial Irrigation and Reclamation Subcommittee, 16 percent of the total.

The same four states elected eight senators. Half of them served on the Senate Interior Committee, and one was chairman.

On upper Colorado River questions the upper basin state delegations might expect support from most of the representatives and senators from thirteen other reclamation states of the West, with the exception of California. In addition, so long as there was no major rivalry between the Bureau of Reclamation and the Army Corps of Engineers, the upper basin bloc usually enlisted the support of delegations from the states most interested in flood control. All told the upper basin coalition could count on almost a majority of the Senate and more than 150 votes in the House, strength which gave the coalition a good start toward the working majority necessary to authorize the upper Colorado scheme.[129]

Proponents were hardly less well-off in the executive branch, where they were supported by the Bureau of Reclamation whose budget constituted the bulk of the budget for the entire Interior Department. Appropriations for the Bureau amounted to $205 million in 1953, compared to $33 million for the Park Service, which opposed the plan.[130]

The opponent coalition consisted of a smaller government agency and a host of conservation and preservation organizations.[131] The National Park Service was opposed because the dams would flood a part of the National Park System and thus violate "national park principles." Preservation groups like the Sierra Club, the National Parks Association, and the Wilderness Society feared loss of the canyon's natural features and especially the precedent of allowing reclamation projects within the National Park System. As the battle progressed, the opponents were joined by individuals who argued that the dams could not be justified on economic grounds and by southern Californian interests who feared any decrease in the amount of Colorado River water available to them.[132]

The Bureau of Reclamation proposal reached the desk of Interior Secretary Oscar Chapman, and was approved in June 1950 over Park Service objections. A number of western Democrats faced stiff opposition in 1950, and President Truman personally asked Chapman to approve the project.[133] Secretary Chapman did not, however, release the report for official interagency comment as required by law. The delay gave preservationists an opportunity to marshal their forces with the surreptitious support of the National Park Service.

Late in 1950 Chapman asked for the resignation of National Park Service Director Newton Drury. Although his ouster was apparently unrelated to his activities with respect to Dinosaur, it aroused a great outcry from conservationists. In order to placate them, Chapman met with conservation leaders in February 1951 and offered two concessions relevant to preserving Dinosaur National Monument. Chapman banned future water control investigations in the National Park System without specific secretarial approval. This ban would prevent park sites from becoming part of routine reclamation studies, and, therefore, of project proposals. Chapman also agreed to unleash the Park Service to aid preservation organizations in building the case against damming Dinosaur.[134] About the same time he released the Bureau of Reclamation report for review by other federal agencies.

Interagency review revealed a major break in the proponent coalition. The report was heavily criticized by the Army Corps of Engineers. The corps' study supported the view that the proposal had economic and engineering flaws.

This unanticipated opposition made upper basin congressmen anxious, and threats were made to introduce an authorization bill without the approval of the Interior Department if Chapman did not release the report to the Bureau of the Budget soon. The anxiety was well-founded, for Chapman's final recommendation to the Bureau of the Budget was less than enthusiastic. He proposed that either Echo Park or an alternative be built. From the developer's perspective, Chapman's recommendation was too little, too late. The Truman administration was scheduled to leave office in a month, and the entire project was bound to be reappraised.[135]

The new Republican administration proved more hospitable to the Upper Colorado River Project. Within the year, Secretary Douglas McKay, an appointee of President Dwight D. Eisenhower, produced a new report approving the Echo Park dam,[136] and bills to authorize construction had been introduced in Congress.

The House Committee on Interior and Insular Affairs was first to consider the bill. It was approved by a 13 to 12 vote after a move to delete the Echo Park dam had been defeated 13 to 10. The vote was much closer than would have been expected on a reclamation bill from a committee that is systematically receptive to western development projects. Its members must have been influenced by the deluge of mail drummed up by the preservationist organizations. In one month the House committee had received 53 letters in support of the project and 4,731 in opposition, a ratio of nearly ninety to one.[137]

The volume of preservationist mail to the entire Congress was enormous, and on August 11, 1954, House Speaker Joe Martin announced that, in light of the protest, the bill would not be considered by the full House in that session.[138]

Still the proposal remained alive. President Eisenhower called for the bill's passage in his 1955 State of the Union Address. On April 20, 1955, the Senate authorized the Upper Colorado River Project on a vote of 58 to 23 after rejecting the Echo Park elimination 52 to 30. The support of the president and the Senate notwithstanding, the project was in trouble in the

House. In June the House subcommittee bowed to preservationist pressure, reversed its previous stand, and eliminated the Echo Park site.

Upper basin interests realized their entire project was jeopardized by unwillingness of the House to authorize a dam in Dinosaur National Monument. In November the area congressional delegation met with the area governors and pledged to drop the controversial site. Interior Secretary McKay followed this action with the announcement that his department was dropping the Echo Park site from its proposal and would study alternatives.

The preservation of Dinosaur had been accomplished. With the Echo Park site removed, the Upper Colorado River Project won quick congressional approval and was signed into law by the president.[139]

Preservationist opponents of the project had had an opportunity to display their muscle. Even the preservationist organizations were surprised at their strong showing. Their newly discovered support was to be a major incentive to undertake a comprehensive wilderness protection bill—one that they hoped might eliminate the necessity of continual defensive actions on behalf of individual wilderness areas.

SUMMARY

For advocates of wilderness preservation, the years between 1916 and 1955 provided many reasons to rejoice. New men of stature had arisen to give voice to wilderness values. Arthur Carhart, Aldo Leopold, Robert Marshall, and others worked for preservation in and out of government, supported by new organizations like the Wilderness Society and the Izaak Walton League. Competition between the Forest Service and the National Park Service had given preservationists political clout beyond their numbers and resulted in the establishment of substantial areas of administratively designated national forest wilderness. Preservation had not been unchallenged, but, where challenges had been considered critical, preservation had generally prevailed.

Still, problems persisted. De facto wilderness everywhere received constant challenge from the drawing boards of developers. Federal reservations were not immune. National park back country was legally unprotected from roads and recreational developments, and the Park Service was eager to please the traveling public. Roads and recreational developments were forbidden in the national forest wilderness system, but that system relied for its existence upon the continuing good will of the Forest Service. With only administrative protection, national forest wilderness could conceivably be eliminated by a stroke of the agriculture secretary's pen.

In the minds of preservation activists the solution to these problems lay in the creation of a statutory system of protection for selected parcels of the

American wilderness, a positive program of protection to replace an endless series of defensive battles. Increasingly, after the victory at Dinosaur, preservationists felt the time had come to go on the offensive.

NOTES

1. United States Department of Commerce, Bureau of the Census, *Statistical Abstract of the United States* (Washington, D.C.: Government Printing Office, 1968), p. 5.

2. United States Department of Agriculture, Bureau of Agricultural Economics, *Supplement to Major Uses of Land in the United States*, U.S.D.A. Technical Bulletin 1082 (Washington, D.C.: Government Printing Office, 1953), pp. 61-62.

3. United States Department of Commerce, Bureau of the Census, *Historical Statistics of the United States, Colonial Times to 1957* (Washington, D.C.: Government Printing Office, 1960), p. 239.

4. United States Department of Agriculture, Bureau of Agricultural Economics, *Major Land Uses in the United States*, U.S.D.A. Technical Bulletin 1082 (Washington, D.C.: Government Printing Office, 1953), p.69.

5. Department of Commerce, *Historical Statistics*, p. 315.

6. United States Department of Agriculture, Forest Service, *Timber Resources for America's Future*, Forest Resource Report No. 14 (Washington, D.C.: Government Printing Office, 1958), pp. 12-15.

7. Department of Commerce, *Historical Statistics*, p. 352.

8. Herman E. Krooss, *American Economic Development*, 2d ed. (Englewood Cliffs, N.J.: Prentice-Hall, 1966), p. 238.

9. 12 Stat. 489.

10. Donald L. Kemmerer and C. Clyde Jones, *American Economic History* (New York: McGraw-Hill Book Co., 1959), p. 468.

11. 39 Stat. 355.

12. Calculated from United States Department of Commerce, Bureau of Public Roads, *Highway Statistics, Summary to 1955* (Washington, D.C.: Government Printing Office, 1957), p. 78.

13. Department of Commerce, *Historical Statistics*, p. 462. The percentage growth in vehicle miles which appears in the text is an estimate based on the assumption that the 1.76 million vehicles registered in 1914 were driven an average of 5,200 miles each, the per vehicle average in 1921, the first year for which data is available. Since the average number of miles per vehicle increased rapidly in the early years—it had exceeded 8,000 by 1928—the estimate in the text probably understates the actual growth.

14. D. E. Christensen, "The Auto in America's Landscape and Way of Life," *Geography* 51 (November 1966): 339.

15. John Ise, *Our National Park Policy: A Critical History* (Baltimore: Johns Hopkins Press, 1961), p. 183; Robert Shankland, *Steve Mather of the National Parks* (New York: Alfred A. Knopf, 1951), p. 7.

16. Ise, *Our National Park Policy*, pp. 193-97.

17. 38 Stat. 798; 39 Stat. 432.

18. 39 Stat. 938; Ise, *Our National Park Policy*, pp. 226-27.

19. 40 Stat. 1135; 40 Stat. 1178; 41 Stat. 356.

20. Treadwell Cleveland, Jr., "National Forests as Recreation Grounds," *Annals of the American Society of Political and Social Sciences* 35 (1910): 241-47.

21. Frank A. Waugh, *Recreational Uses on the National Forests* (Washington, D.C.: Government Printing Office, 1918), pp. 27-28.

22. James P. Gilligan, *The Development of Policy and Administration of Forest Service Primitive and Wilderness Areas in the Western United States*, 2 vols. (Ph.D. diss., University of Michigan, 1954), 1: 76.

23. G. Frederick Schwarz, "A Suggestion Regarding National Forest Reserves," *Forestry and Irrigation* 11 (1905): 288-89.

24. While there has been no great increase in total road mileage since the turn of the century, road building was a substantial threat to the wilderness character of most of the western national forests. These were precisely the areas where new construction was most likely.

25. Gilligan, *The Development of Policy and Administration of Forest Service Primitive and Wilderness Areas*, 1: 73.

26. The statement in the text ignores the 375 million acres of Alaska. The disappearance of wilderness in the forty-eight contiguous states was the major concern of early twentieth century preservationists. Support for this proposition may be found in the writing of Aldo Leopold: "The American of moderate means cannot go to Alaska, or Africa, or British Columbia. He must seek his big adventure in the nearby wilderness or go without it." Aldo Leopold, "Conserving the Covered Wagon," *Sunset* 54 (March 1925): 21. The Alaskan wilderness is not ignored in chapter 7.

27. Victor E. Shelford, "Preserves of Natural Conditions," *Transactions of the Illinois State Academy of Science* 13 (1920): 37-58; Francis B. Sumner, "The Need for a More Serious Effort to Rescue a Few Fragments of Vanishing Nature," *Scientific Monthly* 10 (March 1920): 236-48.

28. Sumner, "The Need for a More Serious Effort to Rescue a Few Fragments of Vanishing Nature," p. 236.

29. Gilligan, *The Development of Policy and Administration of Forest Service Primitive and Wilderness Areas*, 1: 78.

30. Arthur Carhart, "Memorandum for Mr. Leopold, District 3," quoted in Donald N. Baldwin, *The Quiet Revolution* (Boulder, Colo.: Pruett Publishing Co., 1972). Baldwin's book is the definitive work on Carhart. Carhart material appearing here is drawn from this source unless otherwise noted.

31. Baldwin, *The Quiet Revolution*, p. 69.

32. Ibid., p. 151.

33. Gilligan, *The Development of Policy and Administration of Forest Service Primitive and Wilderness Areas*, 1: 82.

34. Roderick Nash, *Wilderness and the American Mind* (New Haven: Yale University Press, 1967), p. 185.

35. Aldo Leopold, "The Wilderness and its Place in Forest Recreation Policy," *Journal of Forestry* 29 (1921): 718-21. Among the more accessible of Leopold's later articles on preserving wilderness in the national forests are: "The Last Stand of the Wilderness," *American Forests and Forest Life* 31 (October 1925): 600; "Comments,"

American Forests and Forest Life 32 (1926): 410; "Wilderness as a Form of Land Use," *Journal of Land and Public Utility Economics* 1 (1925): 398-404; and "Conserving the Covered Wagon," *Sunset* 54 (1925): 21.

36. Outdoor Recreation Resources Review Commission, *Study Report 3: Wilderness and Recreation—A Report on Resources, Values, and Problems* (Washington, D.C.: Government Printing Office, 1962), p. 280.

37. Emerson Hough, "The President's Forest," *Saturday Evening Post* 194 (January 14, 1922): 6.

38. Leopold, "The Last Stand of the Wilderness," p. 600. See also Leopold's "Wilderness as a Form of Land Use," and "Conserving the Covered Wagon." For the counterargument and Leopold's rejoinder see Howard R. Flint, "Wasted Wilderness," *American Forests and Forest Life* 32 (July 1926): 407; and Leopold, "Comments."

39. Gilligan, *The Development of Policy and Administration of Forest Service Primitive and Wilderness Areas*, 1: 95. Gilligan is quoting from a personal conversation with Greeley.

40. I have not attempted here to trace the in-service discussions and differences during this period of rapid transition. The best sources on the internal politics of this era are Gilligan, *The Development of Policy and Administration of Forest Service Primitive and Wilderness Areas*; and Baldwin, *The Quiet Revolution.*

41. National Conference on Outdoor Recreation, *Recreation Resources of Federal Lands* (Washington, D.C.: Government Printing Office, 1928). This is the report of the Joint Committee on Recreational Survey of the American Forestry Association and the National Parks Association to the National Conference on Outdoor Recreation.

42. Gilligan, *The Development of Policy and Administration of Forest Service Primitive and Wilderness Areas*, 1: 100.

43. William B. Greeley to District Foresters, December 30, 1926. Quoted in Gilligan, *The Development of Policy and Administration of Forest Service Primitive and Wilderness Areas*, 1: 104.

44. Gilligan, *The Development of Policy and Administration of Forest Service Primitive and Wilderness Areas*, 1: 106; E. W. Tinker, "Wilderness Areas in the National Forests are to be Preserved," in United States Department of Agriculture, *Yearbook* (Washington, D.C.: Government Printing Office, 1928), pp. 610-12.

45. William B. Greeley, "What Shall We Do with Our Mountains?" *Sunset* 59 (December 1927): 14.

46. Ibid.

47. National Conference on Outdoor Recreation, *Recreation Resources of Federal Land*, p. 139.

48. Ibid., pp. 139-40. On February 7, 1928, Congressman Scott Leavitt of Montana introduced a bill to authorize the establishment of national recreation areas within the national forests. The bill died in committee.

49. Gilligan, *The Development of Policy and Administration of Forest Service Primitive and Wilderness Areas*, 1: 121.

50. Ibid., p. 126.

51. Outdoor Recreation Resources Review Commission, *Study Report 3*, p. 20.

52. A mimeographed supplement to the *Forest Service Administrative Manual*, distributed June 29, 1929. Quoted in Outdoor Recreation Resources Review Commission, *Study Report 3*.

53. Gilligan, *The Development of Policy and Administration of Forest Service Primitive and Wilderness Areas*, 1: 126. A year later the term *research reserve* was abandoned in favor of *experimental forests*, *experimental ranges*, and *natural areas*.

54. Ibid., p. 119.

55. United States Department of the Interior, National Park Service, *Annual Report of the Director* (1924), p. 14, quoted in Ise, *Our National Park Policy*, p. 646.

56. Gilligan, *The Development of Policy and Administration of Forest Service Primitive and Wilderness Areas*, 1: 121.

57. The league had been formed in 1922 by a group of fifty-four Chicago area outdoorsmen desiring to "call a halt to resource degradation." Personal letter from Joseph W. Penfold, special programs director, the Izaak Walton League of America, Inc., to the author, February 3, 1972.

58. United States Congress, *The Congressional Record* 69 (April 23, 1928): 5921, 6051.

59. Fort Frances Pulp and Paper Company (Ltd.) to the Minister of Lands and Forests, Toronto, Ontario, August 25, 1920. Reprinted as "Exhibit A" in United States House of Representatives, Report No. 1945 (71st Cong., 2d sess., June 17, 1930): 12.

60. The actual flooding would certainly have been greater than this, for the power interests failed to submit flood estimates for several of the dams. United States House of Representatives, Report No. 1945, p. 6.

61. Lake of the Woods straddles the international boundary between Ontario and Minnesota to the west of the Rainy Lake chain affected by the Backus application.

62. United States House of Representatives, Report No. 1945, pp. 4-6.

63. O. C. Merrill, executive secretary of the Federal Power Commission, to Senator Henrik Shipstead, December 20, 1928. Reprinted in United States Senate, Report No. 1782 (70th Cong., 2d sess., February 15, 1929): 9.

64. The facts of the case are to be found in the documents appended to United States Senate, Report No. 1782, especially the very detailed letter from O. C. Merrill to Representative Walter H. Newton on February 11, 1928.

65. United States Senate, Report No. 1782, p. 8.

66. United States Congress, *The Congressional Record* 70 (February 16, 1929): 3562, 5219; United States Senate, Report No. 1782; United States House of Representatives, Report No. 2814 (70th Cong., 2d sess., March 2, 1929).

67. United States House of Representatives, Report No. 1945, pp. 1-2.

68. United States Congress, *The Congressional Record* 72 (May 7, 1930): 8521.

69. United States Congress, *The Congressional Record* 72 (May 19, 1930): 9149.

70. *Duluth* (Minnesota) *Herald* (June 26, 1930). Reprinted in United States Congress, *The Congressional Record* 72 (July 3, 1930): 12465.

71. United States Congress, *The Congressional Record* 72 (July 3, 1930): 12456-60, 12462-67.

72. Ibid., p. 12465.

73. 46 Stat. 1020.

74. Gilligan, *The Development of Policy and Administration of Forest Service Primitive and Wilderness Areas*, 1: 133-34.

75. Sigurd F. Olson, "Voyageur's Country: The Story of the Quetico-Superior Country," *The Wilson Bulletin* 65 (March 1953): 58.

76. The term is used in President Franklin D. Roosevelt's Executive Order No. 6783 creating the Quetico-Superior Committee.

77. Executive Order No. 6783, Creation of Quetico-Superior Committee (June 30, 1934).

78. Ernest C. Oberholtzer to Franklin D. Roosevelt, December 19, 1936. Reprinted in Edgar B. Nixon, editor, *Franklin D. Roosevelt and Conservation: 1911-1945*, 2 vols. (Hyde Park, N.Y.: Franklin D. Roosevelt Library, 1957), 1: 607.

79. Olson, "Voyageur's Country," p. 58.

80. President's Quetico-Superior Committee, *Report to the President of the United States on the Quetico-Superior Area* (Washington, D.C.: Government Printing Office, 1938).

81. Harold L. Ickes, secretary of interior, to Franklin D. Roosevelt, March 16, 1938; and Franklin D. Roosevelt to Cordell Hull, secretary of state, March 17, 1938. Reprinted in Nixon, *Franklin D. Roosevelt and Conservation*, 2: 200-1.

82. Olson, "Voyageur's Country," p. 58.

83. This episode is discussed below.

84. Robert Marshall, "The Problem of Wilderness," *Scientific Monthly* 30 (1930).

85. Nash, *Wilderness and the American Mind*, pp. 201-3.

86. Marshall, "The Problem of Wilderness," p. 147.

87. United States Senate, *A National Plan for American Forestry*, Document No. 12 (73rd Cong., 1st sess., March 30, 1933), commonly called the Copeland Report after the senator who sponsored the resolution commissioning the study.

88. Gilligan, *The Development of Policy and Administration of Forest Service Primitive and Wilderness Areas*, 1: 176-80.

89. Ibid., chap. 5.

90. F. A. Silcox to Regional Foresters, June 30, 1934. Quoted in Gilligan, *The Development of Policy and Administration of Forest Service Primitive and Wilderness Areas*, 1: 181-82.

91. Gilligan, *The Development of Policy and Administration of Forest Service Primitive and Wilderness Areas*, 1: 185.

92. Fourteen or sixteen by various accounts.

93. Gilligan, *The Development of Policy and Administration of Forest Service Primitive and Wilderness Areas*, 1: 189, 192; Nash, *Wilderness and the American Mind*, pp. 205-6.

94. Gilligan, *The Development of Policy and Administration of Forest Service Primitive and Wilderness Areas*, 1: 181-82; Nash, *Wilderness and the American Mind*, pp. 206-7.

95. Reprinted in Gilligan, *The Development of Policy and Administration of Forest Service Primitive and Wilderness Areas*, 2: 2-3.

96. Ibid., 1: 193.

97. Ironically, the U-3 (a) Regulation governing "Roadless Areas" permitted roads. Title 36, *Code of Federal Regulations*, Cumulative Supplement, paragraphs

251.20 through 251.22 (March 29, 1946). Reprinted in Gilligan, *The Development of Policy and Administration of Forest Service Primitive and Wilderness Areas*, 2: 6-7.

98. Ibid., 1: 195.

99. United States House of Representatives, Committee on Interior and Insular Affairs, Subcommittee on Public Lands, *Wilderness Preservation System, Hearings on H.R. 9070, April 27 through May 1, 1964* (Washington, D.C.: Government Printing Office, 1964), pp. 1139-43. This amounts to nearly 40 percent of all Forest Service lands classified as wilderness, wild, roadless, or primitive. According to the Forest Service, primitive areas were being administered as though they were subject to the more restrictive U Regulations pending their formal reclassification.

100. Richard L. Neuberger, "He Was a Millionaire Who Walked Himself to Death," in United States Congress, *The Congressional Record* 88 (December 14, 1942): A4306-7.

101. Robert Sterling Yard to Bernard Frank, September 13, 1937. Quoted in Nash, *Wilderness and the American Mind*, p. 206.

102. Gilligan, *The Development of Policy and Administration of Forest Service Primitive and Wilderness Areas*, 1: 198-99.

103. Ise, *Our National Park Policy*, pp. 354-55.

104. The national forests are open to prospecting under the mineral laws. With some exceptions the national parks are not.

105. Ise, *Our National Park Policy*, pp. 435-36; Roosevelt to Harold Ickes, secretary of interior, May 4, 1936, reprinted in Nixon, *Franklin D. Roosevelt and Conservation*, 1: 517-18.

106. Ise, *Our National Park Policy*, pp. 434-35; William P. Wharton, president of the National Parks Association, to Roosevelt, July 1, 1937, reprinted in Nixon, *Franklin D. Roosevelt and Conservation*, 2: 84-85.

107. This dialogue took place from 1936 to 1940 on the pages of the *National Parks Bulletin*, organ of the National Parks Association.

108. Ise, *Our National Park Policy*, pp. 371-78.

109. Ibid., pp. 382-85.

110. Ibid., pp. 383-88.

111. Note that the law did not require the agreement of the consulted parties.

112. Ise, *Our National Park Policy*, pp. 385-94.

113. The present Kings Canyon National Park is contiguous with the northern boundary of Sequoia National Park.

114. Ise, *Our National Park Policy*, pp. 396-97.

115. Ibid., pp. 397-404.

116. United States Department of Interior, *Report of the Secretary of the Interior* (Washington, D.C.: Government Printing Office, 1942), p. 160.

117. Ise, *Our National Park Policy*, pp. 449-50.

118. Ibid., pp. 449-52.

119. 54 Stat. 761.

120. Gilligan, *The Development of Policy and Administration of Forest Service Primitive and Wilderness Areas*, 1: 204-5; Forest Service Circular U-164, December 15, 1947.

121. Exclusive of the $181 million required for the completion of national parkways.

122. The following discussion depends heavily on Russell P. Andrews, *Wilderness Sanctuary* (Indianapolis: Bobbs Merrill Co., 1953).

123. Quoted in Andrews, *Wilderness Sanctuary*, p. 4.

124. Ise, *Our National Park Policy*, pp. 471-72.

125. David Brower, executive director of the Sierra Club, to Phillip Sirotkin, September 15, 1955. Quoted in Owen Stratton and Phillip Sirotkin, *The Echo Park Controversy*, Interuniversity Case Program #46 (Indianapolis: Bobbs-Merrill Co., 1959), p. 38.

126. Stratton and Sirotkin, *The Echo Park Controversy*, pp. 3-4.

127. Much of this information is available from a variety of sources. Stratton and Sirotkin, *The Echo Park Controversy*, is the most comprehensive report on the case as a whole. Other significant sources include: Harvey Broome, "Dinosaur National Monument," *Nature Magazine* 44 (January 1951): 34-36; "Will You Dam the Scenic Wild Canyons of Our National Park System?" a preservationist pamphlet distributed by the opponent coalition; "The Meaning of Dinosaur," *Sierra Club Bulletin* (May 1952): 9; Joe Penfold, "Reclamation's Plan for Invasion," *Sierra Club Bulletin* (May 1952): 10-13; U. S. Grant, III, "They Need Water—But They Don't Need Dinosaur Dams," *Sierra Club Bulletin* (May 1952): 14-23; Bernard De Voto, "Shall We Let Them Ruin Our National Parks?" *Saturday Evening Post*, July 22, 1950, and *Reader's Digest* (November 1951); Ise, *Our National Park Policy*, pp. 476-80, 557-60; and relevant congressional and Interior Department documents.

128. The Commission represented the four states of the upper Colorado River basin: Colorado, New Mexico, Utah, and Wyoming.

129. Stratton and Sirotkin, *The Echo Park Controversy*, p. 13.

130. Ibid., p. 17.

131. Opponent organizations included: the American Forestry Association, the American Nature Association, the American Nature Study Society, the Garden Club of America, the Izaak Walton League, the Colorado Forestry and Horticulture Association, the Emergency Conservation Committee, the Federation of Western Outdoor Clubs, the General Federation of Women's Clubs, the National Audubon Society, the National Parks Association, the National Wildlife Federation, the Nature Conservancy [formerly the Ecological Society of America], the Sierra Club, the Wilderness Society, and the Wildlife Management Institute.

132. Stratton and Sirotkin, *The Echo Park Controversy*, pp. 16-21; "Will You Dam the Scenic Wild Canyons of Our National Park System?"

133. Stratton and Sirotkin, *The Echo Park Controversy*, pp. 41, 47.

134. Ibid., p. 51.

135. Ibid., pp. 54-63.

136. Ibid., p. 69.

137. Ibid., pp. 21, 92-93.

138. Ibid., p. 93.

139. Ibid., pp. 93-95; 70 Stat. 105.

It may seem presumptuous for men and women, who
live only 40, 50, 60, 70, or 80 years, to dare to
undertake a program for perpetuity, but that surely
is our challenge.
                    —Howard Zahniser in testimony
                      before the House Interior Committee,
                      April 28, 1964, six days before
                      his death

PREFACE TO A WILDERNESS BILL

In 1954, James P. Gilligan received his doctorate from the University of
Michigan School of Natural Resources. His dissertation was entitled *The
Development of Policy and Administration of Forest Service Primitive and
Wilderness Areas in the Western United States*. It was at that time the only
book-length, scholarly study of wilderness that could be described as
politically oriented. Dr. Gilligan's dissertation was particularly significant
because he made a number of his conclusions public in a speech delivered on
October 26, 1954 to the Society of American Foresters meeting in
Milwaukee, Wisconsin.[1] Gilligan observed that wilderness in America was
doomed to extinction under the prevailing conditions and that prevailing
conditions could not be altered unless preservation interests formed a united
front in support of some positive program of wilderness preservation.

Gilligan's address is important for its physical appraisal of the state of
wilderness preservation, for its analysis of preservation politics, and for its
effect on the preservation movement. As an assessment of the state of
wilderness preservation in the early 1950s the conclusions of the speech are
unassailable, for the dissertation upon which they are based is the most
comprehensive study of the problem undertaken prior to the 1960s.[2]

The Gilligan address painted a bleak picture of the prospects for
wilderness preservation, given existing law and administrative practice.

Even though the consideration of minority wishes has long been an admirable trait of our governing groups [he reported], it is obvious in land use decisions that there is a steady trend favoring mass use over high quality benefits to fewer individuals. This fact, when combined with the irresistible emphasis on dollar rather than social values of our free enterprise economy, points out the tremendous barrier that wilderness preservation confronts.[3]

Gilligan's conclusion that present law and practice cannot preserve wilderness was based on a catalog of exceptions to wilderness management hidden behind large total acreage figures for officially recognized wilderness areas.

Those interested in national forest wilderness preservation are easily lulled into complacency by the soothing and oft-quoted figures of 13 million acres of land reserved in 77 wilderness, wild, and primitive areas throughout the West.[4]

Gilligan examined only a portion of these areas, yet he reported that they contained 200 miles of public roads, 145,000 acres of private holdings, 400 to 500 mining claims of unknown acreage, sixty mines, twenty-four air strips, pasturage for 140,000 sheep and 25,000 cattle, and nearly ninety dams. He also found wilderness areas diminished by boundary modifications that had shifted land suitable to economic development out of the system.

These deletions have largely been offset by the addition of high, rocky zones to each area where there is little possibility of development demands or timber harvest. [This policy] places a peculiar emphasis on maintaining a large national acreage figure for the wilderness system, while at the same time gradually removing areas needed in multiple-use management.[5]

Gilligan found the lack of dedication to wilderness in the Forest Service compounded by the fact that the Forest Service is far from completely sovereign in its own domain. The service is helpless to protect wilderness from exploitation under the Mining Act of 1872 and is not empowered to prevent dam building by the Interior Department.

In the national parks and monuments, the situation was only marginally better. National parks and monuments contained more wilderness than did national forests, and they were, for the most part, protected by law against lumber, water, or mineral development. Still, according to Gilligan, the National Park Service "is subject to the unrelenting pressures of mass use, and retreats gradually behind the cold logic that more areas must be developed to care properly for the public to which the land belongs."[6]

Gilligan's speech was not limited to castigating those who administer the public lands. He reserved equal criticism for wilderness proponents.

Philosophic incantations about wilderness values and the repetitious theme of saving wilderness everywhere are too abstract for the average administrator faced with unshakable realism. Wilderness supporters have been chiefly defense minded, rushing to prevent developments that may have been carefully drawn and justified. The majority of areas now called wilderness exist because recreational or industrial developments have not, as yet, been economically feasible.

If there were well defined purposes and plans for a national wilderness system which could generate common support, the wilderness movement might well be irrepressible. As it is, the disagreement among wilderness proponents is a highly important deterrent to wilderness preservation in this country.[7]

Gilligan concluded with a quiet plea for a united effort to preserve areas of wilderness.

Those who understand the problems of wilderness preservation on Federal lands are convinced that Congressional action is necessary to retain wilderness areas for future generations. It is improbable, however, that Congressional action or tighter administration to retain important wilderness regions can be effected with only the support of uncertain and divided wilderness proponents.[8]

This speech did not go unnoticed among proponents of wilderness preservation. The spring/summer 1955 issue of *The Living Wilderness*, the official organ of the Wilderness Society, reprinted it in full and devoted its editorial space to a reply saying, in part,

His criticisms should inspire us who uphold wilderness preservation to think out our plans and purposes more clearly and to seek more earnestly the certainty and unity among wilderness proponents which he sees as a requisite for the congressional action that is "necessary to retain wilderness areas for future generations."[9]

In a sense, then, the Gilligan speech was a warning to wilderness supporters that disunity and "philosophic incantations" could spell the end for wilderness even if the proponent groups maintained their ideological purity. It was a call for a positive program, and the Wilderness Society responded.

On May 24, 1955, Howard Zahniser, the society's executive secretary, addressed the National Citizen's Planning Conference on Parks and Open Spaces for the American People. His address, entitled "The Need for Wilderness Areas," outlined the kind of program that Gilligan had asserted was necessary. Zahniser proposed a "national wilderness preservation system" which would be composed of areas already under federal ownership. These areas would continue to be administered by the same agencies that already had jurisdiction over them. No new land administration agency would be required. Rather, administrative procedures would be modified so as to protect for all time the wilderness character of these areas. While the system Zahniser envisioned might be augmented by executive order, only an act of Congress could delete areas. The program, simply put, was to set aside those areas that had so far survived the onslaught of civilization as a kind of perpetual living museum, for the enjoyment of all the nation's people.[10]

The Zahniser speech did not merely express the society's position on preservation, but also proffered a specific program that was moderate in tone and perhaps capable of passage. It seemed to anticipate several major objections. It established no new federal administrative agency, scotching objections based on federal bureaucratic proliferation. It involved lands already in federal ownership, thus precluding the necessity of federal appropriations.

The speech attracted immediate legislative attention. On June 1, 1955, less than a week after its delivery, Senator Hubert H. Humphrey of Minnesota inserted the full text of "The Need for Wilderness Areas" in *The Congressional Record*. As Zahniser later explained, Senator Humphrey's interest led to the drafting of a wilderness bill under the auspices of the Citizens Committee on Natural Resources and the Council of Conservationists with the cooperation of the Wilderness Society, the Sierra Club, the National Wildlife Federation, Trustees for Conservation, National Parks Association, Wildlife Management Institute, and others.[11]

On February 29, 1956, Senator Humphrey publicly stated his intention to submit wilderness legislation along the lines of the Zahniser proposal as soon as possible. He had been encouraged to sponsor the legislation by William Magie of the Friends of the Wilderness, a Humphrey constituent. According to Magie, Humphrey never forgave him for the pressures he had to withstand as chief sponsor of the measure.[12] Many residents of northern Minnesota feared that the wilderness bill would damage the tourist trade generated by the Boundary Waters Canoe Area.

COMPREHENSIVE WILDERNESS LEGISLATION IS INTRODUCED IN CONGRESS

On June 7, 1956, Senator Humphrey introduced the nation's first wilderness bill, designated S. 4013. Senators Richard Neuberger and Wayne Morse of Oregon, Margaret Chase Smith of Maine, Herbert Lehman of New York, James Duff of Pennsylvania, Paul Douglas of Illinois, Thomas Kuchel of California, Karl Mundt of South Dakota, and William Laird of West Virginia joined in sponsorship of the bill.

S. 4013 was but the first of four Humphrey wilderness bills. The Wilderness Society, the National Parks Association, the Izaak Walton

League, the Council of Conservationists, the Wildlife Management Institute, the Citizens Committee on Natural Resources, and the Federation of Western Outdoor Clubs all had been consulted on the draft legislation, and had given formal or informal backing to the effort.

These groups were in regular communication with one another as well as with Senator Humphrey. Communication and cooperation among the major preservationist groups was facilitated by there being a few individuals who occupied a host of offices in several organizations. Among the critical individuals were Howard Zahniser, David Brower, and Ira N. Gabrielson. This group of three included half the members of the Council of Conservationists; the president of the Wildlife Management Institute; the chairman, the vice-chairman, and a director of the Citizens Committee on Natural Resources; the executive secretary and the honorary vice-president of the Sierra Club; the chairman, a past chairman, and a member of the executive committee of the Natural Resources Council of America; the executive secretary and one additional member of the Wilderness Society as well as a recipient of that group's Leopold Medal; two members of the National Parks Association; and members of more than a dozen other conservation groups.[13]

The first Humphrey bill, S. 4013, drafted with the aid of these conservation groups, was a strong preservationist document. It would create a national wilderness preservation system consisting of reasonably untouched areas of federal land in national forests, national parks, national monuments, wildlife refuges, and Indian reservations. Within these areas, all commercial enterprise would be banned including farming, logging, the grazing of domestic livestock, mining, and mineral prospecting. The building of roads or other structures would also be banned. The use of motorized vehicles would be forbidden except as necessary for the administration of the areas.

Some nonconforming uses were to be allowed to continue, however, where they were already well established. In this fashion, some toleration was granted to the use of motorboats and airplanes and to livestock grazing. An earlier draft had made some exceptions for mineral prospecting as well, but these had been deleted at the suggestion of the Izaak Walton League.[14]

The proposed legislation was to apply to a large number of areas under the jurisdiction of several federal land management agencies. In every case, the areas would continue to be managed by the same agency, but that agency would be legally bound to administer its areas with a view to preserving their wilderness character to perpetuity.

S. 4013 embraced all four Forest Service protected classifications, but not equally. "Wilderness," "wild," and "roadless" areas were all to be immediately incorporated into the system. "Primitive" areas were to be reviewed by the secretary of agriculture, who would make such modifications in their boundaries as he would generally make in the process of changing primitive to wild or wilderness areas. These primitive areas were to be incorporated into the wilderness system no later than January 1, 1966.[15] Such a procedure might have been expected to lead to a total of about fourteen million acres on Forest Service lands.

Most roadless areas within the forty-nine units of the National Park System would also become a part of the wilderness system. By 1966 this procedure would probably have added about twenty million acres to the system.

Twenty wildlife ranges and refuges were included in the system subject to the same exclusions for necessary roads and installations as determined by the secretary of interior. Another twenty million acres of wilderness might have been added to the system from these lands.

S. 4013 provided for wilderness areas on Indian reservations with the consent of the appropriate tribal councils, but only as long as the appropriate Indian representatives concurred. Therefore, the protection afforded to Indian lands was less substantial than that afforded other areas under the bill.

The Humphrey bill further provided that "any proposed addition to, modification of, or elimination from the National Wilderness Preservation System otherwise than by Act of Congress" would be accomplished by executive recommendation to the Congress.[16] Such a recommendation would become effective if, after 120 continuous calendar days during a single session of Congress, neither house of Congress had passed a resolution of opposition to the proposed change.

S. 4013 contained one additional provision of some significance. It contained language to establish a National Wilderness Preservation Council, consisting of specified government officials, and, by presidential appointment, interested laymen. The concept of a Wilderness Council interested some preservationists, but its functions were largely advisory.

On June 11, 1956, only four days after the introduction of S. 4013, Congressman John P. Saylor of Pennsylvania introduced a companion bill, H. R. 11703, in the House. H. R. 11703 was identical to S. 4013, reflecting the concerted effort by proponents of preservation to demonstrate unity behind a positive program. Representatives Lee Metcalf of Montana, Henry S. Reuss of Wisconsin, and George P. Miller of California introduced similar bills. These legislative efforts to preserve American wilderness received editorial praise from the *Detroit Free Press*, the *New York Times*, and papers in Oregon and Minnesota.[17]

The Humphrey-Saylor bill deviated in only two fundamental ways from the status quo prior to 1956. It gave statutory protection to areas heretofore protected only by administrative order, and it forbade mining and prospecting, thereby removing protected areas from the jurisdiction of the 1872 Mining Act. Most National Park Service areas already enjoyed this exemption.

The Humphrey-Saylor bill had been introduced in the second session of the Eighty-fourth Congress (1956). It was understood that time would not permit passage before adjournment, but advocates of preservation felt that it was still desirable to have the issue before Congress.

WILDERNESS BILL HEARINGS: COMPETING COALITIONS TAKE SHAPE

Humphrey and Saylor reintroduced wilderness legislation early in the Eighty-fifth Congress. By February 11, 1957, similar bills had been introduced by Representatives Barratt O'Hara, John F. Baldwin, Reuss, Metcalf, and Miller.[18]

Humphrey's second bill, S. 1176, had already undergone a number of changes from its predecessor, S. 4013, as preservationists sought to strengthen the bill's language. The most significant change was the immediate inclusion of Forest Service primitive areas in the wilderness system. This arrangement would give the primitive areas full protection of the law pending their review by the secretary of agriculture.[19]

S. 1176 was the first wilderness bill to be afforded hearings. Hearings were virtually assured when Senator James E. Murray of Montana, chairman of the Committee on Interior and Insular Affairs, signed on as a cosponsor of the bill. The committee took two days of testimony in Washington, June 19 and 20, 1957. While the chief group supporters of the bill had already surfaced in the drafting and introduction of the bill, these hearings provided the first systematic opportunity to assess the strength and sources of opposition.

WATER BECOMES AN ISSUE

Some opposition had surfaced prior to the hearings. Mining, lumber, and grazing interests were expected to oppose the bill. Not entirely expected was strong opposition from "water engineers who want[ed] to reserve a right to build water and hydroelectric projects in the wilderness areas."[20] According to newspapers in California, it was this opposition that caused California Senator Kuchel to decline cosponsorship of S. 1176, although he had sponsored the previous Senate bill, S. 4013.[21] Kuchel is reported to have argued that, "the problem of water development of California is so crucial that before any wilderness bill is passed we must have assurance that all necessary water resources are available for development."[22]

The water issue was central to the testimony at Senator Murray's Interior Committee hearings. Of nineteen opposing groups, five represented water interests. Some of those testifying for water development interests were representative of public and quasi-public groups. These groups were well entrenched in the West and were only beginning to confront major opposition to their projects. The Colorado Water Conservation Board, the Colorado State Watershed Conservation Association, and the Upper Colorado River Commission—all veterans of the Echo Park controversy—testified against the bill. Perhaps more damaging, however, was testimony on behalf of the California State Department of Water Resources. The department's resources planning chief, William L. Berry, testified that the California Water Plan ("a master plan for the development of all of California's water resources to meet the ultimate water needs" of a state population expected to reach three times the 1957 total) called for several water storage projects that would conflict with the provisions of the proposed bill.[23] He also argued that such projects would not harm wilderness areas.

In some cases, [said Berry], features of the California water plan must, of necessity, be physically located within areas proposed for inclusion in the National Wilderness Preservation System. There are no feasible alternatives available.

From a reasonable viewpoint, however, there is no necessary conflict between the two. With proper planning, operation, and maintenance, reservoirs can add to the beauty and recreational potential of these areas.

Other features, such as conduits and tunnels, need leave scarcely a visible trace after the completion of construction.

Proper planning, construction, and operation would allow the integration of features of the California water plan into wilderness areas with a minimum disturbance of natural conditions and with a maximum of added recreational value.[24]

The National Reclamation Association took a different approach, claiming that "there are plenty of areas in the West which will always remain primitive and undeveloped without the necessity of the restrictions proposed in this legislation."[25] In view of Berry's prior testimony, however, it is difficult to imagine what sort of areas the National Reclamation Association had in mind.

David Brower of the Sierra Club undertook to refute the needs of the California Water Plan: "It has been my own theory that California is going to run out of fresh air before it runs out of water." Given the opportunity, stated Brower, water will flow downhill. There is no reason why California cannot collect and store its water at lower elevations after it has flowed naturally from the higher wilderness areas. Indeed, the only benefit to be gained by high altitude is a small increase in hydroelectric generation potential. This benefit, according to Brower, was hardly worth the cost to the wilderness.[26]

HEARINGS REVOLVE AROUND BASIC THEMES

The intensity of interest in water development had come as an unpleasant surprise, but the greatest opposition to S. 1176 came, predictably, from organizations connected with commercial forestry, mining, and livestock production. These commodity groups all took the same general approach to the wilderness bill. Their opposition exhibited several major themes.

Opponents of the wilderness bill often began by denying any real need for wilderness legislation. The statement of the National Reclamation Association cited above puts the argument clearly. This approach challenged a basic assumption of wilderness proponents, an assumption set forth in paragraph two of the bill:

The Congress recognizes that an increasing population, accompanied by expanding settlement and growing mechanization, is destined to occupy and modify all areas within the United States, its Territories, and possessions except those that are set apart for preservation and protection in their natural condition.[27]

A second argument proffered by opponents was that the nation's wilderness areas were already well protected. The greater part of the areas at issue were, after all, either within the borders of the National Park System and thus protected by law, or within the National Forest System and under the administrative protection of the Forest Service. While this argument is closely related to the first, it was much more difficult to answer. An outright denial would be unflattering to the efforts of the National Park Service and the United States Forest Service, thus endangering cooperation between those agencies and the bill's institutional sponsors. Preservation proponents had some support in these agencies, but at the policymaking level Eisenhower's interior and agriculture departments were opposed to a statutory wilderness system. The unfavorable reports of these departments were cited by the bill's opponents as expert testimony from those closest to the situation.

The National Park Service was cautious in its opposition. Its director, Conrad Wirth, spoke for the Interior Department. He questioned the appropriateness of many Indian and wildlife refuge lands for inclusion in the National Wilderness Preservation System. He also worried that

the inclusion of the National Parks in a general system of wilderness areas . . . will have the effect of placing National Parks on a less firm foundation of protection than has already been provided by Federal law.[28]

While this concern was clearly one which wilderness proponents might share,[29] further testimony gave evidence for the proposition that preservationists and the Park Service differed on significant issues. Wilderness advocates consider development, particularly road building, to be the very antithesis of preservation, yet the National Park Service is frequently development minded. Wirth's remarks on road building called attention to a conception of wilderness many preservationists would not share:

As we build a road into Wonder Lake in Mt. McKinley National Park, that does not mean that the park is no longer a wilderness. The road is a wilderness road, to bring people into the wilderness.[30]

The Forest Service was more outspoken. The general view of the Forest Service, as enunciated by its chief, Richard E. McArdle, was that "the bill would strike at the heart of the multiple-use policy of National Forest administration."[31] "Although we are sympathetic to the general objective of the bill," he said, "we recommend that it not be enacted."[32] He indicated that the Forest Service would be very pleased with a bill that gave statutory recognition to wilderness preservation as a legitimate national forest use, but without removing the actual decision from the Forest Service.[33]

The response by proponents to the charge that wilderness had sufficient protection was a hedged denial. While applauding the generally exemplary performance of the administrative agencies, proponents stressed that some unfortunate decisions had been made. They pointed to the recent deletion of fifty-three thousand acres from the Three Sisters Wilderness in Oregon, a deletion personally approved by McArdle in the face of opposition from both Oregon senators and three of the state's four congressmen.[34]

Wilderness proponents also argued that purely administrative protection was insufficient to protect the wilderness resource. No law prevents a future secretary of agriculture from abolishing wilderness areas with a stroke of his pen. No law protects national park wilderness from roads and recreational development. The wilderness bill would preclude such possibilities and strengthen the ability of land management agencies to resist pressures for commercial exploitation or development of natural areas.

A third theme heard in opposition was that wilderness users constituted a privileged minority, a special interest with power out of proportion to its number, determined to "lock up" the nation's resources for their own limited use. Radford Hall of the American National Cattlemen's Association testified that the wilderness bill "would serve only the selfish interests of a very minute segment of our citizenry."[35] Stuart Moir, forest counsel for the Western Forestry and Conservation Association, approvingly quoted one of his predecessors, saying,

It is colossal selfishness on the part of those professional forest lovers, who are fortunate enough to travel throughout America's forest regions and sell their descriptions thereof, to want these regions treated as parks for their private delectation, at the expense of the homeless who want lumber at reasonable prices but can never see these parks, and at the expense of those local communities who live by supplying them.[36]

Opponents made much of McArdle's testimony that in 1956 only 1 percent of the fifty-three million recreation visits to the national forests involved use of wilderness areas, although those areas comprise 8 percent of national forest lands.

Related to the special interest argument was the belief that a National Wilderness Preservation Council would establish an institutional base for the wilderness idea, in effect, granting it a privileged status within the national government. The American Forestry Association's chief forester, Kenneth B. Pomeroy, testified that

if such a system is created, with a wilderness council . . . how then can one deny the creation of other resource councils? . . . In the end such councils would function as "built-in lobbies," create stalemates by opposing one another, and greatly impair the administration of the public lands. In fact, estblishment of a wilderness council would open the door for every other special interest.[37]

Later, Howard Zahniser was to testify that the Forest Service did have a timber council, and the Fish and Wildlife Service a wildlife council, as well.[38]

Proponents of wilderness legislation offered a number of related responses. One line of defense was the claim that "wilderness users" constituted a far greater segment of the population than those who actually visited wilderness areas. Zahniser, chief architect of the wilderness bill, made the point by analogy:

Here in Washington, you can go down to the National Gallery of Art . . . on a hot day like this, when it is cool in there, and wander around and have an experience in solitude, but none of us feel that the National Gallery of Art is there for just the few people that happen to be in that gallery at a particular time.

We maintain it for everybody, and, sooner or later, anyone who is concerned can visit it. That is also true of wilderness areas.

The wilderness areas are maintained so every American, now, and in the future, can have the privilege of choosing to visit a wilderness area, if he wishes to do so . . . and the very fact that it is there means a great deal to many people who do not visit it.

. . . A once-in-a-lifetime experience is enough to justify wilderness to anyone who cannot visit it again.[39]

Another line of defense, discussed in more detail below, was that recreational use constituted only the most visible use of areas which served a number of other functions.

ECONOMIC AND NATIONAL DEFENSE PRIORITIES

A fourth basic theme of the bill's opponents intertwined economic development and national defense priorities. The central argument was the immorality of denying anyone the benefits of economic development simply in order to gratify the aesthetic sense of a few. Testimony of A. Z. Nelson of the National Lumber Manufacturers Association is typical of the opponents' position:

When commercial resources are locked up our economy is deprived of additional tax dollars, pay envelopes, and consumer products. Many, therefore, are deprived of economic sustenance so as to provide a very limited number of individuals with wilderness pleasures.[40]

This was perhaps the most consistent argument of the bill's opponents. Lumber, mining, grazing, and other business interests all shared a firm commitment to development:

Conservation should not mean neglect and waste such as this legislation would encourage.[41]

. . . the mining industry is firmly behind the system established by the general mining laws for the location and patenting of mining claims as the means of encouraging and providing for the development of the mineral resources of the public domain through private initiative and enterprise.[42]

We . . . are unalterably opposed to the locking up of natural resources of any kind from development for the public good.[43]

The Chamber [of Commerce of the United States] believes that such lands should be managed primarily for their highest economic use. Other uses should be encouraged only when compatible with the major use.[44]

In general, opponents of the bill argued that they favored the "concept of wilderness," so long as this concept did not embrace any areas that had any significant potential for development.

The economic issue tied in nicely with a major concern of the 1950s, national defense. Opponents tried to establish the principle that any curb on economic development was a curb on the nation's ability to defend itself. It followed from this principle that advocates of wilderness preservation were diffusely traitorous, or vaguely un-American. Testimony on behalf of the American National Cattlemen's Association seems to make this point:

We believe the protection of the stockpile of atomic bombs is more important to the great majority of people on the East Coast than is the fact that a certain hillside in Wyoming has never heard the ring of the woodsman's ax or the putt-putt of a jeep engine.[45]

To the question of national security, proponents responded that the resources of wilderness areas constituted a strategic reserve that could be utilized if the national interest ever demanded it. Under such circumstances, surely the Congress would act to allow the exploitation of these areas. In the meantime, the congressional ban on development contained in the wilderness bill would protect these areas under less extraordinary circumstances.

Supporters of S. 1176 responded to the broader issue of economic development by stressing the limited economic impact of the bill. Howard Zahniser testified, "we have sought to develop a program that could be supported by those who are concerned with natural resources for commodity purposes."[46] He and others repeatedly made the point that the bill embraced no areas that were not already under some form of restriction with regard to development.

Proponents pointed to the fact that total inclusion of all the areas suggested would still amount to less than 2.5 percent of the total area of the United States. They stressed that those areas that remained wild had survived, at least partly, because they were not readily exploitable for economic purposes. No denial of potential economic uses for these areas was made. Rather, proponents extolled the credo first fashioned in reference to the national parks by Newton Drury, former director of the National Park Service: "Surely we are not so poor that we need to destroy them, or so rich that we can afford to lose them."[47]

Supporters of the bill accused their opponents of neglecting a multitude of wilderness values. Wilderness must be valued for recreation, they argued, and the more so as our daily lives become more regimented and mechanized, but it must also be valued for history, education, and science.[48] Large and ecologically undisturbed areas provide a crucial laboratory for the life sciences, allowing scientists to assess human impact elsewhere. In addition, wilderness areas continue to serve economically measurable functions. As watersheds they are frequently superior to areas that have been disturbed.[49]

Proponents admitted that some local economic dislocations might be postponed by developing wilderness areas, but insisted that where economies rested on one-time use of a nonrenewable resource, wilderness development could only postpone the inevitable. Buying time in this fashion, they argued, would not be worth the cost, namely, the destruction of wilderness, a significant national resource. Whatever economic value these lands have, they will be needed more by future generations than they are today.

FLEXIBILITY AND MULTIPLE USE

A fifth argument evident throughout the hearings was related to the economic development theme and had at its core the notions of flexibility and multiple use. These concepts are related. Both refer generally to a style of administration, and the virtues of both were extolled by opponents of preservation who had no desire to see Forest Service administration of the public lands further restricted.

The multiple-use doctrine had become deeply entrenched in the Forest Service since the time of Pinchot. At least some of the bill's opponents interpreted the doctrine to mean that nearly every acre must be managed so as to provide every possible use. Clearly, the logic of this interpretation breaks down occasionally. Building a reservoir precludes logging just as clearly as designating a wilderness does. How then is reservoir construction appropriate to the multiple-use concept, while wilderness is not? A more reasonable position, implicit in the remarks of many opponents of the bill, was that there is some sort of hierarchy of uses in which wilderness preservation, unrecognized by statute as far as the national forests are concerned, is ranked quite low. By this interpretation, however, wilderness is not a violation of the multiple-use principle, but an application of that principle interpreted so as to apply to the national forests as a whole. Thus, S. 1176 did not "strike at the heart of the multiple-use policy" as the Forest Service chief had suggested, but rather it gave wilderness a permanent and official status in the hierarchy of uses.

Wilderness proponents also stressed a view of the multiple-use doctrine applicable to the system as a whole. Some areas may be logged, others devoted to water impoundment, mineral extraction, or wilderness preservation. The very existence of administratively designated national forest wildernesses demonstrated de facto Forest Service adherence to this view of the multiple-use principle.

The notion of flexibility was closely related. Wise-use conservationists insisted that multiple use demands wide latitude in the allowable range of administrative behavior in order to meet changing circumstances. This is a sort of temporal multiple use. The Forest Service must be able to shift from one use to another as conditions dictate.

Preservationists were adamant about this point. To them flexibility spelled the end for wilderness. By contrast, wilderness advocates stressed irreversibility. David Brower appealed to a part of the American intellectual tradition, stating:

Thomas Jefferson, long ago, said that one generation could not bind another; each had the right to set its own course. . . . But deeds are not matching words. This generation is speedily using up, beyond recall, a very important right that belongs to future generations—the right to have wilderness in their civilization, even as we have it in ours.[50]

George Fell of the Nature Conservancy put the point most simply and cogently: "The next generation and the generations following will always have the choice of exploiting the areas we have preserved, but they will not be able to preserve the areas we have exploited."[51]

These five themes have dominated the debate over wilderness preservation. Details have varied as the scene has shifted from the Wilderness Act of the early 1960s to the Alaska Lands legislation of the late 1970s, but the continuing conflict between preservation and development has persisted in manifesting itself in new versions of these well-established themes.

By the conclusion of the hearings, the bill's designers were ready to make minor modifications to placate critics. Howard Zahniser, testifying in behalf of the Trustees for Conservation, said, "We are now ready to suggest some additional changes that are a response to the comments received since last February 11, when S. 1176 was introduced."[52] The changes were minor. They involved agreeing to analytical listing of wilderness areas, in place of an exhaustive list of names, and further clarifying the powerlessness of the National Wilderness Preservation Council. Of more interest is the proprietary attitude Zahniser took toward the bill. While the "we" is indeterminate, it seems to apply to the proponent groups more easily than it does to the bill's congressional sponsors. These remarks seem to suggest that the preservationist groups involved, or their leaders, had sufficient control over proponent forces to make their suggestions tantamount to adoption by the sponsoring senators.

The House held hearings on similar bills a few days later, but neither House nor Senate committee reported a wilderness bill. It is difficult to determine whether this failure is a sign of the strength of the bill's opponents. R. G. Lynch, in the *Milwaukee Journal*, had reported earlier in the spring that proponents would not seek passage in 1957. "Confident in their strength, the backers are taking it slow and easy." According to Lynch, proponents intended to "parade their forces" at hearings both in Washington, D.C., and in the West, and to press for passage in 1958. Advocates were reported to be "united and confident" of passage, but expecting a fight over modifications of the proposal.[53]

MODIFICATIONS TO PLACATE AGENCY OPPOSITION

In 1957 the fight over modifications was just beginning. While neither committee reported a bill, the Senate group was busily at work on one.

During the hearing Zahniser had solicited a request from the committee to prepare comments on the testimony of the Forest Service and National Park Service. These comments included a new draft bill that provided the foundation for Committee Print No. 1.[54] The Zahniser draft reduced citizen representation on the National Wilderness Preservation Council from six to three,[55] eliminated exhaustive listing of national park and national forest wilderness areas, and directed the secretary of agriculture to administer the national forests in accordance with a multiple-use concept applicable to the forests as a whole, specifically recognizing wilderness preservation as a supplementary national forest use.[56]

This draft made one substantial concession to the opposition, not surprisingly, in the direction of placating public agencies rather than commodity groups. The former had been more cautious in their opposition. It also appeared likely that, given agency support, wilderness advocates could overpower commodity-oriented opponents. The new draft gave the president power to authorize "prospecting, mining, or the establishment or maintenance of reservoirs . . . [when] such use . . . will better serve the interests of the United States than will its denial."[57] This change, by Zahniser's own admission, was directed toward overcoming the criticisms of the Department of Agriculture, the Department of Interior, and the California State Department of Water Resources.

Further discussions on the basis of Committee Print No. 1 resulted in Committee Print No. 2, which was introduced as a report by Senator Neuberger on April 15, 1958, and assigned S. 3619 by the clerk.[58] This insertion was not considered a new wilderness bill, but, rather, an opportunity to publicize the wilderness work of the committee and keep the issue in public view. S. 3619 contained one additional concession to the executive agencies, one not likely to please commodity interests. It changed the manner in which additions to wilderness areas could be made. While earlier drafts would have allowed the agencies to make these additions subject to veto by either House, S. 3619 required a concurrent resolution by Congress to overrule such an administrative action.[59]

On June 18, 1958, Senator Humphrey introduced his third wilderness bill, S. 4028. While significantly different from S. 1176, it contained no major changes from Committee Print No. 2. Its major purpose was to give the Senate Committee on Interior and Insular Affairs an opportunity to report out a reasonably clean wilderness bill. Humphrey and his cosponsors, Neuberger and Douglas, expressed the view that the bill had now been substantially perfected and should be reported and passed without further delay.[60]

Proponents had anticipated hearings in the West from the outset,[61] and opponents, seeing their greatest strength there, seconded the idea. Senator Murray obliged both groups during the summer and fall of 1958 with a series of five hearings, four in western states with many areas of de facto wilderness.

The first hearing on S. 4028 was held July 23, 1958, in Washington, D.C. It gave the government departments and national associations an opportunity to remark on the amended wilderness proposal. As the announced purposes were to consider the extent to which the revisions had met the objections of opponents, most advocate groups did not attend, satisfied to send communications reaffirming their support.

As has been noted, the major revisions seemed aimed at the land agencies, and the response of those agencies was the most significant portion of the hearings. S. 4028 found both the Department of Interior and the Department of Agriculture out of the opponents' camp and cautiously favorable to the legislation. Both departments still recommended against the creation of a National Wilderness Preservation Council, and the Agriculture Department requested authority for its secretary to institute insect and disease control programs,[62] but neither advised against passage.

This was a major triumph for proponents of the bill, since opposition of the executive departments most directly concerned with the bill had furnished opponents with a great deal of ammunition against its passage. In 1957 opponents had often quoted the Forest Service chief's statement that "the bill would strike at the heart of the multiple-use-policy." In 1958 the argument could still be made, but without the opposition of the Forest Service—the institutional embodiment of that policy—the argument lost a great deal of its force. Indeed, the arguments based on sound Forest Service administration and multiple use seemed less ubiquitous in 1958 than they had been in 1957.

STRATEGIES OF DELAY

While all of the arguments were repeated, opponents seemed more set upon delay in 1958 than upon defeat. They called for hearings in the West, and for postponement to await the arrival of the Outdoor Recreation Resources Review Commission report due in 1961.[63] Wilderness advocates had been eager for field hearings in 1957, but by the summer of the second session of the Eighty-fifth Congress, they were understandably less eager to begin any process that would allow S. 4028 to die with the expiration of Congress. As to the matter of the Outdoor Recreation Resources Review Commission study, proponents argued that a firm policy would aid the Commission's work. They denied any conflict in passage of a wilderness bill while the Outdoor Recreation Resources Review Commission was deliberating. Senator Neuberger, a sponsor of both bills, denied any conflict most vehemently.

Since no group was in a sound position to prevent western hearings, the committee scheduled four for November. The committee convened in Oregon, California, Utah, and New Mexico for one day's testimony in each state. The western hearings added nothing new to the debate, but did give many local interests an opportunity to express their objections. While actual witnesses expressed opposition more frequently than support, the committee's mail, the great bulk of it from western states, was well over 80 percent favorable.[64]

The only certain result of the western hearings had been anticipated by all concerned: Senate bill 4028 died with the expiration of the Eighty-fifth Congress. The bill's proponents were falling behind schedule, but no signs indicated that interest in wilderness preservation was losing strength.

By February 19, 1959, when Senator Humphrey and seventeen cosponsors introduced S. 1123, seven wilderness bills had been introduced in the House, including one by that body's foremost preservationist, Congressman John P. Saylor of Pennsylvania. The Saylor and Humphrey bills were identical and represented the interests of the preservation community.[65]

The Humphrey-Saylor bill contained a number of changes, again aimed more at soothing the land management agencies than the commodity interests. The secretary of agriculture was given specific authority to take action against insects and disease in wilderness areas and general authority "to protect and preserve the watersheds, the soil, the beneficial forest and timber growth, and all beneficial vegetative cover."[66] In practical terms this meant that the secretary could authorize activities to control fire and game overpopulation. In addition, the secretary of agriculture was given an additional ten years to reclassify primitive areas, bringing the total time allowed for that task to twenty years; and both secretaries were authorized to designate subordinates to serve in their places on the National Wilderness Preservation Council.[67] All this was designed to win support from the Forest Service and Park Service. Any substantial change for the benefit of commodity interests would be directly detrimental to wilderness preservation.

One minor change was made to placate western economic interests. Earlier versions of the wilderness bill had read: "Within the units of this System designated for inclusion by this Act . . . preservation shall be paramount."[68] In S. 1123 this portion was altered so as to state that areas of the system "shall be so protected and administered as to preserve their wilderness character."[69] According to Humphrey:

The substitute is equally satisfactory for wilderness protection purposes but avoids offending western water interests especially, who for well understandable reasons do not want anything considered paramount to watershed protection.[70]

Senator Murray quickly scheduled two additional western hearings in states previously bypassed. The hearings were held in late March and early April in Seattle, Washington, and Phoenix, Arizona. The quick scheduling of these hearings, even before the executive departments had prepared their reports, is indicative of Murray's desire to placate western critics and build an early momentum for the bill's Senate passage.

These hearings represented unfinished business. Many witnesses appeared, and nearly 500 pages of testimony were accumulated, but the major national organizations were conspicuous by their absence.[71] Opponents were vocal, stressing the same issues that had been elaborated in previous hearings. Yet, even in Washington State, individuals without a commodity interest in wilderness areas were nearly unanimous in their support for the pending legislation.

Perhaps the most important outcome of the western hearings on S. 4028 and S. 1123 was a growing realization on the part of the bills' proponents that the opposition was prepared to be intransigent and to exert itself to defeat the measure in spite of all concessions made by the bills' sponsors. The period of amiability came to an end as wilderness supporters saw their proposal losing momentum. Ira Gabrielson, chairman of the Citizens Committee on Natural Resources, put it this way:

we have a fight on our hands. We may as well recognize it. The fight is not against any interest who will be damaged by the proposed bill, but rather it is against the interests who have hopes of raiding the few remaining areas of wilderness for their own purposes whenever the future may offer them a chance.

The very fact that livestock, lumber, and other commercial interests are so ruthlessly fighting this bill is evidence that they are actually opposed to reasonable safeguards for any public areas. Their pious words for wilderness are forgotten when they face a practical program to preserve it.[72]

Indeed, it seems clear that some of the bill's opponents were engaged in purposely distorting its significance and misrepresenting its consequences; others may simply have been misinformed. The National Wildlife Federation's *Conservation News* for March 1, 1959, carried a report, "Battle Call to Save Wilderness," which quoted various speakers at Farm Bureau and livestock association meetings in Colorado and New Mexico:

The bill stops all grazing on wilderness areas and will be used to chase stockmen off the national forests altogether.

It opens the way for expansion of the wilderness system to encompass all national forest lands.

Local people would be deprived of all livelihood. Filling stations, tourist courts, and restaurants would have to shut down.

Three eastern states have tried this bill and it didn't work.[73]

The accuracy of this report in a partisan preservationist journal might legitimately be questioned, but similar misinformation was delivered directly to the Senate committee by opponents of the bill.

It was also evident that the proponent coalition was eliciting potentially serious counterorganization. Charles Judson described the formation of the Western Resources Conservation Council in the Grand Junction, Colorado, *Daily Sentinel*. The group is "a broad association of users of the public domain seeking its fullest development in the interests of recreation, food production, timber harvest, wildlife management, ore body discovery, and water and power development."[74] Leaders of this group had met with Congressman Wayne Aspinall, and in response to his warning that the real battle against the wilderness must be fought in the East and in California, the group had procured the services of the Denver public relations firm, William Kostler and Associates.[75]

Members of the Senate committee were under a great deal of pressure from both proponents and opponents of the bill. There seemed little likelihood that the full Senate would defeat the bill, but the committee was hardly representative of the full Senate. All of its fifteen members were from west of the Mississippi, and many had close ties with the commodity interests that opposed wilderness preservation.

Senator Murray, who was a strong advocate of the bill in committee, made a public issue of those ties:

For 25 years I have fought for the economic development of the West and of the Nation. I have supported measures to aid every industry now opposing the wilderness bill.[76]

Conflicting pressures seemed to foster inaction. The Phoenix hearings had been completed April 2, and by August there had been no action. One possible explanation is that the committee was awaiting the recovery of Wyoming's Senator Joseph C. O'Mahoney, who had suffered a stroke on June 19.[77]

On August 3, the Citizens Committee on Natural Resources attempted to regain some momentum with an open letter to members of Congress. The letter, covering a full page in the *Washington Post* and *Times Herald* newspapers, urged passage of the wilderness bill in 1959. It was signed by eighteen notables, including Karl Menninger, G. Mennen Williams, Eleanor Roosevelt, Adlai Stevenson, and Frederick Brown Harris, the Senate chaplain.[78] The next day the Senate Committee on Interior and Insular Affairs met and agreed to consider the wilderness measure in executive session on August 14. The committee had begun to mark up the bill, when on August 28 it announced that consideration had been postponed until the second session at the request of Senator O'Mahoney, who was still unable to resume his duties.[79]

Committee activity on the bill resumed early in 1960. On February 16, in executive session, O'Mahoney, recovered from his ordeal, offered amendments to S. 1123 that would restrict statutory protection to the fewer than six million acres already designated by the Forest Service as wilderness, wild, or roadless. On April 20, he was joined by Senator Gordon L. Allott in introducing these amendments in the form of a substitute bill.[80] The O'Mahoney-Allott amendments, as well as numerous others offered in executive session, contributed to the delay in committee.

Personnel changes also complicated action on the bill. Senator Richard Neuberger, a dedicated champion of wilderness preservation and member of the Committee on Interior and Insular Affairs, died on March 8, at the age of 47.[81] A month later Senator Murray, also an advocate of wilderness preservation, announced his retirement.[82] Several weeks earlier he had handed over chairmanship of the committee to Senator Henry Jackson of Washington.[83] In a brief space of time, the bill had lost two crucial supporters.

A third factor also intervened. Since the introduction of S. 1123, the Multiple-Use Act of 1960 had made its way through Congress, and had been signed into law.[84] This statute formalized the long-standing policy of the Forest Service with respect to national forest lands. In the process of reaffirming the multiple-use policy, it gave the first general statutory sanction to wilderness preservation in the national forests. Both houses of Congress incorporated this passage into the Multiple-Use Act: "The establishment and maintenance of areas of wilderness are consistent with the purposes and provisions of this act."[85]

Both supporters and opponents of the wilderness bill supported this enactment, the former stressing that it gave legislative sanction to what the Forest Service had already done, and that it was complementary to the wilderness bill; the latter stressing that it gave wilderness no statutory protection.[86] While the wilderness bill was stalled by its critics in committee, neither house was willing to pass the Multiple-Use Act in a form that would be inconsistent with the wilderness bill.

S. 1123 required technical amendments to take cognizance of the Multiple-Use Act, and these, along with the multitude of major and minor amendments considered by the committee in executive session, demonstrated the need for a clean wilderness bill. The new bill was introduced by Senator Murray on July 2 and designated S. 3809.[87] While it contained nearly thirty changes, only three were of any significance. All mention of wilderness on Indian reservations was dropped from the bill, as was the provision for a National Wilderness Preservation Council. More important, in an attempt to placate western interests, especially lumbermen who had expressed fear of "never-ending aggressive expansion of wilderness reservations under the wilderness bill procedures,"[88] the new bill stipulated that after a fifteen-year period, during which the executive branch could make alterations in the wilderness system subject to congressional veto as previously provided, additions to the system could be made, "only by Act of Congress."[89]

Even as he introduced S. 3809, Senator Murray admitted that "the prospects for finding adequate time for final consideration by the committee have become very discouraging."[90] Indeed, the Eighty-sixth Congress expired without a report on the bill.

The situation in the House was gloomier still. The chairman of the House Committee on Interior and Insular Affairs, Wayne Aspinall of Colorado, a committed foe of the preservation concept, had let it be known that there would be no action by his committee until a bill was passed by the Senate.[91]

THE SENATE PASSES A WILDERNESS BILL

Action on the wilderness issue picked up with the beginning of the new Congress, the Eighty-seventh. Six wilderness bills were introduced in the first three days of the new session, including two that were destined to see a good deal of action.[92] With the new year, the chairmanship of the Senate Committee on Interior and Insular Affairs had passed officially to Senator Clinton Anderson, also a supporter of the wilderness bill. Anderson introduced the new Senate bill, S. 174, on January 5 with thirteen cosponsors, including Senator Humphrey; Senator Jackson, now second-ranking Democrat on the Committee on Interior and Insular Affairs; Senator Kuchel, second-ranking Republican; and Senator Maurine Neuberger, elected to fill the seat of her late husband. S. 174 was considerably rearranged, but was, nevertheless, substantially the same bill as its immediate predecessor, S. 3809.

The new year also brought a new administration to power in Washington. The Kennedy administration took a greater interest in conservation than had its predecessor. Only one month after assuming office, John F. Kennedy addressed Congress on natural resource policy.[93] His speech contained an endorsement for the pending wilderness bill. Thus, for the first time, wilderness preservation became a part of the president's program. The following day Senator Anderson, stressing "the need to act now," announced that hearings on S. 174 would be held promptly.[94] The hearings followed predictable lines. Concerned interest groups reiterated their positions. The new Agriculture and Interior secretaries reflected the new president's commitment to a wilderness policy. Stewart Udall of Interior and Orville Freeman of Agriculture strongly recommended passage.

On July 27, having completed consideration on the bill, and having agreed to several amendments sponsored by Senator Frank Church of Idaho, the Committee on Interior and Insular Affairs reported favorably on the wilderness bill, S. 174. Senators Henry C. Dworshak, J. J. Hickey, Barry Goldwater, and Gordon Allott filed a minority report expressing major objections.[95]

The bill, as reported, required the Secretary of Agriculture to report on the primitive areas within ten years. Presidential recommendations based on these reports would be subject to veto by either house of Congress. The other significant amendments made minor concessions to commodity interests. One allowed limited prospecting to continue in wilderness areas. The other established an Alaskan Land Use Commission to advise secretaries of the land-administering departments on development.[96]

The bill reached the Senate floor on September 1, 1961. It withstood its first floor test when, on September 5, the Senate defeated, by a role call vote of 41 to 32, a surprise motion by Senator Allen Ellender to commit the bill to the Committee on Agriculture and Forestry, which he chaired.[97] Bills involving the public domain are regularly referred to the Committee on Interior and Insular Affairs, and those involving acquired lands under the jurisdiction of the Department of Agriculture to the Committee on Agriculture and Forestry. Ellender's claim to the bill rested on the fact that thirteen thousand of the fourteen million acres of Forest Service land subject to inclusion in the National Wilderness Preservation System were not a part of the public domain. Senator Ellender's motion was widely interpreted as an attempt to delay the bill, rather than as a serious contention that it had been misassigned. The bill's proponents noted that the Committee on Interior and Insular Affairs had been considering legislation of this type for several years without complaint from Chairman Ellender.

On the motion of Senator Metcalf, the committee amendments were agreed to *en bloc*. The Senate then proceeded to adopt a number of minor amendments with the approval of Senator Church, the bill's floor manager.[98] Debate on the bill was lively and occasionally misinformed, with Senators Allott, Dworshak, Goldwater, and Wallace F. Bennett holding for the opposition.

Three significant amendments were offered by Senator Allott. The first would have required an affirmative concurrent resolution of Congress to approve each addition to the wilderness system beyond the wilderness, wild, and roadless areas of the national forests.[99] Under the Allott amendment additions would face essentially the same hurdles as new legislation. The motion to amend was defeated by a 53 to 32 roll call vote the following day.[100]

A second debilitating amendment, giving power to authorize nonconforming uses of wilderness areas in the national interest to the appropriate secretaries rather than exclusively to the president, was similarly defeated.[101] The third, stating that the bill would not limit the authority of the Federal Power Commission to grant licenses for hydroelectric projects in national forest areas was accepted by the Senate with the approval of Senator Church.[102]

Senator Bennett introduced an amendment dealing with reclamation and power developments in national monuments, and for a time it appeared that the "Battle for Dinosaur" would be restaged on the Senate floor. Eventually, however, the amendment was withdrawn.[103]

The debate was concluded on September 6, 1961, and the Senate proceeded to pass S. 174 by a vote of 78 to 8.[104] As anticipated, preservation had the votes on the Senate floor, and S. 174 was dispatched to the House.

DELAY AND DISILLUSIONMENT IN THE HOUSE

True to his word, Congressman Aspinall immediately ordered hearings on the bill. Testimony was taken in three western states in late October and early November.[105] Then, after some delay—ostensibly to wait for the Outdoor Recreation Resources Review Commission's *Study Report No. 3*—five days of testimony were taken in Washington, D.C., from May 7 to 11, 1962.[106]

While opponents of a strong wilderness bill had repeatedly urged delay to await the forthcoming reports of the Outdoor Recreation Resources Review Commission, those reports provided them scant consolation. The Commission Report included a recommendation for wilderness legislation, which Congressman Saylor repeated for the *Congressional Record*.

There is a widespread feeling, which the Commission shares, that the Congress should take action to assure the permanent reservation of suitable areas of National Forests, National Parks, wildlife refuges, and other lands in Federal ownership.[107]

Equally significant were the conclusions and recommendations of the Commission's *Study Report No. 3* on "Wilderness and Recreation," which was released on April 16, 1962.[108] The report recommended:

Congressional legislation which specifically authorizes establishment of wilderness areas within Federal agency jurisdictions, and management activities to perpetuate wilderness conditions. This should include restrictions on mineral entry, mining, and water development, limiting these activities to those clearly in the national interest.[109]

The report concluded with the following observation:

It is difficult to avoid the conclusion that new legislation, specifically directed at and with clear mandates toward preserving wilderness units both in the National Forests and in the National Park System, will be necessary if wilderness areas are to be maintained.[110]

This report, too, Congressman Saylor brought before the full House.

The Interior Committee's Washington hearings attracted much greater participation than had the most recent Senate hearings. The political situation in the House was remarkably similar to that which had earlier prevailed in the Senate. There was a consensus that the House would act favorably on a wilderness bill if it could be gotten out of committee. The committee leadership, however, was firmly opposed to wilderness preservation.

Even with the favor of chairmen Murray and Anderson in the Senate, the bill had taken five years from first submission to passage. The House committee seemed even less hospitable to preservation than its Senate counterpart. Opponents saw a renewed opportunity to defeat the measure. Supporters realized that they must be victorious again to be victorious at all. As a consequence, nearly all the major national organizations with a stake in the wilderness bill were present to testify before Congresswoman Gracie Pfost's Subcommittee on Public Lands.

By May 11 the subcommittee had recorded 1,762 pages of testimony, more than four times the amount the Senate Committee on Interior and Insular Affairs had heard on S. 174, but something less than the nearly 2,500 pages the Senate committee had heard since it began considering wilderness legislation.

Testimony from proponents of wilderness preservation stressed the concessions that had already been made in S. 174 as well as the full range of preservationist themes that had been brought before the Senate committee. Opponents also repeated their arguments and demanded more concessions. Many opponents proposed amendments that would dilute the bill, ranging from specific exemptions for their own commodity interests, to revisions that would leave the wilderness less protected than if the bill were simply defeated.

A few general changes in the tone of testimony were apparent. For the first time, the secretaries of agriculture and interior were heard arguing for a stronger wilderness bill.[111] Opponents seemed to sense that some bill would pass. There was less talk of defeating the bill, more vague praise of the "wilderness concept," and greater acceptance of wilderness preservation where no commodity interest was at stake. Still, mining and petroleum interests, which by their nature cannot pinpoint the areas of value to them, continued to insist on free rein to carry on their activities everywhere. The concessions made by the bill's proponents may have won over some legislators, but they did not significantly blunt the attack of the major organizations opposing the bill.

Although it was expected to be July before Congresswoman Pfost's subcommittee would meet to mark up a House bill, Congressman Aspinall, chairman of the full committee, had promised action. "We'll get a wilderness bill of some kind out of committee," he said, "and we expect it to go through the House this year."[112]

Aspinall took an active role in the subcommittee's deliberations. The wilderness bill was first considered June 29, at which time Aspinall offered a substitute bill by way of amendment to H.R. 776.[113] This substitute was adopted.

On August 9 the subcommittee approved H.R. 776 as amended and sent it to the full committee. While H.R. 776 had been introduced early in the Eighty-seventh Congress by Congressman Saylor, the amended bill bore scant resemblance to its parent. As amended, the entire text had been replaced by new language. Only areas already classified wilderness, wild, and canoe were to be preserved.[114] Some commercial activity was permitted, including mining for a period of ten years. Furthermore, the wilderness classification of every area would be reviewed every twenty-five years to determine its continued appropriateness.[115]

Under the Aspinall substitute the entire wilderness bill was made Title II of an act that forbade all major changes in federal land classifications by the executive branch. Title I incorporated most of H.R. 8783, a bill introduced by Aspinall to reclaim a large measure of the authority over public lands that had been delegated to the executive branch over the years. This bill had been opposed by the land administration agencies,[116] and by the Justice Department, which characterized the bill as "objectionable from the standpoint of infringement of the constitutional powers of the executive branch."[117]

Title II, the "Wilderness Act," sustained two significant changes before the full committee. The committee approved an amendment by Congressman John E. Chenoweth extending the authority of the mining laws over wilderness areas until December 31, 1987, and an amendment by Congressman John Henry Kyl giving the secretary of agriculture authority to allow a ski development on 3,500 acres of the San Gorgonio Wild Area, California.[118]

The full committee voted to report the bill August 30. Then, in an unusual action, it adopted a resolution introduced by Congressman Alfred J. Westland "binding," in Aspinall's words, "the chairman to bring the measure before the House in accordance with the procedures provided by Rule XXVII—the suspension of rules procedure."[119] This procedure was presumably recommended

as one to avoid having emotions take over and undo the work of the committee. He [Westland] foresaw through this procedure the possibility of getting a bill through the House to get it into conference where the two bills from the Senate and the House can be reconciled and brought back with a conference report that we can pass.[120]

Operating under this mandate by the committee, Aspinall approached the Speaker on September 13 for approval of the bill. The Speaker, John W. McCormack, asked for assurance that the bill could muster the required two-thirds majority, and when Aspinall voiced his doubts, suggested he "make application for a hearing before the rules Committee."[121] McCormack had been urgd by many preservationists, including Spencer Smith of the Citizens Committee on Natural Resources and Ira Gabrielson, president of the Wildlife Management Institute, to deny Congressman Aspinall's request.[122]

Aspinall declined to convene his committee, which presumably could have given him new instructions had there been a desire to do so. Instead, he went before the full House on September 20 and denounced the supporters of wilderness preservation. Calling his bill "an attempt at a compromise," he announced to the members that

the extremists have now demonstrated that they have no desire to compromise, and in their reckless and ruthless demand to rule or ruin, they have created an atmosphere which makes [im]possible the enactment of any wilderness legislation during this Congress.[123]

He denounced fifteen proposed amendments published in *The Living Wilderness*,[124] suggesting that wilderness proponents had waited until the bill reached the floor so that they could substitute the Senate bill and subvert the committee system.

Not one of these amendments [he reported] was ever offered in the subcommittee or full committee, and to my knowledge not one of them was ever brought to the attention of any member of my committee.[125]

The next day Congressman Saylor presented a rather different picture of the events of the previous weeks. In a speech that characterized Aspinall as less than candid, he suggested that the chairman had contrived the entire affair for his own purposes. An avowed foe of wilderness preservation, Aspinall had "insisted on complete secrecy during the deliberations . . . and those of us favoring the original bill were precluded from discussing the matter with the outside proponents."[126] The fifteen amendments originally released by the Citizens Committee on Natural Resources came only one week after the first glimpse preservationists had of the new H.R. 776. Saylor reported that he had not brought the amendments before the committee because they would have restored the sense of his original H.R. 776, which had just been deleted in its entirety by the committee. He concluded:

Mr. Speaker, the chairman's explanation of the House Interior Committee action just [will] not wash. The failure to bring the wilderness bill to the floor for full consideration is the responsibility of the committee leadership. Their refusal is due to the fear that when the House has the opportunity to work its will, the result will not be of their choosing.[127]

The House Committee on Interior and Insular Affairs' report on the Aspinall wilderness bill[128] was finally filed on October 3, 1962, just ten days before the Eighty-seventh Congress adjourned. With no rule granted—or requested—it was never placed on the calendar, and the hopes for passage of a wilderness bill in 1962 expired with adjournment.

THE SENATE ACTS AGAIN

The Eighty-eighth Congress (1963-64) promised to be a re-creation of the Eighty-seventh where wilderness legislation was concerned. Senate passage was considered certain. Congressman Aspinall's committee was still the major obstacle.

Senator Anderson, chairman of the Senate Committee on Interior and Insular Affairs, introduced S. 4 on January 14, 1963 with the support of twenty-one cosponsors representing both parties and every section of the country.[129] S. 4 was identical to S. 174 as it had passed the Senate in 1961.[130] Senator Anderson was eager to pass the bill early so as to give the House an extended period of time to act without being threatened by the expiration of another Congress.

Hearings were held in Washington on February 28 and March 1. They were remarkably brief by wilderness bill standards. Most organizations offered only written statements, which were brief reiterations of their well-known positions.[131] Still, there were two changed circumstances that altered the tactics of the opposing coalitions. One change benefited the preservation cause; the other did not. The Outdoor Recreation Resources Review Commission report had been issued, and it was all the supporters of a wilderness bill could have wanted. Opponents had argued that no wilderness bill should be passed while the commission's work was in progress. If opponents had hoped that the report would recommend against wilderness preservation, they were disappointed. The report recommended a wilderness bill. Although the bills' opponents had lost a tactical advantage with the issuance of the commission report, they had gained one with the introduction of Aspinall's version of the wilderness bill, H.R. 776. Opponents who had claimed to support wilderness preservation "in principle" could now argue that they supported an actual wilderness bill. Neither shift of advantage between preservation and development forces had any impact in the Senate, however. The battle lines were already well drawn, and the outcome was not in doubt.

On April 3 the bill was favorably reported to the Senate with five minor amendments.[132] The vote in committee was 11 to 5.[133] The bill was endorsed by the departments of Interior and Agriculture, the Bureau of the Budget, and the Federal Power Commission. Senators Allott, B. Everett Jordan, Peter H. Dominick, and Milward L. Simpson signed minority reports favoring a bill along the lines of the Aspinall substitute.[134] The bill was made pending business the following day and debate began on April 8.

Senator Dominick, acting for Senator Allott, sponsored three crucial challenges to the committee bill. The first would have extended the applicability of the mining and mineral leasing laws through 1977. A second provided that any primitive area not reclassified after ten years time would lose its protected status. The third would have given the appropriate departmental secretary authority to approve nonconforming uses of wilderness areas, rather than investing this power in the president. Each weakening amendment was defeated by the Senate.[135]

A final amendment by Senator Dominick was modeled on the Aspinall substitute. In conformity with the view that Congress must reassert its constitutional right to control the disposition and use of the public lands, the amendment would have required affirmative congressional action on each executive recommendation for that recommendation to take effect.

In substantive terms, the question had become one of how difficult it was to be to enlarge the National Wilderness Preservation System beyond the wilderness, wild, and canoe areas immediately encompassed by the legislation. Leaving reclassification in the hands of the executive subject to congressional veto would leave the future size of the system largely to the discretion of the administration in power during the ten-year review period. It could conceivably approach sixty million acres. With the Kennedy administration in Washington and strongly supportive of preservation this option seemed more appealing to the wilderness lobby. On the other hand, requiring congressional approval for each addition to the system seemed to guarantee little or no growth beyond the original eight million acres. The wilderness bill had already proven to be a long, hard struggle for preservationists. It seemed unlikely that many additions could surmount the succession of obstacles that had to date prevented passage of any wilderness bill.

The Dominick amendment was defeated and the Senate proceeded to pass the measure by a vote of 73 to 12.[136] The Senate had acted, as expected, but the major hurdle still lay ahead.

COMPROMISE IN THE HOUSE

A great number of bills had been introduced into the House, many of them very similar. When House hearings commenced at Olympia, Washington, on January 9, 1964, there were twenty-two bills being considered. By the time the hearings reached Washington on April 27, there were two more. These twenty-four bills fell into three broad groups.

One group included S. 4 and a number of similar bills introduced by long-time supporters of wilderness legislation. Congressman Saylor's H.R. 930 was the prototype for this group of measures. Insiders saw little chance that any bill from this group could survive committee. Congressman Walter S. Baring, chairman of the Public Lands Subcommittee, had refused to schedule hearings on them, and Congressman Aspinall agreed with him on the matter. Baring had promised the American Mining Congress that there would be no wilderness bill unless "proponents are willing to move in the direction of the compromise offered by the House committee last year."[137]

Baring's remarks resulted in the introduction of several new bills, some sponsored by members who had already introduced stronger measures. These scaled-down bills were the price of hearings in the House, but some congressmen went further than others to placate foes of wilderness preservation.

Congressman Saylor was the first to introduce a new bill, H.R. 9070.[138] Saylor sought to test the validity of the congressional control issue raised by the Aspinall substitute. Saylor had always maintained that congressional control over the federal lands was not the real issue. On June 27, 1963 he told the House:

Now some of the same people who seven years ago opposed the wilderness bill for usurping bureau prerogatives are saying that it is giving the bureaus authority and surrendering congressional prerogatives. Such may seem to be inconsistent. Actually they are very consistent—consistently opposed to proposals that will preserve wilderness.[139]

He went on to promise:

Any proposals that provide for more positive congressional action will have our support if they likewise insure the protection as wilderness of the areas provided for in the act until Congress does take further positive action.[140]

Saylor's new proposal combined a strong wilderness bill with complete congressional control. It incorporated only as much area into the wilderness system as did the Aspinall substitute,[141] but provided for maintenance of the status quo ante on all other areas until Congress acted one way or the other.[142]

Other new bills went much further in meeting the demands of wilderness foes. Congressman John D. Dingell's H.R. 9162 was typical. H.R. 9162, like the Saylor bill, required an act of Congress for any addition to the wilderness system beyond wilderness, wild, and canoe areas. Unlike the Saylor bill, however, it did not protect the status quo of primitive, park, and refuge areas beyond the ten-year review period following the bill's passage. H.R. 9162 also extended the applicability of the mining laws to December 31, 1973.[143]

These three bills, H.R. 9070, H.R. 9162, and S. 4, differing widely in their potential consequences, shared center stage as the House Interior Committee commenced its deliberations.

Although little new was to be said at the 1964 wilderness bill hearings, the testimony compiled over a period of four months in Olympia, Denver, Las Vegas, and Washington, D.C. filled nearly 1,400 pages.

One minor issue nearly overshadowed the debate on the bill's merits. Since 1941 various developers had desired to create a ski complex in the region of San Gorgonio Mountain, California. This area had been classified "primitive" in 1931 by the Forest Service. The 1947 decision against ski development reiterated that within the area "wilderness was the predominant value."[144] The area was reclassified "wild" in 1955. As recently as October 16, 1963, Forest Service Chief Freeman had again rejected an application for this type of development at San Gorgonio. A good deal of testimony was devoted to this issue, and most of the committee's mail took a stand on it.

It had become apparent in the preceding Congress that the major issue was how far preservationists would have to compromise their bill to gain the approval of Aspinall's committee. Both Saylor's H.R. 9070 and Dingell's H.R. 9162 were obvious attempts to meet House committee objections. The Saylor bill had been developed with the cooperation of the Wilderness Society and was the last of a long line of preservationist bills revised to meet various objections. The Dingell bill, on the other hand, had been negotiated with Chairman Aspinall and the executive departments before its introduction in the House. For this reason, it was widely believed that the Dingell bill would be the basis for the committee's considerations.[145]

The House committee hearings made it clear that, for the most part, the gap between proponents and opponents of previous bills had been closed, and that the interested organizations, like the legislators, were in a compromising mood. The departments of interior and agriculture reiterated their strong support for a wilderness bill and said they could support the Dingell bill, providing it was amended to preserve the status quo in the primitive areas in the event that Congress failed to reclassify them during the ten-year review period.[146]

Without such an amendment the wilderness bill could be made the vehicle for the elimination of nearly 40 percent of the area to which the Forest Service had given administrative protection.[147] Congressman Dingell himself, in a letter to Chairman Aspinall, and in an appearance before the committee, urged the amendment of his bill to preserve the status quo in the administration of the primitive areas.

Conservation organizations, like the Citizens Committee on Natural Resources, the Izaak Walton League, the Sierra Club, and the Wilderness Society, admitted their preference for S. 4 or H.R. 9070, but chiefly addressed their remarks to the Dingell bill, which they assumed had the best chance of passage. The conservation spokesmen indicated that the Dingell bill would be acceptable providing the primitive areas were protected in their present state of administration.[148]

Regular opponents of wilderness preservation also seemed willing to settle on H.R. 9162, though it should be noted that, for the National Reclamation Association and the three major timber interests,[149] this acceptance was predicated on their belief that the Dingell bill would terminate the primitive designation after ten years if Congress had not acted.[150] The American Farm Bureau Federation, a long-time opponent, supported either H.R. 9070 or H.R. 9162, saying wilderness legislation "needs to be passed to prevent further designations of wilderness areas by Executive order."[151]

Still, some things never change. The American National Cattlemen's Association argued that no wilderness bill was necessary and that any wilderness bill before the report of the Public Land Law Review Commission was premature.[152]

Howard Zahniser, now the executive director of the Wilderness Society, was present for the final public hearing, as he had been for the first.[153] Allowing others to argue the legal technicalities, he attempted to reiterate the basic need for wilderness and the opportunity for its preservation. In many respects, his statement summarized his own efforts. "It may seem presumptuous," he said, "for men and women, who live only 40, 50, 60, 70, or 80 years, to dare to undertake a program for perpetuity, but that surely is our challenge."[154] Six days later, Howard Zahniser died, at the age of 58, the victim of a heart that had not been strong for several years.

The fate of the wilderness bill in the House rested with Chairman

Aspinall, and his behavior was no comfort to wilderness advocates. On April 30, just four days before Zahniser's death, Aspinall had appeared to be incensed over a *Washington Post* editorial that blamed him for the House's failure to pass a wilderness bill.

Those people and those writers and those individuals who consider that the action of last Congress was the action of the chairman of this committee and not the action of the committee itself just do not know what they are talking about and never have, and if they continue in this mode of operation, my opinion is that we will end up without any legislation.

Now, the editorial this morning appearing in the *Washington Post* was just about as dangerous, as far as killing wilderness legislation, as any article could be.

. . . .

Once again I had put myself in the position where I thought I was about ready to accept some leadership to get the bill out, but if I have to work with individuals who can put before the public such unworthy, untrue statements of conditions as they really are, then, of course, I am about ready to withdraw and let the chips fall where they will.

We have members of this committee who are absolutely opposed to any wilderness legislation. They have good reason; and we have some members of this committee who are for any kind of wilderness legislation. They would lock up anybody's property. It would not make any difference whether it upset the economy of a State government, or the economy of a region. They just do not care. They are so selfish. Then we have a great many moderates who would like to see some kind of decision arranged, but I can tell you, friends of the wilderness program, you may not be responsible for what some of your friends are doing, and I know there is a lot of truth in the old adage: "God protect us from our friends. We can take care of our enemies." If you cannot do a better job of putting before the American people the facts as they really are, then we might just as well shut the door and go on with something else.[155]

Preservationist sympathizers could hardly consider such remarks very encouraging. Less than a week later, however, after Zahniser's death, Aspinall sounded more conciliatory. In a tribute to Zahniser on the House floor, he seemed to indicate that his committee would produce an acceptable wilderness bill.

As frequently happens, [he said] Howard did not live to see the fulfillment of one of his prime objects: The legislative establishment of a National Wilderness Preservation System. However, he knew that his main battle had been won.[156]

The Subcommittee on Public Lands, chaired by Congresswoman Pfost, met in executive session on June 1 to mark up the bill. On the second of

June, it surprised most observers by reporting out an amended version of H.R. 9070—the Saylor bill. The subcommittee amendment allowed mining activity for twenty-five years after the act's passage.

Two other amendments were made by the full committee. By a vote of 14 to 11 it deleted the San Gorgonio Wild Area from the bill and ordered the secretary of agriculture to classify approximately 3,500 acres for a ski development.[157] This overruled the decisions against such development dating from 1947.

The second amendment cast serious doubt on the sincerity of those opponents who had couched their opposition in the necessity for congressional control over the public lands. The Saylor bill as amended by the committee would allow the executive branch to declassify areas now classified primitive, subject, in cases where a large acreage was involved, to a congressional veto within sixty days.[158] The committee thus proved to be willing to give the executive branch more power over deletions than S. 4 had given over additions.

PASSAGE OF THE 1964 WILDERNESS ACT

The work of the full committee was substantially undone on the House floor. A Saylor proposal to restore the San Gorgonio Wild Area to the wilderness system was passed 73 to 39.[159] A second Saylor amendment, to eliminate the authority granted the executive branch to declassify administratively portions of the primitive areas not suitable for preservation as wilderness, was adopted by a vote of 67 to 38.[160]

Thus amended, the wilderness bill, for years an exceedingly controversial measure, was adopted by a 374 to 1 roll call vote.[161] Following its adoption, it was renamed S. 4 and returned to the Senate. The report of the ten conferees[162] largely followed the House version of the bill. In the only significant change, the conferees set forward the date on which wilderness would be closed to appropriation under the mining laws, from 1990 to 1984.[163] The Conference Report was agreed to by both Senate and House on August 20, 1964, and signed by President Lyndon B. Johnson on September 3, 1964.[164]

SUMMARY

After several years of effort in Congress, the preservation community had succeeded in passing comprehensive wilderness legislation. Gilligan's call for well-defined plans and an end to philosophic incantations had been answered. The preservation lobby had marshaled the strength manifested in the battle to save Dinosaur and focused it to produce the Wilderness Act of 1964.

In its final form the Wilderness Act made statutory wilderness of the 9.1 million acres classified by the Forest Service as "wilderness," "wild," or "canoe" areas. Equally important, it protected the wilderness character of the national forest "primitive" areas until Congress decided whether permanent statutory wilderness designation was in order.

The system established was small, but it had the potential to grow. Years of struggle lay ahead, but the foundation had been well laid. Congress had committed itself "to secure for the American people of present and future generations the benefits of an enduring resource of wilderness."[165] To implement its commitment Congress had established a "National Wilderness Preservation System" and made a 9-million acre down payment.

NOTES

1. This speech was printed in the proceedings of the convention where it was delivered, reprinted in *The Living Wilderness* (Spring/Summer 1955), and again in United States Congress, *The Congressional Record* 102 (July 11, 1956): 12314-16. Citations here are from the *Congressional Record*.

2. Only the Outdoor Recreation Resources Review Commission, *Study Report 3: Wilderness and Recreation—A Report on Resources, Values, and Problems* (Washington, D.C.: Government Printing Office, 1962) is of comparable value as an assessment of the state of preservation at a given time. This study report was produced by the Wildland Research Center at the University of California under the direction of James P. Gilligan.

3. United States Congress, *The Congressional Record* 102 (July 11, 1956): 12314.

4. Ibid.

5. Ibid., p. 12315.

6. Ibid.

7. Ibid.

8. Ibid., p. 12316.

9. "Wilderness and Democracy," *The Living Wilderness* (Spring/Summer, 1955), reprinted in United States Congress, *The Congressional Record* 102 (July 11, 1956): 12313.

10. The speech is reprinted in United States Congress, *The Congressional Record* 101: A3809-12.

11. United States Senate, Committee on Interior and Insular Affairs, *National Wilderness Preservation Act, Hearings on S. 1176, June 19-20, 1957* (Washington, D.C.: Government Printing Office, 1957), p. 198.

12. William Magie, executive secretary, Friends of the Wilderness, to Craig W. Allin, February 4, 1972. William Magie interview, May 27, 1972, Moose Lake Landing, Ely, Minnesota.

13. This information is available in standard biographic sources.

14. United States Congress, *The Congressional Record* 102 (June 7, 1956): 9778.

15. Ibid., p. 9775.

16. Ibid., p. 9776. The Indian lands noted in the preceding paragraph are an exception to this provision.

17. Ibid., pp. 9778, 10980, 11838.

18. The Senate bill, S. 1176, was cosponsored by Senators William Neuberger, Margaret Chase Smith, Wayne Morse, Paul Douglas, Karl Mundt, James Murray, Alexander Wiley, Joseph Clark, Frank Lausche, Henry Jackson, and Warren Magnuson. The House bills listed in the text are, respectively, H.R. 500, 361, 540, 906, 1960, and 2162. United States Congress, *The Congressional Record* 103 (January 3, 1957): 70, 72-73, 81, 229, 321.

19. Senate Interior Committee, *Hearings on S. 1176, June 19-20, 1957*, pp. 1-8.

20. James McClatchy, "Bill to Form Wilderness Preserves Appears Again," *Sacramento* (California) *Bee*, February 19, 1957. Reprinted in ibid., p. 393.

21. Ibid.

22. James McClatchy, "Water Developers Fight Wilderness Area Proposal," *Sacramento* (California) *Bee*, February 19, 1957. Reprinted in Senate Interior Committee, *Hearings on S. 1176, June 19-20, 1957*, p. 394.

23. Senate Interior Committee, *Hearings on S. 1176, June 19-20, 1957*, p. 283.

24. Ibid.

25. Ibid., p. 331.

26. Ibid., pp. 348-49.

27. S. 1176 reprinted in ibid., p. 1.

28. Senate Interior Committee, *Hearings on S. 1176, June 19-20, 1957*, pp. 107-11.

29. The National Parks Association, long-time supporter of the National Park System, and usually of the Park Service, denied that the wilderness bill would in any way weaken existing protections for areas of the National Park System. Ibid., p. 317.

30. Ibid., p. 379.

31. Ibid., p. 11.

32. Ibid., p. 9.

33. Ibid., pp. 10-11. This was accomplished in 1960 with the passage of the Multiple-Use Act, 74 Stat. 215.

34. Senate Interior Committee, *Hearings on S. 1176, June 19-20, 1957*, p. 106.

35. Ibid., p. 398.

36. Ibid.

37. Ibid., p. 149.

38. Ibid., p. 158.

39. Ibid., pp. 153-54.

40. Ibid., p. 152.

41. Radford Hall, American National Cattlemen's Association, in ibid., p. 398.

42. Howard Gray, chairman, American Mining Congress, in ibid., p. 327.

43. Ibid., p. 329.

44. Unsigned statement on behalf of the United States Chamber of Commerce in Senate Interior Committee, *Hearings on S. 1176, June 19-20, 1957*, p. 414.

45. Radford Hall, executive secretary, American National Cattlemen's Associa-

tion, in Senate Interior Committee, *Hearings on S. 1176, June 19-20, 1957,* pp. 398-99.

46. Senate Interior Committee, *Hearings on S. 1176, June 19-20, 1957,* p. 154.

47. Ibid., p. 258.

48. Howard Zahniser, "A Statement on Wilderness Preservation in Reply to a Questionnaire," March 1, 1949, is the best overall statement on wilderness values. Reprinted in ibid., pp. 165-97.

49. "The Wilderness: A Major Water Resource," *The Living Wilderness* (June 1946). Reprinted in ibid., pp. 159-65.

50. Senate Interior Committee, *Hearings on S. 1176, June 19-20, 1957,* p. 354.

51. Ibid., p. 313.

52. Ibid., p. 155.

53. R. G. Lynch, "Which Way the Wilderness? Part 1: Nature Lovers Battle to Preserve the Wilds," *Milwaukee Journal* (June 9, 1957). Reprinted in ibid., p. 221.

54. Howard Zahniser, "Improvements in the Wilderness Bill," in the United States Congress, *The Congressional Record* 104 (April 15, 1958): 6343.

55. The land management agencies had expressed concern that private members of the National Wilderness Preservation Council could outvote the representatives of the agencies.

56. Senate Interior Committee, *Hearings on S. 1176, June 19-20, 1957,* p. 270.

57. Ibid., p. 274.

58. S. 3619 was not meant to be a bill, but the bill clerk assigned it a bill number as a part of his routine duties. In order to end the confusion, Senator Neuberger received unanimous consent to have the new bill, S. 3619, indefinitely postponed.

59. United States Congress, *The Congressional Record* 104 (April 15, 1958): 6341. See Section 2(f) of the bill.

60. United States Congress, *The Congressional Record* 104 (June 18, 1958): 11551-58.

61. R. G. Lynch, "Which Way the Wilderness?" in Senate Interior Committee, *Hearings on S. 1176, June 19-20, 1957,* p. 221.

62. United States Senate, Committee on Interior and Insular Affairs, *National Wilderness Preservation Act, Hearings on S. 4028, July 23, 1958* (Washington, D.C.: Government Printing Office, 1958), pp. 8, 44-53.

63. Ibid., p. 28. The Outdoor Recreation Resources Review Commission had been created earlier in the session. It was given the task of assessing outdoor recreational potential and need for 1976 and 2000 A.D. See 85 Stat. 470.

64. United States Senate, Committee on Interior and Insular Affairs, *National Wilderness Preservation Act, Hearings on S. 4028, November 7, 10, 12, and 14, 1958* (Washington, D.C.: Government Printing Office, 1959), pp. 2-6. These hearings were held in Bend, Oregon; San Francisco, California; Salt Lake City, Utah; and Albuquerque, New Mexico.

65. Cosponsors of the Humphrey bill were Senators Neuberger, Robert Byrd, Clark, Douglas, William Langer, Mundt, Lausche, Mike Mansfield, Thomas Martin, Morse, Murray, William Proxmire, Jennings Randolph, Smith, Wiley, Harrison Williams, and Hugh Scott. The House bills and their sponsors were: H.R. 713, Baldwin; H.R. 1867, Miller; H.R. 1873, O'Hara; H.R. 1885, Reuss; H.R. 1929, Metcalf; H.R. 1960, Saylor; and H.R. 2187, George McGovern.

66. United States Congress, *The Congressional Record* 105 (February 19, 1959): 2640.

67. Ibid., pp. 2638-43.

68. Ibid. 102 (June 7, 1956): 9775.

69. Ibid. 105 (February 19, 1959): 2641.

70. Ibid., p. 2639.

71. United States Senate, Committee on Interior and Insular Affairs, *National Wilderness Preservation Act, Hearings on S. 1123, March 30 & 31, April 2, 1959* (Washington, D.C.: Government Printing Office, 1959). These hearings were held in Seattle, Washington, and Phoenix, Arizona.

72. Ibid., p. 259.

73. Ibid., pp. 415-16.

74. Charles Judson, "Anti-Wilderness Fighters Begin Battle," *Grand Junction* (Colorado) *Daily Sentinal* (March 1, 1959). Reprinted in ibid., p. 418.

75. Ibid.

76. United States Congress, *The Congressional Record* 105 (February 19, 1959): 2689.

77. "Wilderness Bill," *CQ Weekly Report* 19 (September 4, 1959): 1208.

78. United States Congress, *The Congressional Record* 105 (August 3, 1959): 14916-18.

79. "Wilderness Bill," *CQ Weekly Report* 19 (September 4, 1959): 1208.

80. United States Congress, *The Congressional Record* 106 (April 20, 1960): 8320.

81. Ibid. (March 9, 1960): 5024-25.

82. He died a year later at the age of 84.

83. Senator Murray to Senator Kuchel, March 25, 1960. Reprinted in United States Congress, *The Congressional Record* 106 (April 5, 1960): 7307.

84. 86 Stat. 517.

85. United States Congress, *The Congressional Record* 106 (July 2, 1960): 15564.

86. Ibid., p. 15565.

87. Ibid., p. 15567.

88. Ibid., p. 15565. The words are those of Senator Murray.

89. Sectons 2(e) and 2(f) of S. 3809. Reprinted in ibid., pp. 15567-69.

90. United States Congress, *The Congressional Record* 106 (July 2, 1960): 15565.

91. Ibid. 108 (September 20, 1962): 20201.

92. The bills and their sponsors were: H.R. 293, Baldwin; H.R. 299, Charles Bennett; H.R. 496, Miller; H.R. 776, Saylor; H.R. 1762, John Dingell; S. 174, Anderson, Jackson, Kuchel, Lausche, Humphrey, Neuberger, Proxmire, Randolph, Scott, Williams, Douglas, Byrd, Wiley, and Clark.

93. February 23, 1961. See the *New York Times*, February 24, 1961, p. 12.

94. United States Congress, *The Congressional Record* 107 (February 24, 1961): 2653.

95. United States Senate, Report No. 635 (87th Cong., 1st sess., July 27, 1961).

96. Ibid.

97. United States Congress, *The Congressional Record* 107 (September 5, 1961): 18047-64.

98. Ibid., pp. 18070-71, 18383-87.

99. Ibid., p. 18108.

100. Ibid. (September 6, 1961): 18367.

101. Ibid., p. 18378. The amendment was defeated by a roll call vote of 51 to 35.

102. Ibid., p. 18380.

103. Ibid., pp. 18380-83.

104. Ibid., p. 18400.

105. The places and dates of the hearings were: McCall, Idaho, October 30-31, 1961; Montrose, Colorado, November 1, 1961; and Sacramento, California, November 6, 1961.

106. United States House of Representatives, Report No. 2521 (87th Cong., 2d sess., October 3, 1962). United States House of Representatives, Committee on Interior and Insular Affairs, Subcommittee on Public Lands, *Wilderness Preservation System, Hearings on S. 174, etc., May 7-11, 1962* (Washington, D.C.: Government Printing Office, 1962).

107. United States Congress, *The Congressional Record* 108 (May 1, 1962): 7482.

108. Outdoor Recreation Resources Review Commission, *Study Report 3.*

109. Ibid., p. 14.

110. Ibid., p. 316.

111. House Subcommittee on Public Lands, *Hearings on S. 174, May 7-11, 1962,* pp. 1062-79.

112. "Recreation Legislation Moving Toward Enactment," *CQ Weekly Report* 22 (July 6, 1962): 1145.

113. United States Congress, *The Congressonal Record* 108 (September 20, 1962): 20202.

114. Forest Service terminology for natural areas has gone through several changes over the years. Changes that do not affect management policy are ignored here. The original L-20 Regulation created "primitive" areas. It was followed by the U Regulations, which created "wilderness," "wild," and "roadless" areas, but left the "primitive" areas intact pending reclassification. There were only three "roadless" areas in the national forests, all in northern Minnesota's canoe country. These were consolidated into the Boundary Waters Canoe Area eliminating the "roadless" classification without affecting the area's management. Most of the wilderness bills of the period include the BWCA but exempt it from their most restrictive clauses. This exemption was in deference to the constituents of Senator Humphrey whose support was considered critical.

115. "Wilderness System," *CQ Weekly Report* 22 (August 17, 1962): 1369.

116. United States House of Representatives, Report No. 2521, pp. 57-65.

117. Ibid., p. 62.

118. "House Committee Approves Modified Wilderness Bill," *CQ Weekly Report* 22 (September 7, 1962): 1488.

119. United States Congress, *The Congressional Record* 108 (September 20, 1962): 20202. Under the suspension of rules procedure in the House a bill must be approved by the House leadership. No amendments are permitted, and the approval of two-thirds of those voting is required for passage.

120. United States Congress, *The Congressional Record* 108 (September 20, 1962): 20202. The words are those of Aspinall.

121. Ibid., p. 20203.

122. "Wilderness Bill Crisis," *The Living Wilderness* 26 (Spring/Summer, 1962).

123. United States Congress, *The Congressional Record* 108 (September 20, 1962): 20202.

124. *The Living Wilderness* 26 (Spring/Summer, 1962).

125. United States Congress, *The Congressional Record* 108 (September 20, 1962): 20202-3.

126. Ibid. (September 21, 1962): 20266-67.

127. Ibid.

128. United States House of Representatives, Report No. 2521.

129. United States Congress, *The Congressional Record* 109 (January 14, 1963): 190.

130. Actually, one word had been changed. "Forest Superintendent" was changed to "Forest Supervisor" to correspond to Forest Service terminology.

131. United States Senate, Committee on Interior and Insular Affairs, *National Wilderness Preservation Act, Hearings on S. 4, February 28-March 1, 1963* (Washington, D.C.: Government Printing Office, 1963).

132. United States Senate, Report No. 109 (88th Cong., 1st sess., April 3, 1963).

133. "Wilderness System," *CQ Weekly Report* 23 (April 12, 1963): 562.

134. United States Senate, Report No. 109, pp. 34-44.

135. United States Congress, *The Congressional Record* 109 (April 9, 1963): 5887-932.

136. Ibid., p. 5940.

137. Walter S. Baring, "The Wilderness Bill," speech before the American Mining Congress, September 17, 1963, Biltmore Hotel, Los Angeles, California. Reprinted in ibid. (October 3, 1963): 18606-7.

138. United States Congress, *The Congressional Record* 109 (November 7, 1963): 21430.

139. Ibid. (June 27, 1963): 11930.

140. Ibid.

141. Saylor's bill would add the wilderness, wild, and canoe areas. By virtue of administrative actions since H.R. 776 was reported, these classifications now contained slightly more acreage.

142. United States Congress, *The Congressional Record* 109 (November 7, 1963): 21435.

143. United States House of Representatives, Committee on Interior and Insular Affairs, Subcommittee on Public Lands, *Wilderness Preservation System; Hearings on H.R. 9070, H.R. 9162, and S. 4, April 27-May 1, 1964* (Washington, D.C.: Government Printing Office, 1964), pp. 1058-62.

144. United States House of Representatives, Report No. 1538 (88th Cong., 2d sess., July 2, 1964): 11-12.

145. There was also speculation that a Democratic Congress and administration would rather have Democrat Dingell's name on a major bill than Republican Saylor's.

146. House Subcommittee on Public Lands, *Hearings on H.R. 9070, H.R. 9162, and S. 4, April 27-May 1, 1964*, pp. 1069-72.

147. Ibid., pp. 1139-43.

148. Ibid., pp. 1180, 1228, 1236, 1299.

149. The American Pulpwood Association, American Paper and Pulp Association, and the National Lumber Manufacturers Association.

150. House Subcommittee on Public Lands, *Hearings on H.R. 9070, H.R. 9162, and S. 4, April 27-May 1, 1964*, pp. 1362, 1367, 1381.

151. John Taylor for the American Farm Bureau Federation. Ibid., p. 534.

152. House Subcommittee on Public Lands, *Hearings on H.R. 9070, H.R. 9162, and S. 4, April 27-May 1, 1964*, p. 354.

153. Zahniser had been present at all nineteen hearings, regardless of location, over an eight-year period.

154. House Subcommittee on Public Lands, *Hearings on H.R. 9070, H.R. 9162, and S. 4, April 27-May 1, 1964*, p. 1205.

155. Ibid., pp. 1291-92.

156. United States Congress, *The Congressional Record* 110 (May 6, 1964): 10214.

157. *New York Times*, June 11, 1964, p. 33. When the bill came to a final vote in committee, this provision provoked the only deviation from a unanimous report. Congressman Pat Martin of California, a strong advocate of the wilderness bill, voted present in protest over the San Gorgonio deletion. Other wilderness bill supporters, led by Congressman Saylor, voted for the report expressing confidence that San Gorgonio would be restored in conference with the Senate. *New York Times*, June 19, 1964, p. 12.

158. United States House of Representatives, Report No. 1538, pp. 2-3.

159. United States Congress, *The Congressional Record* 110 (July 30, 1964): 17451-56.

160. Ibid., pp. 17456-57.

161. The dissenting vote was cast by Congressman Joe Pool, a Texas Democrat; however, there were twenty-six announced pairs.

162. Senators Jackson, Anderson, Church, Kuchel, and Allott, and congressmen Aspinall, Harold T. Johnson, Compton I. White, Saylor, and Rogers C. B. Morton.

163. United States House of Representatives, Report No. 1829 (88th Cong., 2d sess., August 19, 1964).

164. Public Law 88-577; 78 Stat. 890.

165. The Wilderness Act, Section 2(a).

George Catlin's "Buffalo Hunt": In 1832, artist George Catlin wrote of his "contemplations on the probable extinction of buffaloes and Indians" and imagined that they might be preserved in a "Nation's park." *(Courtesy of Yale Collection of Western Americana, Beinecke Rare Book and Manuscript Library.)*

Mammoth Hot Springs in 1871: The first photographs of Yellowstone were taken by William H. Jackson during the Hayden Expedition and contributed to the park's creation the following year. *(Courtesy of the National Park Service.)*

Members of the 1871 Hayden Expedition to the Yellowstone *(William H. Jackson photograph, courtesy of the National Park Service.)*

Bison Skulls circa 1875: The near extinction of American bison in the nineteenth century stimulated public concern for wildlife conservation and the eventual creation of national wildlife refuges. *(Courtesy of the Burton Historical Collection, Detroit Public Library.)*

Teddy Roosevelt and John Muir: In May of 1903 President Roosevelt visited Yosemite and went camping with John Muir. *(Courtesy of National Park Service Historic Photograph Collection.)*

Gifford Pinchot: Friend of President Teddy Roosevelt and the first chief of the Forest Service, Gifford Pinchot's utilitarian view of conservation put him at odds with preservationists like John Muir. *(Courtesy of the Library of Congress.)*

Hetch Hetchy in early 1900s: The flooding of this valley in Yosemite National Park for a municipal water supply was denounced by John Muir and stimulated the movement to create a National Park Service. *(Photo by Isaiah West Taber, courtesy of the Sierra Club.)*

Steven T. Mather: The first director of the National Park Service, he brought an entrepreneurial spirit to national park development, enlarging the system but often at the expense of naturalness. *(Courtesy of National Park Service Historic Photograph Collection.)*

Wawona Tunnel Tree, Yosemite National Park: Although cut before creation of the Park Service, it was one of many departures from nature preservation endorsed by the Park Service in its enthusiasm to attract automobile tourists. *(Photo by Henry G. Peabody, 1929, courtesy of the National Park Service Historic Photograph Collection.)*

Arthur Carhart in Superior National Forest: The earliest wilderness advocate within the ranks of the Forest Service, Arthur Carhart was responsible for recommendations against development in the Trapper's Lake area of the White River National Forest, Colorado, and roadless areas of Superior National Forest, Minnesota. *(Courtesy Forest History Society, Durham, North Carolina.)*

Aldo Leopold: Celebrated as the "Father of the National Forest Wilderness System" for his 1921 plan to preserve 574,000 acres of the Gila National Forest, he was also a cofounder of the Wilderness Society, a pioneer of wildlife management and an influential environmental author. *(Courtesy of the Wilderness Society.)*

Robert Marshall, author, adventurer, bureaucrat, and principal founder of the Wilderness Society, Marshall was the most effective champion of the wilderness movement during the 1930s. *(Courtesy of the Wilderness Society.)*

Howard Zahniser, executive director of the Wilderness Society and unofficial author of the Wilderness Act, he died just months before final passage. *(Courtesy of the Wilderness Society.)*

Echo Park, Dinosaur National Monument: The threat of dams in the 1950s galvanized efforts to introduce bills to create a National Wilderness Preservation System. *(Courtesy of the U.S. Geological Survey.)*

Senator Hubert Humphrey: The Minnesota Democrat introduced the first wilderness bill in 1956 and remained a champion of the cause through passage of the Wilderness Act in 1964. *(Courtesy of the U.S. Senate Historical Office.)*

Congressman John P. Saylor: In 1956 the Pennsylvania Republican introduced the first wilderness bill in the House of Representatives. He was also instrumental in passage of the Wild and Scenic Rivers Act. *(Courtesy of Special Collections and Archives, Indiana University of Pennsylvania.)*

Congressman Wayne Aspinall: The Colorado Democrat chaired the House Interior and Insular Affairs Committee. His control of a key committee and effective representation of mining interests made him a formidable obstacle to passage of wilderness legislation.
(Courtesy of the Penrose Library, Denver University.)

Senator Frank Church: The Democrat from Idaho was floor manager for the Wilderness Act and chief Senate sponsor of wild and scenic rivers legislation. *(Courtesy of U.S. Senate Historical Office.)*

President Lyndon Johnson and Congressman John Saylor: The handshake commemorates signing the National Wild and Scenic Rivers Act, October 2, 1968. *(Courtesy of Special Collections and Archives, Indiana University of Pennsylvania.)*

President Lyndon Johnson signs the Wilderness Act, September 3, 1964. *(Courtesy of U.S. Fish and Wildlife Service.)*

Bridger Wilderness, Bridger-Teton National Forest: Named after mountain man Jim Bridger, this superlative western wilderness in the Wind River Mountains of Wyoming was established by the Forest Service and given statutory protection by the Wilderness Act of 1964. *(Photo by Craig W. Allin.)*

Linnville Gorge Wilderness, Pisgah National Forest: This tiny treasure in the Smoky
Mountains of North Carolina is one of only three eastern wilderness areas included in the
Wilderness Act of 1964. *(Photo by Craig W. Allin.)*

Rogue River Wild and Scenic River in Oregon: One of the original river segments protected by the Wild and Scenic River Act of 1968. *(Photo by Lee Webb, courtesy of the U.S. Forest Service.)*

Boundary Waters Wilderness: This million-acre portion of the Superior National Forest
has been subjected to more legislation, more litigation, and more use than any other
wilderness area in the United States. *(Photo by Craig W. Allin.)*

Congressman Morris Udall: The Arizona Democrat led the fight for passage of the Alaska National Interest Lands Conservation Act of 1980. *(U.S. Government photo.)*

Senator Mike Gravel: The Alaska Democrat successfully fought Alaska lands legislation to a standstill. President Carter responded by creating 56 million acres of new national monuments in Alaska. *(Courtesy of U.S. Senate Historical Office.)*

Cecil B. Andrus: interior secretary in the Carter Administration, his withdrawal of 110 million acres of federal land in Alaska and the subsequent creation of 56 million acres of national monuments and 38 million acres of national wildlife refuges were instrumental in overcoming opposition to the Alaska National Interest Lands Conservation Act.

(Courtesy of the U.S. Department of Interior.)

Senator Paul Tsongas: The Democrat from Massachusetts became point man for Alaska lands legislation in the Senate.
(Courtesy of U.S. Senate Historical Office.)

President Carter signs the Alaska National Interest Lands Conservation Act, December 2, 1980. *(Courtesy of the Jimmy Carter Presidential Library.)*

Mount McKinley (Denali): Encompassing the highest peak in North America, the Denali Wilderness was established by the Alaska National Interest Lands Conservation Act in the heart of Denali National Park and Preserve. *(Photo by Craig W. Allin.)*

Wrangell-Saint Elias Wilderness: Established in the Alaska National Interest Lands Conservation Act of 1980, the nation's largest wilderness area is bigger than New Jersey. *(Courtesy of Diane Taliaferro, photographer.)*

Alaska's Arctic National Wildlife Refuge: The Alaska lands legislation designated much of the refuge as wilderness, but the Coastal Plain was excluded because of its potential for oil and gas development. *(Photo by Cathy Curby, courtesy of the U.S. Fish and Wildlife Service.)*

> It is hard enough to design public policies and programs
> that look good on paper. It is harder still to formulate
> them in words and slogans that resonate pleasingly in
> the ears of political leaders and the constituencies to
> which they are responsive. And it is excruciatingly
> hard to implement them in a way that pleases anyone
> at all, including the supposed beneficiaries or clients.
> —Eugene Bardach
> *The Implementation Game*

Passage of the Wilderness Act altered the operations of three of the nation's
four major land management agencies: the Forest Service in the Department
of Agriculture and the National Park Service and the Fish and Wildlife Service[1] in the Department of the Interior.[2] In every case the administrative
response to the Wilderness Act was a product of the act's provisions,
clientele pressures, and the agency's own sense of its mission. These forces
differed for each agency.

WILDERNESS MANAGEMENT IN THE NATIONAL FORESTS

The historic mission of the Forest Service has been the management of the
nation's resources for "multiple use" so as to produce the "greatest good for
the greatest number." This was the dream of Gifford Pinchot, the first director of the Forest Service, and it remains the dominant theme of Forest Service management. When the service received its mandate in 1905, it was
only natural that it should see its mission as one involving primarily commodity exploitation, albeit a scientifically-based and conservation-minded
exploitation. In the agency's early years this view was strengthened by its
regular association with the commodity interests that came to transact
business on a regular basis with the government's tree company. When,
after World War I, Americans expressed an interest in using national forests
for recreation, the service found the idea relatively congenial to the
multiple-use doctrine so long as recreational use did not interfere with the

more important commodity uses. Even wilderness preservation of a sort
was embraced as consistent with multiple use, but the "primitive areas"
created by the service typically had low commodity potential, at least in the
short run. What is more, their creation was designed to placate preservationists, a new element in the Forest Service's clientele, and to slow expansion of the rival National Park Service. And while wilderness preservation
was consistent with service policy because the Washington headquarters
said it was, many old-line foresters in the field never accepted wilderness
preservation as wholly appropriate. Under the circumstances, a degree of
resistance to the provisions of the Wilderness Act was to be expected.

The act had greater immediate effect on the Forest Service than it had on
the Interior Department agencies. All the lands that Congress chose to place
directly into the wilderness system in 1964 were national forest lands.[3] As a
result, it was the Forest Service that had the immediate task of developing
regulations for wilderness management. The regulations, which were ready
in 1966, provide an insight to the Forest Service attitude about wilderness
management.

The Wilderness Act left some matters to the discretion of the agency.
These included the regulation of aircraft and motorboats where their use
had already become established, and measures for the control of fire, insects, and disease. There was an additional grant of discretion in the act's
special management provisions for Minnesota's Boundary Waters Canoe
Area. Section 4 of the Wilderness Act called upon the Forest Service to administer the BWCA in "accordance with the general purpose of maintaining, without unnecessary restrictions on other uses, including that of
timber, the primitive character of the area, particularly in the vicinity of
lakes, streams, and portages."[4] In each of these areas of discretion, the
Forest Service attempted to meet the standards of the Wilderness Act in a
manner that would involve the least possible change from its historic land
management practices.

In the BWCA, for example, the department carried forward the historic
administrative distinction between "interior" and "portal" management
zones. There is not much to distinguish one zone from the other in terms of
topography, but the interior zone has traditionally been managed as
wilderness.[5] Timber harvest, including clear cutting, has continued in the
portal zone since 1964, though the cutting is restricted in order not to be
noticeable from lakes or portages. The Wilderness Act required no changes
in the management of BWCA timber, and the Forest Service chose to make
none.

Forest Service management also allowed the use of snowmobiles over
those lakes and portages in the BWCA where in warmer seasons it allowed
the use of motorboats. Snowmobiles might be considered hard-water boats,

but their use was limited before 1964, and the service was not obligated to approve.

Clearly, the general direction of policy in the BWCA was not changed much by the Wilderness Act. The service endeavored to accommodate as many interests as possible. The dominant clientele pressures at the local level came from companies with timber contracts and from local users who preferred motorboat and snowmobile access. Continuing the historic policy left these interests largely satisfied. Policy continuity also pleased most professional foresters who would have been reluctant to see so large an area devoted to single-use management.[6]

Circumstances in the BWCA have always been unique. Policies adopted for those circumstances are not necessarily pursued in the rest of the Forest Service realm. Unlike the BWCA, most of the "wilderness" and "wild" areas placed into the wilderness system had had the careful scrutiny of the Forest Service. They were smaller in size and had fewer commodity values. The management practices in these areas before 1964 were already consistent with the provisions of the Wilderness Act. After 1964, however, the service used its discretion to further restrict wilderness use, creating a policy of "purity" beyond the requirements of the statute.

The purity policy manifested itself in every aspect of wilderness management. It dictated minimum interference with natural damage from fire, insects, and disease. In his study of the Forest Service, Glen O. Robinson summarizes the policy this way:

Usually insect and disease control is not undertaken unless the danger threatens to spread to other lands, or unless the epidemic presents a greater threat to wilderness values than does the method of control. The stated policy on fire is a bit vague . . . but in general the policy appears to be similar to that for insect or disease control, one which aims for a less aggressive control of fire in wilderness areas where it poses no danger to lands outside the area or to life and property within.[7]

The purist attitude is also present in the administration of motor vehicle policy. In April 1967 Forest Service Chief Edward P. Cliff told the Sierra Club's Wilderness Conference that "only where absolutely necessary will the Forest Service or its cooperators make administrative use of equipment generally prohibited to the public by the Wilderness Act."[8] He went on to cite examples where administrative tasks, generally accomplished by motor vehicle elsewhere, were being accomplished by snowshoe, ski, or horse travel within the wilderness.[9]

Purity has sometimes been carried to an extreme that many find offensive. On one occasion, when two members of an Outward Bound program died within a national forest wilderness area, a local official of the Forest Service refused to allow the use of a helicopter to transport the bodies, because dead bodies presented no emergency sufficient to justify the non-conforming use. The local decision in this matter was overruled by Washington, but the example serves to stress the devotion to purity in wilderness administration.[10]

WILDERNESS MANAGEMENT IN THE NATIONAL PARKS
AND WILDLIFE REFUGES

For the Interior Department agencies the circumstances following passage of the Wilderness Act were somewhat different. Neither the Park Service nor the Fish and Wildlife Service managed lands that had been designated as instant wilderness by Congress. Nevertheless, each had a mandate to develop regulations for the management of such areas once they were designated.

The historic mission of the National Park Service is stated in the National Park Service Act of 1916: "To conserve the scenery and the natural and historic objects and the wild life therein, and to provide for the enjoyment of the same in such a manner and by such means as will leave them unimpaired for the enjoyment of future generations."[11] From the beginning Park Service leadership has recognized that the parks' only real constituency was the traveling public. One result has been an extraordinary emphasis on "enjoyment" in national park management. If the tourists are happy, the Park Service will thrive; therefore, by all means make the tourists happy. To accommodate the desires of tourists, the Park Service evolved a management policy that stressed developments for the convenience of the consumer. Those developments included paved roads, fancy hotels, and, in extreme cases, swimming pools and golf courses. The desire to please the tourists also motivated a good deal of official gimmickry. To improve on the natural surroundings the service cut roads through giant sequoias, pushed fires over cliffs, fed garbage to bears in front of grandstands, and poured chemicals into geysers in order to stimulate eruptions.[12]

Clearly, the Wilderness Act presented something of a threat to the mass merchandising mentality of the Park Service. Large areas of Park Service wilderness would severely restrict management discretion. Predictably, the agency's primary reaction to the Wilderness Act was an attempt to minimize its impact. In fact, the "National Park Service Wilderness Management Criteria,"[13] which were presented to the Sierra Club's 1967 Wilderness Conference, indicated no major change in management plans for the parks as a result of the Wilderness Act. In accompanying remarks Park Service Director George B. Hartzog denied that the proponents of the Wilderness Act had meant any change in park policy. Calling attention to the Wilderness Act's declaration that its purposes were to be "supplemental to the purposes for which . . . units of the National Park System are established and administered . . . ," Hartzog concluded, "in the wilderness legislation, Congress has not changed its long-established policies for the management and use of the National Parks."[14] "To assume that the Wilderness Act establishes new standards and new criteria for National Park wilderness, replacing the old and time-tested wilderness standards and criteria of the Service, would jeopardize the whole National Park concept."[15] While the director did not explain how the park concept would be jeopardized, his management criteria seemed to be designed to protect wilderness values from degradation by anyone not associated with the Park Service. Historic administrative techniques including the use of motorized vehicles, fire roads, lookout towers, and patrol cabins were all explicitly approved by the criteria, as was some manipulation of the fauna and flora. The Park Service viewed its personnel as professional wilderness managers and interpreted the Wilderness Act to present the minimum possible interference with professional prerogatives.

While both the Forest Service and the Park Sevice seemed somewhat concerned that the commandments of the Wilderness Act might cramp their style, the Fish and Wildlife Service (FWS) found the act more congenial.

The historic mission of the Fish and Wildlife Service has been the protection of critical habitat for wildlife. But all wildlife have not been equally cherished. Most refuges have been created to protect the supply of game species for hunters, and hunting organizations have been the primary clientele for the service. As a consequence, the FWS viewed the Wilderness Act as a tool to control more effectively the use of refuge areas for the benefit of the protected species. Since the Wilderness Act did not make wilderness areas wildlife sanctuaries, it presented no significant threat to the FWS's hunter clientele.

While the Forest Service and the National Park Service were reluctant to implement the Wilderness Act, the Fish and Wildlife Service seemed almost enthusiastic. By April 1967 it had identified 80 percent of the total refuge acreage for wilderness study, and Assistant Director Noble Buell was predicting even more. No specific regulations for wilderness management had been developed, but the service looked forward to using provisions of the Wilderness Act to tighten its management control. Indeed, Buell expressed the hope that nonconforming uses explicitly permitted by the act, like grazing, prospecting, and mining, might be eliminated as Congress considered legislation for wilderness areas within the National Wildlife Refuge System.[16]

WILDERNESS REVIEWS IN THE INTERIOR DEPARTMENT

A second administrative task mandated by the Wilderness Act was more complex, involved greater discretion, and aroused far greater controversy.

The act had made the "wilderness," "wild," and "canoe" areas of the national forests instant wilderness, but proponents had hoped for a far more substantial system as a result of the required reviews of potential wilderness areas. Both the Interior and Agriculture departments were charged with reviews, but the nature of the charge differed.

The task of the Interior Department was both more comprehensive and simpler to describe: the secretary was to

> review every roadless area of five thousand contiguous acres or more in the national parks, monuments, and other units of the national park system and every such area of, and every roadless island within, the national wildlife refuges and game ranges [and to] report to the President his recommendation as to the suitability or non-suitability of each such area or island for preservation as wilderness.[17]

In short, he was required to study every substantial roadless area in the national park and wildlife refuge systems and to make recommendations for wilderness additions. These recommendations were to be reviewed at the White House and forwarded to the Congress, which had reserved for itself the final decision in all wilderness designations. The review process was to be completed by September 1974, ten years after the effective date of the legislation.

The Park Service entered into the review process with a considerable lack of enthusiasm, clearly aware that wilderness designation constituted an undesirable limitation of management options in the affected areas. As a consequence, reviews lagged behind schedule, and the areas recommended for inclusion in the wilderness system were far smaller than preservationists had proposed. Members of the conservation community charged that the Park Service was using the review process to set aside large tracts of land for park developments. Developments, especially those which would cater to the auto tourist, were seen as essential to the task of attracting ever greater numbers of visitors to the parks; visitors, in turn, were essential to convince the Congress that increased appropriations and more areas were desirable.

The first case that came to review under this procedure is most instructive. It concerned the Great Smoky Mountains National Park in North Carolina and Tennessee, the heart of the largest remaining wilderness area east of the Mississippi and, ironically, the most heavily used of the major parks nationwide. The park is now bisected by one major highway with two significant spur roads. The bulk of the area consists of two large segments of roadless wilderness.[18] The Park Service proposal called for a second major transmountain highway, numerous feeder roads, and six small areas of wilderness comprising in their totality less than half the area of the park.[19] To wilderness proponents it appeared that the Wilderness Act was being made the vehicle for dismantling the existing wilderness in Great

Smoky Mountains Park. Opposition to the Park Service plan was spearheaded by leaders of the Appalachian Trail Conference as well as the preservationist regulars: Sierra Club, Wilderness Society, National Audubon Society, National Parks Association, and the Izaak Walton League. Preservationists condemned the proposal at hearings in the area, and in June 1969 a delegaton of 100 called upon Interior Secretary Walter J. Hickel and urged the plans be dropped. Hickel responded by ordering a new plan from the National Park Service. It was completed in January 1971. It still put substantial emphasis on new visitor accommodations, but the transmountain road was eliminated in favor of a scenic loop skirting the park's boundary.[20]

As the review process proceeded throughout the parks, two issues developed that put the service at odds with the preservation lobby. One involved the service's zoning methods, the other its treatment of so-called inholdings, privately owned parcels within park boundaries. The service utilized a system of land management zones explained as follows by Director Hartzog: "Class I—high-density recreational areas; Class II—general outdoor recreation areas; Class III—natural-environment areas; Class IV—outstanding natural areas; Class V—primitive areas, including, but not limited to, those recommended for designation under the Wilderness Act; and Class VI—historical and cultural areas."[21] This scheme presented two problems for preservation interests. First, Director Hartzog's remarks made clear that the service contemplated Class V (primitive) lands that it would not recommend for wilderness designation. Second, the very existence of Class III (natural-environment) areas worried preservationists. Hartzog attempted to allay those fears saying that the Class III lands neither "meet our criteria for park wilderness," nor are they "intentionally reserved for future intensive development."[22] Rather, Class III lands provide a "buffer" or "transition" zone between developed and primitive areas, a "wilderness threshold."[23] In his introduction to *Preserving Wilderness in Our National Parks*, Anthony Wayne Smith, president and general counsel of the National Parks and Conservation Association, expressed the preservationist view that the Park Service transition or buffer zones only served to minimize the areas protected.

The Association rejects the proposition that wilderness is a region which lies wholly beyond the sights and sounds of civilization. The Wilderness Act contains no such requirement, and the origin of the phraseology is to be found in regulations developed by the Bureau of Outdoor Recreation. To apply this sights and sounds test is inevitably to reduce the size of wilderness areas in the parks and reduce protection. . . . The Association has felt that the actual purpose of the so-called wilderness thresholds, whether acknowledged or not, is really to reserve such areas for road, parking lot, and facility development in the future.[24]

Indeed, Hartzog's remarks on the subject give substantial support to Smith's concerns.

The only facilities planned in these natural-environment lands are the minimum required for public enjoyment, health, safety, preservation, and protection of the features, such as one-way motor nature trails, small overlooks, informal picnic sites, short nature walks, and wilderness-type uses.[25]

Clearly, the NPS and the wilderness lobby disagreed over what constituted "natural-environment lands" and "wilderness uses."

The second issue which divided the Park Service from preservationists concerned private inholdings.[26] According to Park Service policy, "unless acquisition by the United States is assured, inholdings will be excluded from the area classified as wilderness."[27] The service has suggested that when these inholdings have been acquired, it may then recommend their inclusion in the wilderness area. However, it takes an act of Congress to place lands in the wilderness system, and it is improbable that these relatively insignificant additions would ever be made unless they had the good fortune to be included in an omnibus package of wilderness proposals. Since the policy of excluding inholdings is not required by the Wilderness Act, which makes specific provisions for inholdings in wilderness areas, preservationists feared that the Park Service was utilizing inholdings to open corridors and create enclaves in the wilderness which might eventually be developed to the detriment of surrounding wilderness. This fear was compounded by the fact that the Park Service also carved out enclaves within the wilderness for activities of its own which the Wilderness Act would have permitted. It excluded Crater Lake and Yellowstone Lake from wilderness proposals so that it could use motorboats to patrol the lakes. It excluded "22 nine-acre enclaves" in Kings Canyon and Sequoia national parks to accommodate equipment to measure rainfall.[28] None of these exclusions was necessary under the terms of the Wilderness Act unless the Park Service had additional development plans.

The Park Service was required by law to review and recommend. The evidence suggests that it went about that task in a fashion that was designed to minimize its loss of administrative discretion and to protect large areas for possible intensive development in the future. Such a policy guaranteed that the service would be able to respond to the demands of its auto-tourist clientele. Doing so meant that wilderness recommendations would be modest compared to the desires of the preservation lobby.

The situation in the Fish and Wildlife Service was not much different. The FWS derived its primary political support from sport hunters, and its lands were devoted primarily to preserving habitat for game species. As wilderness reviews proceeded, the FWS determined that in some areas the additional restrictions of the Wilderness Act would be beneficial. Where this was the case, wilderness recommendations were made. In spite of the recommendations of the Interior Department, few areas of national park and wildlife refuge lands have been formally incorporated into the wilderness system. Recognizing that the parks and refuges have substantial protections even without wilderness designation, organizations devoted to wilderness preservation have focused the attention of Congress on wilderness reviews within the national forests where the stakes are higher.

PRIMITIVE AREA REVIEWS AND THE ISSUE OF CONTIGUOUS LANDS: THE POLITICS OF ALLOCATION IN THE FOREST SERVICE

Like the secretary of the interior, the secretary of agriculture was charged by the Wilderness Act to review and recommend. On the face of it the task of agriculture was far more modest. "The Secretary . . . shall . . . review . . .each area in the national forests classified . . . as 'primitive' and report his findings to the President."[29] The question was simply what to do with the "primitive" areas. These areas, originally set aside in the 1920s and 1930s and never reclassified as "wilderness" or "wild," had been a focus of debate during passage of the Wilderness Act. They had been identified as wilderness of a sort, but the L-20 Regulation under which they were created had been fairly soft on nonconforming uses, and the possibility existed that they required substantial boundary revisions. The compromise incorporated in the Wilderness Act gave the "primitive" areas statutory protection while they were studied by the Forest Service. The secretary had ten years to complete the review, but Congress put no time limit on its own deliberations. Thus the "primitive" areas were not officially designated as "wilderness," but no change could be made in their management "until Congress has determined otherwise."[30] Forest Service management of the "primitive" areas was identical to its management of "wilderness" and "wild" areas; so, as a practical matter, the effect of the statute was to guarantee wilderness management for the "primitive" areas.

This apparently simple mandate was complicated substantially by further language in Section 3(b): "Nothing herein contained shall limit the President in proposing, as part of his recommendations to Congress, the alteration of existing boundaries of primitive areas or recommending the addition of any contiguous area of national forest lands predominantly of wilderness value." Some preservationists thought that this language required wilderness management far beyond the boundaries of the primitive areas. They argued that if road building or logging were allowed on undeveloped lands contiguous to primitive areas, it would illegally "limit the President in . . . recommending the addition of any contiguous areas of national forest lands." Was the Forest Service free to develop wild lands contiguous to primitive areas and thus limit the president's options, or was it bound by law to preserve the wilderness potential of these contiguous areas?

The Forest Service adopted the former view—indeed, some have suggested that it deliberately set out to develop as many contiguous areas as possible to reduce the possibility of future wilderness designations. Such developments did take place, but they were not part of any agency-wide policy to limit wilderness acreage. In fact, the first Forest Service proposal to come before Congress called for an increase of over 90 percent in the size of the San Rafael Primitive Area in California.[31] Increased acreages were the norm in the early primitive area reviews. In the first five years the service recommended an increase of 25 percent in the total acreage of the areas reviewed.[32]

Still, if contiguous lands had substantial commodity potential, the Forest Service was under great pressure to allow their development. Torn between preservation and commodity interests in its clientele, the service tried to please both, generally by increasing the total acreage of wilderness areas and simultaneously removing areas with economic potential. Wilderness enthusiasts charged the service with a policy of "wilderness on the rocks" for its exclusion of wooded valleys and accused it of "wilderness preventive logging" for its inroads into contiguous areas of de facto wilderness.[33] Jack Shepard's muckraking study of the Forest Service claims that "all along the Rockies . . . overcutting of timber had quicky become the dominant use of the National Forests."[34] Areas where controversies of this nature arose included the Alpine Lakes and Glacier Peak areas in Washington, the Joyce Kilmer Memorial Forest in North Carolina, the Bob Marshall Wilderness in Montana, Idaho's Magruder Corridor, and the Gore Range-Eagles Nest of Colorado. All over the country the desire of citizen groups to preserve major areas of contiguous wild country hampered the ability of the Forest Service to manage its timber empire according to institutional norms.

MAGRUDER CORRIDOR AND EAST MEADOW CREEK

Battles over the Magruder Corridor and East Meadow Creek are illustrative of the conflict over contiguous areas. The Magruder Corridor is the center of the largest stretch of de facto wilderness in the lower forty-eight states, an area of more than 3.5 million acres, larger than the state of Connecticut. The corridor encloses a little-used road that is bounded on the north by the 1.8 million acre Selway-Bitterroot Primitive Area and to the south by the 1.2 million acre Idaho Primitive Area. Both were created during the 1930s while Robert Marshall was influential in headquarters politics at the Forest Service. In 1956 local conservationists proposed a giant River of No Return Wilderness to be composed of the two primitive areas. The road would remain open, but they hoped it would not be the cause of any significant deletion in the protected area. The Forest Service had other plans. It proposed to delete 500,000 acres from the Selway-Bitterroot Primitive Area including 292,000 along the road. Hearings were held and the matter was discussed within the Department of Agriculture. In 1963 Secretary Orville L. Freeman announced the creation of a Selway-Bitterroot Wilderness Area comprising 1,240,000 acres. The Forest Service had had its way. In the process of conversion from a "primitive" to a "wilderness" area, Selway-Bitterroot had lost more than half a million acres including the critical Magruder Corridor area that connected Selway-Bitterroot with the Idaho Primitive Area to the south. Preservation interests were partially appeased by the creation of a Salmon River Breaks Primitive Area composed of 200,000 acres that had been deleted from Selway-Bitterroot. This was small compensation, however, for loss of the Magruder Corridor severed the connection between Selway-Bitterroot and the Idaho Primitive Area. The largest de facto wilderness area in the lower forty-eight states was now bisected by lands the Forest Service intended for multiple-use management.

When the Wilderness Act was passed in 1964, it made the Selway-Bitterroot area instant wilderness. The Salmon River Breaks and Idaho primitive areas were designated for review, and the Magruder Corridor became an example of "contiguous" wilderness. Both preservation and development interests wanted the corridor. Local forest officials allied with the developers, advertising the advantages of multiple use and working to activate the political muscle of commodity groups like the Northwest Mining Association and the Inland Empire Multiple-Use Committee. In August 1966, under pressure from senators Church of Idaho and Metcalf of Montana, Secretary Freeman appointed a committee to study the area and recommend policy to govern its use. The committee, under the chairmanship of Dr. George Selke, a Freeman advisor, recommended that the area's primitive nature should be maintained. Freeman ordered the Forest Service to implement the recommendations of the Selke committee and preserve the area. Instead, the forest supervisor circulated a proposal calling for substantial road building, logging, and recreational development throughout the corridor. The supervisor's proposal rejected the wilderness alternative as an "unnecessary loss of harvestable timber," arguing that "the wilderness concept, as proposed by the Wilderness Act, would be compromised [by] the proximity of the wilderness to roads and improvements."[35] Ironically, the same report discounted the intrusion that the projected developments would make on nearby wilderness. One student of the controversy concluded that the quality of wilderness becomes a concern for the Forest Service only when it provides a rationale for removing areas from wilderness designation.[36]

Having apparently lost the battle in the executive branch, preservationists turned to Congress. In 1971 they prevailed on senators Church and Metcalf to introduce legislation to protect the area. After nine years of struggle the Congress finally settled the status of the Magruder Corridor. During the summer of 1980 it passed legislation that not only restored the Magruder Corridor to the Selway-Bitterroot Wilderness but also established a 2.2 million-acre River of No Return Wilderness adjoining the Corridor on the south. The adjacent Selway-Bitterroot and River of No Return areas now provide statutory wilderness protection to an area of over 3.5 million acres in central Idaho.

Preservation organizations that fail to reach their objectives through the administrative process increasingly work to have administrative decisions overturned elsewhere. Congress provided the alternative arena where supporters of the preservation of Magruder Corridor could triumph. Increasingly, however, preservationists were resorting to the courts. The case of East Meadow Creek provides a second example of conflict between the Forest Service and preservationists over an area of de facto wilderness. Here Colorado citizens took the service to court and won a major victory.

East Meadow Creek is the name applied to about 2,400 acres of land adjacent to the Gore Range-Eagles Nest Primitive Area in Colorado, just eight miles north of the town of Vail. In March 1969 the supervisor of White River National Forest, in which the area is located, advertised the sale of timber from within the East Meadow Creek area, and a variety of plaintiffs filed suit to stop the proceedings.[37] Since the suit was without precedent, and since standing in environmental cases is a cloudy area of the law,[38] the plaintiffs included individuals and groups with every conceivable type of interest in the case. The plaintiffs alleged that the Forest Service was in violation of Section 3(b) of the Wilderness Act. East Meadow Creek was contiguous to the primitive area and met the minimum standards of wilderness. Thus, the plaintiffs argued, the Forest Service was compelled to study the area and forward its recommendations to the president regardless of what those recommendations were. The Forest Service was also compelled to protect the wilderness character of the area until such time as the president and Congress had made a final determination as to its permanent status. All this was essential, according to the plaintiffs, in order to guarantee an unfettered decision by the president and Congress according to Section 3(b).

The Forest Service responded with a multitude of defenses,[39] but the district court swept them aside, giving expansive interpretation to the Wilderness Act and upholding the plaintiffs' allegations. The Forest Service appealed the decision, but the Court of Appeals for Tenth Circuit unanimously affirmed the lower court finding, and the Supreme Court declined to review. The 1971 circuit court decision stated that allowing unbridled discretion to the Forest Service "would render meaningless the clear intent of Congress . . . that both the President and Congress shall have a meaningful opportunity to add contiguous areas predominantly of wilderness value to existing primitive areas for final wilderness designation."[40] The Forest Service did what it could to minimize the impact of the decision. Management memoranda were issued that gave it a narrow interpretation, and the service announced that it would only be bound by the decision within the jurisdiction of the Tenth Circuit Court. Nevertheless, it is difficult to underestimate the significance of the decision. A federal Circuit Court had interpreted the Wilderness Act to require the Forest Service to preserve contiguous wild lands so that the president and Congress could decide whether they merited entry in the wilderness system. The precedent was devastating to the service's ability to manage the forests in keeping with its own institutional norms. And while the precedent was clearly more important than the 2,400 disputed acres of the East Meadow Creek, preservationists ultimately saved the creek as well. The court's decision gave Congress the last word, and in June 1976 Congress created a 134,000-acre Eagles Nest Wilderness Area including the entire East Meadow Creek area.

CITIZEN PARTICIPATON THREATENS THE FOREST SERVICE

The battles over the Magruder Corridor and East Meadow Creek are symptomatic of a much broader problem for the Forest Service. In the late 1960s and early 1970s the Forest Service was on the defensive almost everywhere, caught in an ever-tightening vise between preservationists, who demanded greater wilderness acreage, and commodity interests, especially lumbermen, who demanded ever-increasing allowable cuts from public forests. Historically, commodity interests were dominant in the agency's clientele, and policy could be expected to be solicitous of their concerns. The Wilderness Act had changed all that. The institutional priorities of the service still favored commodity concerns, but the act had unleashed preservation forces in ways completely unforeseen prior to its passage. Fundamental resource management decisions, which once had been the exclusive prerogative of the Forest Service, were now opened to public participation and final determination by Congress. From the perspective of the agency, the national forests were getting out of control.

The culprit in the Wilderness Act was Section 3(d). In language unprecedented in public land law, the act required both public notice and public hearings prior to any administrative decision to alter the wilderness system. The agency was not only required to solicit public comment, but also to transmit the response to the president and Congress along with agency recommendations. This language applied equally to the Interior and Agriculture departments, but caused greatest difficulty to the Forest Service, whose decisions were most controversial. Citizen participation effectively undermined one of the great weapons of the administrative arsenal—secrecy, the internal control of information. Under most circumstances an administrative decision, even one that requires review at the highest levels, can be systematically presented so as to foreclose options. The longer a policy decision can be kept a matter of strictly internal interest to the agency concerned, the greater the momentum that decision will acquire and the more difficult it will be to overturn it at any point in the political process.

From the point of view of the administering agencies, the impact of the Wilderness Act's public participation requirement was to turn loose a horde of amateur land managers with an interest in preservation. These amateurs did not restrict themselves to commenting on the studies that the Forest Service and other agencies had made; they made their own. Local preservation groups all over the country organized to perform systematic surveys of potential wilderness areas, often in greater detail and with greater accuracy than the overworked staff of the Forest Service could manage. As a result, citizen wilderness proposals sometimes provided the most complete information available to decision makers on particular parcels of federal land. This information could not be buried in the administrative process; the Wilderness Act required its transmission to the president and Congress.

Another problem existed for the Forest Service. These citizen groups refused to limit their studies to areas the service was willing to consider for wilderness designation. They studied anything that looked like wilderness to them, and if the Forest Service proved not to be sympathetic, then maybe their local congressman would be. After all, Congress had reserved the final decision to itself. The tactics of local preservationists have not gone unrewarded, for Congress has repeatedly gone beyond the recommendations of the Forest Service in an attempt to satisfy the desires of these amateur managers.

The possibility of public participation in land management decisions was enhanced still further with the passage of the National Environmental Policy Act (NEPA) signed into law on the first day of the 1970s.[41] Again it is doubtful that many members of Congress realized the revolutionary potential of the act. Section 102 required an Environmental Impact Statement (EIS) for any "major Federal actions significantly affecting the quality of the human environment"; and most important for the preservation lobby, every EIS was to contain a "detailed statement . . . on . . . any irreversible and irretrievable commitments of resources which would be involved in the proposed action should it be implemented."[42] This statement was to be available to the public. Indeed, the guidelines of the Council on Environmental Quality, which administers the act, go further, specifying substantial notice and public hearings in many cases. With characteristic understatement the council concluded that "these provisions for review and comment . . . have opened to public participation many Government decisions that were previously made informally and without prior public notice."[43]

NEPA added yet another weapon to the arsenal of statutes with which preservationists now attacked the service's management of the national forests. The Minnesota Public Interest Research Group (MPIRG), an advocacy group, successfully argued that a number of decisions to sell timber from the portal zone of the Boundary Waters Canoe Area, when taken together, constituted a major federal action significantly affecting the quality of the human environment and thus required an environmental impact statement.[44]

In West Virginia the Izaak Walton League of America struck an even more devastating judicial blow to Forest Service procedures. The suit involved the Monongahela National Forest where preservation-minded citizens objected to the clear cutting of timber, a practice which has some merit in terms of silvaculture but which is less than pleasing aesthetically. In the National Forest Organic Act of 1897 preservationists found the language required to bring clear cutting to a halt. The Fourth Circuit Court ruled that under the act the service could harvest and "sell only timber that is dead, physiologically mature, and of large growth, and that each tree sold must be individually marked and removed from the forest."[45] Forest technology of the mid-1970s made such a constraint untenable.

The court's decision created an impasse which all parties agreed required a congressional solution. A year later that solution was at hand. The National Forest Management Act of 1976[46] was the product of hard bargaining between commodity and conservation forces in Congress. The new law gave statutory permanence to the national forest system and set broad requirements for its administration. In the process conservationists were able to insist upon standards to protect both plant and animal communities within the forests, protections for lakes and streams, and limitations on the practice of clear cutting.

THE FOREST SERVICE PURITY POLICY

Consider the plight of the Forest Service. Congress had given itself the last word on what is to be wilderness and what is not. The Wilderness Act had loosed a horde of preservationists on the forests. They were making studies and recommendations for wilderness preservation beyond what the Forest Service believed to be prudent, and Congress was listening. Courts had forbidden development of contiguous wild lands, enjoined the harvest of timber while environmental impact statements were prepared, and concluded that clear cutting is a violation of the service's organic act. All these things seriously diminished the ability of the service to provide the nation with timber and meet other commodity production goals.

To preserve a degree of administrative control over the forests, it became necessary for the Forest Service to limit the impact of wilderness preservation on commodity production. To accomplish the task, spokesmen for the service placed increasing emphasis on the "purity principle." The principle was justified by reliance on Section 4 of the Wilderness Act, which bars motor vehicles, permanent structures, roads, and commercial activity. Section 4 sets standards to guide administration of the wilderness areas that Congress has designated, and the Forest Service has been scrupulous in its efforts to meet those standards in its management plans. Increasingly, however, the Forest Service insisted on using the management criteria of Section 4 as a minimum standard of admission to the wilderness system. Applying this standard resulted in areas with an old road's or an abandoned mine's being excluded from consideraton for wilderness preservation, a result Congress did not intend.

Congress wrote admission standards into the Wilderness Act, but they are found in Section 2(c), not Section 4. Section 2(c) established that, for the purposes of the Wilderness Act, "wilderness" is

an area of undeveloped Federal land retaining its primeval character and influence, without permanent improvements or human habitation, which is protected and managed so as to preserve its natural conditions and which (1) generally appears to have been affected primarily by the forces of nature, with the impact of man's work substantially unnoticeable; (2) has outstanding opportunities for solitude or a primitive and unconfined type of recreation; (3) has at least five thousand acres of land or is of sufficient size as to make practicable its preservation and use in an unimpaired condition; and (4) may also contain ecological, geological, or other features of scientific, educational, scenic, or historical value.[47]

In making the national forest "wilderness," "wild," and "canoe" areas instant wilderness, Congress determined that these areas met the standards, yet many contained precisely the features that the Forest Service argued would disqualify areas for wilderness study: abandoned roads and railroads, old mines, and areas of commercial logging in an earlier era.

The practical argument for the Forest Service's position is that admitting areas that are less than pristine would set a precedent for violation of the more pristine areas already admitted. According to one Forest Service spokesman, "the standards for wilderness classification and the standards for wilderness management must be the same. They cannot be different. They cannot be separated."[48] Without the highest of admissions standards, he argued, "the country would eventually find itself with half-baked 'wilderness' all over the National Forest System." Such a policy would "effectively mortgage much of the multiple-use potential of the entire National Forest System."[49]

Many writers and a number of congressmen have expressed the view that the purity policy cannot be justified by the statute.[50] When viewed from the perspective of the agency's interests, however, the Forest Service approach was reasonable. Purity in administration generally pleased preservation proponents and served to remind commodity interests that their political support was essential to resisting massive additions to the wilderness system. By the same token, the actual opportunity cost of forgone commodities was rather small. The purist in admissions and purist in administration policy was a logical defense against uncontrolled growth of the wilderness system. The Forest Service is not uninterested in wilderness preservation, but it has a multitude of competing interests to balance, and every legislative enactment that restricts its management options increases the pressure under which it must operate. In addition, the service's fear of massive land withdrawals for wilderness is not without merit. If every large acreage "with the impact of man's work substantially unnoticeable" qualifies as a potential wilderness, then by modest estimate something on the order of seventy million acres might be affected, well over a third of the entire National Forest System. If the use of such an area were to be restricted, even temporarily for the purposes of a wilderness review, the impact on the service's ability to manage forest resources would be devastating.[51] It is no wonder then that supporters of the agency's policy worried about mortgaging the forests' multiple-use potential.

As satisfying as the purity doctrine may have been to professional forest managers and commodity-oriented interests, it could not stand against the increasing national sentiment for wilderness preservation. It received the expected criticism from the preservation press, but it was also under attack in Congress and at the White House.

Responding to public and preservation pressure, members of Congress, including some who had been instrumental in passing the Wilderness Act, publicly criticized the Forest Service policy as a misapplication of the law. The sentiment was particularly strong among members of the congressional Interior committees whose jobs included oversight of the wilderness system.

The Forest Service was also under pressure from the White House. In the spring of 1971 the Council on Environmental Quality circulated a draft executive order that would have required the Forest Service to identify all areas "that appear to have the character of wilderness as defined in Section 2(c) of the [Wilderness] Act" and protect the status of those areas until Congress and the president could determine their fate.[52] The draft was a major threat to Forest Service operations. By requiring the service to use the standard of Section 2(c) rather than its own purity principle, the order would have tied up the entire roadless inventory of the national forests—a disaster for multiple-use and commodity interests and for the perceived institutional integrity of the Forest Service.

RARE I: ONCE OVER LIGHTLY

The Forest Service objected strenuously to the draft executive order, and it was never issued. It is possible that the order was dropped in exchange for a promise from the Forest Service that it would conduct its own roadless area inventory. Whether or not there was an explicit bargain, the Forest Service found it prudent to study its roadless domain, isolate wilderness study areas, and thus free the remainder of its management areas for multiple-use forestry. Since some wilderness review seemed inevitable, the Forest Service settled for a quick, comprehensive look that would serve to speed up both wilderness designations and development options.

In its actual implementation, however, this Roadless Area Review and Evaluation (RARE I)[53] proved to be more quick than comprehensive, as even the Forest Service eventually admitted. The entire review was conducted in a ten-month period from August 1971 to June 1972. The task was enormous, and it was complicated by many areas' being snowbound during the field stages of the process. Shepard claims that the reviews were superficial and allowed commodity-minded regional foresters to select millions of acres of de facto wilderness for immediate road building and timber harvest. In an extreme case, just 1.5 percent of the de facto wilderness in Wyoming's Bridger National Forest was preserved for further study—13,500 acres out of 950,000.[54] This selection process was abetted by massive corporate lobbying against wilderness designations. The Forest Industries Council alone is reported to have spent four to five million dollars in the effort.[55]

In January 1973 the Forest Service announced its preliminary recommendations. They proposed wilderness study status for 235 of the 1,449 areas that had been reviewed. These areas constituted approximately 11 million acres from among the 56 million studied. The preservation community was disappointed, and more so because sixty-one of the areas totaling 4.7 million acres had already been designated for wilderness study by the Forest Service or by Congress. New recommendations amounted to only 6.3

million acres.[56] Only three areas had been selected in the eastern United States, and they totaled less than 50,000 acres. The purity policy was still in force.

Following the January announcement, the preservation lobby generated over 8,000 letters in support of increasing the wilderness study acreage, and when the final recommendation was announced on October 15, 1973, it had grown to 12,289,000 acres in 274 separate areas.[57]

Preservationists had not expected to be satisfied with the results of RARE I. In anticipation of that disappointment, the Sierra Club and others had filed suit in federal court to force the service to protect the entire fifty-six million acres until they could be thoroughly studied. In August federal judge Samuel Conti granted a preliminary injunction to that effect. The injunction spurred negotiations between the litigants, resulting in an out-of-court settlement where the Forest Service promised an environmental impact statement consistent with NEPA before any roadless area was released to multiple-use management. The agreement meant the Forest Service would reconsider the wilderness preservation option before other development would be authorized.[58]

From the perspective of the Forest Service, the Sierra Club settlement and the so-called Conti decision which preceded it robbed RARE I of much of its usefulness. There was little point in having made the inventory if it had not put to rest the question of what areas were to be studied for wilderness preservation and what areas were not. RARE I's failure to solve the problem of wilderness allocation was further demonstrated by passage of the Eastern Wilderness Areas Act of 1975, which explicitly repudiated the purity principle and admitted sixteen eastern areas to the wilderness system.[59]

RARE II: IF AT FIRST YOU DON'T SUCCEED . . .

The RARE I process was now a shambles, and even the service admitted that the process "was found to have some weaknesses."[60] These included deficiencies in the completeness of the inventory, the feasibility of public participation, and the methodology used to select study areas.[61] To the difficulties with RARE I were added new procedural requirements on administrative behavior found in the National Environmental Policy Act, the Forest and Rangeland Renewable Resources Planning Act, and the National Forest Management Act. The ultimate result was "a morass, a tangled web of procedural complications" which prevented expeditious decision making in forest management and infuriated commodity interests.[62]

With the encouragement of a new presidential administration, the Forest Service set out to salvage the situation. It embarked on RARE II—a second look at the entire inventory of national forest roadless areas.

Presidential elections often presage a change of mood in important matters of public policy, and wilderness is no exception. The advent of the Kennedy administration in 1961 gave a substantial boost to the preservation movement while Wilson's succession to office in 1913 guaranteed the "damnation" of Hetch Hetchy. The arrival of the Carter administration marked a similar change of mood in 1977. Presidents Nixon and Ford had not been antagonistic to wilderness preservation. They had seen to the timely completion of the primitive area studies and made substantial wilderness recommendations to Congress. Nevertheless, both presidents had important allies among those with a commodity stake in the national forests, and, for the most part, they were cautious in their recommendations for additions to the National Wilderness Preservation System.[63]

The tone of the Carter administration was set in the president's May 23 message to Congress on protection of the environment. Carter cited the Wilderness Act as a "landmark of American conservation policy" and called for prompt expansion of the system "before the most deserving areas of federal lands are opened to other uses and lost to wilderness forever." The president endorsed "all of the more than 24 million acres of wilderness proposals submitted to Congress by previous Administrations" and called for the enlargement of some of them.[64] The mood of the new administration was also apparent in the appointments of Secretary Bob Bergland and Assistant Secretary M. Rupert Cutler in the Agriculture Department. Cutler, who had been associated with preservation organizations, became the departmental overseer for the Forest Service.

Under this new management, the Forest Service formally abandoned its commitment to using the purity principle as a test of admission to the wilderness system. In testimony before a House Interior subcommittee, Assistant Secretary Cutler called the nation's wilderness a "vanishing resource" and promised that the department would pursue its protection "with a new sense of urgency."[65] This sense of urgency would include a willingness to be more flexible about possible inclusion of wilderness areas which are less than pristine—a willingness present from the beginning in congressional majorities but notably absent in the Forest Service.

The increased concern for wilderness preservation at the highest levels of the administration helped to make RARE II a more intelligent and comprehensive survey than its predecessor. It was undertaken with greater preparation, an improved methodology, and more centralized control. One measure of the new effort was that the Forest Service now found sixty-seven million roadless acres to inventory, eleven million more than were reviewed during RARE I.

Both commodity and preservation groups watched the RARE II process unfold with a mixture of hope and concern. Commodity interests hoped that RARE II would allow the service to release vast areas of de facto wilderness which had been nearly frozen by legal challenges and political pressures. They feared that the new Carter administration would cave in to the preservation lobby and recommend wholesale additions to the wilderness system. One commodity organization, the American Plywood Association, alerted its member firms with the headline, "Wilderness Issue Out of Control."[66] The preservation community hoped RARE II would produce major new wilderness recommendations, but feared that any lands not designated would be lost to preservation permanently.

The concerns of both groups were well founded, for the ultimate purpose of RARE II was to produce the final administrative recommendation as to what portion of the national forests Congress should admit to the wilderness system. The Forest Service presumed that unrecommended lands could be released for multiple-use management at the same time that new wilderness areas were created. By pushing the wilderness decision out ahead of the regular land-use planning process for the forests, the service hoped it could determine wilderness allocations according to national interests, and that future land-use planning could take the wilderness decision as a given. This was no small task and the lobbying from both sides was intense. At one point Secretary Bergland himself was forced to intervene and tell lobbyists for both sides to ease up and let the service do its job.[67]

RARE II results were formally announced January 4, 1979, by Assistant Secretary Cutler. The Forest Service recommended classification of 36.1 million acres of the inventory—58 percent of the total—as nonwilderness. Predictably, spokesmen on both sides of the issue expressed disappointment, although the consensus opinion was that industry had fared rather better than expected.[68] When the final administration proposal was presented in April, it followed the Forest Service's recommendation closely. In spite of the protests of preservation spokesmen, 36 million acres were opened to immediate development; 15.4 million acres were recommended for wilderness status, and a third of that acreage was in Alaska. By the spring of 1979 it was clear that the fate of RARE II lands in Alaska would probably be determined by Alaska lands legislation, which was already working its way through Congress. Outside of Alaska the administration recommended fewer than 10 million acres in wilderness designations, while it released almost 29 million for multiple-use management. An additional 10.6 million acres were reserved for future decision. Three million reserved acres were in Alaska; most of the remaining 7.6 million were in the overthrust belt, a geological formation paralleling the Rocky Mountains and considered to have high potential for mineral and fuel development.

The recommendations displeased the preservation community and likeminded members of Congress. As bills based on the RARE II inventory began to be introduced in Congress, it was clear that preservationists would push for statutory protection of lands beyond those recommended by the Carter administration. In California, the administration of Governor Edmund Brown, Jr. was also displeased with the Carter administration recommendations. In July it filed suit against the Department of Agriculture to halt plans for development of de facto wilderness within its borders. The following January a federal district judge in California ruled that the Forest Service had failed to comply with the environmental impact statement requirements of the National Environmental Policy Act.[69] The decision raised questions about the sufficiency of the entire RARE II process. It also seemed to suggest that the courts might prevent the release of lands designated for nonwilderness if the preservationists would file suit.

Neither preservationists nor developers wanted the RARE II inventory tied up indefinitely in litigation. Both sides began positioning themselves for a legislative showdown. Preservationists preferred an area by area approach with Congress considering bills covering those areas most immediately threatened by development. This approach would take a number of years and allow preservation forces to concentrate on a few areas at a time. Development interests had different ideas. On December 10, 1979, Congressman Thomas S. Foley of Washington introduced legislation which would have brought the wilderness allocation process in the national forests to an abrupt halt. His bill, entitled "The National Forest Multiple-Use Management Act of 1980," would mandate immediate nonwilderness management for the 36 million acres recommended for nonwilderness by the administration and nonwilderness management by January 1, 1985 for any area in the national forests which had not been given statutory wilderness protection by that time—whether the area had been recommended or not. If enacted Foley's legislation would have effectively sealed the size of the national forest wilderness system at whatever acreage it included on January 1, 1985. Foley's position as Chairman of the House Agriculture Committee suggested that his effort must be regarded seriously, but the bill developed little support beyond its fifty-four cosponsors.

In an effort to revive his bill's prospects, Foley introduced a second version. His "National Forest Roadless Areas Act" attempted a compromise with preservation forces. It would have designated all the RARE II wilderness recommendations as statutory wilderness and mandated nonwilderness management for the remainder of the national forests. Preservation forces in the House rejected the bargain and Foley's efforts to accomplish legislative release nationwide were abandoned in favor of attaching similar language to individual RARE II bills.

While the preservation lobby was unwilling to make any compromise with developers that would put a permanent cap on the wilderness allocation process, there was a clear need for some mechanism that would free the Forest Service to pursue multiple-use management practices in areas not designated as wilderness. Compromise language negotiated for an omnibus California wilderness bill appears to have resolved the issue in a fashion that both developers and preservationists can accept. Compromise language in the California bill would have lifted the federal court injunction and declared the environmental impact statement to be sufficient to meet the standards of NEPA. In order to confirm the availability of nondesignated lands for nonwilderness uses, the compromise stated that the lands need not be managed so as to preserve their suitability for wilderness designation.[70] Clearly, this form of legislative release does not *require* the Forest Service to manage the lands for nonwilderness uses. The California wilderness bill expired with the end of the ninety-sixth Congress, but the compromise language developed in it was instrumental in reaching agreements on RARE II bills for Colorado and New Mexico, which were passed late in 1980.

SUMMARY

The Wilderness Act placed new constraints on the activities of the Forest Service, the National Park Service and the Fish and Wildlife Service. Each agency attempted to implement the law so as to minimize disruptions in its normal operation or its pattern of interest group support. A decade and a half after passage of the Wilderness Act each agency had taken steps toward developing useful and innovative management techniques to implement the congressional mandate to administer wilderness areas "for the use and enjoyment of the American people in such a manner as will leave them unimpaired for future use and enjoyment as wilderness."[71]

While management practices are of critical concern, they have taken second place to the politics of allocation.[72] The Wilderness Act required each agency to review its wilderness holdings and recommend additions to the National Wilderness Preservation System, but most attention has focused on the process in the Forest Service. The Forest Service faced a double predicament not shared by the Interior Department agencies. First, preservation was not the agency's primary mission. Its responsibility included managing the national forests so as to provide a continuous stream of forest products into the national economy. As a result substantial forces are arrayed to make sure that this development mandate is fulfilled. Those forces include development-minded industries and interest groups as well as many members of the agency's professional staff. Second, the primitive area reviews required by the Wilderness Act proved to be more complex than the reviews required of the Interior agencies and more controversial as well. As a result, the Forest Service was required to make its wilderness recommendations in an environment where the stakes were high and the rules were unclear and everchanging. Such circumstances invite dispute, and the Forest Service has had its share. The difficulties associated with the primitive area review proved so great that the service was eventually induced to undertake an investigation of its entire roadless inventory—not once, but twice. The final effort (RARE II) appears to have paved the way for further controversy as preservationists continue to push for increased wilderness allocations and developers attempt to put a halt to the allocation process. Whatever the eventual outcome, the process of wilderness allocation in the national forests is likely to continue for many years.

NOTES

1. The official title of the agency concerned with the management of the wildlife refuges in 1964 was the Bureau of Sport Fisheries and Wildlife. In 1974 its name was changed to the Fish and Wildlife Service. I have used the current name throughout to avoid confusion.

2. The massive landholdings of the Bureau of Land Management were ignored in the Wilderness Act.

3. These were the 9.1 million acres classified by the Department of Agriculture in 1964 as "wilderness," "wild," and "canoe" areas under the U Regulations. See chapter 3.

4. The Wilderness Act, Section 4(d)(5).

5. Jack Shepard, *The Forest Killers—The Destruction of the American Wilderness* (New York: Weybright & Talley, 1975), p. 69.

6. The BWCA is by far the largest wilderness area east of the Rockies.

7. Glen O. Robinson, *The Forest Service* (Baltimore: Johns Hopkins University Press, 1975), p. 182.

8. Cliff's remarks are published in Maxine E. McCloskey and James P. Gilligan, editors, *Wilderness and the Quality of Life* (San Francisco: Sierra Club Books, 1969), p. 11.

9. Helicopters were permitted, however, where there was a precedent prior to 1964. See ibid.

10. Robinson, *The Forest Service*, p. 181.

11. 39 Stat. 535.

12. Roderick Nash in John C. Hendee, George H. Stankey, and Robert C. Lucas, *Wilderness Management* (U.S. Forest Service, Miscellaneous Publication No. 1365, 1978), p. 32.

13. These regulations were issued in August 1966. They are reprinted in McCloskey and Gilligan, *Wilderness and the Quality of Life*, pp. 245-47.

14. Ibid., p. 15.

15. Ibid., p. 17. Hartzog is almost certainly wrong in his conclusion that the Wilderness Act was not to affect national park management. See the discussion of

the evolution of the act in chapter 4. Also Roderick Nash has gone so far as to conclude that "the Wilderness Act must be understood as an expression of American dissatisfaction with how the National Parks were being managed." See Hendee, Stankey, and Lucas, *Wilderness Management*, p. 39.

16. McCloskey and Gilligan, *Wilderness and the Quality of Life*, pp. 25-29.

17. The Wilderness Act, Secton 3(c).

18. The term *wilderness* is used somewhat loosely here, for the area of the park was extensively logged in an earlier era.

19. Michael Frome, *Battle for the Wilderness* (New York: Praeger Publishers, 1974), p. 177.

20. Ibid., p. 184. At year's end in 1980 Great Smoky Mountains National Park still had no congressionally designated wilderness, but the most recent recommendation of the Park Service, made in the fall of 1979, called for wilderness designations of 466,000 acres—90 percent of the park's total.

21. McCloskey and Gilligan, *Wilderness and the Quality of Life*, p. 19.

22. Ibid., p. 21.

23. Ibid., p. 22.

24. National Parks and Conservation Association, *Preserving Wilderness in Our National Parks* (Washington, D.C., 1971), p. xiv.

25. McCloskey and Gilligan, *Wilderness and the Quality of Life*, p. 22.

26. Many, if not most, of the larger units of the park, forest, and refuge systems are compromised to some degree by private ownership of lands within the nominal boundaries of these units. These inholdings exist either because policymakers find them desirable, or, as is more frequently the case, because Congress has provided neither the money nor the condemnation authority that would be required to acquire them. The problem for the older units is complicated by the fact that Congress has, in recent years, earmarked the bulk of its appropriations for acquisitions in the more recent additions to these conservation systems.

27. Jeffrey P. Foote, "Wilderness—A Question of Purity," *Environmental Law* 3 (Summer 1973): 259-60.

28. Ibid., p. 260.

29. The Wilderness Act, Section 3(b).

30. Ibid.

31. Frome, *Battle for the Wilderness*, pp. 150-52.

32. United States House of Representatives, *Fifth Annual Report on the Status of the National Wilderness Preservation System*, Document No. 58 (91st Cong., 1st sess., January 23, 1969), p. 17.

33. Frome, *Battle for the Wilderness*, p. 154; Shepard, *The Forest Killers*, pp. 236-38.

34. Shepard, *The Forest Killers*, p. 238.

35. Quoted in Boyd Norton, "The Oldest Established Perennially Debated Tree Fight in the West," *Audubon* 74 (July 1972): 69.

36. Ibid.

37. Peter I. Kain, "The Battle for East Meadow Creek," *American Forests* 75 (October 1969): 39.

38. The decisions of the Supreme Court in *Sierra Club v. Morton, SCRAP v. In-*

terstate Commerce Commission, and others demonstrate the confusion in this area of the law.

39. The Service argued: (1) Timber management is by law within the discretion of the Forest Service and thus not reviewable in court. (2) Plaintiffs were without standing to sue. (3) The suit was prohibited by the doctrine of sovereign immunity. (4) The injunction requested would not protect the area, because the mining laws still prevailed. (5) There was no material issue of fact presented, and the Forest Service was thus entitled to prevail as a matter of law. See Earl S. Wolcott III, *"Parker v. United States:* The Forest Service Role in Wilderness Preservation," *Ecology Law Quarterly* 3 (Winter 1973): 153.

40. 448 F.2nd at 797. Quoted in Wolcott, *"Parker v. United States,"* pp. 156-57.

41. Public Law 91-190; 83 Stat. 852.

42. Ibid.

43. Council on Environmental Quality, *Environmental Quality—1972* (Washington, D.C.: Government Printing Office, 1972), p. 237.

44. *Minnesota Public Interest Research Group v. Butz,* #358 F. Supp. 584 (D. Minn. 1973) affirmed 498 F.2nd 1314 (8th Circuit, 1974). Quoted in "Note: Wilderness Management and the Multiple-Use Mandate," *Minnesota Law Review* 59 (November 1974): 175.

45. *Izaak Walton League v. Butz,* 5 ELR 20573 (August 1975). Quoted in Council on Environmental Quality, *Environmental Quality—1976* (Washington, D.C.: Government Printing Office, 1976), p. 87. See also *New York Times,* August 23, 1975, p. 26.

46. Public Law 94-588; 90 Stat. 2949.

47. The Wilderness Act, Section 2(c).

48. Richard J. Costley, "An Enduring Resource," *American Forests* 78 (June 1972): 11.

49. Ibid., p. 55.

50. See especially Foote, "Wilderness—A Question of Purity;" "Note: Wilderness Management and the Multiple-Use Principle"; and the various congressional hearings on eastern wilderness bills.

51. The Forest Service is required by law to practice sustained yield forestry. In simple terms it may harvest lumber only as fast as replacement trees can be grown. If harvestable trees take fifty years to grow, then the service may cut only one-fiftieth of its trees each year in order to maintain the resource. Trees located in wilderness areas which are off-limits to logging are not counted in the service's inventory. As a consequence any reduction in the acreage where lumber may be cut in a given year produces a proportional reduction in the actual number of logs which may be cut throughout the national forests. Any unexpected wilderness withdrawals would create a lumber shortage and drive up prices.

52. Quoted in Shepard, *The Forest Killers,* p. 251. See also Frome, *Battle for the Wilderness,* p. 162.

53. Since there was eventually to be a RARE II, I use the term RARE I here even though it was not used at the time.

54. Shepard, *The Forest Killers,* p. 252.

55. Ibid.

56. Ibid., p. 256.

57. *CQ Weekly Report* 31 (October 20, 1973): 2786.

58. Council on Environmental Quality, *Environmental Quality—1974* (Washington, D.C.: Government Printing Office, 1974), p. 200.

59. See chapter 6.

60. Testimony of M. Rupert Cutler, Assistant Secretary for Conservation, Research and Education, Department of Agriculture, in United States Senate, Committee on Energy and Natural Resources, *Roadless Area Review and Evaluation (RARE II)* (Washington, D.C.: Government Printing Office, 1978), p. 5.

61. "RARE II Wilderness Attribute Rating System: A User's Manual," in Senate Committee on Energy, *Roadless Area Review and Evaluation*, pp. 95-97.

62. Cutler in Senate Committee on Energy, *Roadless Area Review and Evaluation*, p. 5.

63. This caution did not prevent the endorsement of popular bills with limited commodity implications, such as the Eastern Wilderness Act.

64. *CQ Weekly Report* 35 (May 28, 1977): 1064.

65. United States House of Representatives, Committee on Interior and Insular Affairs, *Endangered American Wilderness Act, Hearings on H.R. 3454, May 2 and 6, 1977* (Washington, D.C.: Government Printing Office, 1977), III: 95-96.

66. Quoted in Charles Clusen and Douglas Scott, "The Endangered American Wilderness Act," *Sierra Club Bulletin* 62 (June/July/August 1977): 8.

67. Tim Mahoney and Jody Bolz, "RARE II: A Test for Forest Wilderness," *Living Wilderness* 42 (April/June 1978): 12.

68. *CQ Weekly Report* 37 (January 20, 1979): 96.

69. *Wilderness Report* 17 (January 24, 1980): 1.

70. *Wilderness Report* 18 (August 12, 1980): 5.

71. The Wilderness Act, Section 2(a).

72. Wilderness management techniques have been the subject of great debate and numerous journal articles. This debate is beyond the scope of this volume, but it may be of interest to readers. The best single source on the state of the art in wilderness management is John C. Hendee, George H. Stankey, and Robert C. Lucas, *Wilderness Management* (U.S. Forest Service, Miscellaneous Publication No. 1365, 1978). Readers of this volume should be aware that the principles and practices described are a compendium of the more innovative approaches being used in various localities, not a description of routine management practices across the country.

LEGACY OF THE WILDERNESS ACT: THE NEW MOOD IN CONGRESS $\quad6$

> Conservation of the natural resources of America
> cannot be achieved by half-baked measures.
> —Congressman John P. Saylor
> May 19, 1966

If the passage of the Wilderness Act in 1964 was a victory for preservation sentiment over the demands of developers, then Congress in the remainder of the decade proved it was no fluke. It had been almost fifty years between the passage of the National Park Service Act and creation of the National Wilderness Preservation System. Now new systems of preservation were created on an accelerated schedule. Scenic rivers, national trails, and endangered species legislation were adopted during the period from 1966 to 1973. Each was a manifestation of the new congressional mood—a willingness to see marginal sacrifices in economic advantage in order to preserve the last remnants of America's natural and historic past. The national ecological consciousness of the late 1960s and early 1970s strengthened the political forces of preservation.

Supporters of wilderness preservation had frequently argued that a major benefit of wilderness was the preservation of endangered species of wildlife. With wilderness designations affecting less than 1 percent of the nation's land, it was clear to most conservationists that a broader form of protection was essential to prevent the extinction of native species. Congress took the first steps toward providing that protection in the Endangered Species Preservation Act of 1966.[1] This act gave expression to the increasing public concern for wildlife and authorized the expenditure of government funds to provide habitat for endangered species.

Congress strengthened the protection for endangered species with the Endangered Species Conservation Act of 1969.[2] The 1969 act prohibited the importation into the United States of any animal threatened by global extinction. This statute was designed to deny American markets for any animal whose species was threatened. While some members of the environmental lobby have suggested that the act is counterproductive,[3] it was the clear intent of Congress to strengthen the protection afforded to endangered species.

Both the 1966 and 1969 statutes were of fairly limited scope. By 1973 Congress was ready for a more comprehensive attack on the problem. In a tone reminiscent of the National Environmental Policy Act, the Endangered Species Act of 1973 declared that "all Federal departments and agencies shall seek to conserve endangered species and shall utilize their authorities in furtherance of the purposes of this Act."[4] Each agency is required to utilize "all methods and procedures which are necessary" to prevent the extermination of "any member of the animal kingdom."[5] Here, indeed, is wildlife conservation legislation based on ecological and preservationist principles, a major break from the nation's previous preoccupation with the conservation of "game" species.

The significance of this legislation is best demonstrated by the case of the nation's best known obscure fish—the snail darter. In 1973 a University of Tennessee zoologist discovered the rare fish in a portion of the Little Tennessee River scheduled to be inundated by the completion of the Tennessee Valley Authority's Tellico Dam. Opponents of the dam seized on the snail darter as the last chance to halt construction. In 1976 they filed suit in federal court arguing that completion of the dam would violate the Endangered Species Act by destroying the darter habitat. Both the circuit court and the Supreme Court agreed with the dam's opponents, in spite of the fact that the dam had been authorized and construction begun before the law was passed. The courts ruled that to complete the project now would be illegal unless Congress saw fit to grant a statutory exemption for Tellico.

The congressional response was to create a special panel of high-level federal bureaucrats with the power to make exceptions in the application of the Endangered Species Act. To the surprise of most congressmen, the panel's first decision was *not* to exempt the Tellico Dam—leaving it, in effect, as a multimillion-dollar concrete monument to the nation's commitment to species preservation.

Declaring a winner in this controversy is most difficult. Congress eventually proved unwilling to allow the dam to stand 95 percent completed and approved legislation which will allow the project to be finished. President Carter opposed such an exemption but declined to veto the legislation in hopes that Congress would be more favorably disposed to his priority proposals. Supporters of the Tellico Dam won out, but it is not at all clear that the snail darter lost. It has been transported to a new habitat and is reported to be thriving.[6]

What is most remarkable about the snail darter story is not that the dam was eventually completed, but that its completion was an issue at all. As recently as 1963 the very idea that a three-inch fish of no known use to man might be sufficient cause to halt construction of a dam, almost ten years after it was begun, would have seemed preposterous. It remained preposterous to many in the late 1970s, yet the tide of preservationist sentiment was sufficiently strong to cause Congress to adopt a variety of tactics to allow the construction of the dam without the unpleasant task of a record vote against this very popular little fish.

RIVER PRESERVATION

While endangered species has attracted greater public attention, the wild and scenic rivers legislation of the late 1960s is closer kin to the Wilderness Act. Indeed, the cast of characters associated with the rivers legislation is almost identical to that of the Wilderness Act. The first wild rivers bill was introduced in Congress by Senator Frank Church of Idaho who had served as floor manager of the Wilderness Act. A similar, but stronger, measure was introduced in the House by Pennsylvania's "Mr. Conservation," Congressman John Saylor. The primary adversary was once again Congressman Wayne Aspinall of Colorado, chairman of the House Interior Committee. There are similarities in legislative history, as well. The Senate acted first, passing the legislation twice before it managed to spur the House to action.

These similarities are striking but superficial. While congressmen made frequent comparisons with the Wilderness Act during the debate, a fundamental difference exists in the nature of the political process that created wild and scenic rivers legislation. Congress had debated wilderness legislation in the context of management categories already established by the Forest Service. These categories were accepted as legitimate by all sides during the debate. The result was that debate concerned whether specific categories of areas should or should not be designated wilderness, not whether specific parcels should be. In the final compromise "wilderness," "wild," and "canoe" areas were given immediate designation; "primitive" areas were not.

In the case of rivers, there was no preexistent set of categories to shape the debate. Any congressman might reasonably propose that some river segment in his district be included or excluded from the protections of the proposed act. Without strong administrative categories, it was possible, at least in theory, to give every congressman what he and his constituents most desired, and to a substantial degree that is what Congress did.[7]

Unlike the Wilderness Act, wild rivers legislation had its origins in the executive branch. It was the conservation component of President Johnson's Great Society Program. In 1961, at the suggestion of the National Park Service, a Senate Select Committee on National Water Resources had recommended that "certain streams be preserved in their free-flowing condition," but the matter was not really on the national agenda until President Johnson endorsed the idea in his 1965 State of the Union Address and in a separate presidential message on natural beauty. Presidential endorsement followed a joint study of river resources by the secretaries of Agriculture and Interior. In 1963 they compiled a list of 650 rivers or river segments that might be worthy of preservation. Sixty-seven of these were designated for field study, and the result was a list of 22 candidates for preservation. Senator Church's original bill rested heavily on these studies, much to the consternation of some of his colleagues. According to Church his bill was "patterned after, and intended to be a working partner to the Wilderness Act."[8] It called for immediate designation of six rivers, two of them, the Salmon and the Middlefork of the Clearwater, in Idaho. Senator Simpson of Wyoming raised immediate objection to the inclusion of a segment of the Green River in his state. He was the first of a great many senators and congressmen who felt constrained to object that a river in their district had—or just as often had not—been designated in the bill. Senator Simpson had some reason for concern. Proponents of rivers legislation had relied on the judgment of the executive agencies as to the suitability of including any particular river. They had not solicited advice from affected Senate colleagues, and some confusion erupted as to the degree of communication that had taken place between state and local officials and congressional delegations, on the one hand, and the departments of Agriculture and Interior, on the other. When the Church bill was reported from committee in January of the following year, the Green River and the Suwanee (Georgia and Florida) had been demoted to so-called study status, and the Eleven Point (Missouri) had been elevated to an immediate designation. Each change was at the request of an affected senator. Wild rivers preservation was ultimately to express the "pork barrel" principle, giving each senator or congressman what he wants in his district. Dams, reservoirs, and other river developments have historically been allocated by Congress in order to meet the political needs of the incumbent congressmen. There is a certain consistency, therefore, in the extension of this principle to govern the nondevelopment of rivers. Once it was clear to the Senate that everyone was to get his own way on his own turf, most opposition withered. Indeed, the only serious matter that emerged in the debate was the question of whether the legislation would in any fashion alter the respective powers of the nation and the states to control the waters of the West. Water politics in the West is complex and the stakes are high, but all agreed that the bill under consideration would not upset the legal status quo. The bill's prohibition of dams in designated areas was a major change in national policy, but so long as designations were all consistent with local interest, the policy change was of small consequence to individual senators. This lack of concern is evident in the wide margin by which the bill passed the Senate. The record vote of January 18, 1966, showed 71 in favor and 1 opposed.[9]

The Senate bill was introduced in the House and referred to the Interior Committee, but Congressman Saylor, the committee's ranking member and the preeminent preservationist in the House, found it unsatisfactory. Saylor quoted approvingly from the president's speech of February 8, 1965:

Those who first settled this continent found much to marvel at. Nothing was a greater source of wonder and amazement than the power and majesty of American rivers.

He endorsed the president's call to "preserve free-flowing stretches of our great scenic rivers before growth and development make the beauty of the unspoiled waterway a memory." But he found the actions to be less satisfactory than the words. Characterizing the administration bill recently passed by the Senate as "fainthearted" and "timorous," he declared, "the conservation of the natural resources of America cannot be achieved by half-baked measures." He proceeded to introduce a "strong scenic rivers bill" endorsed by the major preservation organizations.[10]

The Saylor bill proposed fifteen rivers for immediate preservation, sixty-six others for study, and withdrew the power of the Federal Power Commission to license dams on any of them until Congress had had the opportunity to act in each case. The bill used a classification system based on the degree of wildness of the stream and allowed for the reclassification of streams that might be restored or improved. It was, by any standard, the strongest river preservation bill ever introduced in Congress. It was also an effort to stake out a bargaining position for the inevitable battle with Chairman Aspinall in the House Interior Committee. Aspinall, however, had let it be known that he did not consider wild rivers to be "priority legislation,"[11] and his committee did not report any river protection bill in the Eighty-ninth Congress.

The impact of the Saylor bill was felt first in the Senate where it forced a reevaluation of the "administration bill" passed in 1966. Senator Church reintroduced the Senate-passed bill in the first days of 1967; he had thirty-eight cosponsors. By the time the bill had emerged from committee, however, it had been amended to incorporate many of the Saylor bill features. The committee version of S. 119 was titled, "Wild and Scenic Rivers Act," and embodied the Saylor distinctions based on degree of wildness. Seven rivers were proposed for immediate inclusion in the wild category and an additional five in the scenic category. Twenty-seven were designated for further study. In other respects the new S. 119 followed closely the language of its Senate predecessor; its conservation provisions being of the sort Congressman Saylor had called "half-baked." The Senate committee reported August 3, 1967, and five days later the Wild and Scenic Rivers Act was again approved by the Senate. The vote was 84 to 0.[12]

In anticipation of Senate action some movement could be detected in the House. Congressman Aspinall had signaled his intent to consider the matter by submitting his own scenic rivers bill.[13] The Aspinall bill was predictably the weakest bill yet seen in terms of conservation, giving only four rivers immediate designation. In spite of its limited coverage, Interior Secretary Stewart Udall endorsed the Aspinall bill, creating the impression in the minds of some conservationists that he had sold out to the man whose committee controlled most Interior Department legislation. That judgment was probably too harsh. It is more probable that departmental support was used to cement Aspinall's willingness to report some river preservation measure. That a spirit of conciliation was alive in the chamber is beyond doubt. On July 1, 1968, after prolonged discussion in committee, Congressman Saylor was able to introduce a new bill[14] cosponsored by twenty-two other members, including Chairman Aspinall.

Two days later the committee issued a favorable report on the bill, and on July 15 an effort was made to pass it under the suspension of the rules procedure. This same procedure had been used by Aspinall to torpedo the Wilderness Act in 1962. Motivation for use of the procedure here is unclear, although the outcome was somewhat predictable. Congressmen who had taken no particular notice of the committee's work on wild and scenic rivers legislation suddenly discovered that their districts were to be affected by one or another of the proposals. Aspinall and others made it quite clear that the committee had granted every request by individual congressmen when the matter affected their districts, yet it was apparent that no systematic attempt had been made to gain the approval of each affected representative prior to bringing the bill to the floor. Now, before the House on a suspension of the rules procedure, amendments that might have satisfied individual concerns were out of order and a two-thirds majority was required for passage. That majority was not achieved.[15]

Midsummer is dangerously close to the projected adjournment of Congress in election years, and the House Rules Committee, which normally controls the chamber's agenda, was apparently reluctant to schedule the bill for debate. Having already failed to pass under the suspension of the rules procedure, the bill's future was not bright. Many conservationists were unwilling to see the matter die, however, and a group, spearheaded by Congressman John Culver of Iowa, petitioned the Rules Committee to reconsider its stand and schedule the bill so that it could be considered under normal procedures and could be amended on the floor. The pressure was successful and on September 10 the Rules Committee approved the bill for consideration with amendments in order. Two days later the House passed a slightly amended Wild and Scenic Rivers bill by a vote of 267 to 7. The conference committee split the difference between Senate and House bills. The final version created three categories of river, wild, scenic, or recreational, depending on the level of development. Under it, the executive departments would determine the river category while Congress retained the decision to include a river in the act's provisions. In the designation of specific rivers the conferees followed the practice of both House and Senate, including only those rivers and river segments which had the approval of the state's senators and the local congressman. The resulting Wild and Scenic Rivers Act designated eight rivers for immediate inclusion and twenty-seven others for study.[16] The bill became law with the signature of President Johnson October 2, 1968.[17]

Following the bill's passage the Interior and Agriculture departments established an interagency steering committee to implement the act. Within the two departments, the Forest Service, National Park Service, and Bureau of Land Management have the major responsibilities for administration of designated rivers and making the required studies. In the years since the act's passage Congress has designated additional rivers in both the "instant" and study categories. Indeed, proposed additions to the system are sometimes grouped together to gain broad support in much the same fashion that dam and harbor proposals always have been.[18] While not as restrictive as the Wilderness Act in its provisions, the Wild and Scenic Rivers Act has provided an ongoing mechanism to preserve a number of our nation's streams in a near natural condition. Perhaps equally important, it provides a tool for preservation forces interested in preserving a particular river from unnecessary development. The kinds of "uneconomic" values once totally ignored in the calculus of cost/benefit have received congressional recognition, and this, in itself, is likely to affect the development decisions of resource planners both private and public.

WILDERNESS TRAILS

Hiking clubs in the Northeast were the first advocates of scenic trail preservation. The concept took on national significance in 1921 when Benton MacKaye first proposed a kind of super trail which would run the length of the Atlantic Coast.[19] In 1925 several hiking groups joined together to implement the MacKaye proposal. They formed the Appalachian Trail Conference, which has been the moving force behind the development and protection of the Appalachian Trail ever since.

The early history of the Pacific Crest Trail is very similar. It began in 1932 with a proposal by Clinton C. Clark for a mountain trail to parallel the

Pacific Coast. Before long a Trail Conference was formed to support the project. Eventually, the federal government became an active partner in both of these major trails. The route of the Pacific Crest Trail was almost entirely over federal lands, so governmental cooperation was essential. In the East, the Appalachian Trail was largely on private lands, but both the Forest Service and the Park Service endorsed the project and assisted it where federal lands were involved. For half a century both trail conferences were remarkably successful, and each was interested in federal legislation to protect their accomplishments and, perhaps, to set aside other wilderness trails as well. National trails legislation had been introduced in Congress as early as 1945, but it had not received serious attention.[20]

In 1966 the scenic trails concept got the national attention it had previously lacked. In a February message on preserving our natural heritage, President Johnson endorsed federal legislation to protect trails of national significance. About the same time the Bureau of Outdoor Recreation released a study which predicted substantial growth in the numbers of people walking for pleasure and suggested that a national system of trails would provide inexpensive recreational opportunities.[21] The president's speech and the bureau's study were followed in February 1967 by the introduction of new national trails legislation. The bill, which had been drafted in the Interior Department, was sponsored by Chairman Jackson of the Senate Interior Committee and by Congressman Roy Taylor, a prominent member of the House Interior Committee. With such prominent support, the outlook for national trails legislation was bright.

The bill passed the Senate with only minor modifications. The Senate version designated four trails for immediate inclusion in a system of national scenic trails: the Appalachian Trail extending 2,000 miles from Maine to Georgia, the Continental Divide Trail extending 1,200 miles from Glacier National Park on the Canadian border to Bridger National Forest in Wyoming, the Pacific Crest Trail extending 2,350 miles from Canada to Mexico, and the Potomac Heritage Trail extending 825 miles along the banks of that historic river. Eleven other trails were designated for further study and possible inclusion at a later date.

The House Interior Committee under the chairmanship of Wayne Aspinall was predictably unwilling to support a measure as strong as the Senate bill. Instead, it reported a more modest bill establishing only one national trail, the Appalachian, and designating fourteen others for study. Like the wild rivers legislation of 1968, the national trails bill came to the House floor late in the evening of July 15 under the suspension of the rules procedure. Unlike the more controversial rivers legislation, it received the necessary two-thirds approval and was sent to conference with the Senate. The conference report, which won quick approval in each house, designated the Appalachian and Pacific Crest trails for immediate inclusion in a national trails system and designated fourteen other trails for study. The resulting National Trails System Act was signed by President Johnson on October 2, 1968.[22]

Thus, in the decade following the passage of the Wilderness Act Congress had created a national system of protection for wildlife, free-flowing rivers, and wilderness trails. Congress had also, in the National Environmental Policy Act, created a system of protection for the general environment. Increasingly, Congress found itself willing to forgo some marginal economic enterprise for the sake of preserving a sample of our heritage. This willingness was a function of the increasing scarcity, and thus increasing value, of natural environments. It is also a tribute to the countless individuals who have worked in the sometimes thankless task of representing noneconomic values to the nation's decision makers.

WILDERNESS CRISIS: THIS TIME IT'S THE GRAND CANYON

The legislative process decreed by our founding fathers is cumbersome and slow. Because it is, we must view with particular awe the ability of Congress to establish four major preservation systems in less than a decade. More frequently, it takes some sort of crisis to force Congress to redirect its legislative energies and act on behalf of the American wilderness. And what one Congress has done, a succeeding Congress can undo. So it has frequently been with the national parks.

In the mid-1950s preservation organizations had coalesced for the successful battle to prevent the damming of Dinosaur National Monument by the Bureau of Reclamation. By the mid-1960s the bureau was ready to do battle again. In August 1963 it announced a water project of incredible scale. The Pacific Southwest Water Plan would divert huge quantities of water from the Pacific Northwest to the water-hungry Southwest. Such a project was presumably necessitated by the continuing population boom in the Southwest and by the fact that the bureau had already diverted every available ounce from the overworked lower Colorado River.[23] Treaty commitments to Mexico prevent us from draining the Colorado dry.

If the Colorado could not supply the water the Southwest would need, its hydroelectric potential could be tapped to produce the power needed to pump water in from Washington and Oregon. To that end dams would be built in Bridge and Marble canyons. While neither dam was in the National Park System, the lakes created would flood thirteen miles of river within the Grand Canyon National Park and forty miles within the adjacent national monument. All the development forces that had been arrayed against Dinosaur were now arrayed against the Grand Canyon, and one more.

Stewart Udall, an interior secretary with remarkable conservationist sensitivity in most matters, was from Arizona. His younger brother Morris, a notable conservationist in his own right, had recently been elected to the Congress. The water problem was real, and the Udall brothers, pressured by the president from above and by the bureau and constituents from below, gave their support for the dams. The Udall defections would be difficult to overcome, but preservationists had one thing going for them —the Grand Canyon, the Park Service's number one attraction, one of the seven wonders of the natural world. The game was now for the ultimate stakes and the preservation lobby knew it. Sierra Club Executive Director David Brower told Roderick Nash, "If we can't save the Grand Canyon, what the hell can we save?"[24]

The evidence as to the damage the dams would do to the park was never clear. The development-minded majority on the House Interior Committee claimed, "It would be unthinkable that the [Interior] committee would take any action that would materially harm the grandeur and the beauty of the Grand Canyon."[25] They denied that the national park was meant to be a wilderness and argued that the lake behind the downstream dam would provide a "water highway" to "permit hundreds of thousands of people annually to visit and view an area now open to only a handful of daring riverrunners."[26] No one denied that the ecology of this stretch of the river would be changed. The dam's proponents argued that it would be immeasurably improved, rendered safe and accessible to families in power boats. The committee made much of the fact that none of the changes they proposed would be visible from any spot frequented by tourists. They accused the preservation lobby of painting "a picture of devastation and ruin wholly unsupported by the facts."[27]

No doubt, the rhetorical flourishes of the preservation forces did lead some Americans to visualize the Grand Canyon, filled to the rim, a kind of super bath tub. The damage would not, of course, have been that dramatic. Nonetheless, conservationist concern was not unfounded. The downstream dam would flood many miles of the canyon, putting a stop to the processes of erosion that are a part of the canyon's ecosystem and inundating some of the most significant geological features of the lower canyon. The upstream dam had the potential to be even more damaging. By impounding and releasing water just 12.5 miles upstream of the park boundary, it would cause sudden and violent changes in water level in the canyon, creating danger for hikers, boaters, and campers, and destroying fragile canyon-bottom habitat. Preservationists on the committee and in interested organizations were simply not prepared to join in the majority's conclusion that "the project plan will retain an undisturbed stretch of the Colorado River, 104 miles in length," between the two projects.[28]

It is difficult to gauge the probabilities of the plan's passage in the summer of 1966. The forces which a decade earlier had assured that the Interior Department and the Interior Committees would support flooding Dinosaur would most probably be sufficient to achieve the same objective here. The politics of reclamation is a politics dominated by local development interests and a construction-minded federal agency. In 1956 conservationists had succeeded in pushing the decision out of the reclamation subsystem and onto the floor of Congress where the diffused nationwide opposition could for the first time coalesce to overpower the geographically concentrated forces of development. Some observers foresaw the same result in 1966. *Newsweek*, for example, concluded on May 30 that "despite strong support from Arizona Democrats like Sen. Carl Hayden and Rep. Morris K. Udall, brother of Interior Secretary Stewart L. Udall, the dams face an upstream struggle to win authorization."[29] Even the president's budget bureau recommended deferring one of the two dams. But conservation organizations, like the Sierra Club, were taking no chances. The Sierra Club bought full-page advertisements in the *New York Times* and other major papers. The ads carried the banner, "Now Only You Can Save Grand Canyon From Being Flooded . . . For Profit," and concluded with this message: "Remember, with all the complexities of Washington politics and Arizona politics, the ins and outs of committees and procedures, there is only one simple, incredible issue here: This time it's the Grand Canyon they want to flood. *The Grand Canyon*." The ad contained coupons to clip and send to the president, Secretary Udall, Congressman Aspinall, and others, an invitation to contribute, and the reminder that "all contributions and membership dues are deductible."[30]

Preservationists thought they were taking no chances, but they were wrong. The following day a federal marshal delivered a notice to the club's headquarters in San Francisco announcing that its tax exemption was suspended and an investigation was being initiated concerning permanent revocation. Some conservationists suggested that the Internal Revenue Service (IRS) had been put up to it by the Interior Department or Chairman Aspinall, but that allegation was never substantiated.

It is difficult to assess the impact of this episode on the probability that the dams would be approved, but there is no doubt that the confrontation between the Sierra Club and the IRS attracted more attention than the ads ever could have by themselves. Many apparently saw the Sierra Club as engaged in a David versus Goliath struggle with the IRS and sympathized with the underdog. In August the Club reported that its membership was growing at the rate of 1,000 per month, more than 20 times its historic rate of growth.[31]

Preservation forces had a second advantage as well. As the full implications of the Pacific Southwest Water Plan became apparent, there were defections from the ranks of project supporters. The announced intent to divert water from the Northwest cost the support of representatives of the relatively water-rich areas of the West. Secretary Udall found himself faced with a disgruntled Park Service, desertions from the ranks of usually dependable reclamation supporters, only partial support from the White House and the Bureau of the Budget, and a frontal assault from his frequent allies in the conservation movement. The combined pressure of these forces, strengthened by the public outrage over the IRS action against the Sierra Club, proved too much for the secretary, and the 1966 version of the project died. In February 1967 Secretary Udall transmitted to the new Congress a draft of the administration's new proposal. The new draft eliminated any commitment to the interregional water diversion contemplated by the Pacific Southwest Water Plan, and it proposed *no* new dams on the Colorado River. The proposals pleased preservation interests and those concerned over the possible loss of water resources from the Pacific Northwest, but the opposition from most of the Colorado River Basin was harsh. Udall was castigated as a traitor to reclamation in newspapers throughout the Southwest.

A bill similar to the administration's new proposal was reported favorably by the Interior Committee and passed the Senate on a voice vote August 7, 1967. Even in success several senators felt that protection for the Grand Canyon required strengthening. Senator Jackson introduced an Interior Department bill that would have expanded the national park by 68,000 acres, and Senator Clifford Case of New Jersey proposed to encompass the entire canyon. Case and Congressman Saylor in the House proposed to expand the park, not by 68,000 acres but by 536,000. The Grand Canyon, said Case, belongs "to all the people of the world. . . . The highest and best use of the canyon," he concluded, "would be to keep it as it is, undammed, undemeaned, and undiminished."[32] With the eventual protections for the park built into the reclamation legislation, the proposals for immediate park expansion were allowed to expire with the end of the Ninetieth Congress.

The Senate-passed bill was sent to the House where Chairman Aspinall could be expected to use his substantial influence to restore the excised dams. Aspinall's own bill (H.R. 3300) eliminated the Marble Canyon Dam but continued the downstream project at Bridge Canyon. By the time it had emerged from committee, however, H.R.3300 had no provisions for Colorado River dams, and the committee majority was willing to argue, contrary to their arguments of the previous year, that the dams were not, in fact, an essential feature of the project.[33] On the matter of dams in the Grand Canyon, there was no longer any dispute. Section 605 of the eventual statute prohibited any dam on "the main stream of the Colorado River between Hoover Dam and Glen Canyon Dam until and unless otherwise provided by Congress."[34]

HELL'S CANYON TOO

The Grand Canyon episode was not the only effort to dam a wild river in the years after the Wilderness Act. A very similar scenario was played out over Hell's Canyon on the Snake River, which divides Oregon from Idaho. Like those for the Grand Canyon, plans to develop the Hell's Canyon hydropower potential had a long history, dating back at least to 1947 when the Army Corps of Engineers completed a study of potential projects on the Columbia River and its tributaries, including the Snake.[35] Bills to authorize federal dams in the canyon were introduced regularly after 1952, and several private companies were also interested in the sites. Conservationists showed no interest in the area until 1959 when the Oregon Izaak Walton League was alarmed by the threat to migratory fish populations. Dams upstream and downstream from Hell's Canyon were decimating the salmon runs, and the IWL feared that further dam construction would make the rivers virtually impassible to this important fish species.

The Federal Power Commission granted a license to the Pacific Northwest Power Company for construction of a dam and reservoir in 1964, but the license was contested in court by another company interested in the river's development. After a three-year struggle the Supreme Court remanded the decision to the FPC for further study, with Justice William O. Douglas reminding the bureaucrats that the best dam in Hell's Canyon might be no dam at all. Having fought to a draw of sorts in the courts, the competing power companies joined forces and made a joint application to the FPC for a Hell's Canyon power project. The FPC eventually granted the license requested, but noting that several bills had been introduced in Congress to preserve this stretch of the river, the FPC put a moratorium on construction until December 31, 1975 to allow Congress to work its will in the matter.

Permanent moratorium bills passed the Senate twice but failed in the House. By the mid-1970s as the FPC deadline approached, preservationist thinking was gravitating toward the idea of a Hell's Canyon National Recreation Area (NRA) with substantial portions protected by the Wilderness and Wild Rivers acts. The Senate passed a Hell's Canyon NRA bill, but the House failed to follow suit. As the final year of protection under the FPC moratorium began, passage of some sort of measure seemed probable. The administration backed a proposal to make 68 of the canyon's 101 miles a component of the National Wild and Scenic Rivers System, but resisted the more encompassing NRA legislation with substantial wilderness designations as premature. The Forest Service had wilderness recommendations under advisement for a large portion of the adjoining area, but was loath to have a congressional decision on the matter until the evidence of governmental mineral surveys was available. The administration position was reasonable and ought not to be construed as antipreservation, but the wishes of the land management agencies were to prove less compelling in the corridors of Congress than the stand of the area's congressional representatives.

In the Senate, legislation for a substantial NRA was sponsored by both senators from each of the affected states, Idaho and Oregon, and was passed substantially intact by the full Senate. In the House, the cast of characters had altered dramatically since the battles over the Grand Canyon. Heroes and villains of the preservation movement had passed from the scene.

Wayne Aspinall was the first to go. In 1972, after fourteen years at the helm of the House Interior Committee, the seventy-six-year-old Aspinall succumbed to a combination of old age, environmental politics, and an unfriendly reapportionment at the hands of a Republican-controlled state legislature. Aspinall fell to the primary efforts of a thirty-eight-year-old, environmentally oriented, law professor, who, in his turn, lost the general election to a Republican. Thus, as so often happens in the American congressional system, a distant decision by a handful of primary voters changed the complexion of natural resource politics for the nation. Aspinall's chief adversary on the House committee, John Saylor, departed the scene shortly thereafter. In 1973 the *Almanac of American Politics* assessed his political position and concluded, "About the only thing that would end Saylor's House career is retirement; he is 66 in 1974."[36] John Saylor died a few months later at the height of his political popularity.

There was every reason to believe that this changing of the guards in the House would mitigate the level of conservation conflict in that chamber. James Haley of Florida, the new chairman of the House Interior Committee, was perhaps even less hospitable to conservationist positions than was Aspinall. He was also less expert in the committee's subject matter and from a constituency where the stakes were lower, and he could be expected to exercise far less dictatorial control over the committee than did his predecessor. At seventy-three years of age his tenure as chairman would not be a long one.

Haley's committee reported out a moderate proposal for Hell's Canyon. It followed the general thrust of the Senate bill in establishing a large NRA including some instant wilderness, but it acceded to the administration position to the degree that it proposed immediate Wild and Scenic river status for only the 68 miles recommended. The proposal passed the House, and the two chambers were able to reconcile their differences without resort to a conference committee. Congress clearly had its way, and preservation triumphed. In final form the act encompassed the entire 101-mile river segment in an NRA, complete with large areas of instant wilderness and areas for further wilderness study.[37] Many congressmen were undoubtedly impressed by the frequently repeated testimony that the hydropower from

Hell's Canyon would be sufficient to postpone a power shortage in the Northwest for less than a year, clearly, too small a return for loss of what is quite probably the deepest canyon on the face of the earth. The movement to preserve the Snake River free-flowing through Hell's Canyon had maintained its momentum in spite of the Arab Oil Embargo of 1973-74, administration attempts to handle the issue through narrower legislation, and industry desires to tap the mineral, as well as the hydrological, potential of the area. The decision was clearly symptomatic of a new national concern with preservationist politics and cause for alarm on the part of mining, timber, and energy companies with business interests in the public domain's resource base.

RUNWAYS IN THE WILDERNESS

These were not the only interests to suffer at the hands of preservationists in the years since 1964. In Florida, preservationists turned their fire on a sometime ally, the transportation industry. Political alliances of preservation forces and dominant transportation interests have occasionally sprung up. The Central American Steamship Company, and later the Southern Pacific Railroad, contributed to the preservation of Yosemite. The Northern Pacific Railroad helped preserve Yellowstone, and the Great Northern Railroad worked to create Glacier. Steven Mather was able to enlist the support of the auto and highway lobby in the early days of the National Park Service. In the late twentieth century it was air travel that marked the cutting edge in transportation, and it was air travel that, in its turn, posed a threat to wilderness resources. In Florida's Everglades and in New Jersey's Great Swamp, preservation forces beat back politically potent attempts to replace wilderness with runways.

In the case of the Everglades, the jetport had few supporters outside the local Miami community. The federal government had a recognized commitment to the preservation of Everglades National Park, and the state of Florida was concerned that its location might alter the south Florida ecosystem, including the park, and work a long-term detriment to the state's tourist trade.[38] Support for the project came from the Dade County Port Authority which promised "the greatest jetport man has ever envisioned."[39] Such a development clearly meant an economic bonanza for segments of the south Florida economy. State and local forces were undermined in their efforts to prevent the development by the jetport's location and its methods of finance. The airport site was six miles north of Everglades National Park in an unprotected area of Big Cyprus Swamp and on private lands; it was to be financed in stages by local bond issues and its own revenues. Neither the federal government nor the state could conveniently exercise control over the project by means of land-use regulation or funding.[40] The Federal Aviation Administration (FAA) could deny the papers necessary for airport operation, but in the 1960s environmental concerns were not yet on the FAA's agenda. Indeed, with the exception of the Department of Transportation, of which the FAA is a part, the federal government was "institutionally unaware" of the proposed development.

In June 1969 Senator Jackson held hearings on the jetport threat to the Everglades in order to drum up support for the National Environmental Policy Act, which he had introduced. Testimony at the hearings painted a portrait of massive bureaucratic fragmentation and negligible or nonexistent consultation. Neither the Port Authority nor the FAA had attempted to bring federal or state conservation agencies into the decision-making process although Section 4(f) of the Department of Transportation Act required it.[41] The Senate hearings directed national attention to the plight of Everglades Park and resulted in a joint federal and state study which concluded, as conservationists had warned, that "development of the proposed jetport . . . will destroy inexorably the south Florida ecosystem and thus the Everglades National Park."[42] In January 1970 the departments of Interior and Transportation, Governor Claude Kirk of Florida, and Mayor Stephen Clark of Miami signed an agreement calling for a new site for the jetport. The training use which had already begun at the Everglades site would be allowed to continue on a temporary basis, but eventually the airfield would be allowed to disintegrate.[43]

Everglades National Park has always lived on borrowed time because it is on the receiving end of south Florida's River of Grass. Without the waters' flowing into the park from unprotected areas, the ecology of the area would be devastated by the first annual dry season. Park borders may be sacrosanct, but unless the water supply is protected, the park will die. The jetport controversy had captured public attention in the early 1970s, and Congress moved to attempt a more permanent solution. All legislative solutions take time, but with the jetport safely relocated, near consensus on saving Big Cyprus Swamp emerged. The president endorsed the plan, as did the entire Florida congressional delegation. The state of Florida passed legislation declaring the area to be of critical concern and appropriated $40 million to assist the federal government in acquiring title. Indeed, Senator Lawton Chiles noted that the proposal's supporters "include the local governments concerned, the State of Florida, the Department of Interior—the Republican Federal Administration and Democratic leaders of the Congress and in Florida—Florida's most ardent conservation organizations, and the Greater Miami Chamber of Commerce."[44] The House bill went so far as to provide for legislative condemnation of virtually all private property in the 570,000-acre area, a tactic used amid great debate in the establishment of

Redwood National Park. The Senate determined such extreme measures were unnecessary, but joined with the House in expressing the belief that acquisitions in Big Cyprus Swamp were a high priority. Interchamber differences were resolved in the same mood of consensus and general mutual congratulation that prevailed at the bills' original passage in each of the chambers. President Ford's signature in September 1974 established the nation's first National Preserve. The word *preserve* is significant. Although certain uses were to be allowed to continue, the central purpose of the Big Cyprus Preserve was preservation of the Big Cyprus and the hydrologically linked Everglades National Park. Consistent with the preservationist emphasis, the act provided for study of the area's suitability for wilderness designation.[45]

If the preservation of the Everglades, which was undertaken in the 1970s, is remarkable for the degree of cooperation that the project developed, the preservation of New Jersey's Great Swamp is remarkable for its very success. Like the Everglades, the Great Swamp fell under the eye of a powerful governmental airport builder, in this case the New York Port Authority, operator of La Guardia, JFK, and Newark airports and a host of other transportation facilities. Unlike the Dade County Authority, New York's had no real alternative to the swamp site; and unlike the Everglades, the Great Swamp had no national recognition as an irreplaceable national treasure. The Great Swamp's survival was almost entirely the work of local aficionados. Their perseverance resulted not only in preventing the airport from being built, but also in the establishment of a Great Swamp National Wildlife Refuge containing the nation's first national wildlife refuge wilderness area.[46]

EASTERN WILDERNESS

These threats to western rivers and eastern swamplands had come largely from regional development interests. These interests were frequently aided by federal agencies without any significant conservation mission. The Federal Power Commission is charged by law to develop rivers by licensing dams. The FAA is charged to promote air travel by licensing airports. Prior to 1970 a lack of environmental consciousness was to be expected from these agencies. A more subtle, but also more closely watched, threat to wilderness resulted from a lack of commitment to wilderness on the part of the very agencies charged to administer it—the Fish and Wildlife Service, the Park Service, and the Forest Service. The agencies were frequently less aggressive in designating potential wilderness areas than the preservation lobby would have wished. The Forest Service, in particular, came in for criticism by preservationists on this score, and in a number of important cases the dispute was carried into the Congress for final adjudication.

Congress was forced to confront the purity issue regularly as the Forest Service brought in its primitive area recommendations. The Forest Service frequently justified modest wilderness proposals on the grounds that areas not recommended failed to meet the standards of the Wilderness Act. Preservationists almost always brought in larger proposals, and Congress often made substantial additions to the Forest Service recommendations. A more general problem for preservation interests was that the Forest Service standard for wilderness precluded, by its own admission, any additional areas east of the Great Plains, although the greatest demand for the recreation resources of wilderness was in the East in proximity to most of the nation's population.

The Forest Service was over a barrel. It was interested in catering to the obvious need for primitive recreation in the eastern national forests, but to admit that an area once harvested for timber, mined, or farmed might be admitted to the wilderness system, was to admit that any area in the national forests might be admitted. Clearly, no Congress would ever contemplate a wilderness system so vast, but any hint that the entire system might qualify suggested the possibility of an injunction from the federal courts requiring a multiple-use moratorium while the areas were studied. The service could not be expected to welcome dramatic reductions in its management options for the national forests, but this was precisely the specter that haunted the issue of wilderness in the eastern national forests.

An internal memorandum, dated September 1971, to the chief of the Forest Service from the regional foresters for the East and Midwest, suggests the direction in which policy was evolving in the Forest Service. The memorandum cited increased interest in primitive recreation and noted that this interest was "increasingly translated into proposals for new wilderness classifications" in spite of the fact that "there are simply no remaining candidate areas for wilderness classification in this part of the national forest system."[47] The memo went on to recommend the establishment of "Wildwood-Heritage areas" which might be given a variety of other labels such as "Pioneer," "Frontier," or "Wild." It also suggested that Forest Chief John R. McGuire might make such a proposal to the Sierra Club's 1971 Wilderness Conference. McGuire chose not to go that far, but he did reiterate the Forest Service policy that no areas in the East qualified for protection under the Wilderness Act and asked for suggestions on some alternative form of classification.[48]

The situation confronting the Forest Service on eastern wilderness areas in 1971 and 1972 was in many respects similar to the situation it confronted on de facto wilderness areas, generally, during the same period. Enormous public pressure was gathering for congressional designation of wilderness areas not recommended or even studied by the Forest Service, and countervailing pressure was coming from commodity interests. Congress had given the impression that it was prepared to exercise its wilderness creation prerogatives in a fashion sympathetic to wilderness proponents. The Forest Service response was RARE I, the first survey of all de facto wilderness areas in the national forests. De facto wilderness constituted fifty-six million acres, even by the fairly restrictive interpretation of the service. This would have been a disastrous time for the Forest Service to admit to a new standard of flexibility as to what might qualify for wilderness protection. The de facto wilderness survey might well have doubled.

President Nixon increased the public pressure on the Forest Service in his environmental message to Congress in 1972. He bemoaned the lack of wilderness in the East and directed "the Secretaries of Agriculture and the Interior to accelerate the identification of areas in the Eastern United States having wilderness potential."[49]

The Forest Service needed some way out of its dilemma, and a separate system for the eastern national forests seemed a logical solution. Senators George Aiken and Herman Talmadge and Congressman John Kyl, friends of the Forest Service, obliged the service by the introduction of national forest "wild areas" bills that would create a separate category of preserved space east of the 100th meridian. The wild areas proposal would, in effect, have written the service's purist policy into law by recognizing that eastern national forests cannot meet the criteria of the Wilderness Act. The Aiken-Talmadge bill enshrined a congressional finding that, "few areas of the National Forest System located in the Eastern United States, which were acquired largely from private ownerships, meet the criteria set forth for wilderness by the Wilderness Act of 1964 because of the past works of man."[50] While Chief McGuire was careful to say that the Forest Service was neutral on this proposal, it clearly was a Forest Service bill. It had been drafted by the service, and lower echelon employees were active in its support. George Alderson, legislative director for Friends of the Earth, reported that he had been present when a Forest Service spokesman had actively pushed the proposal among representatives of the major preservation groups. He also reported "persistent efforts by Forest Service officials at the local level to seek support for 'wild areas' instead of wilderness."[51] This activity took the form of "listening sessions" that were conducted throughout the eastern United States to gauge public opinion—sessions described by Senator Church as characterized by "blatant and obvious bias."[52] The service mailed something in excess of three thousand invitations for nine such listening sessions in early 1972. A four-page memo that accompanied the invitation made it clear that the question was one of finding the best *alternative* to the Wilderness Act for protecting eastern national forest areas. According to Senator Church "the Forest Service got back a lot of the carbon copy they had spooned out in advance. . . . A great many people . . . were all for something called a 'wild areas system.' "[53] But a great many had also spotted a preferable alternative. Senators Jackson and Church had introduced legislation that would establish eastern wilderness areas under the Wilderness Act. The Forest Service internal memorandum of August 16, 1972, which summarized the proceedings of the listening sessions, stated that: "About 50% of those who supported a Wild Area System did so only to the extent that it should be included under the Wilderness Act." The memo stated further that, "Many people expressed real concern that the Forest Service was too strict in their interpretation of the 1964 Act," and that "the introduction of the Jackson omnibus bill (S. 3792) was a serious handicap for the Forest personnel at a couple of meetings."[54]

It is hard to avoid the conclusion that the Forest Service was actively advancing the Aiken-Talmadge bill. Apart from the bill's recognition of the Forest Service view in the purity debate, the Aiken-Talmadge bill was probably perceived as preferable because it was being handled by the Senate Agriculture and Forestry Committee. Most Department of Agriculture business comes before this committee, and the department undoubtedly finds its interests better served there than in the Interior Committee.

This change in committee arena was made possible by the complex jurisdictional rules under which committees of Congress operate. The Agriculture and Forestry Committee has jurisdiction over "forestry in general, and forest reserves other than those created from the public domain,"[55] while the Interior Committee has jurisdiction over the public domain from which the western national forests were created. It had been appropriate, therefore, for the Wilderness Act to have been handled in the Interior Committee, and a belated attempt to have it referred to the Senate Agriculture Committee had been rebuffed.[56] By 1972 there was considerable precedent for Interior Committee consideration of "wilderness" measures, but the interest of the Forest Service in an alternative to the Wilderness Act for the East provided an opportunity for Aiken and Talmadge to introduce legislation "to establish a system of wild areas within the lands of the National Forest system" and claim jurisdiction for their own Agriculture Committee.

Whether the Aiken-Talmadge initiative was antiwilderness was much disputed in conservation circles. Writing in 1976, Allen Smith of the Sierra Club concluded that "in general, the members of the Agriculture committees were not receptive to Wilderness designation, and were proposing wild areas as a less protective, more easily exploited, land-preservation system."[57] On the other hand the Agriculture Committee approach won the approval of Joe Penfold, conservation director of the Izaak Walton League. Penfold argued that wild areas legislation would not preclude considering eastern areas for designation under the Wilderness Act where that was appropriate, and that the protections given would be as strong or stronger than those afforded by the Wilderness Act.[58]

There is support for Penfold's position in the language of the Agriculture Committee's bill. While it created only one "instant" wild area, and designated none for specific study, it terminated many of the nonconforming uses allowed under the Wilderness Act, like grazing and mining, and provided the authority to consolidate the government's property using condemnation procedures if necessary. Penfold was also correct in his observation that Congress had created a precedent for multiple levels of wildness in its passage of wild and scenic rivers legislation with "wild," "scenic," and "recreational" river segments. The real problem for preservationists was not that wild areas would be less well protected, but rather that the combination of strict protection, Agriculture Committee jurisdiction, and the lack of any specific list of study areas would result in few areas being designated. These problems notwithstanding, the legislation was reported by the committee on September 22 and passed by the Senate without debate on the 26th.[59] Senator Jackson's bill did not receive any action in the Senate, and neither the Jackson nor the Aiken-Talmadge bill was acted upon in the House.

The Ninety-third Congress opened with a flurry of activity on eastern wilderness. Many bills were submitted to both the Agriculture and Interior committees. The Agriculture Committee promptly reported S. 22, a reintroduction of the previously passed Aiken-Talmadge bill, but the Interior Committee requested and received assurance that S. 22 would be delayed until it could hold hearings on S. 316. S. 316 was a revised version of the so-called Jackson omnibus bill of the previous Congress and differed from S. 22 fundamentally in that it established wilderness areas under the Wilderness Act.[60] The hearings on S. 316 provide a chronicle of the debate over wilderness purity between the majority of the Senate Interior Committee and most of the preservationist lobby, on the one hand, and the Forest Service, on the other. S. 316 as reported by the committee in December was a strong preservationist bill. Management of the eastern areas was to be "in accordance with the provisions of the Wilderness Act,"[61] except that grazing and mining were prohibited and condemnation procedures were approved. More important, the bill specified nineteen areas of instant wilderness and an additional thirty-nine study areas. By prior arrangement, S. 316 was then referred to the Agriculture Committee where an attempt would be made to reach some accommodation between advocates of the two approaches.

During the months of discussion on S. 316, the administration had endorsed a Forest Service bill, "The Eastern Wilderness Amendments of 1973," which specified fifty-three study areas and amended the 1964

Wilderness Act to specify that less than pure areas could only be considered east of the 100th meridian.[62] The administration bill also sought to deprive preservationists of their victory in the East Meadow Creek case by specifying complete multiple-use management authority for the secretary of agriculture "within areas not designated *by him* for review,"[63] and by discontinuing the protection afforded to study areas if the president chose not to recommend them. These latter provisions were, of course, unsatisfactory to the preservationist forces. In the early years of Wilderness Act deliberations they had pressed for a system where the president could create wilderness areas, but only Congress could abolish them. They were not disposed to reverse that process.

After several months of negotiation, during which the Department of Agriculture amended its draft bill so as to create sixteen instant wilderness areas and thirty-seven study areas, the interested members of the Agriculture and Interior committees developed a compromise package which was presented to the Senate. Negotiations had been difficult and near collapse on several occasions, and all hands concurred in the judgment that agreement had finally been reached and the legislation saved largely through the efforts of Senator Aiken of Vermont. Many of his colleagues praised his efforts, and several suggested the Eastern Wilderness Areas Act would stand as a monument to his long and distinguished Senate career. The compromise bill was an amalgam of S. 22, S. 316, and the administration proposals. At first glance the preservationists seemed to have gotten the best of the bargain. The new bill established nineteen instant wilderness areas and forty study areas. It eliminated grazing and mining, not just in the eastern areas, but throughout the entire wilderness system. In principle, of course, this was precisely what preservationists should prefer. In practice the Wilderness Society and the Sierra Club, as well as the Izaak Walton League and the National Wildlife Federation, denounced this attempt to create a uniform administrative system for all national forest wilderness. Since 1964 the preservationist lobby had proven itself consistently pragmatic where wilderness allocation was concerned; this was no exception. The Forest Service had used the purity principle for years to minimize the acreages qualifying for preservation. The preservationist lobby was not about to join in purifying the western wilderness areas of nonconforming uses at the expense of alienating supporters. Too much purity meant too little wilderness.

Readers who have become cynical about the motives of wilderness managers may have entertained the notion that this attempt to purify the entire national forest wilderness system might be some sort of plot hatched by the Forest Service and members of the Agriculture and Forestry Committee. If it was, the committee members showed little commitment to the project, for both Aiken and Talmadge endorsed amendments offered by Senator Jackson to restore the status quo on nonconforming uses in the West. With the adoption of the Jackson amendment, the only real concern of wilderness proponents was that study areas would be protected for only six years, once presidential recommendations had been made, rather than "until Congress decides otherwise." Still, this concession seemed a small price to pay, and general assurances were offered that, if it proved necessary, the requisite committees would be favorably disposed toward a legislative extension of the time limit. This compromise package was endorsed by the Senate May 31, 1974, and forwarded to the House where passage was anticipated.

The House Interior Committee reported December 16. The House bill avoided most of the areas of controversy in the Senate. It designated sixteen areas of instant wilderness and seventeen areas for wilderness study. It provided limited powers of condemnation for inholdings, but made no amendment whatsoever in the 1964 Act. The House passed the measure two days later and the Senate agreed to the House version, thus eliminating the necessity of a conference impossibly late in the session. Preservation organizations had proven themselves most adept in the politics of legislation. The Eastern Wilderness Areas Act of 1975 was ultimately more responsive to the desires of the Wilderness Society and the Sierra Club than it was to the Forest Service. The service's purity principle was implicitly repudiated, and the eastern United States had increased its total of designated national forest wilderness areas fivefold.

ENDANGERED AMERICAN WILDERNESS

The Eastern Wilderness Areas Act may have repudiated the purity principle, but it had little obvious impact on Forest Service management policy. Congress had, after all, repudiated the purity principle several times over, first and most importantly in the legislative history surrounding the passage of the original Wilderness Act. When the service's first Roadless Area Review and Evaluation failed to identify, even as study areas, a number of de facto wilderness areas of substantial interest to preservationists across the country, Congress was again called upon to come to the rescue. The result was what came to be called the Endangered American Wilderness Act. The purpose of this legislation was to set aside significant wilderness areas in the West which had been classified as multiple-use lands under RARE I. These lands were endangered by logging, mining, and off-road-vehicle use, of course, but in the most direct sense the threat to these lands was the management of the United States Forest Service. Steve Young of the National Audubon Society voiced typical preservationist complaints to the Senate's Subcommittee on Parks and Recreation in the fall of 1977: "The whole process [of Forest Service land-use planning] has been biased against wilderness designations. Development decisions can be made on the lower agency levels, while any proposal to conduct wilderness studies must be cleared all the way to the District of Columbia before the proposed action can even be made public . . . a wilderness study proposal can be vetoed before the public is even aware of the proposal. It's no wonder that so much controversy has erupted in the last few years."[64] Yet, by the time that this testimony was delivered, the attitude in the Forest Service had begun a substantial change. Testifying for the new Carter administration, Assistant Secretary Cutler announced: "We recommend the enactment of S. 1180, the Endangered American Wilderness Act of 1977, if amended to designate a larger number of wilderness areas."[65] With this statement the Department of Agriculture, in effect, endorsed legislation to protect portions of the American wilderness from its own constituent bureau, the Forest Service. The Department of Agriculture was still interested in commodity developments, to be sure, but the mood on wilderness was clearly conciliatory. Passage of the Endangered American Wilderness Act in 1978 may mark the end of the debate over purity between legislators and administrators.

BLM WILDERNESS

In the interval between passage of the Eastern and Endangered Wilderness acts Congress passed two particularly significant statutes. The National Forest Management Act of 1976 (chapter 5) was essential to free the Forest Service from the burdens of the Organic Act of 1897 as interpreted by the court in *IWL v. Butz*. The other was a product of a more evolutionary process.

From the very beginning of the nation, the United States government had found itself proprietor over an extensive public domain. From the cession of the western land claims of the original thirteen colonies until 1976, something in excess of three thousand land laws were enacted to control the management and disposition of the federal lands. By the midpoint of the twentieth century, after more than 100 years of evolution in public land law, the nation's lands were governed by a complex and often contradictory mass of statutes. And in spite of the plentitude of laws, major questions were left unanswered. This is not surprising, for the public domain, throughout most of its history, was seen as something temporary. As decisions were made that certain lands would remain under federal control, systems of management were prescribed for those lands: national forests, national parks, national wildlife refuges, national monuments, lands devoted to reclamation and flood control projects and to military reservations. Always these lands, reserved and dedicated to some useful purpose,

were provided with an administrative agency and generally with some congressionally mandated set of management practices. The General Land Office, and its successor, the Bureau of Land Management (BLM), was charged
with the administration of the leftovers.

By the 1960s it seemed probable that the bulk of the remaining public
domain would remain public. With the exception of Alaska, vast and virtually undeveloped, the national mood favored retention over disposal of
what remained. Very little else was obvious, however; and therefore, in the
same month that Congress created the National Wilderness Preservation
System, it established a Public Land Law Review Commission (PLLRC) and
charged it to study the public lands and their administration and to make
recommendations to Congress. The commission was composed of six
members each from the Senate and House Interior committees and six
presidential appointees. It was chaired by Congressman Wayne Aspinall,
and included in its membership most of the individuals whose names have
been prominent here in the formulation of congressional wilderness policy:
Senators Allott, Anderson, and Jackson, and Congressmen Baring, Kyl,
Saylor, Taylor, and Udall. The PLLRC, being a product of the Interior committees, was also a product of the public land states. Congressmen John
Saylor of Pennsylvania and Roy Taylor of North Carolina were the sole
representatives of states or districts east of the Mississippi.

The commission's report, *One Third of the Nation's Land*, issued in 1970,
reached the obvious conclusion that "at this time most public lands would
not serve the maximum public interest in private ownership."[66] It went on
to recognize the desirability of the "national forests, the National Park
System, the National Wildlife Refuge System, and the parallel or subsidiary
programs involving the Wilderness Preservation System, the National
Riverways and Scenic Rivers Systems, national trails, and national recreation areas."[67] Far more controversial was the commission's recommendation that Congress should "assert its constitutional authority by . . . reserv-
ing unto itself exclusive authority to withdraw or otherwise set aside public
lands."[68] The commission reached the conclusion that executive reservations were typically made without "adequate study" or "proper consultation," and recommended that all such executive designations be recon-
sidered.[69] These conclusions and recommendations are, of course, quite
consistent with Chairman Aspinall's frequently expressed desire to expand
the scope of congressional control over the public lands.

Where wilderness was concerned the commission gave preservationists
cause for both concern and optimism. Concern grew out of recommendations that seemed to place a high priority on the economic return of the
federal lands, and, particularly, the recommendation that "there should be
a statutory requirement that those public lands that are highly productive

for timber be classified for commercial timber production as the dominant use."[70] To many conservationists this was an obvious encouragement to those land managers intent on a policy of "wilderness on the rocks." On the other hand, a planning and dominant-use mentality, such as that exhibited by the commission, might work to the advantage of wilderness preservation as well. The commission called attention to the existence of lands in the national forests and in the public domain that might qualify as wilderness and called for systematic inventory and review of all such areas so that appropriate recommendations might be made to Congress.[71]

Many of the land laws of the 1970s have been influenced by the commission's report, but none is more important than the Federal Land Policy and Management Act of 1976.[72] It declared a general policy of retention of the public lands and provided a comprehensive organic act for their management by the Bureau of Land Management, amending or repealing over 300 public land laws in the process. Of particular interest was the first statutory provision for wilderness study of BLM lands. Section 603 of the act required review of the entire roadless inventory of the BLM for possible wilderness values—some 90 to 120 million acres according to the Council on Environmental Quality. These reviews are to be completed by 1991, and while the study areas are not "frozen" in terms of development, the intent of Congress is clear that apart from the effect of the mineral laws they are to be managed "so as not to impair the suitability of such areas for preservation as wilderness."[73] This language was incorporated into the statute over the objections of the Interior Department that a wilderness review of every area over 5,000 acres would impose an unreasonable burden on the department. The administration had proposed to study only areas in excess of 50,000 acres and to do so without any deadline.[74] Congressman Aspinall got his way on the matter of executive withdrawals. The statute placed limits on them and provided that major withdrawals are subject to congressional veto by concurrent resolution. Existing withdrawals are to be studied over a fifteen-year period, but lands in all the major conservation categories are exempted from this provision. This massive exemption virtually guaranteed that no harm would come to preserved wilderness in spite of this flexing of congressional muscle. Since 1964 wilderness designations per se have been made only by act of Congress in any case.

In each age our technology produces new affluence and greater interest in wilderness preservation. In the latter part of the twentieth century no wilderness is untouched by the works of man. Global air pollution consisting of combustion by-products and radioactive fallout from weapons testing is more than sufficient to work some change everywhere on earth. Congress recognized this indirect sort of threat in the 1977 Clean Air Act Amendments. A major bone of contention in air pollution legislation has always been the extent to which air quality would be allowed to deteriorate in order to allow industrial growth in relatively undeveloped—and thus relatively clean—airsheds. The 1977 Amendments provided for the division of clean air areas into three classes based on the level of degradation that would be permitted. Congress demonstrated its commitment to the wilderness resource by designating large national parks and wilderness areas as the only federally mandated Class I (minimum degradation) areas.[75]

EXPANSION OF PARK WILDERNESS

In the years following the passage of the Wilderness Act national park wilderness was not a high priority for the conservation movement. Important battles had to be fought and won—over protection of the Grand Canyon and the Everglades, over creation of North Cascades, and over creation and protection of Redwood in California. The question of what portion of the established parks was to be designated wilderness was never as pressing as what portion of the forests. Nevertheless, 1978 did see significant national parks wilderness legislation utilizing the omnibus bill approach which had proven an effective conservation tool.[76]

What was eventually to become the National Parks and Recreation Act of 1978 began in the House with the usual collection of special purpose bills of small consequence piling up in an Interior subcommittee. With more than eighty such bills to consider, Congressman Phillip Burton of California introduced an omnibus bill of over 150 pages designed to accomplish a variety of purposes, including adding substantially to national park wilderness and to the National Wild and Scenic Rivers System (NWSRS). Senator James Abourezk of South Dakota had, in the meantime, introduced a considerably more modest proposal restricted in the main to raising appropriations ceilings for various units of the National Park System. The Burton bill provided for designation of wilderness areas in 14 units of the National Park System, the largest being a 2,022,221-acre preserve in Yellowstone—91 percent of the total park acreage. The politics of omnibus legislation is a politics of expediency and, therefore, a politics of consensus and congressional courtesy. As such, the Burton bill did not attempt to handle the entire backlog of national park wilderness proposals. Still, if successful, it would have increased national park wilderness almost sixfold, from fewer than 1.2 million acres to almost 7 million. In eight of fourteen cases the Burton bill designated acreages larger than those recommended by the administration; in the remaining six the area equaled the administrative recommendation. In three cases the designations were even larger than the latest recommendation from local citizens' groups associated with the preservation movement.

The wilderness provisions of the bill were quickly decimated, however, as the Interior Committee deleted provisions related to Yellowstone and Grand Teton national parks totaling almost 2.2 million acres. Congressmen from Wyoming and Montana were uniformly opposed to the designations. Their attitudes were reiterated on the floor of the House as Congressman Max Baucus of Montana argued for his amendment to eliminate a million acre wilderness designation in Glacier National Park. "Our National Park System contemplates motorized use; that is, people are permitted—indeed encouraged—to drive through the parks. Also the National Park Service sets aside certain areas for development in the wilderness. . . . Wilderness is a separate system from the National Parks. I do not think that we should mix the two." Wyoming Congressman Teno Roncalino echoed the sentiments. "To do this to Yellowstone or Glacier National Park, where our two states lead the nation in visitors, is to set back the wilderness concept itself. There has got to be some place left where people can go in a car."[77] Mr. Baucus's amendment passed, as did others offered by the representatives of the immediately affected districts. The Burton bill, stripped of several wilderness and wild river proposals, was passed by the House on July 12, 1978, by a vote of 341 to 61.

The House bill was, according to Congressman Burton, "subject to a few minimal senatorial complaints,"[78] and a modified version was substituted for a Senate-passed bill on October 4. The modification contained eight of the original fourteen wilderness designations. One week later Congressman Burton substituted the House language for yet another Senate-passed bill. The Senate had acted on a number of measures, each of which generally accomplished a purpose similar to that accomplished by a part of the omnibus bill. By substituting the entire omnibus package for the language of each of these Senate bills, Burton kept the measure alive and intact as the Congress neared an end. Each substitution involved some amendment to the previous measure as Senate and House differences were minimized. As the end of session neared there was also pressure to make major additions to the package covering the Boundary Waters Canoe Area or the Alaska lands question, but Burton correctly perceived these additions as a threat to the passage of the omnibus legislation and resisted them. Senator Abourezk brought a revised version of the omnibus bill to the Senate on October 12, where it passed on a voice vote. The House concurred the following day. In final form the National Parks and Recreation Act of 1978 established eight national park wilderness areas totaling 1,974,000 acres and more than doubled the total acreage of designated wilderness in the National Park System. It also made a major addition to the National Wild and Scenic Rivers System, designating eight new river segments as a part of the system and an additional seventeen for study. The act tripled the size of the National Trails

System, adding the Continental Divide Trail from Canada to Mexico as the nation's third National Scenic Trail, and establishing a National Historic Trail category consisting of the Oregon, Mormon Pioneer, and Lewis and Clark trails in the western United States and the Iditarod Trail in Alaska. Finally, fifteen new units were added to the National Park System, and the Mineral King Valley was attached to Sequoia National Park.

In making Mineral King a part of the national park, Congress laid to rest one of the oldest preservationist issues in the West. In recognition of the continuing interest of Disney Productions and others in developing the valley for skiing, the House committee had directed the secretary of interior to consider this alternative in his management plan for the area. The Senate, on the other hand, was prepared to buy Disney out, if necessary, to prevent the valley's development. The final language indicates an unambiguous preservationist victory: "The Congress recognizes that the Mineral King Valley area has outstanding potential for certain year-round recreational opportunities, but the development of permanent facilities for downhill skiing within the area would be inconsistent with the preservation and enhancement of its ecological values."[79]

THE BOUNDARY WATERS WAR

Congressman Burton's labor on behalf of the omnibus park legislation in 1978 did not prevent his involvement in one additional preservation battle of substantial importance—a battle over the future of the Boundary Waters Canoe Area. The BWCA has probably consumed greater space here than any comparably sized piece of the American landscape. As the recipient of many types of legislative and administrative protection over the years, the BWCA fits no neat category; it is sui generis. It lies in the domain of the Forest Service, but has been singled out by Congress for special protections not applicable to other forest areas. It has never been a national park, though congressmen have talked of making it one, and it has enjoyed certain protections against development not shared by national parks while other forms of development allowed there are forbidden in the park system. Congress included it in the National Wilderness Preservation System under the 1964 act, but as a special case. The area has been given unprecedented protection by executive order and has spawned significant litigation under both the Wilderness Act and NEPA. It is the nation's second largest wilderness area outside Alaska, and the most heavily used. When combined across the international boundary with Ontario's Quetico Provincial Park, it forms a wilderness of more than two million acres. It has been a laboratory for management techniques that will be required to preserve the wilderness resource in the face of ever-increasing demand for wilderness recreation. It is the nation's only substantial lakeland preserve. All of these things have combined to make the BWCA a kind of barometer of the state of health of American wilderness.

Congressional action in 1978 was necessitated by a confluence of pressures on the area. In the period since 1964 the "Battle for the Wilderness" in northern Minnesota occasionally took on the appearance of a war. Threats to the area's wilderness character came from three sources: continued timber harvest, minerals exploration and the concomitant possibility of future mining, and recreational overuse, especially by motorboat and snowmobile.

The timber threat to the BWCA resulted from paragraph 4(d)(5) of the Wilderness Act which said, in effect, that although the BWCA was to be part of the wilderness system, no change was to be made in the policy of timber management. The language which made the BWCA an exceptional case under the Wilderness Act had been inserted at the behest of Senator Humphrey, the bill's original sponsor, after it became clear to him the degree to which full wilderness status would alienate his northern Minnesota constituents. Logging has continued in the BWCA since 1964, although the no-cut area has been twice increased by action of the secretary of the interior. Even with these increases approximately 25 percent of the remaining virgin timber in the BWCA is located in the portal zone and available for harvest.[80] Although the no-cut zone was expanded under the direction of Agriculture Secretary Freeman of Minnesota, all cutting of virgin timber dismayed preservationists concerned for the future of the area.

In 1973 the Minnesota Public Interest Research Group filed suit in federal court under NEPA to halt the sale and cutting of virgin timber, claiming that the activities of the Forest Service in this matter constituted a major federal action significantly affecting the human environment and therefore requiring an environmental impact statement.[81] The district court found for the plaintiffs even though the timber sale had been contracted prior to the passage of NEPA. The court enjoined further logging wherever virgin timber was involved. Its decision was sustained by the Eighth Circuit Court the following year.[82] The Forest Service prepared the environmental impact statement, determined that continued cutting of virgin timber was acceptable, and MPIRG, now joined by the Sierra Club, went back to court. The new suit was based on the terms of the Wilderness Act. The plaintiffs argued that the Wilderness Act had zoned the BWCA as wilderness and that conflicting uses were therefore precluded. It was a weak argument from a legal standpoint. However illogical it might have been for Congress both to put the BWCA into the wilderness system and to specify that wilderness status would not serve to protect it from logging, motorboats, and mining, that is precisely what Congress had done. Amazingly, federal district court judge Miles Lord did not see it that way. "The court feels," concluded Justice Lord, "that the Forest Service interpretation of the Wilderness Act is not warranted. . . . Where there is a conflict between maintaining the primitive character of the BWCA and allowing logging or other uses, the former must be supreme."[83]

The mineral threat was perhaps more ominous. The Superior National Forest area had long been known to have low grade copper-nickel deposits. With the demand for these minerals growing, the holders of mineral rights in the area became restless. In the summer of 1969, George St. Clair, a New York mineral rights owner, had a camp established within the interior zone for prospecting purposes. He violated the regulations for the area in occupying the site beyond the fourteen-day camping limit, and in January 1970 the Forest Service confiscated the gear that had been abandoned there. In the meantime St. Clair had notified the Forest Service that he intended to bring in heavy equipment for the purpose of exploratory drilling. The Forest Service made it clear that it did not approve of the operation and that it would do what it could to prevent it. The mining loophole in the Wilderness Act is large, however, and it was not clear that the Forest Service had sufficient authority to prevent the drilling. The oldest institutional defender of the canoe country, the Izaak Walton League, filed suit shortly thereafter. Justice Philip Neville's finding, which may have influenced that of Justice Lord later the same year, was that mining and prospecting were contrary to the objectives of the Wilderness Act and that where such conflict exists, the wilderness purpose must dominate.[84] The decisions of the Federal District Court in Minnesota bought time for conservationists, but they failed to stand the test of appeal. While eventually overturned, these decisions on nonconforming uses of the wilderness attracted national attention and increased congressional interest in granting the BWCA full wilderness status.

Even more intractable than the problems of mining and logging were those of recreational overuse. A 1978 article in the *Duluth News-Tribune* began: "For all practical purposes the Boundary Waters Canoe Area has become a hotel without a roof."[85] The comment was prompted by the announcement that the Forest Service was imposing a reservation system for the area's two thousand back country campsites. The newspaper might well have said, "motel without a roof," because the great majority of the campsites in the BWCA were still legally accessible by motorboat. The Wilderness Act had allowed the continuance of motorboat use at the discretion of the secretary of agriculture in areas like the BWCA where such use was already well established, and the Forest Service, responsive to local pressure, had made minimal attempts to restrict motor use.

With logging, mining, and overcrowding all seriously threatening the wilderness character of the BWCA, Congress prepared to act. The first scenes were acted out in the House where Congressman James L. Oberstar, whose district encompasses the BWCA, and Congressman Donald Fraser of Minneapolis both introduced BWCA bills. The Oberstar proposal was drafted with the aid of the Forest Service and with sensitivity to the desires of local residents who depend upon multiple use of the area for both pleasure and profit. Under the Oberstar proposal the BWCA would be enlarged slightly, with 60 percent of the total area to be designated wilderness and 40 percent to become a new national recreation area where motorboats, snowmobiles, and timber harvest would be accommodated but mining would not. Preservation forces examined the Oberstar proposal and found it wanting. The result was the Fraser bill, drafted in large measure by the Sierra Club. It made the entire BWCA a full-fledged wilderness area and also banned mining operations.

Many members of Congress were apparently prepared to back any compromise that the Minnesota delegation could produce on this matter, but compromise would not be easy. The Minnesota delegation met for breakfast on March 31, 1977, to discuss the matter. Both Fraser and Oberstar presented their proposals. Oberstar had made some concessions toward a larger wilderness area but still embraced the two-zone concept. Senator Humphrey, who presided at the meeting, read a study by the Library of Congress that was critical of both House proposals and called for a more comprehensive approach. Everyone endorsed an attempt to combine the two proposals, but no one would commit himself in advance to support the outcome.[86]

As the battle heated up, bumper stickers proliferated. Around Ely, Minnesota, a major gateway to the BWCA, the most popular was, "Sierra Club—Kiss My Axe."[87] Tempers ran high as a House subcommittee took two days of hearings in Minnesota. The July 7 hearings in St. Paul produced support for the wilderness, but July 8 in Ely was another matter. Environmentalists were hanged in effigy, and local wilderness supporters were intimidated by threats of violence. Buildings were burned and in the bars there was talk of burning the forest.[88] One local resident described it as a "small war."[89] The message was loud and clear to the congressmen: "Leave *our* woods alone." In a sense both congressmen Oberstar and Fraser were too closely tied to the constituents they represented to be able to negotiate effectively with "the enemy." So, following the hearings congressmen Bruce F. Vento of St. Paul and Burton of California wrote a compromise package. The Burton-Vento compromise, introduced in the spring of 1978, preserved Oberstar's two-zone concept in form but was really closer to the Fraser proposal. The entire BWCA would become wilderness, and the area surrounding the present road corridors into the BWCA would be designated as a national recreation area. Limited use of motorboats, and even more limited use of snowmobiles, would be allowed in the area designated wilderness.[90] The major impact of the recreation area designation would have been the prohibition of mining, and the recreation area concept was soon dropped in favor of the more descriptive "mining protection area."

The crucial House vote came June 5 on a motion to substitute the Burton-Vento measure for the Oberstar bill. The compromise language prevailed over the desires of the local representative by a vote of 213 to 141, and the House proceeded to pass the measure 324 to 29.

The compromise package was delivered to the Senate where discussion focused on the level of motorboat use that would be permitted. Minnesota's senators favored less restrictive language, similar to what had been in the defeated Oberstar proposal. Once again it appeared that the legislation might founder, but Senator Abourezk, chairman of the Parks and Recreation Subcommittee, prevailed upon local leaders of the opposing coalitions to attempt to produce a compromise which both could support. The motor recreation and resort coalition was represented by Ron Walls of the Boundary Waters Conservation Alliance. Charles Dayton of the Friends of the Boundary Waters Wilderness represented the interests of the preservation lobby. Three days of intensive negotiation produced the "Dayton-Walls Compromise," which more than doubled the area left open to motorboats in the House bill but still left motor recreation substantially reduced from 1977 levels. The Dayton-Walls compromise was quickly approved by both House and Senate, and the BWCA was returned to a more highly protected, but still unique, status in the National Wilderness Preservation System.

SUMMARY

The political struggles described in this chapter demonstrate the remarkable power preservation interests have had in the legislative arena since 1964. Preservation victories have been commonplace in spite of the enormous resources which developers are able to bring to bear on the process. The root cause of this preservationist success is a receptive national mood made possible by the increased prosperity the nation has enjoyed since the end of World War II.

Between 1950 and 1978 the national population increased by 43 percent to 218 million. The economy grew at an even more rapid rate. In the same twenty-eight years, per capita Gross National Product in constant 1972 dollars increased by more than 80 percent from $3,500 to $6,343.[91] In spite of the abnormally high inflation rates of the 1970s, the percentage of American families with incomes below the poverty level remained a relatively stable 11 or 12 percent, less than half the rate for the 1950s.[92] This affluence was expressed in a predictable fashion by an increase in the percentage of personal consumption expenditures going to recreation. The $11.1 billion spent for recreation in 1950 constituted 5.8 percent of all personal consumption. By 1977 the recreation expenditure had increased to $81.2 billion, 6.7 percent of a much larger total consumption.[93]

On a more superficial level preservation successes are a result of the growth and political maturation of the preservation lobby. Its strength derives from its representation of a position which has become popular in the nation at large, but it has also been blessed with a leadership cadre skilled in practical politics and capable of maximizing its advantages. It is the skill of the leadership cadre that is primarily responsible for presenting a unified preservation voice in Washington and subverting the natural tendency for each of a dozen major groups to go its own direction. Preservationists should also credit Congressman Aspinall for much of their success in the years following passage of the Wilderness Act. Aspinall, more than any other individual, was the seasoned adversary against whom preservation forces were forced to struggle. His opposition to preservationist policies forced the preservation lobby to develop its political resources. His legacy in the Wilderness Act, the requirement that all additions to the system be by act of Congress, precipitated the creation of a network of organizations at the grass roots which has become a significant force in American politics. Intergroup cooperation and grass-roots organization would prove critical to the effort to preserve Alaskan wilderness.

NOTES

1. 80 Stat. 926.

2. 83 Stat. 275.

3. Some preservationists argue that certain species may be saved only if they are imported to the United States and nurtured here.

4. 90 Stat. 913.

5. Council on Environmental Quality, *The Evolution of National Wildlife Law* (Washington, D.C.: Government Printing Office, 1977), pp. 370-411.

6. Ann Pelham, "Tellico Go-ahead," *CQ Weekly Report* 37 (September 29, 1979): 2140.

7. Academics call this pattern of legislative decision making "distributive." It has obvious electoral advantages for incumbents.

8. United States Congress, *The Congressional Record* 111 (March 8, 1965): 4290.

9. United States Congress, *The Congressional Record* 112 (January 18, 1966): 536.

10. Ibid. (May 9, 1966): 10043.

11. United States Congress, *The Congressional Record* 114 (February 5, 1968): 2072.

12. United States Congress, *The Congressional Record* 113 (August 8, 1967): 21751.

13. H.R. 8416.

14. H.R. 18260.

15. United States Congress, *The Congressional Record* 114 (July 15, 1968): 21461.

16. United States House of Representatives, Report No. 1917 (90th Cong., 2d sess., September 25, 1968). United States Congress, *The Congressional Record* 114 (September 25, 1968): 28010-15.

17. Public Law 90-542; 82 Stat. 906.

18. The National Parks and Recreation Act of 1978, which is discussed later in this chapter, is a good example of this type of coalition politics.

19. Benton MacKaye, "The Appalachian Trail—An Experiment in Regional Planning," *Journal of the American Institute of Architects* (October 1921).

20. Nature Conservancy, *Preserving Our Natural Heritage*, 2 vols. (Washington, D.C.: Government Printing Office, 1976), 1: 253-54.

21. United States Department of the Interior, Bureau of Outdoor Recreation, *Trails for America: Report on the Nationwide Trail Study* (Washington, D.C.: Government Printing Office, 1966), pp. 20-21.

22. Public Law 90-543; 82 Stat. 919.

23. The portion of the Pacific Southwest Water Plan actually before Congress in the mid-1960s was called the Central Arizona Project. Information on this dispute is generally indexed under the latter name.

24. Roderick Nash, *Wilderness and the American Mind* (New Haven: Yale University Press, 1973), p. 230.

25. United States House of Representatives, Report No. 1849 (89th Cong., 2d sess., August 11, 1966), p. 36.

26. Ibid., p. 37.

27. Ibid., p. 35.

28. Ibid., p. 42.

29. *Newsweek*, May 30, 1966, p. 27.

30. *New York Times*, June 9, 1966, p. 35.

31. Ibid., August 7, 1966, p. 50.

32. United States Congress, *The Congressional Record* 113 (May 4, 1967): 11763.

33. United States House of Representatives, Report No. 1312 (90th Cong., 2d sess, April 24, 1968).

34. Public Law 90-537; 82 Stat. 885.

35. William Ashworth, *Hell's Canyon* (New York: Hawthorn Books, 1977), pp. 70-71.

36. Michael Barone, et al., *The Almanac of American Politics, 1974* (Boston: Gambit, 1973), p. 875.

37. Public Law 94-199; 89 Stat. 1117.

38. David Brennan, "Jetport: Stimulus for Solving New Problems in Environmental Control," *University of Florida Law Review* 23 (Winter 1971): 377.

39. Quoted in Howard Bloomfield, "The Everglades: Pregnant with Risks," *American Forests* 78 (May 1970): 27.

40. Brennan, "Jetport," pp. 379-80.

41. United States Senate, Committee on Interior and Insular Affairs, *Everglades*

National Park, Hearings June 3 and 11, 1969 (Washington, D.C.: Government Printing Office, 1969).

42. Quoted in Paul Brooks, *The Pursuit of Wilderness* (Boston: Houghton Mifflin Co., 1971), p. 127.

43. Bloomfield, "The Everglades," p. 24.

44. United States Congress, *The Congressional Record* 120 (September 9, 1974): 30472.

45. Public Law 93-440; 88 Stat. 1258.

46. See Cam Cavanaugh, *Saving the Great Swamp* (Frenchtown, N.J.: Columbia Publishing Co., 1978).

47. Quoted in George Alderson, "Antiwilderness Plot Revealed," *Not Man Apart*, reprinted in United States Congress, *The Congressional Record* 119 (January 16, 1973): 1251-52.

48. Ibid.

49. Council on Environmental Quality, *President's 1972 Environmental Program* (Washington, D.C.: Government Printing Office, 1972), p. 10.

50. S. 3973, 92nd Congress.

51. United States Congress, *The Congressional Record* 119 (January 16, 1973): 1252.

52. Ibid., p. 1251.

53. Ibid.

54. Quoted by Senator Church in ibid.

55. United States Senate, Report No. 1214 (92nd Cong., 2d sess., September 22, 1972), p. 6.

56. See chapter 4.

57. *Sierra Club Bulletin* 61 (October 1976): 20.

58. United States Congress, *The Congressional Record* 118 (June 13, 1972): 20572-73.

59. Ibid. (September 26, 1972): 32186ff.

60. Ibid. 120 (May 31, 1974): 17184.

61. Section 7 of S. 316.

62. United States Senate, Report No. 1599 (93rd Cong., 2d sess., December 16, 1974), p. 27.

63. Ibid. Emphasis added.

64. United States Senate, Committee on Energy and Natural Resources, Subcommittee on Parks and Recreation, *Endangered American Wilderness Act of 1977, Hearings on S. 1180, September 19-20, 1977* (Washington, D.C.: Government Printing Office, 1978), p. 44.

65. Ibid., p. 16.

66. Public Land Law Review Commission, *One Third of the Nation's Land* (Washington, D.C.: Government Printing Office, 1970), p. 1.

67. Ibid.

68. Ibid., p. 2.

69. Ibid., pp. 1-2.

70. Ibid., p. 92.

71. Ibid., pp. 198-99.

72. Public Law 94-579; 90 Stat. 2743.

73. Ibid., p. 2785.

74. United States Senate, Report No. 983 (94th Cong., 2d sess., June, 1976), p. 91.

75. Public Law 95-95.

76. See, for example, legislation on wild and scenic rivers, eastern wilderness areas, and so-called endangered wilderness areas.

77. United States Congress, *The Congressional Record* 124 (July 11, 1978): H 6399.

78. Ibid. (October 4, 1978): H 11535.

79. Public Law 95-625, Section 314(h). Many of the documents relevant to the passage of the National Parks and Recreation Act of 1978 are gathered together in *Legislative History of the National Parks and Recreation Act of 1978* compiled by the House Interior Subcommittee on National Parks and Insular Affairs (Washington, D.C.: Government Printing Office, 1978).

80. Sierra Club, North Star Chapter, *A Wilderness in Crisis—Boundary Waters Canoe Area* (Minneapolis: Sierra Club, 1970), p. 26. Sigurd F. Olson, "Wilderness Besieged: The Canoe Country of Minnesota," *Audubon* 72 (July 1970): 32.

81. *Minnesota Public Interest Research Group v. Butz*, 358 F. Supp. 584, 623, 630 (D. Minn. 1973) quoted in John J. Kearns III, "Environmental Law—Eighth Circuit Applies Reasonableness Standard to Review Agency Decision Not to File Environmental Impact Statement," *Fordham Law Review* 43 (March 1975): 665.

82. *Minnesota Public Interest Research Group v. Butz*, 498 F. 2nd 1314 (8th Cir. 1974) quoted in Kearns, "Environmental Law," p. 656.

83. Jack Shepard, *The Forest Killers—The Destruction of the American Wilderness* (New York: Weybright & Talley, 1975), p. 270.

84. *Izaak Walton League v. St. Clair*, 353 F. Supp. 698 (D. Minn. 1973) cited in "Note: Wilderness Management and the Multiple-Use Mandate," *Minnesota Law Review* 59 (November 1974): 173.

85. "One Use is Enough," *Duluth* (Minnesota) *News-Tribune*, January 4, 1978, reprinted in United States Congress, *The Congressional Record* 124 (June 5, 1978): H 4939.

86. Leo Schumacher, "A History of the Effort to Preserve the Boundary Waters Canoe Area," (Unpublished manuscript, Cornell College, 1977).

87. Personal observation by the author.

88. Richard Liefer, "Boundary Waters Wilderness: Local Versus National Interest," *Des Moines* (Iowa) *Register*, July 23, 1977. Philip Shabecoff, "Wilderness Plan Rouses Minnesota Lake Country and Poses Hard Questions About Land Use Policy," *New York Times*, July 28, 1977. Both articles are reprinted in United States Congress, *TheCongressional Record* 124 (June 5, 1978): H 4936-37 and H 4940-41.

89. Shabecoff, "Wilderness Plan Rouses Minnesota Lake Country."

90. "BWCA Compromise," *St. Paul* (Minnesota) *Sunday Pioneer Press*, March 26, 1978, reprinted in United States Congress, *The Congressional Record* 124 (June 5, 1978): H 4940.

91. United States Department of Commerce, Bureau of the Census, *Statistical Abstract of the United States* (Washington, D.C.: Government Printing Office, 1979), p. 438.

92. Ibid., p. 462.

93. Ibid., p. 440.

There is one other asset of the Territory not yet
enumerated, imponderable, and difficult to appraise,
yet one of the chief assets of Alaska, if not the
greatest. This is the scenery. There are glaciers, mountains, and fjords elsewhere, but nowhere else on earth
is there such abundance and magnificence of mountain, fjord, and glacier scenery. For thousands of
miles the coast is a continuous panorama. For one
Yosemite of California Alaska has hundreds. The
mountains and glaciers of the Cascade Range are
duplicated and a thousand-fold exceeded in Alaska.
The Alaska coast is to become the show-place of the
earth, and pilgrims, not only from the United States,
but from far beyond the seas, will throng in endless
procession to see it. Its grandeur is more valuable than
the gold or the fish or the timber, for it will never be
exhausted.

—Henry Gannet
"General Geography"

The history books of the present generation probably continue to call the
Alaska purchase of 1867 "Seward's Folly" precisely because it is so obvious
to modern Americans that it was no folly. The $7.2 million purchase price
seems a trivial sum for 365 million acres of land, amounting as it does to a
little less than 2 cents an acre. Incredibly, the price we paid for Alaska may
have been a good deal less than the price we said we paid. The American
government was beholden to the Russian fleet which had performed a show
of naval strength on behalf of the Union at a time when there was fear that
the British and French might ally themselves with the Confederacy. After
the Civil War had come to an end, the Russian and American governments
were both looking for a mechanism by which the American indebtedness
could be unobtrusively paid. The Alaska purchase provided the opportunity. Russian colonization had not progressed far in Alaska. The interior was

almost completely unknown and "widely believed to be a vast snowbound wasteland, worthless, and barren of life—except for a few polar bears, walruses, and aborigines who lived in igloos."[1] The Russians were quite ready to part with the territory that had netted them little wealth and was distant and difficult to administer. According to a 1971 article in the American Bar Association *Journal*, Americans paid only $1.4 million for the actual purchase of Alaska. The remaining $5.8 million was payment for the wartime services of the Russian navy.[2] If this account is accurate, the actual market value of Alaska in 1867 was something less than 0.4 cents per acre.

To the extent that the Alaska purchase was to be an economic speculation, it was clearly one that would take many years to bear fruit. Accordingly Seward's Folly receded from the public mind and was largely ignored for the next 100 years. For the first 17 years of American rule, until passage of the Organic Act of 1884, Alaska had no government at all. Even in 1884 there was little interest in Alaska's governance. The major accomplishment of the Organic Act was Congress's declaration that Alaska would be ruled by the laws of Oregon, which it was until 1900. Still the Organic Act did give passing attention to the Alaska natives who had been completely ignored in the negotiations with Russia. Section 8 of the act gave informal recognition to native land claims, but postponed any permanent disposition indefinitely. It reads in part: "Indians or other persons . . . shall not be disturbed in the possession of any lands actually in their use or occupation or claimed by them, but the terms under which such persons may acquire title to such lands is reserved for future legislation by Congress."[3] If gold had not been discovered in 1880, it is doubtful that even the limited provisions of the Organic Act would have been enacted. It was to be 87 years before Congress would fulfill the promise of the Organic Act and specify the terms under which natives could acquire title to their traditional lands.

The discovery of gold was the first indication of the mineral potential of Alaska and the first serious threat to native use and occupation of the land. The riches proved to be limited, however, and the gold rush was mostly a memory by 1910.

The permanent legacy of the gold rush was a change in Alaska's demography. In 1880 Alaska had 33,000 inhabitants, virtually all of them Alaska natives. By 1910 the native population had declined to 25,000 and had been supplemented by the arrival of 39,000 non-natives. The Alaska natives have been an Alaskan minority ever since. World War II brought the military to Alaska. With the troops came a new surge of immigrants from the lower forty-eight states. The state's total population was 75,000 in 1940 as the war boom began and 230,000 when statehood was achieved just nineteen years later.[4]

STATEHOOD

The Statehood Act[5] was the result of extensive local lobbying by the new Alaskan immigrants who believed correctly that they could profit from the economic benefits that would accompany statehood. By the time it was passed in 1958 the military boom was over in Alaska and the economy was in a serious state of decline. Congress dealt with Alaska's economic malaise by creating a package of statehood benefits without precedent in the nation's history. Alaska was given full title to the submerged lands of its continental shelf estimated at 35 to 45 million acres. It was allowed to select 104 million acres of federal lands for their economic potential and was given full title to all minerals on state-selected lands. The Alaskan land grant far exceeded the total land grants given to the seventeen western states upon their admission to the union. To sweeten the package still further, the state received 90 percent of the revenues from mineral leasing on lands which remained in federal ownership—twice the percentage other states receive.[6]

Native interests were largely ignored as the federal government conveyed this bounty to the state, and congressional intention is hard to determine. On the one hand, the state had clearly been given the right to select 104 million acres of public domain. On the other, Alaska had disclaimed, both in the Statehood Act and in her constitution, "all right and title to any lands or other property not granted or confirmed to the State . . . and to any lands or other property (including fishing rights), the right or title to which may be held by any . . . Natives, or held by the U.S. in trust for said Natives."[7] Apparently no one saw state selections and native rights as mutually exclusive except the natives. As the state began making selections that intruded on native claims, the natives responded by filing suits and petitioning Congress. In 1961 the Supreme Court interpreted the Statehood Act to preserve the status quo with respect to native claims, but also ruled that since the United States had clearly given the state the right to select, selections could continue. According to the Court aggrieved natives could sue the United States for damages caused by the state selection.[8] This decision may have been good law, but it was far from satisfactory as a solution to the problem of native claims.

The major native populations—Aleuts, Eskimos, and Indians—set aside historic rivalries and organized themselves politically into the Alaskan Federation of Natives (AFN). By 1966 the AFN was prepared to claim virtually the entire state on behalf of all Alaska natives.[9] The prospect was a judicial nightmare, with every parcel transferred to the state an invitation to litigation. In December 1966 Secretary of Interior Udall called a halt to all federal land transactions, including the state selections, so that Congress could settle the native claims issue. When Congress proved unwilling to handle the matter promptly, the temporary "land freeze" was replaced by

Public Land Order No. 4582, withdrawing all vacant, unappropriated, and unreserved public lands in Alaska from appropriation under any land law until December 31, 1970. With 95 percent of the state's land still in federal ownership, the land freeze virtually prohibited significant economic development. Alaska's Governor Walter J. Hickel attempted to have the Public Land Order set aside in the courts, but he was ultimately unsuccessful, and Alaska's lands remained "frozen."

The stakes were raised dramatically in February 1968, when an Atlantic-Richfield Company (ARCO) well, Prudhoe Bay No. 1, struck oil. In rapid succession another ARCO well and one owned by British Petroleum confirmed the find. Alaska's North Slope was a major oil field, if only a means could be found to get the oil to market. Plans were begun immediately for what was to become one of the greatest feats of construction ever undertaken—a Trans-Alaskan Pipeline to link the North Slope oil fields with an ice-free, deepwater port somewhere in the south of Alaska, a distance of almost 800 miles. There were three serious obstacles to such an undertaking: first, such a pipeline had never been constructed; second, such a pipeline would have to be built across federal land, which was frozen to allow Congress to settle the native claims; and finally, such a pipeline would be an intrusion on wilderness comparable to the transcontinental railroad of a century earlier.

Both the wilderness intrusion and the untried nature of the project dismayed environmentalists, and several conservation groups vowed to put a halt to the project. What had begun as a simple administrative freeze to allow Congress to settle native claims was now intermixed with issues of technology, energy self-sufficiency, and ecological and wilderness preservation. To complicate the matter further, incoming President Nixon appointed the man who had challenged the land freeze in court, Alaska's Governor Hickel, to replace the man who had issued the freeze, Interior Secretary Udall. Nixon's appointment of one of the contestants in a major land struggle to the Interior Department post paralleled President Wilson's appointment of Franklin K. Lane a half-century earlier. Lane's appointment spelled defeat for the effort to preserve Yosemite's Hetch Hetchy Valley in 1913. Congress, however, was not eager to hand over the enormous powers of the secretary's office to Hickel without attaching strings. During confirmation hearings the Senate Interior Committee extracted a promise from Hickel that the Public Land Order would not be modified or rescinded without the approval of the Senate and House Interior committees. This promise provided Congress with two years to handle the native claims issue before the freeze would expire allowing the state to resume land selections and the department to issue a permit for pipeline construction. Secretary Hickel's past performance as governor and his public pronouncements left little doubt that he would act in the interests of Alaskan development as soon as the opportunity presented itself.

Eight oil companies had formed a consortium to build the pipeline. They were used to getting what they wanted from the Interior Department, and no one seriously doubted that the necessary permit would eventually be granted. The oil companies were so confident that they purchased and took delivery of $200 million worth of pipe for the work, long before the permit was approved. This show of confidence led some conservationists and pipeline opponents to speculate that the Interior Department had given secret assurances to the oil companies. More likely, the oil companies simply were willing to bank on the prospect that the government would behave much as it always had in similar matters. There might have been less confidence had the oil companies fully understood the engineering, ecological, economic, and political difficulties inherent in their proposal. The early expectation was that the pipeline would be completed in 1972 at a cost of $900 million. Settlement of the native claims and litigation over the permit eventually delayed completion until 1977. By that time project costs had increased tenfold to $9 billion.

If the land freeze itself had been insufficient stimulus for a settlement of the native claims, the discovery of oil provided added incentive. If the pipeline was to be built and the oil shipped, then a right of way would be necessary across 800 miles of public lands, most of them claimed by the Alaska natives. A settlement of the native claims was now seen as a necessary prerequisite for the development of Alaskan oil. Suddenly, everyone with a vested interest in oil had a vested interest in the native claims settlement. After 100 years of delay, Congress put the native lands claims near the top of its list of priorities.

A NATIVE CLAIMS SETTLEMENT

A host of settlement plans circulated in Washington during 1970. Logically, the most generous to the natives was the plan introduced by the Alaskan Federation of Natives. It called for a grant of forty million acres and $500 million plus a perpetual 2 percent royalty on all minerals leased from lands owned by the federal government at the time of statehood. Village, regional, and statewide corporations would be established to manage the natives' new assets. At the opposite extreme of generosity was the proposal of the Alaska State Chamber of Commerce and the nearly identical official state of Alaska position. Both called for a grant of about ten million acres in and around present native villages. The chamber also endorsed an "equitable and just" monetary settlement to be paid entirely by the federal government. So long as the federal government was paying it all, the state was willing to endorse the AFN demand of $500 million. Neither of these plans, however, provided the natives with any continuing royalty from mineral leasing. This omission is particularly important to the state because of the generosity of the Statehood Act. Because the state could anticipate 100 percent of the royalties from its own land selections and 90 percent from lands which remained in federal ownership, any provision giving natives a cut of mineral royalties would tend to drain state, rather than federal, coffers. The state was not about to endorse any plan for settling native claims that would have the effect of renegotiating the Statehood Act to the state's disadvantage.

Between these extremes several additional proposals were receiving substantial attention. There was the recommendation of the Federal Field Committee, a government study group, calling for a grant of five million acres, $100 million, and a 10 percent royalty on all revenues from the public lands over a ten-year period. The Department of the Interior proposed granting ten million acres and $500 million. Alaska's senators proposed minimal land grants, between five and ten million acres, and a package of cash and royalties that would be worth $1 billion over ten years. What is most apparent about each of these proposals is its similarity to the state of Alaska and chamber of commerce proposals and its distance from the plan endorsed by the AFN. While it is impossible to fix accurate dollar values for land grants, subsistence use, or the various royalty packages, it is difficult to avoid the conclusion that the total dollar value of the AFN proposal was at least twice that of the next most generous competitor. Most political observers of the period saw the AFN proposal as a negotiating position and assumed that the final settlement would see substantially reduced payments, especially in outright land grants.

The Senate Interior Committee had given extensive consideration to settlement bills throughout the Ninetieth Congress (1967-68), but the task had foundered for lack of definitive information on the nature and background of the issue.[10] To resolve this problem Chairman Jackson asked the Federal Field Committee for Development Planning in Alaska to prepare a study that would provide the necessary information and suggest a framework for settlement. The Field Committee study, *Alaska Natives and the Land*, and accompanying proposals were routed to the Interior Department and incorporated into a draft bill.

The Senate committee reported a settlement bill June 11, 1970, claiming that it had built "upon the best features of all of the bills which have been considered by the Committee over the last four years."[11] The bill was a compromise, but it followed most closely the desires of the Interior Department and the state of Alaska. Each had advocated a land grant of ten million acres and a cash payment of $500 million. The committee bill followed this formula, but made one major concession to the AFN position.

The federation had proposed a perpetual 2 percent royalty on mineral leasing. The committee granted the royalty, not in perpetuity, but until an additional $500 million had accrued to the natives. Since the royalty was no longer open-ended, the committee package can be summarized as ten million acres and $1 billion—no small amount, but a far cry from the AFN proposal.

Senate floor consideration began on July 14. The bill found support from both of Alaska's senators and was passed the following day on a vote of 76 to 8. The only major issues raised in the debate concerned whether or not the provisions of the settlement could be considered paternalistic and whether the mineral leasing, which would provide the native royalty funds, should be on a competitive or noncompetitive basis. This latter argument was of greater concern to mineral interests than to natives since the native cut was set at $500 million in any case.

Of no apparent concern during the floor debate was the implication of the proposed act for the Alaskan wilderness. Yet the bill did address the matter. Section 18(a) prohibited native selections in existing national parks, wildlife refuges, and forests totaling almost fifty million acres. Since these areas had already been reserved for a specific purpose by Congress, the prohibitions were noncontroversial. More important were the provisions of Section 23. This section instructed the interior secretary to study "all unreserved public lands in Alaska . . . which are suitable for inclusion as recreation, wilderness, or wildlife management areas within the National Park System and the National Wildlife Refuge System."[12] The secretary was to make recommendations to Congress based upon this study. Clearly, someone was thinking about the future of conservation in Alaska, but Section 23 was a very poor vehicle to assure that future. The secretary was given three years to make his recommendations. If he took the full time allotted, Congress would have only two years to act on the recommendations before the lands would be "unfrozen" and available to commercial development. Congress is not noted for its ability to deal with matters of this magnitude and complexity in so short a span of time. A second problem was even more pressing. The immediate threat to Alaskan wilderness came from state selections, and Section 23 stated "nothing in this section shall restrict the land selection rights of the State."[13] These conservation provisions were never debated. Apparently their inadequacy came to the attention of the conservation community only after the bill had been passed by the Senate. Once aware of the problems, the preservation lobby was happy to see the bill referred to the House and forgotten.

By 1971 the full impact of a native claims settlement act was appreciated in the conservation community. Legitimate concerns for doing justice to the natives had distracted many observers from close scrutiny of secondary ef-

fects. A settlement act would not only dispose of some 10 to 40 million acres
of federal land, but would also end the land freeze. With Public Land Order
4582 canceled, the state could continue its selection of 104 million acres, and
private parties would be free to appropriate public lands, particularly
mineral lands, under various public land laws. The net effect would be an
overnight shift from a development freeze to a development free-for-all involving most of Alaska. Conservationists had two major concerns if Alaska
land development were allowed to occur without any systematic land-use
planning. First, it seemed highly probable that the pattern of land ownership in Alaska would become a disorganized patchwork of federal, state,
native, and private control. Such a situation would preclude systematic
resource management and prevent future Congresses from establishing new
national parks, forests, and wildlife refuges except by condemning and
purchasing lands that had recently belonged to the United States. The prospects for substantial additions to these conservation systems would be
reduced dramatically once the necessary land base had been removed from
the public domain. The Alaskan wilderness and those who cherish it would
be the losers. The second fear concerned the pending pipeline. While many
conservationists would have gladly put a stop to the entire project, most
recognized that some pipeline would eventually be built. Preservationist
disputes with the Interior Department notwithstanding, far better to have
the pipeline built across federal lands with strict environmental controls
than to allow the state to select a pipeline corridor and supervise the project
itself. Needless to say, the state of Alaska had not convinced most conservationists that it had either the will or the resources to control the major oil
companies in such a venture.

The conclusion drawn in the conservation community was that a settlement act must contain strict land-use planning provisions and allow the
American people to make some "selections" of their own before they were
saddled with nothing but leftovers.

When the matter came before the Ninety-second Congress in 1971, the
House was the first to act. Preservation's major advocates on the House Interior Committee, John Saylor and Morris Udall, worked hand in hand with
the major conservation organizations to incorporate a "public interest" land
selection. The Saylor-Udall proposal would have directed the secretary of
the interior to withdraw up to fifty million acres suitable for "potential inclusion as recreation, wilderness, or wildlife areas" within the nation's four
major conservation systems: the National Park System, the National Forest
System, the National Wildlife Refuge System, and the National Wild and
Scenic River System. Five areas would be set aside directly by the proposal.
This approach was defeated in the committee by a vote of 26 to 10.[14]

The committee bill did recognize the conservationist concerns in a limited way. An amendment approved in the full committee would have continued the land freeze in general until a comprehensive land-use plan could be prepared. Loopholes in this plan made it insufficient from the point of view of conservationists. Native and state selections would be allowed to proceed unhindered, and the secretary of the interior would be allowed to make additional exceptions at his discretion. The committee majority argued that to do more would be to add language that was clearly not germane to a bill designed to settle native claims. In dissent, John Saylor made the preservationist case that the proposed Alaska Native Claims Settlement Act (ANCSA) was not simply a bill to settle claims but was also a bill to open up Alaska; it was "the first step in a long series of actions which will profoundly affect the future economic, social, and political development of the State."[15]

Having lost the battle in committee, the conservation community turned its attention to the House floor and to the White House. On September 30, 1971 leaders of twelve environmental organizations, including the National Wildlife Federation, the Sierra Club, and the Wilderness Society, wrote an open letter to President Nixon warning that "speculators and exploiters" had been using the Native Claims Settlement Act as a vehicle to accomplish the "unrestricted exploitation of America's last frontier."[16] Even the National Rifle Association (NRA) joined in the appeal which called upon the president to resist the bills which were being reported from the Interior committees of Congress. The letter was to no avail. Equally futile was the attempt by congressmen Udall and Saylor to substitute their plan for the committee bill on the House floor. The Saylor-Udall amendment was defeated on a roll call vote of 178 to 217. A second conservation-oriented amendment offered by Congressman Dingell was also defeated. It would have increased the level of protection against intrusions into existing wildlife refuges. The net result was a political nightmare for preservation interests. The House bill as amended provided less protection for existing wildlife refuges and national forests than the Senate bill of one year earlier. By increasing the land grant to the Alaska natives to forty million acres, it also increased the magnitude of the threat to wild Alaska. Yet for most House members, it was unthinkable to vote against the bill and by doing so to appear to vote against the legitimate interests and needs of the Alaska natives. It was 1971 and Indian rights were significantly more popular than they had been a century earlier in the American West. Final passage on October 20, 1971, was by a comfortable margin of 334 to 63.

The following day the Senate committee reported a version of the bill showing little more sensitivity to the land-use planning issue and to the need to preserve critical environments in the public domain. The previous Senate bill had directed the secretary of the interior to study lands suitable for inclusion in the National Park and National Wildlife Refuge systems and make recommendations to Congress. Recommended additions would have been withdrawn, but the withdrawal would not have been effective against the three major threats to the wilderness in 1970: native selections, state selections, and grants of right of way for things like pipelines. The 1971 version showed only slight modification. The secretary was allowed to withdraw lands for national forests as well as for national parks and wildlife refuges, but the withdrawals were for a maximum of two years and were not effective against the immediate threat of state selection. The major change in the bill was the creation of a North Slope Recreation and Transportation Corridor on federal lands. The committee claimed to take no position on whether or not the Trans-Alaska Pipeline should be built, but argued that if it were, it should be on federal lands. Keeping the pipeline corridor under federal control would ensure that federal environmental standards would be applied to any possible construction and that the corridor would also be accessible for public recreational use.[17]

Preservationist lobbying had increased with the defeat of the Saylor-Udall initiative in the House. That lobbying apparently bore fruit when the bill reached the floor. Senator Alan Bible, chairman of the Subcommittee on Parks and Recreation, rose to explain to the chamber that the nation's foremost conservation organizations had expressed reservations about the section of the bill dealing with withdrawals for public reservations. He proposed an amendment endorsed by Chairman Jackson to "insure that what I understand to be the committee's intent is made perfectly clear in the language of the bill."[18] Senator Bible called his amendment "reasonable and noncontroversial,"[19] but it was a major change in the legislation. It reversed the selection priorities of the committee's bill. Under the Bible amendment, the secretary of the interior was to study Alaskan lands for possible addition to the National Park and National Wildlife Refuge systems, and his recommendations were to take precedence over state and native selections. If Congress concurred with the secretary's recommendations and added lands to parks and refuges, the state and the natives would be allowed additional selections elsewhere in lieu of those relinquished. If Congress failed to act within five years, the land would then revert to unreserved status and the state and native selections would be established. The Bible amendment was passed with little debate as was the entire bill. For the first time one house of Congress had accepted language that gave the secretary's recommendations for additions to conservation units a higher priority than state and native land selections.[20]

CONSERVATION PROVISIONS OF ANCSA

The House and Senate bills were referred to a conference committee. What emerged is the subject of continuing controversy. What had been Section 24 of the Senate bill, became Section 17 of the Alaska Native Claims Settlement Act of 1971.[21] Interpretation of Section 17 would determine the future of conservation in Alaska. The relevant portions of this section are reproduced in Appendix B.

Subsection (d)(1) terminated the land freeze originated by Secretary Udall and provided in its place a legislated freeze for a period of ninety days. This period allowed the interior secretary to make withdrawals "under authority provided for in existing law to insure that the public interest in these lands is properly protected."[22] These withdrawals have no effect on native and state selections in the areas around native villages. By inference these same withdrawals would affect other native and state selections, although Senator Theodore F. (Ted) Stevens argued the contrary case to the Senate the following March.[23]

Subsection (d)(2), paragraph (A), directed the secretary to withdraw up to eighty million acres suitable for addition to one of the four conservation systems. This paragraph specifically prohibited state and native selections in the withdrawn areas except on lands adjacent to native villages.

Paragraph (B) of this subsection required that the secretary's withdrawals be made within nine months and provided that "lands not withdrawn under paragraph (A) or subsection 17(d)(1)" shall be available for state selection and other forms of appropriation. This paragraph provides additional evidence that (d)(1) withdrawals generally take priority over state and native selections.

Paragraph (C) required the secretary to make recommendations to Congress for additions to the four conservation systems and provided that lands withdrawn, but not recommended, would become available for state selection and other uses. Paragraph (D) gave Congress five years to act on the secretary's recommendations and provided that the withdrawal of lands not recommended would terminate at the end of two years from the act's passage.

The final paragraph of subsection 17(d)(2) stipulated that state and native selections may be made on any lands withdrawn under subsection (d), but that these selections would not be made effective so long as the lands in question were withdrawn. If Congress accepted the recommendatons of the secretary of the interior and incorporated selected lands into a conservation unit, then the state and native corporations would be allowed to make other selections in lieu of those foreclosed to them.

Prodevelopment and Alaska state interests apparently interpreted the intent of Section 17 to be withdrawal of not more than eighty million acres that would affect native and state selections. The language of the section seems to provide for the withdrawal of up to eighty million acres under (d)(2) and an unspecified additional acreage under (d)(1). Some conservationists seized upon this apparent oversight to urge the secretary to reserve as much as fifty million acres under (d)(1) as well as eighty million under (d)(2). To Senator Stevens such a result was patently absurd. In March 1972 he asked his colleagues:

By what stretch of the imagination can anyone assume that the conference committee which contained three members from Alaska and was chaired by the distinguished Representative from Colorado (Mr. Aspinall), chairman of the Interior and Insular Affairs Committee, who opposed the Udall-Saylor amendment, could possibly approve such a bill?[24]

Senator Stevens's reading of the intent of the conference committee may have been accurate—it is hard to imagine the conferees approving unlimited secretarial withdrawals under (d)(1)—but his reading of the resultant statute was clearly erroneous.

The state of Alaska may well have recognized the danger to state selection inherent in the language of (d)(1), for in January 1972, without warning, it proclaimed selection of its entire remaining allotment under the Statehood Act, some seventy-seven million acres. The state took the position that the ANCSA had given it immediate authority to resume selection and that the congressional land freeze imposed by subsection (d)(1) did not preclude state selections.[25] This interpretation is at least questionable, for subsection (d)(2)(B) says in part, "All unreserved public lands *not* withdrawn under . . . subsection 17(d)(1) shall be available for selection by the State."[26] Such a provision would be meaningless if lands which are withdrawn were also to be available for state selection. Nevertheless, the state's attempt to seize the initiative apparently gained it some bargaining advantage.

ALASKA LANDS BATTLE TAKES SHAPE

Interior Secretary Rogers C. B. Morton announced preliminary withdrawals two months later and final withdrawals in September. The final withdrawals totaled more than 240 million acres. Under subsecton (d)(2)) 79 million acres were withdrawn, and an additional 47 million under (d)(1). Another 4.5 million acres were tied up in pipeline corridors mandated by the act, and 112 million acres were withdrawn to provide a pool from which the natives could select their 40 million acres. Many of the (d)(1) and (d)(2) withdrawals conflicted with the recently announced state selections, and Alaska filed suit in federal court to have the conflicting withdrawals set aside. Alaska had lost a previous suit over the Udall land freeze and seemed to be on substantially weaker legal grounds in this instance. Nevertheless, the suit did serve to initiate negotiations between the state and the Interior Department resulting in an out-of-court settlement in which Alaska gained some concessions. In a "Memorandum of Understanding Between the State of Alaska and the United States," dated September 1, 1972, Secretary of Interior Morton and Governor William A. Egan agreed to an exchange of sorts.[27] The secretary made some of his preliminary (d)(2) withdrawals available for state selection and converted another portion to (d)(1) status. The total area affected was about 14 million acres. In return the state relinquished 35 of the 77 million acres selected in January.

The act had given the secretary until December 19, 1973, to make his recommendations to Congress for additions to the nation's four conservation systems. Secretary Morton's proposals alienated everyone. Alaskan officials were infuriated by the recommendation of certain (d)(1) lands for inclusion. They claimed a violation of the Memorandum of Understanding and filed suit again. Conservation organizations that had fought for the (d)(1) and (d)(2) provisions in the law were outraged by the secretary's proposal of three new national forests on (d)(2) lands totaling over eighteen million acres. Preservation organizations argued that the intent of (d)(2) was to place land chiefly valuable for recreation, wilderness, and wildlife into appropriate conservation systems. Commodity exploitation under multiple-use management, such as that provided by the Forest Service, was supposed to be the fate of BLM lands that would remain in federal ownership after all the authorized selections had taken place. The Forest Service had committed itself to the designation of wilderness study areas within three years after the creation of these new national forests, but this was no guarantee that substantial areas of Alaskan national forests would be designated wilderness. Indeed, nowhere in the proposed legislation was any statutory wilderness designated. Instead, the secretary was mandated to make recommendations according to the procedures in the Wilderness Act. Three years were provided for this task to be accomplished.[28]

Conservation organizations, which had assumed that their task would be the defense of the Interior Department's proposals for additions to the conservation systems, now set out to draft recommendations of their own. The conservationist proposal eliminated any new national forests, increased the allocations of lands to the other systems, and provided a ten-year review period for wilderness designations during which the lands would have to be administered so as to preserve their suitability for wilderness designation.[29] The total designations encompassed by the conservationist proposal were over 106 million acres, a substantial increase over the 83.5 million proposed by Secretary Morton.

While legislation was introduced in Congress the month following publication of the secretary's recommendations, neither the Nixon nor the Ford administrations gave it high priority, and the first three of the five years Congress had given itself to act on the matter slipped by without a bill reported in either house. This passage of time probably worked to the advantage of preservation forces. The lapse in public attention allowed the preservationist organizations to refine their proposals, educate their memberships, and build the legislative machinery for an all-out drive to preserve the greatest possible expanse of America's last wilderness.

Preservation organizations poured a large measure of their resources into the Alaska lands issue. Conservationists had been studying the wilderness potential of Alaska lands since the formation of the Alaska Wilderness Council in 1967. These studies were among the first efforts at systematic land-use planning in Alaska. When the Field Committee was asked to report on the Alaska lands question by Chairman Jackson, its chairman, Joe Fitzgerald, went to the Alaska Wilderness Council for help. Access to the Field Committee spurred preservationist-minded studies of the Alaskan landscape before 1971. Following passage of ANCSA, study activities were expanded, and by the time Congress was ready to give the matter serious consideration, the preservation lobby had done its homework. The result was H.R. 39, introduced by Congressman Morris Udall in January 1977.

H.R. 39 was the work of the preservation community, but it differed substantially from previous preservationist proposals. More than 8 million acres had been added to the 106 million specified in the 1974 draft, with enlarged reservations for all but the Forest Service. Even more important, by 1977 the conservation community had decided that Alaska was no longer a great unstudied giant. Enough was known to designate wilderness areas immediately. It was hard to imagine a better vehicle for congressional designation of wilderness than the present one. Since the legislation would create major new units in the nation's conservation system, logic suggested that the job be completed by designating wilderness additions before public interest in Alaska waned. The drafters of H.R. 39 responded to this logic with Title VI, which for the first time added actual wilderness designations to a comprehensive Alaska lands bill. The wilderness proposals totaled more than 146 million acres. The bill designated 32 of approximately 50 million acres in preexistent conservation units and all of the 114.6 million acres of additions.[30] If enacted, the addition to the National Wilderness Preservation System would be more than ten times the total size of the system in 1977—14.43 million acres.

The preservation lobby also made use of the relative disinterest in Alaska lands legislation between 1973 and 1977 to build grass-roots support for a strong preservationist measure. The conservation magazines provided the primary vehicle for this effort, carrying descriptions of the Alaskan landscape most often accompanied by glossy full-color photographs. The areas that the preservation lobby had singled out for new national parks and wildlife refuges were pictured and described in glowing terms. By 1977 the grass roots of the preservation community had been sensitized to the Alaskan issue.

The period of respite also provided an opportunity to build a politically potent lobbying institution to handle the Alaska measure. The Alaska Coalition had its official beginning in 1971 during the Native Claims controversy. It coasted along as a minor star in the conservation coalition until January 1977, when staff from the National Audubon Society, Wilderness Society, Sierra Club, National Parks and Conservation Association, and Defenders of Wildlife met "and decided Alaska was the most important conservation issue of the century."[31] Coalition politics involving the preservation regulars is not uncommon, but the scope of cooperation on Alaska was unprecedented. Each of the organizations present pledged money, office space, and staff support, and the Alaska Coalition emerged as an environmental giant. It was the primary institution through which the fight to pass H.R. 39 would be fought.

Another major advantage to the preservation coalition during the period from 1973 to 1977 was an improved political climate. This improvement was manifested in both executive and legislative arenas. At the White House, President Carter succeeded President Ford. Environmentalists had high hopes for the new administration and early presidential appointments seemed to confirm these hopes. Secretaries Cecil D. Andrus at interior and Bergland at agriculture seemed more sympathetic to environmental and conservation concerns than their predecessors, and recognized members of the conservation community were appointed to important posts below the secretarial level. While the same Interior Department bill that had been introduced in 1974 remained before the Congress, it was widely understood that the new administration would support expanded reservations once it had had the opportunity to study the matter and formulate its own policy.

In Congress the outlook was equally propitious. Personnel changes brought a more favorable climate to the House Interior Committee. James Haley, who had served largely without controversy as chairman since the political demise of Wayne Aspinall, retired in 1976. So did second-ranking Roy Taylor of North Carolina. This would have delivered the interior chairmanship to Harold (Bizz) Johnson of the First Congressional District in California. California's First Congressional District is enormous, covering more than one-fifth of the state's land. It is mountainous and sparsely populated, the kind of place where the frontier mentality might still persist. True to form, its congressman produced a record on the Interior Committee that made him relatively unpopular with environmentalists. He was politically reminiscent of Aspinall. Johnson's certain chairmanship was complicated when Jim Wright of Texas was elected Majority Leader. In accepting the post Wright vacated the chairmanship of the Public Works Committee, leaving Johnson in line for that post as well. Faced with an Interior Committee that had become uncomfortably environmentalist in orientation and a more hospitable panel at Public Works, Johnson chose the latter. This move resulted in the promotion of Morris Udall to the interior chairmanship. Nothing could have pleased the preservation lobby more. Differences over the Grand Canyon notwithstanding, Udall was the most obvious inheritor of the mantle laid down by John Saylor. Saylor had been a most vocal advocate of conservation legislation and had exercised great influence on his colleagues, but, as a Republican, he had never held the critical chairmanship. In Udall conservationists had both a political ally and a spokesman with a national reputation.[32]

Clearly, the delay in bringing Alaska lands legislation to the floor had worked to the political advantage of the preservationist coalition. With a new president, a new committee chairman, a new lobbying organization, new public interest, and a new proposal to support, the conservation community was greatly optimistic about the prospects for Alaska.

With Udall at the helm, H.R. 39 became the primary vehicle for arguing the Alaska lands issue. The Alaska Coalition won an important procedural fight almost immediately. The Interior Committee voted to create a subcommittee on General Oversight and Alaska Lands. Giving the issue to a new subcommittee rather than an existing one allowed Udall to dictate majority membership. Preservationists had reason to hope that the new subcommittee chaired by John F. Seiberling of Ohio would effectively represent their interests. Seiberling had excellent conservation credentials and was a cosponsor of H.R. 39.

PRESERVATION TRIUMPHS IN THE HOUSE

With strong support from both committee and subcommittee chairmen, the House got off to a fast start on what promised to be a long road to passage of an Alaska lands bill. The subcommittee held hearings regularly for five full months beginning and ending in Washington, D.C. Sixteen cities were visited in Alaska and five in the lower forty-eight. Testimony was taken from over two thousand witnesses who compiled a hearing record of sixteen volumes and over seven thousand pages. The testimony from these field hearings presents an interesting picture of the distribution of opinion on wilderness preservation. Early in the century during the debate on the Hetch Hetchy Valley, Senator James A. Reed had remarked that the outcry on behalf of the valley was proportional to the distance from it. His observation supports the proposition that wilderness is most valued by those who most perceive its scarcity. The testimony from the Seiberling subcommittee hearings demonstrated the point once again. The locations of hearings were divided into five categories based on an intuitive notion of their distance from the Alaskan wilderness. Closest to the wilderness are the Alaska native villages. These are followed by the small settler towns, Sitka, Juneau, and Ketchikan, dependent on extractive industries and the larger cities of "urban" Alaska, Anchorage and Fairbanks. Farther still are Denver and Seattle in the West, and Atlanta and Chicago in the older and more densely settled portion of the lower forty-eight states. A sample of the testimony from each category of location reveals the geographical distribution of support for wilderness preservation generally and H.R. 39 specifically. Eighty-nine percent of the sample took a clear positon for or against the kind of substantial wilderness designations embodied in H.R. 39. Of those who expressed an opinion, the percentage favorable to wilderness was as follows:

Native villages	0%
Settler towns	16%
Urban Alaska	56%
American West	88%
American East	100%[33]

If there are any surprises here, they are, first, the incredible strength of the relationship between location and attitude toward wilderness and, second, that Alaska's major cities actually produced propreservation majorities for the hearings. It is hard to avoid the inference that the preservation lobby was working effectively in support of a prowilderness turnout. In fact, several members of the Chicago sample indicated that they had learned of the hearings or been sensitized to the issue by the Sierra Club.

While the hearings progressed around the nation, the Carter administration was working to perfect its own Alaska recommendations. They were presented to the subcommittee during the final set of hearings in September. The Carter proposals were, of course, less dramatic than those embodied in H.R. 39, but they were by far the most generous recommendations ever made by an American administration. The new proposals involved a total of 92 million acres and expanded the acreages proposed by the Ford administration for parks, wildlife refuges, and wild and scenic rivers. More important, the administration embraced the preservation ideal of designating substantial "instant" wilderness. It proposed designation of more than 43 million acres in new and existing units and proposed wilderness study for the remaining additions.[34] The administration had proposed 100 million fewer acres of instant wilderness than did H.R. 39, but the preservation lobby was pleased. The administration recommendations were compromises in which preservation had done rather well. H.R. 39 was the preservationist wish list, a position from which to negotiate.

To understand the negotiations that followed, it is essential to examine the strengths and weaknesses of the proponent and opponent coalitions. The proponent coalition is easily characterized because it showed remarkable unity. The heart of the proponent effort was the Alaska Coalition, which grew with the undertaking. By the time the battle was fully joined in Congress, the coalition contained virtually the entire preservation lobby. Important member organizations included the Appalachian Mountain Club, American Rivers Conservation Council, the Cousteau Society, Defenders of Wildlife, Environmental Defense Fund, Environmental Policy Center, Federation of Western Outdoor Clubs, Friends of the Earth, National Audubon Society, National Parks and Conservation Association, Natural Resources Defense Council, Sierra Club, and the Wilderness Society. The coalition also boasted support from significant Alaskan conservation groups including the Alaska Conservation Society, Alaska Center for the Environment, Brooks Range Trust, Denali Citizens Council, Fairbanks Environmental Center, Southeast Alaska Conservation Council, and the Trustees for Alaska.[35] Rounding out the coalition was a host of sportsman's organizations and a number of influential groups with less specific interests in Alaska: the Garden Club of America, United Auto Workers, Oil Chemical and Atomic Workers International Union, and the National Council of Senior Citizens. The latter groups are of particular interest because they represent constituencies that are generally depicted as being against wilderness preservation. The National Wildlife Federation, the nation's largest conservation group, remained technically independent of the coalition but in fact cooperated closely with the member organizations.

At the height of its activity the Alaska Coalition mounted the best organized, best financed lobbying campaign in the history of conservation. The combined resources of the supporting groups and the response to direct mail solicitations allowed the coalition to engage in a host of techniques generally reserved for the better financed opponents of wilderness preservation. Grass-roots organizers traveled throughout the country building a network of supporters. Movement leaders estimated a minimum of ten thousand people nationally were actively working for Alaskan preservation and claimed substantial responsibility for the overwhelming proconservation turnout during the Seiberling subcommittee hearings. The grass-roots network was fed by direct mail information and by a twenty-four-hour "Alaska Coalition Hotline" from which activists could obtain daily updates on the congressional situation. These tactics allowed the coalition to deluge Congress with constituent mail on Alaska lands. According to some sources the mail volume on this issue was the greatest since the great civil rights debates of the early 1960s.[36]

In Washington, the staff was sufficiently large to achieve a degree of specialization unprecedented in environmental or conservation lobbying. Ten full-time lobbyists worked the congressional corridors and offices. A separate staff was devoted to the effort to activate the media. Grass-roots organizers had specific regional beats. At crucial times the resources were found for such mind-boggling tasks as "calling the members of the Wilderness Society whose congressmen are undecided."

The resources available to the coalition were unprecedented for a conservation organization, but success cannot be explained totally by the group's resources or even by the sophistication with which those resources were used. The coalition's opponents had greater resources.

The central organization in the opponent coalition is the state of Alaska itself, representing the interests of development-minded immigrant Alaskans. The state's major advantages in this struggle were its ability to finance its efforts through taxation, its obvious and legitimate interests in economic development within its jurisdiction, and the support of powerful and well-financed commodity interests. Disadvantages included its small population base, its distance from the District of Columbia and isolation from the lower forty-eight states, and the apparent inability of its congressional delegation to cooperate on tactics in spite of their agreement on the issues.

Joining the state of Alaska in opposition to H.R. 39 was a host of local organizations. Preeminent among them was Citizens for the Management of Alaska's Lands. This big-budget lobbying committee represented development and commodity interests in the state. More colorful, and probably a good deal less effective, was the so-called REAL Alaska Coalition composed of about forty Alaskan sportsmen's groups. Mining and petroleum interests were also active in opposition, although most of their activities were supported by the individual companies directly involved, rather than by industry-wide organizations like the American Mining Congress or the American Petroleum Institute.

Both the proponent and the opponent coalitions were well organized and active by the time Congressman Seiberling's subcommittee commenced field hearings in 1977. At the conclusion of those hearings Seiberling and the subcommittee staff produced a new version of H.R. 39. The subcommittee draft was a compromise between H.R. 39 as introduced and the proposals of the Carter administration. It had the support of most of the Interior Committee Democrats including Chairman Udall. The subcommittee draft designated an addition of 102 million acres to the four conservation systems in Alaska, and created 81 million acres of instant wilderness in new and existing national parks, forests, and wildlife refuges.

The position of the state of Alaska was best represented by Senate Bill 1787, which had been introduced by Senator Stevens and which had the support of Alaska Congressman Don Young and many of the committee's Republicans. The Stevens-Young proposal would have placed only about twenty-five million acres into the four conservation systems. The primary task of the subcommittee during mark-up would be to choose between these dramatically different proposals.

Subcommittee Chairman Seiberling had hoped to complete the mark-up process in 1977, but he deferred to the wishes of Congressman Lloyd Meeds of Washington who asked for a delay until the first of the year so that he could study the competing measures and perhaps produce one of his own. The delay displeased conservationists, the administration, and the committee leadership, all of whom feared that it would work to the advantage of the bill's opponents. They were no happier when they saw the Meeds proposal in January. Meeds described his work as an attempt to find a compromise between the subcommittee draft and the Stevens-Young approach. Chairman Udall described it as "divisive as hell."[37] The Meeds amendment would have reduced the total acreage added to conservation systems to seventy-nine million and the total wilderness designations to ten million acres.

The major danger for the preservation forces was that the Meeds proposal would attract the support of Republicans and enough marginal Democrats to influence the mark-up process seriously. The Meeds proposal did attract conditional support from Congressman Don Young and from several development interests, but it went down to defeat in the subcommittee on a vote of 10 to 7. Other amendments of smaller individual significance but substantial cumulative impact were pressed by Congressman Young. According to Chairman Seiberling, Young offered eighty-nine amendments in the course of the bill's consideration in committee and eighty-five were accepted.

An important result of the debate over competing versions of the bill was to delay the work of the committee. It finally reported on April 7, 1978.[38]

The Native Claims Settlement Act had established a deadline of December 18, 1978, for congressional action. If that deadline was not met, then, according to the terms of the law, the (d)(2) reservations would revert to unreserved public domain susceptible to selection by state and natives and to appropriation under the public land laws. Some opponents of H.R. 39 had suggested that passing no bill would be preferable to passing H.R. 39, and the approaching deadline provided increased bargaining leverage to those so inclined.

The Interior Committee report on H.R. 39 stressed balance and compromise. It went out of its way to point out the degree to which it had receded from the extreme conservationist position embodied in H.R. 39 as introduced. The major compromises included cutting the total acreage from 115 to

95 million acres and cutting the designation of instant wilderness from 146 million to 74 million acres.[39] In redrawing the boundaries of conservation areas, the committee endeavored to exclude areas of oil and mineral potential wherever possible. The result, according to the committee, was a package that included only 30 percent of the lands with mineral potential and only 4 percent of the lands with oil and gas potential in conservation units. Other changes in the bill expressly recognized valid existing mineral claims and protected the right to develop them. Committee compromises also provided for sport hunting and commercial guiding in certain additions to the National Park System. Table 3 provides a systematic comparison of the major features of competing Alaska lands bills during the Ninety-fifth Congress.

Although the committee bill drew back significantly from the extreme wilderness conservation expressed in H.R. 39 as introduced, it was still a strong Alaska wilderness bill. As indicated in the table, the committee version generally placed more land into conservation units than had been suggested by the administration. The wilderness provisions were more encompassing except in the case of the national forests, where the Department of Agriculture recommendation of February 1978 included more wilderness than proposed by H.R. 39. The department later determined that its calculations had been in error and that it would be necessary to reduce the area devoted to wilderness if logging in the forests were to remain at present levels. The committee ensured no diminution in the established logging enterprises by cutting the wilderness designation by more than a third. Where there was no preexistent industry with a stake in the resources of the land, the committee was more solicitous of wilderness preservation, designating over 80 percent of the fifty million park acres and over 40 percent of the seventy million acres in refuges as wilderness. Almost all of the remaining area in these two systems was designated for wilderness study. Following the tradition of the primitive areas in the national forests, this latter designation would have required separate congressional action to designate further wilderness but would have protected the wilderness character of the area until Congress had acted.

The preservation lobby should have been very pleased, and it was. The original H.R. 39 had been a negotiating instrument. Preservationists were able to compromise in dramatic fashion and still retain a strong wilderness bill. The committee, under Chairman Udall, had reported a bill that recognized the preservation position on most major issues. It designated large areas of instant wilderness and designated wilderness study for most of the rest of the (d)(2) lands. It created no new national forests and explicitly embraced the preservationists' argument that all (d)(2) lands were intended for a greater degree of protection than that afforded by the multiple-use

Table 3   ALASKA LANDS BILLS IN THE NINETY-FIFTH CONGRESS, 1977-1978
ACREAGE ADDED TO CONSERVATION SYSTEMS BY COMPETING PROPOSALS

Conservation System	Original H.R. 39	Carter Adminis- tration	Stevens/ Young	House Interior Committee	House H.R. 39	Senate Energy Committee	Senator Gravel
National Park System (NPS)	64.4	41.8	10.5	43.2	42.7	44.3	28.7
National Wildlife Refuge System (NWRS)	46.4	45.2	8.0	50.8	76.8	35.8	17.9
National Forest System (NFS)	0.0	2.2	5.7	3.3	2.7	8.4	3.7
National Wild and Scenic Rivers System (NWSRS)	4.1	2.5	1.0	1.7	1.7	—a	1.0
Total New Acreage in the Four Conservation Systems	114.9	91.7	25.2	99.0	123.9	88.5	51.3
Wilderness Designations in New and Pre- existent Conservation Units	146.5	48.9	0.0	74.3	65.6	37.2	—b

SOURCES: United States Congress, *Congressional Record* 124 (July 13, 1978): S 10763-64; Senate Report No. 1300 (95th Cong., 2d sess., October 9, 1978), p. 104; Alaska Coalition, *Comparison of Substitutes*, Part 1; *New York Times*, May 20, 1978, p. 22.

NOTE: All figures are in millions of acres.

aThe Senate Committee specified rivers but did not indicate the number of acres involved.

bGravel's proposal would have created some wilderness in national forests, but no acreage was specified.

management of the Forest Service. The most undesirable feature of the bill from the standpoint of the conservation lobby was Title IX. It allowed the Interior Department to conduct mineral information studies including core drilling everywhere in Alaska, including national park and national wildlife refuge wilderness areas. Title IX also included provisions for opening the nonwilderness portions of these systems to actual exploration and extraction under certain circumstances. The procedure created to accomplish this was cumbersome and required both a secretarial recommendation and a joint resolution by Congress with the concurrence of the president. Since such a procedure is tantamount to passing a new law, which Congress can always do, the loophole for economic development created by Title IX is smaller than it looks.

Under the complex jurisdictional rules of the House, a favorable report from the Interior Committee was insufficent to send this measure to the floor. The Committee on Merchant Marine and Fisheries shared responsibility by virtue of its jurisdiction over the Wildlife Refuge System. The Fisheries Committee provided a new opportunity for Congressman Young to dilute the preservation features of H.R. 39. He was partially successful. The committee reported amendments that would increase the size of the National Wildlife Refuge System in Alaska to more than seventy-seven million acres, but it proposed only twenty million acres of instant wilderness.[40] Probably more important, the work of the Fisheries Committee consumed an additional five weeks.

When the bill reached the House floor in mid-May, both Meeds and Young were eager for the opportunity to alter it further. The complex parliamentary situation under which the bill was considered offered ample opportunity. It is a routine function of the House Rules Committee to establish a customized set of procedures called a "rule" to facilitate consideration of important pieces of legislation on the House floor. Such rules generally specify the length of time a measure may be debated and whether or not amendments are in order. The rule adopted for the consideration of H.R. 39 gave the House its choice of three basic bills, each of which could be amended on the floor. The first was the so-called consensus substitute. It was the product of negotiations within the majority leadership and followed the Fisheries Committee report where wildlife refuges were concerned and the Interior Committee report on other matters. The second option was the Meeds substitute, which closely resembled the Meeds proposals that had been defeated in the Interior Committee. The third option was the Udall substitute, a version closer to that reported by the Interior Committee and preferred by the conservation community.

Three hours of general debate passed on the evening of May 17. Discussion was low keyed, and fewer than two dozen representatives were in attendance. Still, it served to put the House on notice that the parliamentary situation would be a mess and that Congressman Young would give full support to the Meeds substitute. The next day's debate was nasty and emotionally charged. Opponents of the legislation characterized it as feudal and colonialistic, a clear violation of states' rights in general and the Statehood Act in particular. Setting aside federal conservation lands was even likened to a policeman tearing a baby from its mother's arms. In his own flourish of rhetorical excess Congressman Seiberling alluded to the similarity of territorial demands by Congressman Young and by Adolph Hitler. Emotion aside, it was a day of triumph for the Alaska Coalition and its supporters in the House. The bill's opponents complained openly about the "little caribou buttons," the symbols of support for the Alaska Coalition that were much in evidence about the floor and in the galleries. Congressman William M. Ketchum expressed dismay that the House leadership was unwilling to follow the lead of the chamber's obvious expert on Alaska, Congressman Young. According to Ketchum," all you [Mr. Udall] have to do is to say the word 'wilderness' and everybody jumps."[41]

The strength of preservation forces was demonstrated in the voting on amendments. Fewer than 100 congressmen remained on the floor during debate, but when it came time to vote, the forces were available to beat back debilitating amendments by Young and Meeds by margins of more than 100 votes. The most critical amendment offered during the course of the debate was one by Congressman Meeds in an effort to reduce the area of designated wilderness from approximately sixty-five million acres in the "consensus substitute" to thirty-three million acres. By restricting wilderness designations exclusively to areas of the National Park System already protected from commodity exploitation, the Meeds wilderness amendment would have gutted the wilderness provisions of the bill. The Meeds amendment passed by 38 to 30 on a divison of those present, but when Congressman Udall demanded a record vote, the result was 119 in favor and 240 opposed.

The decisiveness of the Meeds defeat fostered negotiations behind closed doors, and when Congress reconvened on Friday, Chairman Udall was able to report that agreement had been reached by Udall, Seiberling, Meeds, and Young that no further significant amendments would be proposed or supported by any of them. Congressman Young would have the opportunity to move to recommit the Udall substitute to committee with orders to report out the Meeds substitute. By a parliamentary device the House would then be provided the opportunity to vote first on the Meeds substitute and then the Udall proposal. A bargain had been struck and everything proceeded according to plan. The Meeds substitute was defeated by a record vote of 242 to 67. Final passage was an even more lopsided 277 to 31.

The 1978 bill passed by the House proposed to add 124 million acres to the four conservation systems as follows: NPS, 42.7 million; NWRS, 76.84 million; NFS, 2.74 million; and NWSRS, 1.67 million.[42] The total area designated for instant wilderness was 65.55 million acres.[43] The substantial increase in the size of the total package was the result of an amendment passed by voice vote to make the National Petroleum Reserve a wildlife refuge without changing the primary purpose of the area.

The preservation lobby had a stunning victory in the House, but the legislation was dragging in the Senate and a tough battle loomed to gain Senate approval before the statutory deadline of December 18, 1978.

DELAY AND DISILLUSIONMENT IN THE SENATE

An important metamorphosis had taken place in the Senate since the days of the Wilderness Act. Back in the fifties and sixties the Senate Interior Committee, under the leadership of men like Anderson, Jackson, Church, and Metcalf, had been the foremost advocate of wilderness preservation. The House Committee under Aspinall had been more resistant. In the late 1970s the tables had clearly turned. Personnel changes in the House had created a propreservation shift. Personalities passed from the scene in the Senate committee as well, but the important shift was the result of committee reorganization in the early 1970s. The reorganization consolidated jurisdiction over energy in the old Interior Committee now redesignated Energy and Natural Resources. The result was a shift in emphasis in the committee, as control over the public lands became the committee's secondary concern after the national energy dilemma. The new concern with energy might be expected to make the committee particularly sensitive to the arguments of oil companies that wilderness designations would cripple the energy search. The new energy responsibilities and Washington's greater economic ties with Alaska than with any other state both contributed to Chairman Jackson's reluctance to take a strong leadership role in pushing a conservation-oriented bill in the Senate.

Chairman Jackson had promised to get Alaska lands legislation out promptly, perhaps as early as June, but both Alaska senators had expressed strong opposition to the bill passed by the House and threatened a filibuster. Equally important, Senate Majority Leader Robert Byrd had stated his reluctance to schedule floor debate for the measure if it emerged from committee under the threat of filibuster.[44]

It was inevitable that in an election year the Alaska lands controversy would dominate Alaska state politics. Most interesting was the primary contest for the Republican gubernatorial nomination between incumbent Governor Jay Hammond and former Governor and Interior Secretary Walter Hickel. While both men could be counted upon to uphold vigorously state interests in the Alaska lands controversy, in local parlance Hickel was the "boomer" (committed to rapid development) and Hammond was the "greenie" (committed to environmentally sound development). Almost any version of H.R. 39 was likely to be unpopular with a majority of development-minded Alaskans, and the primary Hickel strategy was to saddle Hammond with responsibility for it. Senator Stevens and Congressman Young, who had doggedly pursued strategies of nibbling away at anti-development sections of the Alaska lands bills, had apparently earned great popularity for their efforts and did not attract serious opposition. Hickel associated himself with Senator Gravel in the view that all available tactics should be used to defeat Alaska lands legislation in the Senate. The Hammond approach called for continuing work to produce an acceptable bill—the approach of Congressman Young and, increasingly as the summer progressed, the view of Senator Stevens as well.

Mark-up progressed at a snail's pace in the Senate committee, hampered by the crush of energy legislation and the parliamentary tactics of Senator Maurice R. (Mike) Gravel. The week of July 10 Gravel angered many of his colleagues by objecting to routine unanimous consent agreements that would have allowed the Energy Committee to meet while the Senate was in session. Such meetings are generally contrary to the rules of the Senate, but routinely approved to prevent the work of the chamber from grinding to a halt. This procedural strategy angered Majority Leader Byrd. He had expressed some sympathy for the desires of the Alaska senators on the lands measure, but he had no sympathy for anyone who would disrupt the Senate's scheduled work.

The evening of July 13 Gravel was ready to go even further. The Senate was considering a bill dealing with White House employees when Gravel was recognized. He announced to his colleagues that he intended to speak "at some length"[45] and planned to continue until at least 9:00 A.M. the following morning. His strategy was to keep the Senate in session so as to prevent the Energy Committee from meeting to continue mark-up on the Alaska lands bill. Gravel reasoned that if the committee could not meet while the Senate was in session and the Senate could be kept in session, then the committee simply could not meet at all. The pressure would presumably force the Senate to postpone consideration of the measure until 1979 when he felt a compromise more to his liking could be arranged. Gravel indicated that he would discuss the Alaska matter until he was tired; then he was prepared to introduce the text of a two-volume biography of Gerald Ford as an amendment to the pending legislation. He told his colleagues that "this legislation deals with the White House, and I picked this amendment especially because I think it would be valuable, and I think that the desk will begin to start reading it when I get tired."[46] By forcing a full reading of the amendment Gravel could oblige the staff of the Senate to conduct his filibuster for him. This was a remarkable use of the filibuster, one designed not to thwart the legislation on the floor, but to hold the entire chamber hostage over the proceedings of a single committee. The strategy did not sit well with Majority Leader Byrd, who invoked a little-used rule allowing the majority leader and minority leader jointly to authorize a committee meeting while the Senate was in session. Even in defeat Gravel did not soon relinquish the floor. Senator Stevens intervened to tell the Senate that he wanted the committee mark-up to go forward so that he could further work for Alaska's interests and to ask Gravel to reconsider his tactics. On one occasion he reminded Gravel that "in 200 years plus, the Senate of the United States has never enacted a bill that affected only one State when both Members from that State opposed it."[47] Further, he suggested "the Senate is more likely to abide by the tradition . . . if we, in turn, abide by the tradition of the Senate."[48] The senior senator from Alaska did eventually desist, but not before he had made it clear that he was prepared to use the rules in every way that he could imagine to thwart passage of an Alaska lands bill. His tactics had successfully called the nation's attention to the strength of his convictions on the issue, but they had also alienated the majority leader and quite possibly Alaska's other senator as well.

This episode demonstrates the growing inability of senators Gravel and Stevens to agree on a strategy to protect Alaskan interests from what they perceived to be the environmental excesses of the Alaska lands bills. At one point Stevens had been inclined to join Gravel in using every available tactic to defeat any Alaska lands bill, but by mid-July he was pursuing a different approach. Although he affirmed on July 18 that he would join Senator Gravel in a filibuster unless an acceptable compromise could be worked out,[49] Stevens was increasingly devoted to a bargaining strategy. His new approach was identical to that of Alaska's only congressman, Don Young. He worked tirelessly to modify the bill in committee, offering amendments designed to make the measure more palatable to the state of Alaska and Alaskan development interests.

Stevens's shift in strategy was probably due at least in part to the perception, which must have become clearer as the summer progressed, that the Carter administration had both the authority and the will to act if Congress failed to pass the legislation. Secretary Andrus had already told reporters in Alaska that "if no law is enacted, the people who will suffer will be the Alaskans."[50] It was well known that Interior Department lawyers were examining several existing statutes to determine the exact range of authorities under which the interior secretary or the president could act to protect those lands being considered until Congress could complete its work. As clarity began to emerge from the situation, the utility of preventing legislation prior to the December 18 deadline became less and less apparent.

Three statutes appeared to create executive authority for land withdrawals. The Antiquities Act of 1906 gave the president the authority to create national monuments. While it is doubtful that Congress contemplated use of this law to set aside large reservations, the precedent for doing so was well established. Teddy Roosevelt had used the authority of the act to set aside the Grand Canyon and Lassen Peak early in the century.[51] Of more recent origin, but perhaps equally useful for withdrawal purposes, was the Federal Land Policy and Management Act.[52] This "BLM Organic Act" required the secretary of the interior to study all BLM roadless areas in excess of five thousand acres for wilderness potential. It would appear that under this statute the secretary could designate vast tracts in Alaska to be protected as wilderness while the department and Congress determined which areas should be permanently designated as parts of the National Wilderness Preservation System. An additional possibility was presented by a 1956 act. Early wildlife refuges had been established by executive order and after 1910 under the general authority of the Pickett Act.[53] With the passage of the Fish and Wildlife Act of 1956,[54] the secretary of the interior was empowered to take necessary steps to protect fish and wildlife, including the establishment of refuges. While a use of any or all of these authorities in Alaska would involve acreages large beyond precedent, the executive branch had ample legal power to act in the absence of congressional legislation.

Senator Gravel's floor tactics constituted only part of the reason for slow progress in the Senate Energy and Natural Resources Committee. The committee was producing, one step at a time, a bill with considerably less appeal for the preservation lobby. Neither development nor preservation interests could command a clear majority and the result was protracted discussions, close votes, and more discussions. As the discussions proceeded it became increasingly apparent that conservationists would probably not be willing to accept the bill that the committee would report. The prospect was, therefore, one of extensive debate on the floor and a House-Senate Conference Committee with major obstacles to overcome. Indeed, one reason Senator Gravel seemed so willing to kill the whole measure was his frequently stated belief that the House conferees would inevitably get the best of the bargain. Still, Senator Stevens's tactics were proving effective. On August 30 the *New York Times* editorialized that under the "weak leadership" of Senator Jackson, the Energy Committee "has been giving the exploiters almost everything they want." *Times* editor John B. Oakes accused the committee of allowing Stevens to dictate the results of its deliberations in spite of the fact that he was not a committee member and was out of step with the views of most Americans.[55]

In mid-September the bill which Chairman Jackson had once promised for June was still in committee, Senator Gravel's goal of preventing any Alaska lands bill was nearer achievement, and Secretary Andrus was making no bones about what the administration would do if Gravel had his way. Speaking to the Nature Conservancy, Andrus called the argument that the administration position would hamper economic development "pure baloney" and repeated his promise to take administrative action if the Congress failed to legislate. "We have no intention, as some have charged, to turn Alaska into some sort of wilderness playground for the rich. And equally, we have no intention of letting Alaska become a private preserve for a handful of rape, ruin, and run developers. Alaska's magnificent resources belong to all Americans for all time."[56]

When the Senate committee finally reported its version of H.R. 39 on October 5, it had produced a compromise that was denounced on all sides.[57] The bill as reported covered about ninety-seven million acres, but the gross figure is deceiving. Substantial acreages were assigned to the Forest Service and the BLM, both multiple-use management agencies. Eight and one-half million acres assigned to the Park Service were given a lower level of protection than they had under the House bill. Wilderness designations were reduced to thirty-seven million acres.

The final hope for a legislated solution in 1978 rested upon informal talks that opened following the Senate committee report. The principal actors in both House and Senate participated in the hope that some sort of informal compromise might be reached that could be introduced on the Senate floor as a substitute, passed, and then approved by the House without amendment. The informal talks would then have served the function of a conference committee. Still, the chances of success were very remote because the two sides were far apart, and Gravel's promise to kill any bill suggested that no compromise would be viable. Then, on October 12, the odds appeared to shift dramatically. In a letter to senators Stevens and Byrd, Gravel indicated that he had altered his position. At the urging of Citizens for the Management of Alaska's Lands and various Alaskan politicians, Gravel said he had decided to work for a compromise measure before Congress adjourned.[58] Suddenly the negotiations showed promise, and they assumed a feverish intensity. Udall and Seiberling accepted a series of amendments that moved the so-called ad hoc conference closer to the Senate version, winning a twelve-million acre increase in total wilderness designations in return. Senator Stevens was so optimistic that he joined a pool, started by the lobbyists who waited outside, predicting that the agreement would be announced at 10:50 A.M. on the 14th.[59] After extensive negotiations over a thirty-six-hour period, all particpants were satisfied that they had produced a package that was better than no bill at all—all participants but one. When agreement seemed assured, Senator Gravel entered the discussions with a demand for rights of way across conservation lands that the other Alaskans felt they could do without, and that Udall and Seiberling were absolutely

unwilling to accept. The meeting disbanded, the legislation lost. Senators
Jackson, John A. Durkin, Stevens, and Gravel all gave reasons for the
failure of the ad hoc conference. All but Senator Gravel concurred that full
agreement had been reached before Gravel changed his mind and sabotaged
the package. Their words were unusually harsh. Senator Stevens charged
Gravel with reneging on the agreement and proclaimed that Gravel must
now bear the responsibility for Antiquities Act withdrawals. Senator
Durkin was even more explicit. "The people of Alaska should know," he
said, "that this compromise foundered on two words, after 47 mark-ups,
and those two words are 'Mike Gravel.' "[60]

One last-ditch effort was made to forestall administrative action on
Alaska lands. The House amended a Senate-passed bill setting aside
wilderness in the lower forty-eight states, substituting language that would
have extended the deadline for congressional action by one year and allowed
the legislators one more chance. Gravel would have none of it. He insisted
once again that no bill would pass regardless of the consequences, and made
clear his intent to block passage of the extension by filibuster if necessary.
The Senate leadership was forced to withdraw the measure without a vote,
and the protection of Alaska's "national interest lands" was left to the
administration.

AN UNPRECEDENTED PRESIDENTIAL PROCLAMATION

The administration was quick to make good on promises proffered by
Secretary Andrus and President Carter. The first step was a secretarial
order from Andrus withdrawing 110 million acres for a period of three
years under the authority of the Federal Land Policy and Management Act
of 1976.[61] Two weeks later President Carter invoked the Antiquities Act of
1906 to provide further protection for 56 of the 110 million acres withdrawn
by Andrus. Unaided, the secretarial withdrawal would have expired in
three years. The seventeen national monuments created under authority of
the Antiquities Act were permanent. Such a designation could only be undone by an act of Congress that could be vetoed by the president. In one
swift act the president more than doubled the size of the National Park
System, and adroitly shifted the political burden from the backs of preservationists to those of developers. The decisions prompted Edgar Wayburn, the
Sierra Club's Alaska specialist, to pronounce Carter the "greatest conservation president of our time."[62]

The monuments were not the only blow to development interests. Under
presidential direction Secretary Andrus at interior began the process mandated by law to create forty million acres of new national wildlife refuges,
and Secretary Bergland at agriculture withdrew eleven million acres of land
in existing national forests to prevent mineral entry and state selection.

Conservationists were delighted; many Alaskans were not. There were public protest demonstrations in Alaska sponsored by the REAL Alaska Coalition, and Governor Hammond filed suit. The suit charged that the administrative actions by President Carter and his cabinet officers were illegal and asked the court to grant Alaska 41 million acres of land that the state had selected but the federal government had not approved. There was little prospect that the suit would prove successful. The (d)(2) withdrawals mandated by the Alaska Native Claims Settlement Act of 1971 had expired on December 18, 1978, but several layers of withdrawal orders remained in effect. All the (d)(2) lands had also been withdrawn under the (d)(1) provisions of the Settlement Act which contained no time limit. All roadless areas under the management of the Bureau of Land Management, most of the state, were withdrawn from most uses by Section 603 of the BLM Organic Act while their potential for wilderness preservation was studied by the Department of the Interior. The controversial actions of the president and cabinet secretaries had added two additional layers of protection to the 121 million acres involved in the struggle to pass Alaska lands legislation.

Governor Hammond's suit may have been motivated by considerations other than winning in court. Peter Scholes, Alaska coordinator for the Wilderness Society, speculated that the state actions were designed to boost Hammond's reelection prospects, by taking a tough stand with the federal government, and to force the Interior Department to enter negotiations over state selections. If so, the first goal was accomplished; the second was not. Hammond won reelection easily, but the administration felt secure enough in the multiple layers of protection that it had provided for the national interest lands to rebuff any overtures to negotiate.[63]

There was strong evidence in early 1979 that the Alaska lands issue was not about to go away. In spite of the permanence of the management decisions which the Carter administration had taken and was continuing to take, conservationist spokesmen continued to insist that the most desirable outcome was a legislated solution along the lines of their 1977 proposal. The issue's major antagonists were not ready to let the matter drop either. While conservationists were elated with the efforts of the administration, they still had less than they wanted. A legislated solution would allow them to designate substantial additions to the National Wilderness Preservation System—something no presidential action could accomplish. Many also felt that the presidential actions had so strengthened their position that they could win a tougher presrvation measure in 1979 than had been possible in 1978. On the other side of the issue, the state of Alaska and its allied interests found the new status quo untenable and required new legislation to set the matter right. The state appropriated two million dollars to fight the battle in Washington and stepped up its efforts accordingly. Commodity interests, mining and oil companies preeminent among them, also increased their efforts. And they had a new ally in 1979. The Organization of Petroleum Exporting Countries (OPEC) determined that the time had come to insist upon substantially higher prices for the crude oil that the United States imported in increasing amounts. The OPEC action, when coupled with other more general market forces, produced a doubling of gas prices between May 1978 and May 1979. Oil industry spokesmen hoped, and conservationists feared, that the gas price squeeze would make massive "lock ups" of possible oil and gas reserves in wilderness areas and national parks political suicide. In a few short months following the presidential proclamations, Alaska appeared to be up for grabs once again.

The issues remained much the same: wilderness areas versus multiple-use areas; how much land and what degree of protection for each of the four systems; the fate of state and native land claims and of the existing national forest lands.

ROUND TWO IN THE HOUSE

Buoyed by the support of the administration, and with the continuous support of the Alaska Coalition and the preservation lobby, Congressman Udall introduced a new H.R. 39 on January 15, 1979. Udall's new bill confirmed the presidential monument decisions, renaming those under the National Park Service as national parks. In all it proposed to provide varying degrees of protection under the four conservation systems for about 110 million acres. The bill would designate 85 million acres of wilderness in new and existing units including the two national forest areas proclaimed to be monuments by the president. Udall found 153 cosponsors for H.R. 39 and seemed confident that it would win House passage. Once again he repeated his charge to the chamber: "Not in our generation, nor ever again, will we have a land and wildlife opportunity approaching the scope and importance of this one. . . . This time, given one great last chance, let us strive to do it right."[64] The victory which Udall and the preservation lobby desired would not be won without a fight. Congressman Meeds of Washington, who had allied himself with Alaska's Don Young in an effort to weaken the 1978 version of H.R. 39, had retired. The battle was taken up by two congressmen from Louisiana, Jerry Huckaby and John Breaux. Huckaby was a member of Udall's Interior Committee; Breaux served on Merchant Marine and Fisheries. Both were among the thirty-one House members who had voted against H.R. 39 in 1978. The battle in the House would eventually become a three-way struggle among proponents of a "Huckaby substitute," a "Breaux-Dingell substitute," and a "Udall-Anderson substitute." Advocates of each would attempt to lay claim to the label H.R. 39.

The Interior Committee acted first, surprising most observers and dismaying the major conservation organizations. By a vote of 22 to 21 it reported out not the bill proposed by its chairman, Mr. Udall, or even a modified version thereof, but rather the Huckaby substitute. Huckaby argued, apparently successfully, that the committee should try to put the Alaska lands legislation to rest as quickly as possible, and that the best way to do that was to report out the measure agreed upon by the ad hoc conference of the previous Congress and sabotaged by Senator Gravel. Every Republican on the committee joined with seven dissident Democrats to produce the one-vote margin of victory.

The committee report on the Huckaby substitute stressed three themes.[65] First, it argued that this bill was in fact the "work product" of the previous Congress and that it had been agreed upon by the members of the ad hoc conference including Udall and Seiberling. Second, it attempted to make the case that this was "a sweeping environmental measure of unprecedented proportions."[66] Finally, the report argued that only this substitute achieved an effective balance between conservation and development.

The committee's twenty-one dissenters filed a 300-page minority report which attempted to refute each of the themes propounded by the Huckaby supporters. They argued that the ad hoc compromise was not the work product of the Senate, which had never had the opportunity to vote on it, and that it was certainly not the work product of the House, which had passed a much stronger measure and explicitly rejected weakening amendments. The Huckaby substitute was more appropriately viewed as the work product of Senator Stevens who had successfully implemented a strategy of delay, sure in the knowledge that he could extract concessions with adjournment threatening that he could not extract otherwise.[67] To the argument that the Huckaby substitute was an environmental measure of unprecedented proportions, the minority responded that it was dramatically weaker than H.R. 39, as introduced by Congressman Udall, than H.R. 39, as passed by the House in 1978, and than the status quo subsequent to the administrative protections granted in 1978. "This 'Huckaby substitute,'" they reported, "has been found flatly unacceptable, not only by us but also by the administration, and by all of America's major membership conservation organizations."[68] The minority made clear that they would carry their fight to the Committee on Merchant Marine and Fisheries and to the floor of the House if necessary.

The Fisheries Committee followed the lead of the Interior Committee and reversed its decision of the previous year, reporting out the Breaux-Dingell substitute rather than the Udall bill. As the House bills emerged from committee and headed toward their final confrontation on the floor, the issue had become less one of acres and more one of the degree of protection from commodity exploitation. Both Huckaby and Breaux-Dingell substitutes designated less wilderness than the Udall initiatives. Equally displeasing to the preservation forces, both bills tended to reduce levels of protection for the parks and wildlife refuges in Alaska. They also committed substantial acreages to land management categories like national reserves, national recreation areas, and national conservation areas. These categories kept the total acreages high, but allowed for increased economic exploitation. The degree to which the differences now rested on complex matters of administrative protection is emphasized by the fact that the gross acreage of the Huckaby and Breaux-Dingell substitutes approximated very closely the overall recommendation of the administration in December 1978,[69] yet were denounced by the administration as "unacceptable."

Even with administration support and more than 150 cosponsors, the Udall bill was now in deep trouble. Both of the committees which shared jurisdiction on this matter had reported bills which most members of the preservation lobby considered less desirable than the status quo. If he was to have a measure that could be adopted as a substitute on the House floor, Udall would need a new compromise proposal and would benefit by a prominent Republican as a cosponsor. He found his cosponsor in John B. Anderson of Illinois, the widely respected chairman of the House Republican Conference. Together with their allies in the Alaska Coalition, they drafted yet another modification of H.R. 39, the Udall-Anderson substitute. While three measures were now in contention, the Alaska lands controversy remained substantially two sided. The Alaska Coalition and the preservation community were firmly united behind the Udall-Anderson proposal. Don Young, chief spokesman for the state in the House, indicated that he could support either the Huckaby or the Breaux-Dingell approach. Table 4 summarizes the provisions of the three measures before the House. The provisions of H.R. 39 as it passed the House in 1978 are included for comparison.

Before the House had the opportunity to act, the debate took a rather unexpected turn. The National Rifle Association entered the fray with guns blazing. The NRA charged that the Udall-Anderson bill was a surreptitious attempt to introduce gun control in America. The charge was evidently based on the fact that a somewhat larger portion of the state would be closed to hunting under Udall-Anderson than under the Breaux-Dingell bill which the NRA favored. These allegations received a lot of informal attention around the House of Representatives in the weeks preceding the floor debate, but the consensus seemed to be that the NRA had overextended itself in an attempt to lend assistance to the efforts of Congressman Dingell, a member of the NRA National Board.

When the Alaska lands issue reached the floor, it came under a complex rule that would allow both committee-reported bills and the Udall-Anderson substitute to be considered. The national press was uniformly predicting a very close contest, and many members commented on that possibility from the floor. So long as the perception remained that the out-

Table 4   MAJOR ALASKA LANDS BILLS IN THE HOUSE, 1979

Conservation Systems	1978 House Bill	Udall-Anderson Substitute	Huckaby Substitute	Breaux-Dingell Substitute
National Park System				
National Parks and Monuments	27.2	27.0	20.5	20.5
National Park Preserves	15.6	17.1	21.6	12.5
National Recreation Areas	0.0	0.0	2.5	0.0
	42.8	44.1	44.6	33.0
National Wildlife Refuge System	76.8	62.4	45.1	87.7
Bureau of Land Management Areas	0.0	0.0	4.4	2.5
National Forest System	2.7	3.3	3.0	3.0
Total New Acreage (exclusive of Wild and Scenic Rivers)	122.3	109.8	97.1	126.2
Wilderness Designations (in new and preexistent conservation units)				
National Park System	41.7	34.0	27.6	22.1
National Wildlife Refuge System	19.9	26.9	20.1	29.7
National Forest System	3.9	6.4	2.9	2.9
Total Acreage Designated Wilderness	65.5	67.3	50.6	54.7

SOURCE: Alaska Coalition, *Comparison of Pending Alaska Lands Substitutes, Part 1—Conservation Units Compared* (April 30, 1979).

NOTE: All figures are in millions of acres.

come was in doubt, it would be sensible for the supporters of each bill to attempt to amend their proposals so as to attract marginal voters. Among the opponents of the Udall-Anderson bill this strategy was clearly being used. Congressman Young had announced that the governor, the state legislature, the two senators, and Alaskans generally could support a bill along the lines of Huckaby or Breaux-Dingell. The supporters of these two bills would attempt to meld them together into a package that would retain the support of development-minded congressmen and attract sufficient marginal members to achieve passage. Although there was a lot of bantering on the floor over which side was doing the most to accommodate the marginal voters, congressmen were in general agreement that neither side would use its votes to prevent the other from adopting amendments to make its proposals more appealing. As this process proceeded it became apparent to the discerning viewer that while the Breaux-Dingell-Huckaby forces were amending their measure to move it toward the Udall-Anderson approach, the Udall-Anderson supporters were subtly doing the opposite.

Breaux-Dingell supporters accepted important amendments to restore the Gates of the Arctic and Wrangells national parks to the size designated in the 1978 House bill. A second amendment to Breaux-Dingell increased the level of protection for the caribou of the Arctic National Wildlife Refuge.[70] The amendment would allow oil and gas exploration to go on, but would require the secretary of the interior to put off leasing the area for production until other areas had been leased. A third major amendment shifted seven million acres of lands classified as wildlife refuge under Breaux-Dingell to park preserve and thus increased their level of protection.[71] Minor amendments also moved the substance of the Breaux-Dingell bill closer to that of Udall-Anderson. These alterations were finally codified in one final amendment to Breaux-Dingell offered by Congressman Breaux. The 479-page amendment replaced the entire text of Breaux-Dingell with language that included all the amendments mentioned above and further accommodated the Huckaby substitute as reported by the Interior Committee. With the adoption of this amendment, the prodevelopment forces in the House had a single proposal behind which they could unite. If it had not been obvious before, it was obvious now, that there were two, not three, fundamental coalitions.

In the preservation coalition, perfecting amendments were also being accepted. One significant amendment placed the Copper River area in Southeast Alaska under wildlife refuge management. This followed the plan of Breaux-Dingell rather than Udall-Anderson, which had given control of the area to the Forest Service, but in doing so it upgraded the level of protection for the area. Breaux-Dingell had originally emerged from the Fisheries Committee with many more acres committed to wildlife refuge status than the competing proposals. This approach had received the blessing of commodity interests, because Breaux-Dingell also gave the wildlife refuges the least protection against commodity development. Most of the late amendments to Udall-Anderson extended refuge status to lands that Breaux-Dingell had included and the preservation lobby had been willing to forgo to achieve a higher standard of protection. Superficially, these acreage additions appeared to make Udall-Anderson more like Breaux-Dingell, and, by inference, more palatable to development interests. Some members of the House erroneously concluded that preservation was being diluted by the changes. But Don Young of Alaska told the assembly, "Let us not kid ourselves," the bill as amended is not "more palatable to the people in Alaska."[72] Young was correct, of course. By adding previously unclassified areas to the refuge system, the preservation forces were strengthening their bill, not weakening it. The fact that these additions took the form of adopting acreages suggested by Breaux-Dingell did not change the fact.

A consistent strategy of the Breaux-Dingell forces had been to focus on the fact that their proposals encompassed the most acres. The greater number of acres was designed to appeal to the environmental community. The Udall-Anderson forces, by comparison, had tried hard to keep the total acreage in their bill down so as not to appear to be environmental extremists. That the floor strategy found both bills being altered in the direction of greater preservation suggests that Breaux-Dingell supporters suspected they were short of votes and that the Udall-Anderson forces were confident of victory. If so, both groups had assessed the situation correctly. When the key vote came on the motion to accept the Udall-Anderson version of the bill, the preservation lobby counted 268 votes, the developers, 157.

There can be no question that the outcome was a major preservation victory. House rules permit one motion to recommit a bill before final passage. It is permissible in such a motion to propose that a bill be recommitted to committee with instructions that it report out a different version. In an effort to salvage something for their efforts, Congressman Keith G. Sebelius of the Breaux-Dingell-Huckaby forces moved to recommit with instructions to report out the 1978 House bill. This vote offered the House a simple choice between the language of Udall-Anderson just passed and the language of the bill the House had passed by a 9 to 1 margin one year earlier. Chairman Udall much preferred the new product and the motion to recommit was defeated easily on a voice vote. With the critical choice between Udall-Anderson and Breaux-Dingell-Huckaby proposals behind it, the House passed the Alaska lands measure by a final vote of 360 to 65.

With the House on record once again in favor of a strong preservation bill, attention turned to the other chamber where development forces could be expected to redouble their efforts. Senator Stevens provided a foreshadowing of the Senate consideration the day following House passage. He told the Senate, "the decisions that were made in the House as they affect my state are catastrophic. . . . I think that the Senate should know that [the House decision to pass Udall-Anderson] is a cause of war as far as this Senator is concerned. . . . I hope no member of the U.S. Senate thinks that the House bill is going to get to the Senate floor with ease. This is going to be the worst battle in the environmental history of the United States."[73] This statement by the more moderate of Alaska's senators suggested an epic battle in the Senate, but two major advantages Stevens and Gravel had shared in 1978 were absent in 1979. First, the presidential proclamation and associated executive branch actions had created a status quo fairly comfortable to preservationists and acutely unpleasant for developers. Second, the 1978 measure had been reported to the Senate late in the Ninety-fifth Congress when the tradition of unlimited debate made obstruction by a single individual effective. Even if Stevens worked effectively to stall the measure in committee as he had done in 1978, it seemed probable that a bill would be reported in 1979. If obstructionist tactics were to keep the measure off the floor in the end-of-session rush, it would likely be reported early in the second session when the full Senate was not pressed with business. At that time even a determined filibuster could be weathered or defeated by a vote of cloture. Whatever the eventual outcome, the next act belonged to the Energy Committee, which was once again swamped with other matters of importance.

ACT TWO IN THE ENERGY COMMITTEE

Three Alaska bills were on the Energy Committee's agenda for 1979. S. 9 had been introduced by Chairman Jackson. It was almost identical to the bill the committee had reported in 1978 and was expected to provide the basis for the committee's work. S. 222 was a more preservation-oriented bill. It had been introduced by senators Durkin, Gaylord Nelson, and William V. Roth with the blessing of the Alaska Coalition and resembled the Udall-Anderson substitute that had passed the House. Finally, there was S. 1176, sponsored by the Alaska senators and designed to revoke the president's national monument proclamations and to limit severely the powers of the administration under the Antiquities Act of 1906 and the Federal Land Policy and Management Act (FLPMA) of 1976.

Chairman Jackson had promised to expedite consideration of Alaska lands legislation in 1979, but in spite of his promise events moved at a snail's pace. It was midsummer before there was noticeable progress. On July 10 the Energy Committee convened long enough to beat back an attempt by Senator Gravel to hold hearings on the bills in Alaska. Alaska lands legislation had been the subject of extensive hearings over several years, and the Gravel proposal was universally interpreted as one more tactic to delay action on the measure. The committee refused to hold the requested hearings, and Senator Jackson predicted that it would complete action and report to the Senate before the summer recess set for August 4.[74] The committee, however, was in no danger of meeting its chairman's deadline.

It was September before the subcommittee on national parks convened to consider S. 1176, the Stevens-Gravel bill. Brief hearings on the proposal provided a forum for Interior Secretary Andrus to denounce the measure and threaten further administrative action under FLPMA unless the Senate hastened to pass protective legislation for Alaska lands. Andrus reported that administrative hearings had been completed for the establishment of forty million acres of wildlife refuges under Section 204(c) of the act and that he was prepared to proceed with the designation if Congress was dilatory. Few members of the committee relished the thought of further executive withdrawals; neither did many support the Stevens-Gravel effort to undo what had already been accomplished. As a result, no effort was made to report S. 1176 from the subcommittee.

Full committee consideration of S. 9 and S. 222 finally got under way on October 9, but the battle had been gathering steam behind the scenes. With the disestablishment bill dead, both Alaska senators had turned their attention to modifying S. 9. Senator Gravel was not a committee member, but he had been invited to participate by Chairman Jackson in recognition of the bill's importance to his state. This year Gravel took full advantage of the invitation and prepared more than forty substantive amendments to the bill. Senator Stevens also had a number of amendments to offer. Stevens's amendments were endorsed by Governor Hammond and many development interests, but, unlike the Gravel amendments, they did not involve wholesale cuts in the acreages proposed by S. 9. Senator Stevens also appeared willing to negotiate over his amendments, while Senator Gravel preferred to see his own go down in defeat, perhaps to further justify the filibuster that he regularly threatened if the committee failed to produce a bill that he considered liveable for Alaska. Meanwhile, Senator Paul E. Tsongas of Massachusetts, who had assumed leadership of the conservation forces on the committee, had prepared fifty amendments supported by the Alaska Coalition.

The preservation lobby and its allies on the committee would have preferred to postpone all substantive amendments to S. 9 until the bill reached the Senate floor. Preservationists believed they had greater support in the full Senate than they had on the Energy Committee. Still, unwilling to see S. 9 further weakened in the committee, they vowed to call up preservation amendments if Gravel insisted on calling up development amendments. Altogether the committee was confronted with the prospect of more than 150 amendments, each of which would require some sort of disposition.

Committee consideration was further hampered by the continuing rift between senators Stevens and Gravel. Stevens took the position that Alaskan development interests would benefit if a bill could be passed in 1979. It would end the uncertainty about what development would be permitted and allow the Senate to vote before preelection jitters set in, giving the Alaska Coalition even greater clout among senators from the lower forty-eight states. Senator Gravel preferred no bill at all.

Gravel had developed a maverick image in the Senate and appeared to relish it. In 1971 he had gained national attention by his attempt to unilaterally declassify the Pentagon Papers by reading them into the *Congressional Record*. A year later he took the podium at the Democratic National Convention to nominate himself for vice president. In 1973 he alienated Chairman Jackson by a surprise move to exempt the court-stalled Trans-Alaska Pipeline from the requirements of the National Environmental Policy Act. With the help of a tie-breaking vote from Vice President Agnew, Gravel prevailed and undercut efforts by Jackson and Stevens toward a comprehensive revision of federal pipeline legislation. In the summer of 1979 many Senate insiders speculated that Gravel's "no-bill" strategy was designed to carry him through to an otherwise uncertain reelection in 1980. If so, the committee provided an excellent forum, for the Alaska legislature was financing the daily telecast in Alaska of committee business.

In spite of Senator Gravel's tactics, the committee made progress on the bill. Some of Gravel's more controversial amendments were summarily defeated. Other amendments by Senator Stevens were adopted. Finally the committee evolved a procedure where committee staff and representatives of senators Stevens and Tsongas met almost continuously behind closed doors to hammer out compromise amendments which were then brought before the full committee for summary approval. After a month of hard bargaining, S.9 was ready for the floor. It was reported by a vote of seventeen to one on October 30, with Senator Tsongas casting the lone dissenting vote.[75]

The bill as reported still bore a remarkable resemblance to the bill the committee had reported a year earlier[76] and differed rather dramatically from the measure passed by the House. Those differences are summarized in table 5. As the table indicates the two bills were in substantial agreement only on the matter of national parks and national park wilderness. The Senate committee bill not only granted protection to twenty-six million fewer acres but also granted lower levels of protection in many instances. More than fifteen million acres in the Energy Committee bill were assigned to the Forest Service or the Bureau of Land Management for multiple-use management. In addition very little wilderness was designated except in the National Park System where the wilderness designation added little additional protection.

The committee bill received the immediate seal of approval from an advisory panel appointed by Governor Hammond to study the matter. The group urged senators Stevens and Gravel to meet with representatives of the House and work out compromise legislation which could be passed by the Senate and the House. Both senators acceded to the advisory panel's request, but Senator Gravel did so with great reluctance.[77] In remarks entered in the *Congressional Record*, Gravel described the bill as "more responsive

Table 5   MAJOR ALASKA LANDS BILLS IN THE SENATE, 1979-1980

Conservation Systems	1979 House Bill	Energy Committee Bill	Tsongas Substitute
National Park System			
National Parks and Monuments	27.0	22.3	—
National Park Preserves	17.0	17.9	—
National Recreation Areas	0.0	2.7	—
	44.0	42.9	44.0
National Wildlife Refuge System	79.5	43.0	81.0
Bureau of Land Management Areas			
National Conservation Areas	0.0	7.8	0.0
National Recreation Areas	0.0	1.0	0.0
	0.0	8.8	0.0
National Forest System	3.4	5.6	2.7
National Wild and Scenic Rivers[a]	(10)	(7)	(10)
Total New Acreage (exclusive of Wild and Scenic Rivers)	126.9	100.3	127.7
Wilderness Designations (in new and preexistent conservation units)			
National Park System	34.1	29.0	34.0
National Wildlife Refuge System	28.1	4.3	27.0
National Forest System	6.4	4.4	5.8
Total Acreage Designated Wilderness	68.6	37.7	66.8

SOURCES: Senate Report No. 413 (96th Cong., 1st sess., November 14, 1979); *CQ Weekly Report* 37 (July 19, 1979): 976-78; *Congressional Record* 125 (November 15, 1979): S 16787.

NOTE: All acreage figures are in millions of acres.

[a]These are the numbers of rivers designated outside of national parks, wildlife refuges, and wilderness areas. The number of acres involved is unspecified and generally rather small. Each bill also designated a number of wild and scenic rivers within other conservation units.

to the needs of Alaska and the nation" than previous bills, but still "extreme" and damaging "to the economic and lifestyle pursuits of Alaskans and the needs of the nation in years to come."[78] Even the panel hedged in its recommendation. It supported passage of the committee bill but indicated that it could accept very few concessions to the House-passed version.

To members of the environmental community, concessions to the House version were absolutely essential if the bill was to be made supportable. In order to facilitate getting them, senators Tsongas and Roth introduced a substitute bill on November 15. The Tsongas-Roth substitute was modeled after the Udall-Anderson bill passed by the House, but it incorporated compromises that Tsongas and Stevens had reached while S. 9 was in committee. Its acreage provisions are compared with those of the House bill and the Energy Committee bill in Table 5.

With the introduction of the Tsongas-Roth substitute, Senator Stevens called off his own efforts to get a bill passed in 1979. While he supported the committee bill, he could not support the Tsongas substitute which he feared the Senate might adopt if S. 9 were called up. Senator Tsongas, for his part, appeared ready to filibuster the committee bill if it were called up in a manner that would prevent a vote on his substitute. Both Stevens, on behalf of the state, and Tsongas, on behalf of the Alaska Coalition, had staked out their positions. Dramatic differences remained to be resolved, and neither side sounded conciliatory. Least conciliatory of all was Senator Gravel who now appeared to back away from even his hedged commitment to S. 9 as reported by the Energy Committee.

With the press of end-of-session business it was clear that there would be no Alaska lands bill in 1979 unless a time limitation agreement could be negotiated to avert a filibuster. In the Senate such negotiations require unanimous consent. There was none, and Congress adjourned without the opportunity for Senate consideration of the committee bill or the Tsongas substitute.

A SURPRISE AGREEMENT

At the outset of the second session in 1980, the Alaska Coalition mounted a drive to get the stalled legislation moving again. Behind the scenes in the Senate, the bill was moving. Without knowledge of the conservation community, Majority Leader Byrd and the principals of the Alaska debate negotiated a time agreement that shocked and dismayed the Alaska Coalition. On Thursday, February 7 Senator Byrd announced the agreement and it received the required unanimous consent. The time agreement allocated a total of twenty hours of debate on the bill among the interested senators and set limits on the number of amendments that might be offered. Senator Tsongas was allowed five amendments; senators Jackson, Stevens, and

Gravel were allowed three each. A two-hour limit was imposed on the debate over each amendment with an additional thirty minutes for amendments to the amendments. At the conclusion of the amendment process Senator Tsongas was authorized to move substitution of the Tsongas-Roth bill for the committee bill as amended.

The agreement seemed to allow the Senate to work its will on the Energy Committee bill under rules that would preclude a filibuster. This was obviously advantageous to the preservation lobby, which felt its strength was greater on the floor than it had been in the Energy Committee. Senator Tsongas, however, had paid a high price for the agreement. The price was a five and one-half month delay in floor action, for the agreement stipulated that the bill would not be called up before July 4.[79]

The preservation lobby was dumbfounded. Alaska Coalition Chairman Chuck Clusen called the decision "incomprehensible,"[80] but, of course, it was not. Tsongas thought he had eliminated the filibuster threat; Gravel and Stevens put greater stock in the value of delay. "Never in my wildest dreams," said Gravel, "did I think we could hold out until late summer. If everything goes to hell in a handbasket, we could probably stop a bill coming out of conference at the end of the session, but we would not be able to stop it now."[81] Senators Stevens and Gravel understood, perhaps better than Senator Tsongas, a recent arrival from the House, the leverage that a vocal minority would be able to exert as the end of the Congress approached.

The unexpected turn of events in the Senate produced the promised reaction from Secretary Andrus. On February 12 he issued orders under Section 204(c) of FLPMA to withdraw 40 million acres in Alaska from development for a period of twenty years. The orders created thirteen wildlife refuges totaling 37.6 million acres to be administered by the Fish and Wildlife Service and four natural resource areas totaling 3.2 million acres to be administered by the BLM. While the term of the withdrawals was twenty years, the withdrawals for wildlife refuge purposes were permanent in effect, because, under existing law, the Interior Department was required to renew them.[82] The new withdrawals brought to 96 million the number of acres given long-term protection by administrative action. By this act the Carter administration created a protected area somewhat larger than its own legislative proposals had originally recommended. Once again delay in the Senate had been greeted with determination in the executive department, as the Carter administration pressured Alaska's senators to grant concessions to preservation.

The time agreement also had an impact on lobby interests. The Alaska Coalition redoubled its efforts on behalf of the Tsongas-Roth substitute. In cooperation with the Americans for Alaska, the Coalition engaged in a carefully choreographed campaign of celebrity lobbying. Singers, soldiers, scientists, and celebrity widows called on selected senators. Among the participants were Laurence Rockefeller, John Denver, Jacques Cousteau, Ansel Adams, and a host of retired government officials including senators Henry Cabot Lodge and John Sherman Cooper, governors Russel W. Peterson, Tom McCall, and Dan Evans, and military officials Elmo R. Zumwalt, Jr. and Paul H. Nitze. The widows of Supreme Court Justice William O. Douglas and former Interior Secretary Rogers C. B. Morton were also active in the lobbying effort.[83] While the preservation lobby called upon its rich relations for help with the Senate, the state of Alaska set out to buy the hearts and minds of average Americans, launching a four-million-dollar effort to influence the constituents of persuadable senators in the forty-eight contiguous states. John Katz, an aide to Governor Hammond, explained that the money would be used for newspaper advertising, because under the Federal Communications Commission's "fairness doctrine" radio and television stations might be required to provide equal time to the environmentalists.[84]

In spite of the efforts of lobbying organizations on both sides of the issue, most members of the Senate displayed greater independence from interest group influence than their colleagues in the House. Major participants in the Senate like Stevens and Tsongas also seemed less firmly tied to the interests of the competing lobbies than their counterparts in the House had been. Stevens was charting his own path, satisfied to support the committee version of S. 9 on the floor, but inclined to offer amendments in conference where he could reasonably anticipate greater support. Any conference committee would be expected to include the chairmen and ranking minority members of the Senate Energy Committee, the House Interior Committee, and the House Merchant Marine and Fisheries Committee, as well as Alaska's two senators and its one representative. With those participants the conference committee would almost certainly be less preservation minded than the Congress as a whole. Senator Tsongas was also plotting an independent course. While the Alaska Coalition continued to stress the big vote on the Tsongas-Roth substitute, Tsongas himself devoted more energies to the five amendments that he was authorized to offer. The five amendments were apportioned out to prominent conservationists in the Senate, and the preservation lobby had little choice but to pitch in and work for their adoption.[85]

Under the time agreement each side had consented to give official notice of its intentions by an exchange of proposed amendments. This portion of the agreement was consummated in May, and there were no surprises. The five Tsongas amendments proposed to decrease the acreage open to sport hunting in the National Park System, designate additional wilderness in the National Forest, National Park, and Wildlife Refuge systems, add fifteen million acres to the Wildlife Refuge System, tighten controls over transportation projects, and designate three additional wild and scenic rivers. The three Stevens amendments proposed to guarantee the prerogatives of the state in fish and wildlife management, facilitate certain land exchanges, and prohibit future executive withdrawals of public lands in Alaska. The amendments to be offered by Senator Gravel proposed to open an additional two million acres of national parks to sport hunting, allow mining claims in conservation areas to be developed until 1984, and convey up to one million acres of submerged lands to native corporations created by the Alaska Native Claims Settlement Act. Senator Jackson had a right to three amendments under the time agreement, but he chose not to offer any.

The agenda was set. Eleven amendments and the Tsongas-Roth substitute had been published for the consideration of the Senate. The efforts of lobbying interests continued, but for most preservation or development-minded citizens across the nation, it was a time to wait.

S. 9 ON THE SENATE FLOOR

The waiting came to an end on July 21 when Senator Byrd called up the Alaska lands bill in accordance with the provisions of the February 7 unanimous consent agreement. That agreement had provided for twenty hours of general debate equally divided among senators Gravel, Stevens, Jackson, and Tsongas. Only Senator Gravel seemed determined to consume all he had been allotted. After brief introductory remarks by Senator Jackson on behalf of the Energy Committee bill, Senator Gravel took control of the floor and proceeded to a rough-and-ready demolition of the committee bill, the Carter administration, and environmentalists generally. Gravel's harangue continued for well over three hours and contained several allegations about the bill's history and provisions which were of very questionable accuracy. At the conclusion of his remarks only he and Senator Stevens remained on the floor.

Stevens took the opportunity to disassociate himself from what Gravel had said, but he also issued a warning to the environmentalists. "This debate, Mr. President, could prove to be a very long debate should any of the Tsongas amendments not be tabled. . . . The complexities of these amendments will require that we offer a series of second-degree amendments."[86] Stevens claimed no intention of acting in a dilatory fashion, yet he made it perfectly clear that if preservationists insisted on their amendments the debate might last indefinitely. This statement was a real threat to preservationist plans. The time agreement limited debate on second-degree amendments to thirty minutes, but it placed no restrictions at all on the number of second-degree amendments that could be offered.

Stevens was followed by Senator Tsongas who offered introductory remarks on behalf of the conservation community. Tsongas called the impending decision on Alaska lands "an extraordinary chance to conserve the natural legacy of all Americans, for all Americans, for all time."[87] Shortly thereafter the Senate recessed for the day.

July 21 had been a day for discussion; July 22 was a day for decision. Under the terms of the time limitation agreement the Tsongas amendments were the first to be considered, and Tsongas had decided to lead off with his wildlife refuge proposal. It was cosponsored by senators Gary Hart, John H. Chafee, Randolph, Culver, and Church, and was probably the most popular of the five Tsongas amendments. It proposed additions to the National Wildlife Refuge System in Alaska totaling about fifteen million acres.

Conservationists expected to win the refuge amendment, but the margin of victory was beyond any expectation. In rapid succession preservationists won three critical votes by convincing margins. A motion by Energy Committee Chairman Henry Jackson to table the wildlife refuge amendment was defeated 33 to 64 on a roll call vote.[88] Many Energy Committee Democrats broke ranks with their chairman to support the refuge amendment. Conservative Republicans like Richard Luger, Roger Jepsen, Robert Dole, Alan Simpson, and Strom Thurmond deserted their Minority Whip, Senator Stevens, to support the measure. Jackson and Stevens were dismayed, but the vote was no fluke. An effort to divert a part of the added acreage to national forest status was defeated by a vote of 30 to 66, and a proposal to reduce the size of the addition failed by a vote of 33 to 62.[89]

For Senator Stevens the margin of defeat on the refuge amendment suggested the possibility that all of the Tsongas amendments might pass the Senate substantially unscathed. Stevens had been prepared to lose the refuge amendment, but he was not about to lose much more. He escalated his rhetoric on the Senate floor, threatening at least eighteen additional second-degree amendments, and making it perfectly clear that even under the time limitation agreement he could bring all proceedings to a halt if he chose to do so. Tempers flared on both sides of the issue. Debate continued throughout most of July 22 and 23 with no sign of progress toward any solution. Once again in 1980 the Senate was in danger of seeing Alaska lands legislation argued to death. Recognizing the futility of continuing, Majority Leader Byrd pulled the Alaska lands bill off the floor late in the day on July 23.

The time limitation agreement had served the purposes of the Alaska senators well. It had delayed consideration of the measure for more than five months, but it had not really prevented a filibuster. Now, late in the session, Senator Gravel might again succeed in talking the measure to death. Senator Stevens presumably still favored passage of the committee bill, but his ability to create stalemate meant increased bargaining advantages even in the face of a Senate that had just demonstrated overwhelming support for preservationist amendments.

The situation was deadlocked. Stevens had demonstrated his ability to kill the bill, but he found the prospect of continuing administrative withdrawals unacceptable. Tsongas had demonstrated that he had the votes, but he would be unable to make use of them unless some accommodation was reached with Stevens. Negotiations began again in earnest and behind closed doors. Principals from the House were called in, and the Senate witnessed something akin to a repeat of the ad hoc conference of 1978. The resulting package, dubbed the Tsongas-Roth-Jackson-Hatfield substitute, pleased neither the Alaska state government nor the Alaska Coalition, but it did have the support of senators Henry Jackson and Mark O. Hatfield, the chairman and the ranking minority member of the Senate Energy Committee. Senator Stevens officially disapproved the package, but his staff assistant had been involved throughout the negotiations, and many Senate insiders believed the resulting compromise was as much the work of Senator Stevens as of those whose names it carried. In any event senators Stevens, Jackson, Roth, Hatfield, and Tsongas all agreed that the new language would be offered as a substitute for the committee bill in lieu of Tsongas-Roth. With at least tacit approval from all interested senators, other than Senator Gravel, the compromise package could presumably pass the Senate by a wide margin.

A serious procedural problem remained, however. The time agreement required that the amendments which had been allotted to various senators be disposed of before Tsongas could offer the substitute. With the new substitute negotiated, neither Tsongas nor Jackson had any interest in calling up their allotted amendments. Stevens called up one amendment. It was passed, and thus attached to the pending Energy Committee bill, with the understanding that similar language would also appear in the Tsongas substitute when it was presented. That left Senator Gravel with a right to three amendments under the time agreement, and the Senate spent most of two days on August 4 and 5 waiting for the senator to dispose of them. Gravel had other plans, and he succeeded in keeping the Senate in session without bringing any of his amendments to a vote. Finally, in frustration, Majority Leader Byrd filed a motion for cloture calling the existing parliamentary situation "obviously futile."[90] The cloture motion meant further delay. In the Senate such a motion cannot be called up for two days after it is filed, and the Senate was scheduled to be in recess August 6 through 15 for the Democratic National Convention.

Senator Gravel had succeeded in stalling Senate action once again, but he had paid a high price for his success. Senator Tsongas reported that senators had approached him offering assistance, not out of support for the bill, but out of concern for the institutional integrity of the Senate. The turning point, according to Tsongas, was an exchange between Gravel and Senator Goldwater of Arizona. Goldwater complained that the Senate was engaged in "horseplay" rather than "the business of America" and asked the chair to exempt members attending committee meetings from Gravel's continuous calls for a quorum. When the request was denied, Goldwater withdrew it, and Gravel seized the opportunity to appeal the ruling of the chair and tie up the chamber for another forty minutes.[91] Most senators were clearly tired of the delaying tactics, but Gravel interpreted the matter differently. "I picked up a lot of respect today," he said. "There were a lot of good vibes on the floor. Senators were laughing, and the cloakroom was just a-howling."[92]

When the Senate reconvened on August 18, a more reflective mood prevailed. Senator Gravel spoke quietly of the founding fathers and the Senate's role as protector of minorities in the constitutional scheme of things. Senator Stevens was in an even more conciliatory mood. He complimented Senator Tsongas for his willingness to bargain in good faith and suggested that the Tsongas-Roth-Jackson-Hatfield substitute granted the state 81 percent of what its legislature had said was necessary. The remarks of both senators exuded a sense of inevitability. Both sides must have accurately gauged the outcome of the impending vote. Later that afternoon, on the first attempt, the Senate voted cloture. The motion required 60 affirmative votes; there were 63 yeas and only 25 nays. Senator Gravel capitulated. "My amendment is pending," he told his colleagues. "I am prepared to call that up at the disposition of the leadership and prepared to proceed at whatever pace the leadership chooses."[93] The rest was anticlimax. The Senate disposed of the remaining amendments. They had become superfluous, for they altered the committee bill, and everyone understood that the committee bill was no longer a serious consideration. Senator Tsongas had the votes, and the new compromise version of the Tsongas substitute had the support of those necessary to assure that the vote would take place.

At last the Senate was prepared to act on an Alaska lands bill. Under the time limitation agreement an additional four hours of general debate were in order on the Tsongas substitute, but the Senate was ready to move on to other things. The Tsongas substitute was approved by a roll call vote of 72 to 16.[94] Final passage was delayed one day to allow additional senators to participate, but the decision had been made. On Tuesday, August 19 only twelve colleagues joined the two Alaska senators in opposing the bill; seventy-eight voted in favor of it.[95] The vote demonstrated broad support for the legislation in the Senate. Democrats supported passage by a margin of 50 to 3, Republicans by a margin of 28 to 11. Even senators representing the eleven contiguous western states with huge federal landholdings voted in favor of the Alaska measure by a vote of 13 to 6. Twenty months after the original congressional deadline for Alaska lands legislation, the Senate had finally passed an Alaska lands conservation bill.

For Senator Gravel it was the end of a four-year struggle to prevent passage. Seven days later it proved to be the end of his Senate career as well. Gravel was defeated in the Alaska Democratic primary, where the Alaska lands bill and Gravel's tactics had been the only significant issues. Commentators expressed varied opinions about the reasons for Gravel's defeat. In all probability the bill's success just one week before the election left Gravel doubly damned. Alaskans who had voiced regular approval for the tactics of Senator Stevens and Congressman Young disapproved of Gravel's approach right along. Once-militant Gravel supporters may well have been disillusioned by his last-minute tactical failure.

FINAL PASSAGE: NOT WITH A BANG, BUT A WHIMPER

The next play belonged to the House, which had twice passed much stronger versions of the bill. The Alaska Coalition and its chief supporters in the House were loath to agree to a bill that differed so dramatically from their own earlier efforts. House members also took umbrage at statements emanating from the Senate which suggested that the House had better settle for the Senate version or risk losing everything. Congressmen Udall and Seiberling objected to the take-it-or-leave-it attitude and indicated that they would give careful consideration before jumping on this particular bandwagon. Many rank and file House members apparently agreed. In a show of institutional pride and support for preservation principles, 111 of them signed a letter addressed to Udall and Seiberling calling the Senate bill inadequate and recommending modifications along the lines of the House-passed measure. Still, to insist on a conference committee to work out the Senate-House differences was tactically dangerous. A conference committee procedure would provide Senator Gravel at least three additional opportunities to filibuster the bill to oblivion. A filibuster could be mounted against the appointment of conferees, against the motion to take up the conference report, and against approval of the report.

To avoid a conference committee, principal proponents of the legislation met informally in September in an effort to negotiate some sort of compromise that could win approval in both the Senate and the House. The effort proved unsuccessful, and on October 4, as the Congress prepared to adjourn for the national elections, congressmen Udall of Arizona and Thomas B. Evans of Delaware introduced a package of amendments which they said conceded far more than they demanded.[96]

Preservation hopes were high for the lame-duck session that would follow in November. Those hopes were dashed the evening of November 4, 1980, as election returns poured in from across the country. In a massive vote of no confidence, the Carter administration and a host of liberal senators were swept from office. It was the economy, not Alaska, that determined the vote in the lower forty-eight states, but the results were no less painful for the preservation community. The Wilderness Society's *Wilderness Report* proclaimed "Election Landslide Stuns Conservationists,"[97] as it reported the defeat of senators Frank Church of Idaho, Gaylord Nelson of Wisconsin, and John Culver of Iowa—all friends of preservation. The Republican party conquered the White House and took majority control of the Senate for the first time in more than twenty-five years.

In the House it was Morris Udall's turn to capitulate. At a press conference the morning of November 12, the first day of the lame-duck session, Udall bowed to "political realities" and announced that he would seek House passage of the Senate bill. The task was accomplished before the day was done. Shortly before 6 P.M. Udall received unanimous consent to bring the Senate bill to the floor. One-half hour later the pleasantries were concluded and what will certainly be the most important single act in the history of American wilderness legislation had been passed—not with a bang, but a whimper. In the brief discussion preceding the voice vote, Congresswoman Millicent Fenwick, a Republican from New Jersey, eloquently expressed the feelings of many preservationists in the House. "Mr. Speaker, I rise in support of this compromise. It is statesmanlike, I imagine. It is disappointing. It is prudent. It has many virtues. And it lacks many others. But I think it is wise at this moment to support it, and we have to accept that which is possible even if it is not perfect. I congratulate the chairman. I was a cosponsor of the Udall-Evans bill. I regret that it is not now before us, but we must accept what we have."[98]

Both preservationists and developers vowed to carry on the struggle, and no one can seriously doubt that there will be future skirmishes over the development or preservation of critical acres in the forty-ninth state. In all probability, however, the major decisions concerning conservation lands in Alaska have now been made. President Carter made it official, signing Public Law 96-487 on December 2, 1980.

ALASKA NATIONAL INTEREST LANDS CONSERVATION ACT

While it was less than preservation forces had hoped for, the Alaska National Interest Lands Conservation Act did more for conservation and for wilderness preservation than any law in human history. The act contains

Table 6   SYNOPSIS OF THE ALASKA NATIONAL INTEREST LANDS
CONSERVATION ACT OF 1980

Conservation Systems	New Acreage	Wilderness Acreage[a]
National Park Service	43.66	32.36
National Parks	(22.34)	
National Monuments	(2.26)	
National Preserves	(19.06)	
National Wildlife Refuge System	54.86	18.56
Bureau of Land Management Areas[b]	2.22	0.0
National Forest System	3.35	5.36
National Wild and Scenic Rivers	1.30	0.0
Total Acreage	105.39	56.28

SOURCE: United States Congress, *The Congressional Record* 126 (August 18,
1980): S 11063-119.

NOTE: All figures are in millions of acres.

[a]Wilderness designations in both new and preexistent conservation units.

[b]The act created one National Conservation Area and one National Recreation Area to be administered by the BLM. These lands are less well protected than those in conservation systems, but special management provisions distinguish them from BLM lands generally.

almost 100,000 words and is as complex as its 449 pages would suggest. Its major conservation features are summarized in table 6. The act added ten units to the National Park System and expanded three existing units. These and other major additions to conservation systems are shown in map 1. The total acreage added to the park system was 43.66 million, 24.60 million in parks and monuments and just over 19 million in national preserves, which are to be administered as national parks except that sport and subsistence hunting and trapping are permitted. The additions brought the total National Park System acreage in Alaska to 50.6 million and increased the total acreage within the National Park System nationwide by almost 150 percent. The addition to national park wilderness was more spectacular still. More than 32 million acres were designated in new and

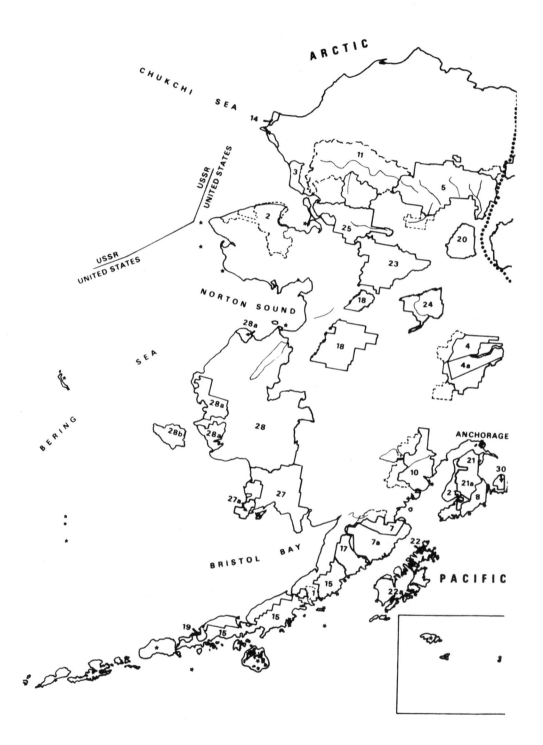

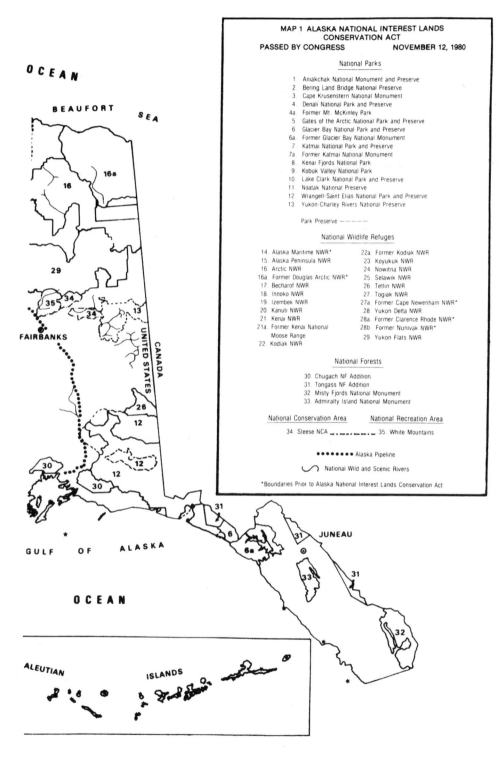

MAP 1 ALASKA NATIONAL INTEREST LANDS
CONSERVATION ACT
PASSED BY CONGRESS   NOVEMBER 12, 1980

National Parks

1.   Aniakchak National Monument and Preserve
2.   Bering Land Bridge National Preserve
3.   Cape Krusenstern National Monument
4.   Denali National Park and Preserve
4a. Former Mt. McKinley Park
5.   Gates of the Arctic National Park and Preserve
6.   Glacier Bay National Park and Preserve
6a. Former Glacier Bay National Monument
7.   Katmai National Park and Preserve
7a. Former Katmai National Monument
8.   Kenai Fjords National Park
9.   Kobuk Valley National Park
10. Lake Clark National Park and Preserve
11. Noatak National Preserve
12. Wrangell-Saint Elias National Park and Preserve
13. Yukon-Charley Rivers National Preserve

Park Preserve – – – – –

National Wildlife Refuges

14. Alaska Maritime NWR*   22a. Former Kodiak NWR
15. Alaska Peninsula NWR   23. Koyukuk NWR
16. Arctic NWR   24. Nowitna NWR
16a. Former Douglas Arctic NWR*   25. Selawik NWR
17. Becharof NWR   26. Tetlin NWR
18. Innoko NWR   27. Togiak NWR
19. Izembek NWR   27a. Former Cape Newenham NWR*
20. Kanuti NWR   28. Yukon Delta NWR
21. Kenai NWR   28a. Former Clarence Rhode NWR*
21a. Former Kenai National   28b. Former Nunivak NWR*
    Moose Range   29. Yukon Flats NWR
22. Kodiak NWR

National Forests

30. Chugach NF Addition
31. Tongass NF Addition
32. Misty Fjords National Monument
33. Admiralty Island National Monument

National Conservation Area   National Recreation Area

34. Steese NCA _._._._.._   35. White Mountains

•••••••• Alaska Pipeline

⌒ National Wild and Scenic Rivers

*Boundaries Prior to Alaska National Interest Lands Conservation Act preexistent National Park System areas, well over ten times the total in the lower forty-eight states.

Additions to the National Wildlife Refuge System were equally spectacular. Ten new units were created; existing refuges were consolidated and expanded. The total refuge addition came to almost 55 million acres, more than one and one-half times the size of the entire system nationwide prior to the Alaska lands legislation. More than 18.5 million refuge acres were also added to the wilderness system, giving them substantial additional protection. Prior to passage of the Alaska National Interest Lands Conservation Act fewer than 800,000 acres in the refuge system had received congressional wilderness designation.

Wilderness areas under Forest Service management were also established. More than 5 million acres in the Tongass National Forest were added to the National Wilderness Preservation System, and a wilderness study area was designated in the Chugach National Forest. The additions increased the total wilderness acreage in the National Forest System by more than 30 percent. The National Wild and Scenic River System also emerged greatly expanded. Before the act twenty-eight river segments had been included in the system, totaling about 719,000 acres. The Alaska National Interest Lands Conservation Act designated twenty-six additional river segments, thirteen within the National Park System, six within the National Wildlife Refuge System, and seven outside the boundaries of other conservation units. The 1.3 million acres involved tripled the land area preserved under the National Wild and Scenic Rivers Act. Section 1317 of the act designated all nonwilderness portions of the National Park and Wildlife Refuge systems as wilderness study area. While this is more than 47 million acres, the land was not given substantial interim protection, and it is reasonable to believe that substantial enlargement of the designated wilderness acreage in Alaska is unlikely for the foreseeable future.

The price of all this success was the release to nonwilderness uses of any remaining lands being studied by the Forest Service under the RARE II process. The act in effect declared the wilderness designation process terminated in Alaskan national forests. It also canceled the effect of the executive proclamations and withdrawals which the administration had used so effectively to pressure Congress to act. One last major concession to the development interests of the state appeared in Section 1326. At the insistence of Senator Stevens the act contained a provision limiting executive withdrawals of federal lands in Alaska to 5,000 acres without the approval of Congress. Carter's monument proclamations and the interior secretary's withdrawals had amounted to more than 100 million acres—2,000 times the size of the new limitation—but even the environmental lobby was not terribly disturbed about shutting the barn door just now. FLPMA and the

Antiquities Act had both seen unprecedented use in the Alaska lands controversy. Conservationists were sorry to see executive withdrawal authority so trimmed in Alaska, but surely the benefits outweighed the price that was now imposed.

It was not everything conservationists had hoped for, but it was a great deal indeed. The Alaska Coalition soon recognized the magnitude of the preservation success. Its "Alaska Hotline" telephone recording for November 13 proclaimed "The greatest Alaska hotline ever. . . . You did it!" To a significant degree, they had.

NOTES

1. Peggy and Edgar Wayburn, "Alaska—the Great Land," *Sierra Club Bulletin* 58 (June 1973): 5.

2. Donald J. Jarosz, "Our Last Frontier," *A.B.A. Journal* (1971), reprinted in United States Congress, *The Congressional Record* 117 (September 14, 1971): 31890.

3. 23 Stat. 24.

4. Wayburn, "Alaska—the Great Land," p. 7.

5. 72 Stat. 341.

6. Robert W. Swenson, "Legal Aspects of Mineral Resources Exploitation," in Paul W. Gates, *History of Public Land Law Development* (Washington, D.C.: Government Printing Office, 1968), p. 742.

7. 72 Stat. 349.

8. *Kake Village v. Egan*, 369 U.S. 60 (1962). The natives were generally conceded to have "aboriginal" or "Indian" title to the lands they occupied or used. In 1955 the Supreme Court clarified the concept of Indian title saying that it was not a property right under the Fifth Amendment and thus did not require compensation if seized by the federal government, but that it was a recognized right of occupancy and use legally protected against intrusion by third parties. In short, only the federal government could extinguish the land claims of the Alaska natives. *Tee-Hit-Ton v. U.S.*, 348 U.S. 272 (1955).

9. Wayburn, "Alaska—the Great Land," p. 8.

10. United States Senate, Report No. 925 (91st Cong., 2d sess., June 11, 1970).

11. Ibid., p. 98.

12. Ibid., p. 42.

13. Ibid., p. 41.

14. United States Congress, *The Congressional Record* 117 (October 14, 1971): 36262.

15. United States Senate, Report No. 925, p. 51.

16. United States Congress, *The Congressional Record* 117 (October 13, 1971): 36144.

17. United States Senate, Report No. 405 (92nd Cong., 1st sess., October 21, 1971): 54-55 and 69-71.

18. United States Congress, *The Congressional Record* 117 (November 1, 1971): 38452.

19. Ibid., p. 38451.

20. The natives were given fewer selection options in most versions of the proposed settlement act than was the state. By the early 1970s most versions gave lands to native villages and also to broader regional native organizations. The villages were required to select lands nearby for village expansion and the actual use of the village inhabitants; they were also given the highest priority in the selection process. The regional organizations would presumably select lands for their economic value as would the state. These selections for economic value are given a reduced priority under the Bible amendment. Since these selections might, if unrestricted, have been made all over the state, they presented a greater threat to wilderness and land-use planning than did the village selections.

21. Public Law 92-203; 85 Stat. 688.

22. United States House of Representatives, Report No. 746 (92nd Cong., 1st sess., December 13, 1971): 25.

23. United States Congress, *The Congressional Record* 118 (March 1, 1972): 6247ff.

24. Ibid., p. 6251.

25. Memorandum to Members of the Senate Interior Committee from Special Counsel Steven P. Quarles, December 9, 1974, in United States Senate, Committee on Interior and Insular Affairs, *Status of Federal Lands in Alaska, Hearings on Management of Lands under the Alaska Native Claims Settlement Act, December 10, 1974* (Washington, D.C.: Government Printing Office, 1975), pp. 6-7.

26. Emphasis added.

27. Reprinted in United States House of Representatives, Report No. 1045 (95th Cong., 2d sess., April 7, 1978): 403-7.

28. S. 2917. United States Congress, *The Congressional Record* 120 (January 30, 1974): 1308-12.

29. S. 2918. United States Congress, *The Congressional Record* 120 (January 30, 1974): 1312-14.

30. These are gross acreages. Net acreages would depend on the extent of established private inholdings. In any event, all acreages cited in the Alaska lands controversy are estimates and should be treated as such.

31. Gail Robinson, "How the Alaska Coalition Pushes Its D-2 Land Lockup," *The Alaska Professional Hunter* 7 (Spring 1979): 3.

32. Udall's race for the Democratic presidential nomination in 1976 had given him a degree of visibility unusual for a member of the House. While the nomination proved elusive, the effort promoted recognition and generated favorable comment in the press.

33. The reader is reminded that these percentages are based upon a sample. The distribution of opinion that they display is dramatic and statistically significant but subject to sampling error. The reader should not jump to the intellectually appealing, but probably false, conclusion that no one in the East testified against the bill and no one in a native village for it.

34. United States House of Representatives, Subcommittee on General Oversight and Alaska Lands of the Committee on Interior and Insular Affairs, *Inclusion of Alaska Lands in National Park, Forest, Wildlife Refuge, and Wild and Scenic Rivers*

Systems, Hearings on H.R. 39, et al., September 15 and 21, 1977 (Washington, D.C.: Government Printing Office, 1977), XVI.

35. The Trustees for Alaska is a group of prominent Americans, the majority of whom have Alaskan addresses.

36. Robinson, "How the Alaska Coalition Pushes Its D-2 Land Lockup," p. 2.

37. United States Congress, *The Congressional Record* 124 (January 14, 1978): 66.

38. United States House of Representatives, Report No. 1045.

39. Wilderness acreages include new wilderness designations in preexistent conservation areas. Ibid., pp. 66-68.

40. Ibid., Part II.

41. United States Congress, *The Congressional Record* 124 (May 18, 1978): H 4243.

42. The Alaska Coalition, *Comparison of Pending Alaska Lands Substitutes* (Washington, D.C., April 30, 1979), Part 1. *New York Times*, May 20, 1978, p. 22.

43. The Alaska Coalition, *Comparison of Pending Alaska Lands Substitutes*, Part 1.

44. *New York Times*, May 19, 1978, p. 12.

45. United States Congress, *The Congressional Record* 124 (July 13, 1978): S 10736.

46. Ibid., p. S 10740.

47. Ibid., p. S 10773.

48. Ibid.

49. *New York Times*, July 19, 1978, p. 8.

50. *CQ Weekly Report* 36 (July 22, 1978): 1876.

51. See chapter 3.

52. See chapter 6.

53. 36 Stat. 847.

54. 70 Stat. 1119.

55. *New York Times*, August 8, 1978, p. 134-35.

56. Ibid., September 17, 1978, p. 17.

57. United States Senate, Report No. 1300 (95th Cong., 2d sess., October 9, 1978).

58. *CQ Weekly Report* 36 (October 21, 1978): 3100.

59. Ibid., p. 3101.

60. United States Congress, *The Congressional Record* 124 (October 14, 1978): S 19140.

61. This was an "emergency" withdrawal authorized by Section 204(e) of the act. It is ironic that Chairman Aspinall and others involved with the Public Land Law Review Commission had supported this act as a means of reasserting congressional control over the public lands after a long history of executive inroads.

62. Edgar Wayburn, "Alaska: President Carter to the Rescue," *Sierra Club Bulletin* 64 (January/February 1979): 22.

63. *Wilderness Report* 15 (December 1978): 1.

64. United States Congress, *The Congressional Record* 125 (January 15, 1979): H 46.

65. United States House of Representatives, Report No. 97 (96th Cong., 1st sess., April 18, 1979), Part I.

66. Ibid., p. 138.

67. Senator Stevens described this strategy of delay in an interview that was

published in the December 1978 issue of *Alaska Industry*.

68. United States House of Representatives, Report No. 97, Part I, p. 380.

69. The administration's most recent recommendations to the Interior Committee called for classification of 123 million acres with wilderness designation for 52 million acres of new and existing units.

70. This is the only area considered to have high potential for oil and gas exploration which the Udall-Anderson proposal declared completely off-limits by granting a wilderness designation. Breaux-Dingell and Huckaby took the position that the area should be explored in an environmentally sound manner and not given wilderness status.

71. Although the exact meaning of the "park preserve" designation underwent some change during the Alaska lands controversy, these areas were generally understood to have the protections of national parks except that sport hunting would be permitted.

72. United States Congress, *The Congressional Record* 125 (May 16, 1979): H 3362.

73. Ibid. (May 17, 1979): S 6121-22.

74. *CQ Weekly Report* 38 (July 14, 1979): 1398.

75. Senator Gravel was a participant in the committee's deliberations, but not a committee member, and therefore, not entitled to vote.

76. See table 3.

77. *CQ Weekly Report* 38 (November 3, 1979): 2449.

78. United States Congress, *The Congressional Record* 125 (November 15, 1979): S 16804.

79. Since Congress would be in recess July 4, the bill could not be called up until late in the month. See generally United States Congress, *The Congressional Record* 126 (February 7, 1980): S 1293-99.

80. *Wilderness Report* 17 (February 18, 1980): 1.

81. Ibid., p. 4.

82. *Federal Register* 45 (February 12, 1980): 9562.

83. *CQ Weekly Report* 38 (August 4, 1980): 2297.

84. *Wilderness Report* 17 (April 25, 1980): 3.

85. The five Tsongas amendments and their cosponsors are as follows: a 1.5-million-acre increase in the designated wilderness within the national forests of Southeast Alaska (Roth and McGovern); an increase in the level of protection for some of the 43 million acres placed in the national park system by the committee bill (Charles Mathias); wilderness designation for the Douglas Arctic Wildlife Refuge and wilderness additions in many of the national parks and wildlife refuges (Nelson and Carl Levin); additions of 15 million acres to the wildlife refuges designated by the committee bill (Hart, Chafee, Randolph, Culver, and Church); tightened regulations for transportation projects and designation of three additional wild and scenic rivers (Proxmire and Thomas Eagleton). See United States Congress, *The Congressional Record* 126 (May 22, 1980): S 5780-85, and (May 28, 1980): S 5889; also *Wilderness Report* 17 (May 27, 1980): 4.

86. United States Congress, *The Congressional Record* 126 (July 21, 1980): S 9422.

87. Ibid., p. S 9430.

88. Ibid. (July 22, 1980): S 9522.

89. Ibid., pp. S 9524 and S 9534.

90. Ibid. (August 5, 1980): S 10792. In routine parliamentary practice, a motion of cloture, when passed, ends debate and causes the matter in question to be brought to an immediate vote. In the United States Senate the matter is not quite so simple. The Senate's tradition of uninhibited debate is apparent even in its cloture rule. A motion for cloture must be made two days before it can be voted upon. It requires sixty votes for passage and still allows a limited amount of additional debate. A cloture motion is an awkward tool, but its passage does serve notice that a strategy of delay cannot succeed in preventing the full Senate from voting on the merits of the matter in question.

91. United States Congress, *The Congressional Record* 126 (August 5, 1980): S 10789.

92. *CQ Weekly Report* 38 (August 9, 1980): 2298.

93. United States Congress, *The Congressional Record* 126 (August 18, 1980): S 11051.

94. Ibid., p. S 11140.

95. Ibid. (August 19, 1980): S 11203.

96. *Wilderness Report* 18 (October 9, 1980): 1.

97. *Wilderness Report* 18 (November 7, 1980): 1.

98. United States Congress, *The Congressional Record* 126 (November 12, 1980): H 10528.

EPILOGUE: WILDERNESS POLICY FOR THE 1980s AND BEYOND

> In Wildness is the preservation of the World.
> —Henry David Thoreau
> *Excursions*

Efforts to preserve the American wilderness are an ongoing story, but the beginning of a new decade under new political leadership is an appropriate time to assess preservation politics—past, present, and future.

In many respects wilderness is just another natural resource. Our world was provided with a limited stock, and people decide how that stock is to be used. In a world dominated by natural environments it is inevitable, indeed desirable, that people should take charge and strive for pleasure, profit, convenience, and comfort. In a wilderness world these things are scarce and worthy of human efforts. Our ancestors confronted a continental wilderness and took the only course open to them. They built the modern world.

Modernization is the dominant theme of our age. Underdeveloped countries strive to achieve it. Overdeveloped countries strive to extend it. Modernization is a process associated with population growth and technological change, with increasing urbanization, mechanization, and interdependence, with specialization and the division of labor. It is also a process that tears people from their traditional roots, fostering alienation and social unrest. It is a process that converts natural to artificial environments, a process which is, by definition, wilderness annihilating.

As a consequence the history of modernizing America is a history of resource use where the first victim was the American wilderness. A profligate use of our natural resources was the necessary first step in modernizing America. It destroyed the American wilderness and created the conditions under which a wilderness ethic could emerge. It made wilderness a scarce commodity.

In the eighteenth and early nineteenth centuries, it was an urbane and literate elite who treasured wild country and urged its preservation, men like Thoreau, Emerson, and Catlin. But as technological progress engulfed more and more of wild America, increasing numbers of Americans began to appreciate the environmental cost. As wilderness became increasingly scarce, interest in its preservation grew. Early political successes, like the efforts to preserve Yosemite and Yellowstone and to set aside forest reserves, were as much the product of more practical motivations as of preservationist fervor, but the idea that the federal government could effectively intervene to preserve natural environments took root and grew. In the twentieth century the idea came of age and manifested itself in eighty years of landmark legislation designed to curb economic excesses and preserve some semblance of wild America. With increasing rapidity Congress and the executive branch responded to America's awakening appreciation of wildness. The Antiquities Act, the National Park Service Act, the Shipstead-Nolan Act, the administrative designation of wildlife refuges and Forest Service primitive areas, and the defeat of such ill-advised governmental developments as the effort to dam Dinosaur were milestones in governmental preservation policy and set the stage for the climactic legislation of the 1960s and 1970s.

The Wilderness Act of 1964 set in motion a process of wilderness review, designation, and preservation that will probably continue for some time. Its progeny include the Eastern Wilderness Act, the Endangered American Wilderness Act, the National Trails Act, the National Wild and Scenic Rivers Act, the Federal Land Policy and Management Act, and the Alaska National Interest Lands Conservation Act. The result of this preservationist success in the political arena is a statutory wilderness system comprising more than eighty million acres. The system is depicted in map 2. An additional area of more than thirty million acres has been mandated for wilderness study by Congress or the executive branch.

The wilderness system in the national forests has grown from the 9.1 million acres set aside by the 1964 Wilderness Act to 25.4 million acres. Almost 10 million acres were added in 1980 alone. The Alaska lands legislation added 5.3 million acres and bills based on the RARE II inventory added an additional 4.4 million acres in the contiguous forty-eight states. The continuing controversy over wilderness designations in the national forests will center upon the results of the RARE II inventory. The advent of a conservative Republican administration and Republican control of the Senate will undoubtedly slow the wilderness designation process, but it is unlikely that RARE II will be repudiated by the Forest Service. It may take many years, but about 8 million acres of additions to national forest wilderness are probable before the allocation process has run its course. At present about 13.5 percent of the 188 million acres in the National Forest System are committed to wilderness preservation. Eventually between 17 and 18 percent of Forest Service land will probably receive congressional wilderness designation.

MAP 2 NATIONAL WILDERNESS PRESERVATION SYSTEM
JANUARY 1, 1981

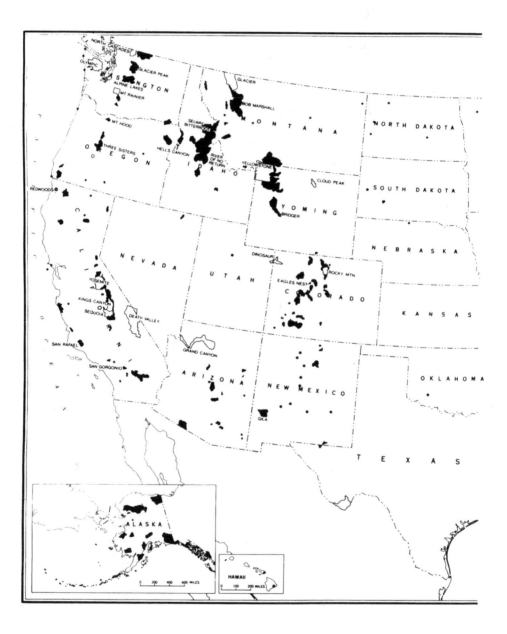

Source: Base map courtesy of the United States Department of the Interior.

The wilderness system in the national parks has been slow to develop. Practical politics produced a dearth of statutory wilderness designation before the Alaska lands legislation. First, environmental organizations have considered national park lands to be relatively immune to development compared to national forest lands and have, therefore, devoted most of their energies to the National Forest System. Second, most legislators had been disinclined to designate national park wilderness unless the local senators and the area's congressman endorse the recommendation. When the stakes were perceived to be very high, as they were in Alaska, BWCA, and River of No Return legislation, the parochial interests of local representatives may be overridden, but legislators were loath to do so over the relatively minor question of whether lands that already have national park protection shall also have wilderness protection.

Before the Alaska lands legislation the National Park Service managed about 30 million acres, exclusive of the president's monument proclamations in Alaska. Less than 10 percent of that total had received congressional wilderness designation. The Alaska National Interest Lands Conservation Act added 43.7 million acres to the park system and 32.4 million acres to park wilderness. As a result, the National Park System has grown to more than 73 million acres of which just over 35 million acres (48 percent) has been designated as wilderness.

The political conditions that have produced minimal congressional wilderness designations in the national parks outside of Alaska will no doubt persist for some time. Park wilderness will continue to grow at a slow pace. In the long term, however, the potential for wilderness additions is excellent. Substantial portions of the largest parks in the lower forty-eight states will eventually be included in the wilderness system. When the process is complete park wilderness may exceed 50 million acres and embrace up to 70 percent of all park system lands.

Predicting the wilderness potential of the wildlife refuge system is difficult. Before 1980 refuge wilderness designations had been relatively inconsequential, amounting to fewer than one million acres. The Alaska lands legislation added almost fifty-five million acres to the thirty million already in the refuge system, creating an eighty-five-million-acre system containing nineteen million acres of wilderness. Disagreement about the proportion of the refuge system that was to be designated wilderness highlighted the controversy over Alaska lands legislation. As long as refuge wilderness designations remain that controversial, major wilderness additions in the refuge system are unlikely. In the long run, however, those controversies may cool. As it becomes clear that substantial areas in the refuge system have minimal value as a source of minerals or other commodity interests, those areas may be added to the wilderness system.

The eventual acreage of designated wilderness on BLM lands is also difficult to predict. In response to the Federal Land Policy and Management Act of 1976 the BLM inventoried 174 million acres in fourteen contiguous western states. On November 14, 1980 the bureau announced that 149 million acres had been determined to lack wilderness characteristics and an additional 24 million acres had been identified as wilderness study areas.[1] These areas will now be subjected to the kind of intensive study that had previously been mandated for Forest Service primitive areas and for the large roadless tracts in national parks and wildlife refuges. These lands may not receive the interim protection that conservationists would prefer. A federal district judge in Wyoming ruled November 7, 1980 that the bureau could not prohibit oil and gas leasing activities even if those activities would impair the area's wilderness characteristics.[2] If mineral developments are allowed to go forward, and if presidential recommendations for BLM wilderness emerge during the Reagan administration, the recommended acreages are likely to be small. Still, it seems probable that from 10 to 20 million acres of present BLM wilderness study areas will eventually find their way into the National Wilderness Preservation System.

If this analysis is correct, Americans can look forward to a National Wilderness Preservation System that will eventually reach 100 to 130 million acres in size. Friends of wilderness preservation will wish there were more. It is doubtful that they will appreciate the magnitude of their accomplishment. Political successes have increased the appetite of the preservation lobby, and legislative outcomes which would have been hailed as great victories ten, twenty, or thirty years ago are greeted with mixed emotions today. An appreciation of what has been achieved requires a historical perspective, a point of view rarely shared by those actively engaged in the political struggle.

On November 11, 1953, Interior Secretary Douglas McKay addressed the Western Governors' Conference in Albuquerque, New Mexico. He defended the administration's public land policy, which he said would continue to be one of gradual transfer of the public domain to private ownership. He argued that the nation's resources are best developed by private enterprise. Many Americans today would agree with the general proposition, but not many would endorse McKay's conclusion that the Interior Department's "basic mission is to dispose of . . . the public domain."[3] On the contrary, the Congress has gone on record in the Federal Land Policy and Management Act as favoring the retention of most lands currently in federal ownership. Congress has placed more than 80 million acres of those lands into the National Wilderness Preservation System, and it is reasonable to anticipate additions of between 20 and 50 million acres before the allocation process comes to an end. Such a wilderness system will embrace about 5 percent of the total land area of the United States. The magnitude of the victory for preservation will be greater than preservationists could have imagined as recently as 1964. That victory will come none too soon, for the time is now within our comprehension when the only wilderness that will remain is the wilderness that has been purposefully preserved. When that time comes, 100 million acres will not seem too much.

REPUBLICANS AND WILDERNESS

The political climate in which preservation has flourished for years has clearly been altered. The new president and new Congress are more conservative, more Republican, and more development oriented than their predecessors. They are more in tune with what the press calls the Sagebrush Rebellion, that collection of commercial and governmental interests in the western states that would like to reduce the influence of the federal government in local affairs and open the public lands to increased commercial development to promote private profit and regional growth.

Nowhere is the philosophical compatibility between the new administration and the interests of the Sagebrush Rebellion more clear than in the appointment of the new secretary of the interior. Reagan's selection of Colorado attorney James Watt appeared to be a clear signal that the president-elect desired a more development-oriented policy at the Interior Department. As president and chief legal officer of the Mountain States Legal Foundation in Denver, Watt had been an active participant in litigation challenging the environmental preservation policies of the federal government. William Turnage, executive director of the Wilderness Society, called the appointment "disastrous," adding "it appears that Reagan is paying off his political debt to the right wing with the environmental issue."[4] Many environmentalists probably shared Turnage's sentiments, but preferred not to alienate the secretary designate with loose talk.

The other key appointment for the politics of wilderness preservation is that of assistant secretary for natural resources and environment in the Agriculture Department. The assistant secretary has supervisory responsibility for the Forest Service, and the man appointed generally reflects the intended emphasis of the administration. Carter's initial appointment had been Rupert Cutler, a product of the environmental movement. While Reagan's assistant secretary has not yet been named, it is almost certain that the nominee will come from a timber industry background.

It is understandable that environmentalists should be dismayed by their prospects under the Reagan administration, but the change in policy is likely to be much less dramatic than the change in personnel. The wilderness constituency is alive and active throughout the country. It is skilled in administrative and adjudicative politics, and the new administration will not be able to ignore it. In addition, to a far greater degree than during the days of Leopold and Carhart, a substantial wilderness constituency exists in the bureaucracy. A host of civil servants who believe in wilderness preservation inhabit the Park Service and the Forest Service, in Washington and in the field. Their numbers will probably increase. Modern forest or park managers are more likely than their predecessors to have been trained in ecology and economics as well as practical forestry, and individuals with strong environmental concerns are increasingly attracted to land management careers. In the 1920s and 1930s top management in the Forest Service had much greater management discretion than it does today, and it still had difficulty getting field personnel to take wilderness preservation seriously. Any modern manager who decided to dismantle the wilderness system would face far greater obstacles. In order to reorient the work of field personnel he would first have to change the legal constraints under which they work. Two decades of wilderness-supportive legislation would have to be undone by Congress. Reagan's opportunity to reorient the politics of preservation lies less in his power to appoint departmental managers than in the ability of a skillful president to motivate and lead the Congress.

The outcome of the 1980 election may make that job easier than most observers had predicted. The political leadership remains substantially unchanged in the House. Representatives Udall, Seiberling, and Burton all retained their seats and their positions of leadership on critical committees and subcommittees. A modest influx of more development-minded representatives may cut into the margins of victory that preservation forces have recently been able to muster in the House, but a propreservation majority will remain.

The Senate is cause for greater concern in the preservation community. The 1981 Senate comprises eighteen newcomers, sixteen of them Republicans. Based on the environmental votes compiled by the League of Conservation Voters, the newcomers are dramatically less likely to support environmental preservation. Environmental support scores were available for the six newcomers who previously served in the House. In each case the score of the senator-elect was lower than that of the incumbent he replaced. The average environmental support score for the newcomers was 26 percent. The average of the eighteen incumbents leaving office was 59 percent.

More important than the overall shift in the chamber is the leadership change resulting from Republican control. The shift makes Senator Stevens of Alaska majority whip and Senator James McClure of Idaho the chairman of the Energy and Natural Resources Committee. McClure is a conservative Republican and friend of western development interests. Under his leadership, and with the votes of six Republicans added to the committee, the

Energy and Natural Resources Committee is likely to be firmly in the camp of the energy and resource industries. Since approval by this committee is necessary for the congressional designation of wilderness areas, very few such designations are likely during McClure's tenure as chairman. The composition of the Senate Energy Committee will likely prove more detrimental to the cause of further wilderness designations than will the makeup of the Reagan administration. For the short term, personnel changes in Congress and the executive branch may devastate the ability of the environmental community to pass new legislation. Preservation forces will find themselves playing defense rather than offense. So long as preservationists control the critical chairmanships in the House, however, the defense is likely to be effective.

In the long run, the future of wilderness preservation will depend less on the partisan control of the Congress or presidency, and more on the tides of public sentiment to which both parties inevitably, if sluggishly, react. During the 1960s and 1970s American policymakers perceived that a host of natural resources were threatened. Clean air, unpolluted rivers and streams, safe drinking water, and tolerable noise levels all received the attention of policymakers. So also did free-flowing streams, back-country foot trails, and the genetic diversity of North American plant and animal communities. The increasing scarcity of these resource values moved lawmakers to protect them, but giving that protection has inevitably meant that other values would suffer at least relative demotion in the pantheon of worth. Since these natural amenities are threatened primarily by the engines of economic development their preservation depends on the willingness of government to regulate that development.

American enterprise easily adjusts to the idea that it must pay for many of the resources that it utilizes: the land upon which it builds, the oil to fire the boilers, or the electricity to run the lights. These resources command a price because they belong to someone else, someone in a position to deny access unless the price is paid. By tradition other resources, equally necessary to the enterprise, have been available without cost: the water to wash away waste products, or the air required to support combustion and the respiration of the work force. These resources, too, belong to somebody else, but because they belong to everybody else, government must determine an equitable and efficient allocation. Access to these resources must sometimes be denied in the interest of the community at large. So the modern era, which produces enormous affluence at enormous cost to the environment, is inevitably characterized by an unprecedented degree of governmental involvement in the process of resource allocation. This in turn produces groans of oppression from the business community, which urges politicians to get government "off its back." The problem is that we can't have it both ways. Freeing business to produce without restraint might well increase business productivity but only at the cost of increased environmental degradation. Increased efforts to preserve wilderness or any other natural amenity are likely to succeed at the cost of reduced production and decreased economic efficiency.

As this is written, in the final days of 1980, the American public seems to be clamoring for more production and fewer natural amenities. At least, that is what the new Republican president and his allies would have us believe. If wilderness preservation has prospered as affluence has grown, then perhaps the 1980 election marks the end of both. The economy is in relatively poor shape, plagued by substantial unemployment and double-digit inflation. If this is the end of American prosperity, then we might well expect that Americans will choose to sacrifice their remaining wilderness to the necessities of economic progress.

I suspect that this is not the case. In the first place, while the economic problems of the nation are undeniably real, Americans as a group are not becoming poorer. What has happened during the decade of the 1970s is that the geometric growth in our affluence that had persisted since World War II has come to a rather abrupt halt. It is not American prosperity that has been shattered by the economic malaise of the 1970s; it is the expectation of ever-increasing wealth. The failure of our economic system to meet our inflated expectations translates real wealth into perceived privation. Perceptions are important, but they are also malleable. Over a period of years the economy will succeed in resuming its previous rate of growth, or, if it does not, the new rate will be perceived as normal. Either way current perceptions of poverty are likely to vanish. In the interim, well wishers of wilderness preservation should not be surprised if they can achieve little beyond what has already been accomplished. Neither should this be a cause for despair. We are very near the point in our national development when the only surviving wilderness will be that wilderness formally protected. Americans have been awakened to its scarcity and they are unlikely to tolerate any wholesale declassification in order to utilize those few resources that have been "locked up."

Americans seem torn between two competing concepts of our place on the planet. We are conditioned by our past successes to believe in the technological fix. This school of thought presumes that as every resource is exhausted, it will be replaced by some new wonder of technology. This view supports the argument that oil conservation is unnecessary, because we have plenty to last us until the advent of breeder reactors and controlled nuclear fusion. In this sort of thinking, wilderness appreciation can be replaced by movies and television and ultimately by pleasure electrodes in our heads, and we will all be the happier for it.

Common sense and the laws of thermodynamics seem to argue for the alternative concept: spaceship earth. Adherents of this concept acknowledge the finite nature of earth resources and reject the inevitability of a technological solution for every problem. This view demands a role of stewardship toward the planet and its resources. We must plan wisely, conserve where we can, and ultimately bring our civilization into greater harmony with the global ecosystem of which it is unquestionably a part.

While the latter view is preferred by environmentalists, it is difficult to guess which view will provide the motive force for Americans and their policymakers in the next generation or two. Whichever view prevails, present wilderness designations are not likely to be undone. If Americans adhere to the concept of spaceship earth, then wilderness will be cherished for its naturalness and for its ability to preserve ecological systems. It will be preserved as a symbol of the natural order to which we must adapt our civilization. If, on the other hand, Americans see science as savior, the anticipated technological fix will make it unnecessary to give serious consideration to plowing up our protected wilderness. The economic gain potentially available by doing so will appear insignificant compared to our ever-increasing ability to accomplish what we want by technological means. To environmentalists the desire to dominate the global ecosystem and remake it in man's image may seem less appealing than the desire to live in harmony with a more natural system, but wilderness preservation is likely to be a part of the American experience under either regime.

NOTES

1. *Federal Register* 45 (November 14, 1980): 75574-75.
2. *Rocky Mountain Oil and Gas Association v. Andrus; Wilderness Report* 18 (December 18, 1980): 6.
3. *New York Times*, November 3, 1953, p. 25.
4. *Wilderness Report* 18 (December 18, 1980): 3.

EPILOGUE TO THE 2008 EDITION

On January 20, 1981, fifty-two American hostages were released in Iran, Ronald Reagan was inaugurated president of the United States, and the first edition of this book was dispatched to the publisher after more than a year's delay waiting for Congress to finish work on the Alaska lands legislation (Chapter 7). Reagan's election the previous November and Republican capture of the Senate for the first time in twenty-five years facilitated closure on a decade of legislative struggle over the future of preservation in Alaska. With the prospect that further delay might cost them everything, congressional conservationists returned for a lame-duck session and settled for what they could get. A lame-duck president, Jimmy Carter, signed the Alaska lands bill with just seven weeks remaining in his term.

In the original epilogue I noted that the political winds had shifted direction, that preservation forces would be less influential in the foreseeable future, and that wilderness additions would come slowly under Republican leadership. Nevertheless, the wilderness system would eventually reach 100 to 130 million acres, and—despite slow forward progress—there was little danger of significant reductions in wilderness protection.

SLOW GROWTH OF THE WILDERNESS SYSTEM

There has been no massive rollback of wilderness protection: the American system of checks and balances makes changing anything difficult. But the less hospitable political climate I foresaw in late 1980 now describes a history of some twenty-seven years and counting. The legislative battles over the Wilderness Act of 1964 and the Alaska National Interest Lands Conservation Act of 1980, which form the backbone of this book, are now well established as bookends on a fifteen-year period of unprecedented environmental progress. George Cameron Coggins observed that the Wilderness Act began "the Age of Preservation."[1] I would suggest that ANILCA marked the end.

Between these two legislative landmarks, Congress approved the Land and Water Conservation Fund Act (1965), the Wild and Scenic Rivers Act (1968), the National Trails System Act (1968), the National Environmental

Policy Act (1969), the Wild Free-Roaming Horses and Burros Act (1971), the Marine Mammal Protection Act (1972), the Endangered Species Act (1973), the Forest and Rangeland Renewable Resources Planning Act (1974), and the Federal Land Policy and Management Act (1976), which extended wilderness preservation to BLM lands. Congress also enacted wilderness additions in thirty-nine states: Alabama, Alaska, Arizona, Arkansas, California, Colorado, Florida, Georgia, Hawaii, Idaho, Illinois, Kentucky, Louisiana, Maine, Massachusetts, Michigan, Minnesota, Mississippi, Missouri, Montana, Nebraska, New Jersey, New Hampshire, New Mexico, North Carolina, North Dakota, Ohio, Oklahoma, Oregon, South Carolina, South Dakota, Tennessee, Texas, Vermont, Virginia, Washington, West Virginia, Wisconsin, and Wyoming. The Congress that rushed to enact the Alaska lands legislation late in 1980 also enacted major wilderness additions for New Mexico and Colorado.

Legislation passed in the last half of 1980 proved not only to be the zenith of wilderness preservation efforts in the United States, but very nearly the end of them. The Reagan Administration identified itself with the anti-Washington, pro-development agenda of the Sagebrush Rebellion and marked the passing of bipartisan cooperation on wilderness preservation. Since then, legislative solutions to the issues of wilderness preservation have been rare, and they have succeeded only under rather specific—some have said miraculous—circumstances. Two cases are worthy of mention.

The first case arose out of the second Roadless Area Review and Evaluation (RARE II) of the national forests (Chapter 5), which satisfied no one. Opponents wanted to finish the national forest wilderness system once and for all. Some were willing to extend wilderness status to the areas recommended by the Carter administration in return for permanently releasing the rest of the roadless acreage for multiple-use management and likely development. But the administration had proposed fewer than ten million acres of new wilderness in the lower forty-eight states, and the preservation community was unwilling to settle for so little.

With the support of wilderness advocates, the State of California sued the Forest Service, alleging violations of the National Environmental Policy Act (NEPA) and challenging the agency's designation of forty-seven areas in California as nonwilderness.[2] The district court ruled that the environmental impact statement (EIS) required by NEPA was inadequate and enjoined the agency from releasing the disputed lands to potential development. In 1982, the ninth Circuit Court of Appeals concurred, concluding that the EIS had failed to provide site-specific analysis or adequately to address public comments. Most telling, the EIS had failed to consider any alternative that would allocate more than one-third of the roadless areas to wilderness when, in the words of the court, "All of the RARE II acreage, by definition, met the mini-mum criteria for inclusion in the NWPS."[3]

The circuit court's decision in *California v. Block* certified the failure of RARE II. The Carter administration's methodology for administrative de-classification of potential wilderness areas was fatally flawed. Once again, the release of wilderness-eligible tracts for multiple uses was enjoined, effectively precluding road building and logging in thirty-six million acres of national forests. With both sides stymied and no enthusiasm for a vastly more compli-cated RARE III, all parties had an incentive to negotiate. Those negotiations bore fruit in 1984 with twenty-one generally state-specific wilderness laws adding more than eight million acres to the wilderness system and replicat-ing a set of compromises initially negotiated for the Alaska, New Mexico, and Colorado wilderness laws that had passed late in 1980. Appropriately, the biggest beneficiary was California, where new wilderness exceeded three million acres. Washington, Arizona, Utah, and Wyoming each gained about one million acres.[4]

California was the key player in the second case as well. The California desert began to attract policy attention in 1967, when environmentalists were appalled by the impact of the first "Barstow to Vegas" off-road motorcycle race, an annual event that attracted thousands of riders through 1974 when the BLM revoked its permit.[5] The possibilities for preservation were enhanced by the Federal Land Policy and Management Act of 1976 (FLPMA), which called for a study of the California desert as well as wilderness review of road-less BLM lands. During the Reagan administration, however, federal policy reversed course. Interior Secretary James Watt sought to roll back acreage in wilderness study areas nationwide. In the California desert the BLM demon-strated a cavalier attitude toward its own resources, renewing the Barstow to Vegas race and approving a cyanide heap-leach open-pit gold mine in an area it had previously designated as "of critical environmental concern."[6]

The renewed threats to environmental protection prompted the first of many bills to protect the California desert. The House of Representatives passed a bill in 1991, but differences between the bill's Senate sponsor, Alan Cranston, and his Republican counterparts[7] continued to preclude action in the Senate.[8] Prospects for passage were improved mightily by the election in 1992. California's two new senators, Dianne Feinstein and Barbara Boxer, were supporters of desert conservation, and under newly elected president Bill Clinton, the Bureau of Land Management was expected to be support-ive rather than resistant.[9] However, the four Republican congressmen who represented local desert districts continued to object to what they saw as a lockup of resources,[10] and they enjoyed considerable support from other western Republicans.

Despite broad support in California and nationally, the California Desert Protection Act of 1994—including seven million acres of new wilderness areas—passed only because Senate Majority Leader George Mitchell was willing to keep the Senate in session beyond its scheduled adjournment in order to break a Republican filibuster.[11] The vote to end debate passed by the bare minimum of sixty votes, including those of seven Republicans, only one of whom represented a western state.[12] Author Frank Wheat called its passage a "miracle."[13] Indeed, it was. With sweeping Republican victories in the congressional elections of 1994 and the election of a development-minded president, George W. Bush, in 2000, if the desert protection act had not passed in 1994, it probably would not have passed at all.

It is no accident that, since 1981, the lion's share of wilderness growth has taken place in California. California epitomizes the New West. Uniquely among the fifty states, it contains both the vast expanses of de facto wilderness that make wilderness system expansion possible and the huge, recreation-oriented, urban populations that make wilderness preservation politically feasible. It takes an act of Congress to designate a wilderness area, but with rare exceptions that act ratifies a local consensus that preservation is desirable. Outside of California, consensus for preservation has been harder to find. As Figure 1 demonstrates, except for the events of 1984 and 1994, the nearly thirty years since passage of ANILCA have been distinctly anticlimactic, and growth of the National Wilderness Preservation System has been painfully slow.

THE PARTISAN PENDULUM

This low level of legislative productivity has frustrated preservation and development interests alike. Opportunities to command legislative majorities and rewrite public land laws have been few. Both sides have shifted their strategies to other arenas: to states, counties, administrative agencies, and courts. The strongly prodevelopment administrations of presidents Reagan, Bush, and Bush pursued administrative strategies, attempting to change the facts on the ground by exerting greater control over agency behavior. The generally propreservation administration of President Clinton did the same. Agencies were reorganized. Science was manipulated. Policy loyalists were appointed and promoted, and agency regulations were rewritten in an effort to achieve the desired policy results. The increasingly politicized agencies wobbled like drunkards, unbalanced by their efforts to produce policies consistent with the alternating ideological preferences of Republican, then Democratic, then Republican administrations.

Since 1981, the primary wilderness battles have been outside of Congress, often triggered by executive agency decisions, and generally concluded—if at

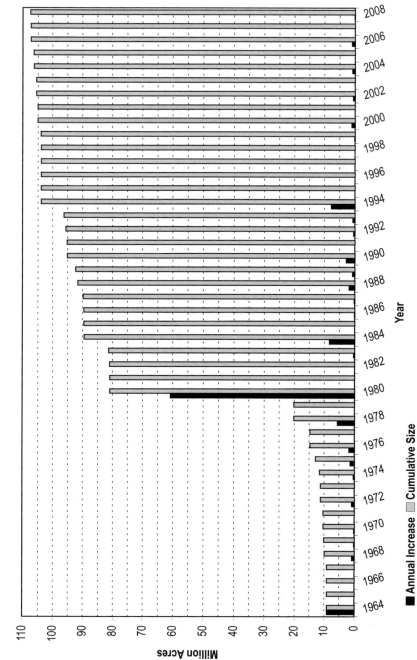

Figure 1: Growth of the National Wilderness Preservation System, 1964–2008

all—in the federal courts. For Republican and Democratic administrations alike, the primary focus has been on roads.

WILDERNESS AND ROADLESSNESS

Nineteenth-century preservation efforts (Chapter 2) were in no significant sense antiroad. The preservation of Yellowstone was motivated by a desire to prevent the curiosities from falling into private hands, and early park promoters encouraged development. In 1872, as the park was being created, *Scribner's* magazine enthusiastically predicted that "Yankee enterprise will dot the new Park with hostelries and furrow it with lines of travel."[14] Railroads were among the earliest promoters and concessionaires in most of the major western parks, and after 1916 the new National Park Service quickly made friends with the automobile. Over the next fifty years, the Park Service constructed scenic highways and catered primarily to automobile tourists. Roads were equally complementary to national forests, where the primary goal was to guarantee a perpetual supply of water and wood products.

The early hospitality to road building—even among preservation proponents—reminds us that the twentieth century impulse for wilderness preservation was not merely a continuation of the forces that had created national parks and national forests in the nineteenth century. A national constituency for "wilderness" preservation arose only after the nation embarked on massive road building triggered by the Federal Aid Road Act of 1916. As noted in Chapter 3, "Foresters favored road building because it improved timber access and fire protection, even though it also provided access to tourists. Park service staff favored road construction precisely because it aided tourist travel" (68).

In contrast to their nineteenth-century predecessors, twentieth-century wilderness champions came to regard roads as the enemy. In Colorado, Arthur Carhart successfully argued to keep the immediate vicinity of Trapper's Lake roadless, and his early proposal of a roadless area in the Superior National Forest of Minnesota was the first step toward preservation of the modern Boundary Waters Canoe Area Wilderness (69-70). In "The Last Stand of the Wilderness" Aldo Leopold wrote, "By 'wild places' I mean . . . big areas wild enough to be free from motor roads, summer cottages, launches, or other manifestations of gasoline."[15]

Paul S. Sutter has recently written an entire book devoted to explaining "how the fight against automobiles launched the modern wilderness movement."[16] Arguments based on single causes inspire some skepticism, but it is beyond dispute that the founders of the Wilderness Society were devoted to roadlessness. In 1946, responding to the heresy that wilderness might be appreciated from an automobile, society co-founder Harvey Broome protested that "roads and wilderness were antithetical," and the very notion that wilderness might be appreciated by automobile "could undermine our entire program and philosophy."[17]

A decade later when Wilderness Society executive director Howard Zahniser sketched out the first draft of what would become the Wilderness Act, prohibition of roads and motor vehicles was a major theme. The Wilderness Act itself remained true to that theme, declaring: "Except as specifically provided in this Act, and subject to existing private rights, there shall be no . . . permanent road within any wilderness area" (Section 4(c)). The areas given immediate statutory protection by the Wilderness Act were in fact roadless, and the vastly larger areas required to be studied for wilderness potential by the Interior Department were candidates for wilderness precisely because they were "roadless" (Section 3(c)).[18] As noted above and for reasons detailed in Chapter 5, the concept of "roadlessness" also became central to thinking about wilderness in the national forests.

It is apparent, then, for reasons both historical and legal, that the modern view of wilderness is inextricably tied to the absence of roads. Roads disqualify an area for wilderness status, so a pro-roads policy serves the purposes of wilderness opponents. By contrast, efforts to preserve roadless areas of public land can be viewed as a form of wilderness protection by proxy.

The politics of wilderness preservation since 1981 has been dominated by two distinct road wars. The first was a bottom-up "roaded areas" initiative aggressively pursued by a handful of western counties and states with initial encouragement from the Reagan administration. It was designed to disqualify areas for wilderness preservation by asserting local authority over historic travel routes. The second was a top-down national forest "roadless areas" initiative promulgated in the final years of the Clinton administration and vigorously resisted by the succeeding Bush administration.

REVISED STATUTE 2477 AND WILDERNESS ROADS

For many, especially in the rural West, wilderness preservation continues to be regarded as the ultimate lockup of resources, a denial of access to the land and of the possibility of economic development. Since 1980, the tool of choice in their war against wilderness has been Revised Statute 2477, one sentence in the Mining Act of 1866 announcing "that right of way for the construction of highways over public lands, not reserved for public uses, is hereby granted."[19] This section was repealed by FLPMA in 1976, with a typical caveat: "Nothing in this Act [FLPMA] . . . shall be construed as terminating any valid . . . right-of-way . . . existing on the date of approval of this Act."[20]

In 1866, of course, very little public land was reserved for any purpose. There were no national parks, no national forests, and no national wildlife refuges. For 110 years, until R.S. 2477 was repealed, people came and went over federal lands. During that same period lands increasingly were reserved for a multitude of purposes. Once lands were reserved, no new R.S. 2477 rights of way could be established, but pre-existing rights of way remained legally valid. This rule was simple enough in principle, but there were two enormous practical complications. First, the law lacked clear definitions. Second, no one was required to keep any records.

How do you determine the existence of a right of way? Some states and counties argued that R.S. 2477 was a general easement: any place where travel has occurred is a highway, and kicking a few rocks or stones aside is construction. Footpaths might be highways for the purposes of R.S. 2477. They argued that mere use may constitute construction and that state courts must decide these matters.[21] In fact, state courts have been very generous in interpreting R.S. 2477 to the benefit of their respective states. In some cases mere words have been construed to be highways. A 1980 opinion by an Interior Department attorney noted that courts in Kansas, South Dakota, and Alaska had concluded that their respective states could perfect R.S. 2477 rights of way along all section lines merely by passing a law saying so—without any construction or any use.[22] Of course, such an interpretation effectively nullifies all the wilderness provisions of the 1980 Alaska lands legislation as well as of the 1976 Federal Lands Policy and Management Act, which had repealed R.S. 2477. Once a R.S. 2477 highway exists, some states and counties asserted virtually unlimited authority to maintain and improve the rights of way.

There was nothing in the federal law explicitly to contradict these claims. R.S. 2477, which is quoted in its entirety above, set no standards. Rights of way were offered, but what constituted acceptance? If a route became well-established, state and local governments might begin to provide maintenance, and a highway number might be assigned. These cases, of course, were never at issue. The potential crisis for wilderness values arose most clearly in the arid lands of the Southwest where off-trail travel is relatively easy on foot, with pack stock, and even by motor vehicle. In desert environments the passage of a single Jeep may leave a trail that is discernible for decades. Does such a Jeep track constitute a highway? Does it establish a right of travel that can be used effectively to prevent the establishment of wilderness areas or to thwart other environmental objectives? These questions remain at the heart of the R.S. 2477 debate.

An Interior Department opinion issued in the final year of the Carter administration had construed state rights under R.S. 2477 narrowly. It concluded that the validity of R.S. 2477 claims was a question of federal law, that "in order for a valid right of way to come into existence, there must have been the actual building of a highway," and that "a highway is a road freely open to everyone."[23] Under such an interpretation, claims would be few. They would be for obvious roads and would be unlikely to provoke any controversy.

During the presidencies of Ronald Reagan and George Bush, policy tilted toward privatization and economic development of public lands. In 1988 a new policy on R.S. 2477 rights by Interior Secretary Donald Hodel encouraged states and counties to be aggressive—many would say excessive—in their claims. Hodel's policy was not broad enough to encompass purely speculative highways, but it set the bar awfully low. Under the Hodel policy a foot trail might qualify as a highway. Clearing vegetation or moving rocks might qualify as construction. Indeed, "the passage of vehicles by users over time may equal actual construction" and "absent evidence to the contrary," R.S. 2477 claims "by an appropriate public body...will be accepted."[24] As long as there was some minimal evidence of construction or travel, claimants would be given the benefit of the doubt.

A number of states and counties took up the invitation, filing thousands of right-of-way claims, many in national parks, wildlife refuges, and wilderness areas.[25] In 1992 Tom Kenworthy of the *Washington Post* reported that in Utah R.S. 2477 is the "best weapon they've ever found against efforts to [preserve] wilderness" and he quoted County Commissioner Dixie K. Thompson saying: "We are going to try to eliminate wilderness in Emery County."[26] Wilderness advocates saw the administration's policy of extreme generosity in approval of rights of way as a conspiracy to eviscerate federal conservation efforts, destroy established wilderness areas, and foreclose new ones.

In 1992 a democratically controlled Congress questioned the Hodel policy, ordering the Interior Department to report on the history of the R.S. 2477 controversy and demanding "sound recommendations for assessing the validity of claims" consistent both with R.S. 2477 and the Federal Land Policy and Management Act, "which mandated policies of retention and efficient management of the public lands."[27] Later that fall Bill Clinton defeated incumbent president George Bush, and it was the more preservation-minded Interior Secretary Bruce Babbitt rather than Secretary Hodel who delivered the report to Congress the following year. The Clinton administration tilted back toward preservation. Babbitt's report to Congress recommended new regulations and declared that the BLM would defer deciding most R.S. 2477 claims until new rules could be established.[28]

Proposed rules published in August 1994 suggested wholesale repudiation of the Hodel policy. They disclaimed rock removal and vegetation clearing as evidence of construction, stating "Construction means...physical modification of land for use by highway traffic."[29] Furthermore, state court judgments would not be regarded as definitive, and even where rights of way were recognized, use might be regulated in service of other land management priorities. It appeared that the Clinton administration was ready to rein in R.S. 2477 claims, but electoral politics was about to produce yet another reversal.

In November Republicans captured majorities in both houses of Congress, improving the legislative prospects for proroad forces. The four Republican senators from Utah and Alaska introduced a Revised Statutes 2477 Rights-of-Way Settlement Act that would have required land managers to act on claims within two years, to file suit in order to deny a right-of-way claim, to have claims determined under state law, and to bear the burden of proof on all legal issues.[30] This radical legislation died in committee,[31] but the new Congress did pass temporary legislation declaring, "no agency of the Federal Government may take any action to prepare, promulgate, or implement any rule or regulation addressing rights-of-way authorized pursuant to section 2477 of the Revised Statutes (43 U.S.C. 932), as such section was in effect before October 21, 1976."[32] Similar language was included in the Interior Department appropriations bill for 1996. Language in the 1997 appropriations bill has been interpreted as a permanent ban:[33] "No final rule or regulation of any agency of the Federal Government pertaining to the recognition, management or validity of a right-of-way pursuant to Revised Statute 2477 (43 U.S.C. 932) shall take effect unless expressly authorized by an Act of Congress subsequent to the date of enactment of this Act."[34]

With administrative rule-making shut down, President Clinton inflamed the controversy by a unilateral display of presidential power. In September 1996, he exercised presidential authority under the Antiquities Act to create a 1.7-million-acre Grand Staircase-Escalante National Monument in south-central Utah. The political establishment in Utah was incensed. In Escalante, Clinton and Babbitt were hanged in effigy.[35] In Salt Lake City, the Utah House ordered an investigation of whether the state could expropriate the Sundance Ranch of Robert Redford, who supported the monument.[36] Back in Washington, the House of Representatives—but not the Senate—passed a measure by Utah Republican James V. Hansen limiting the president's power to create national monuments without congressional approval.[37]

Most significantly, county officials in Utah struck back with what environmentalists viewed as acts of vandalism. County road crews graded sixteen roads on BLM lands without notice or permission. Six of the routes lay within wilderness study areas and nine within the Grand Staircase-Escalante National Monument. The Southern Utah Wilderness Alliance and other environmental groups sued the BLM for failure to enforce federal laws, and the BLM countersued the counties for trespass and damages. Prodded into action, the BLM examined the county right-of-way claims and concluded that fifteen of the sixteen lacked merit.[38] Environmental plaintiffs won a major victory in the district court, which deferred to the agency's findings and found the counties guilty of trespass,[39] but in 2005 the Tenth Circuit Court of Appeals delivered a more nuanced decision that would reshape the R.S. 2477 debate once again.

Meanwhile, back in Washington, the controversy over Grand Staircase-Escalante National Monument did not deter Secretary Babbitt from exploiting the sliver of opportunity regarding R.S. 2477 that Congress had provided in the 1997 appropriations act. In a January 22 memorandum, he acknowledged that no final rule could be adopted without congressional approval. Then he proceeded to revoke the Hodel policy, remind the agencies that his moratorium was still in place, and set out a temporary rule for handling R.S. 2477 claims that put the burden of proof on the claimants.[40] The issue remained stalemated for the remainder of the Clinton presidency.[41]

The controversy heated up again when the 2000 election produced unified Republican control of Senate, House, and presidency for the first time since 1954.[42] The Interior Department was once again less committed to environmental protection and more hospitable to right-of-way claims, but the language Congress had put in place to block the Clinton administration from adopting strict rules now prevented the Bush administration from adopting lenient rules—at least not without some legal dexterity. Suddenly things got very complicated and very secretive. BLM administrative rules were changed to allow states and counties to file quiet title claims in court for rights of way, forcing the federal government to go to court to block them. In 2003 Interior Secretary Gale Norton and Utah Governor Mark Levitt signed a Memorandum of Understanding that allowed the federal government to accede to state right-of-way claims by filing legal disclaimers of interest in the affected property.[43]

These administrative efforts to facilitate state and county claims were effectively superseded by the 2005 decision of the Tenth Circuit Court of Appeals in *SUWA v. BLM*. The court held the burden of proof that a right of way exists rests on the claimant, not on the federal government.[44] Before a right-of-way holder can undertake improvements "beyond mere maintenance," it must notify the federal managing agency, which is obliged to make the "initial determination of whether the construction work falls within the scope of an established right of way."[45] Beyond that, the court declined to defer to agency judgment. It found nothing in the language of R.S. 2477 giving the BLM authority to make binding decisions on the validity of R.S. 2477 rights and ordered the district court to decide for itself whether the counties were guilty of trespass.[46] Since FLPMA presumably protected vested rights as they existed when R.S. 2477 was repealed, the court found all subsequent administrative efforts to interpret those rights lacked legal force, doubly so since administrative decision-making had been permanently barred by the

1997 appropriations act.[47] The court ruled that because "BLM regulations continued to incorporate state law as the standard for recognizing R.S. 2477 rights of way until the repeal of R.S. 2477 in 1976," [48] state law—so far as it does not contradict federal law—remains the standard.

Interior Secretary Gail Norton embraced this relatively state-friendly decision, abolished the temporary regulations adopted under the Clinton administration, and directed Interior agencies to follow the principles established in the court's decision nationwide, "keeping in mind that one of the most important principles is that State law generally must be used to assess R.S. 2477 claims." [49] As a practical matter the rules have been relaxed again. Assuming continuing congressional inability to legislate a solution to the R.S. 2477 issue, whether these rules remain relatively relaxed or are tightened anew may continue to depend on the vagaries of presidential politics.

WILDERNESS BY PROXY: THE ROADLESS AREAS INITIATIVE

As noted above, the Forest Service's second Roadless Area Evaluation and Review (RARE II) failed to settle the issue of which national forest roadless areas ought to be recommended for wilderness. California filed suit to prevent the development of roadless national forest lands, and in 1982 the Ninth Circuit Court of Appeals declared RARE II legally insufficient. The status of many national forest roadless areas was clarified through the legislative process, but a substantial inventory of roadless areas remained undeveloped—potential candidates for development or for future consideration as designated wilderness. During the Reagan and Bush administrations, decision making with respect to these roadless areas proceeded through the traditional, decentralized national forest planning process.

The Clinton administration became concerned that this decentralized process would squander the benefits of national forest roadless areas by increments. In January 1998, Forest Service chief Mike Dombeck proposed suspending most new road construction in roadless areas. The moratorium on road building galvanized the preservation community and generated 119,000 mostly favorable public comments. Public opinion polling confirmed high levels of public support, not merely for the moratorium but for permanent protection of national forest roadless areas.[50] The relationship between roadlessness and wilderness was apparent to all parties. In a July 1998 letter to employees, Dombeck wrote, "Our proposed suspension of road construction in roadless areas will help us develop not only a science-based long-term road policy but one that also reflects the values that society places on wild places, old growth, wilderness, and on intact and unfragmented landscapes."[51]

In 1999 discussions began between the Forest Service and the White House about permanent roadless area protection, and it soon became a presidential priority.[52] On October 13, 1999, President Clinton publicly announced his roadless areas initiative and formally directed Secretary of Agriculture Dan Glickman to develop regulations to provide "appropriate long-term protection for most or all of the currently inventoried 'roadless' areas."[53] The White House clearly saw this as a legacy project and wanted it completed before Clinton left office. To move the process along, the Forest Service structured its environmental impact analysis team under its Incident Command System, originally created for wildfire management.[54] A draft environmental impact statement and proposed regulations were published May 10, 2000, and a final environmental impact statement was issued November 13. The final rules were promulgated January 12, 2001, with an effective date of March 13, 2001.[55]

The final Roadless Area Conservation Rule prohibited most road construction and reconstruction and most timber harvesting on 58.5 million acres of inventoried roadless areas, almost one-third of all national forest lands. According to the Forest Service, the intent was "to provide lasting protection for inventoried roadless areas within the National Forest System in the context of multiple-use management."[56] This protection was justified because, "inventoried roadless areas provide clean drinking water…large, relatively undisturbed landscapes that are important to biological diversity and the long-term survival of many at risk species…[and] opportunities for dispersed outdoor recreation, opportunities that diminish as open space and natural settings are developed elsewhere. They also serve as bulwarks against the spread of non-native invasive plant species and provide reference areas for study and research."[57]

These were not new wilderness areas. Under the Wilderness Act, only Congress can create wilderness areas, but the Forest Service had ample authority under other statutes to place various restrictions on the use of roadless national forest lands. The restrictions imposed here—banning most road building and most timber harvest—were significant steps toward protecting the ecological integrity of the areas in question and preserving the possibility of future inclusion in the National Wilderness Preservation System by Congress.

Eight days later George W. Bush was inaugurated president of the United States. That very day the new administration postponed the effective date of all federal rules not yet in effect. The Clinton rule was allowed to go into effect on May 12, but it was immediately clear that the Bush administration planned to amend or abandon it. On January 8 the Kootenai Tribe of Idaho and various business and recreation groups [58] had filed suit to enjoin enforcement of the Clinton rule on procedural grounds.[59] Despite more than four hundred public meetings and the submission of more than one million written comments, the district court concluded that the public had been deprived of "any meaningful dialogue or input into the process"[60] in violation of the National Environmental Policy Act. The Bush administration declined to defend the Clinton rule in court or to appeal the district court's decision. As a practical matter, the district court's injunction of May 10 provided breathing space for the new administration to fashion an alternative policy.

As with R.S. 2477, the Bush administration operated in unusual secrecy. New policies were implemented beginning May 31, but nothing was published until August. This behavior was particularly ironic considering that a federal court had just found the massive public involvement in preparation of the Clinton rule insufficient. The Congressional Research Service characterized additional directives issued in December as "difficult to interpret"[61] but concluded that they "apparently eliminated the requirement that there be a compelling need for a road and also eliminated requirements for a science-based analysis and a full EIS in all cases."[62]

On December 12, 2002, the U.S. Court of Appeals for the Ninth Circuit reversed the Idaho federal court, finding the Forest Service had complied with NEPA in fashioning the Clinton rule and concluding that the lower court decision "proceeded on an incorrect premise, applied the wrong standard for injunction, and abused its discretion."[63] The Clinton rule had been vindicated by the court, but the Bush administration continued with its somewhat opaque process of modification.

A new roadless area proposal, first published July 16, 2004, provided no protection at all for roadless areas. Instead it described a process to allow state governors to petition for roadless area protection in their respective states. In the meantime, everyone from the chief of the Forest Service to local forest supervisors could authorize road building and timber harvest in roadless areas until forest plans have been completed.[64] As if to reinforce its repudiation of the Clinton rule, six months later new regulations on national forest planning were published in which the terms "roadless area" and "inventoried roadless area" had vanished from the Forest Service vocabulary.[65]

The final Bush roadless rule was issued May 13, 2005. The Forest Service described it as a response to concerns raised by the Clinton rule, although 96 percent of the 1.15 million written comments had supported the Clinton rule, and the vast majority of comments invited by the Bush administration continued to support the Clinton rule.[66] Whereas the Clinton rule had shifted Forest Service policy dramatically toward conservation, the Bush rule tilted dramatically in favor of development, and it did so without any environmental impact analysis. Under the Bush rule there was no national policy of protection for roadless areas. In order for protection to be considered, governors were required to petition within eighteen months, and petitioning was onerous. States were required to provide detailed descriptions and recommendations for roadless areas, not unlike environmental impact analyses. The process appeared time consuming and expensive, and there was no guarantee that the Forest Service would accept the state's recommendation. There were no standards for public participation. A committee was established to review petitions, but there were no standards for reviews or recommendations.[67]

Several governors expressed concern that the process was unnecessarily vague and burdensome. Wyoming Governor Dave Freudenthal, whose state had sued to enjoin the Clinton rule, remarked, "the feds are transferring a kind of political planning responsibility without any of the authority, and frankly without probably some of the information you might need to make the decision."[68] Despite the burdens, a number of governors did submit petitions for roadless area protection. Virginia, North Carolina, South Carolina, New Mexico, and California petitioned for protection of all their roadless areas; Idaho and Colorado sought protection for some. The Forest Service approved the petitions of the three eastern states.[69]

Other states—led by California, Oregon, and New Mexico, and joined by various environmental organizations—filed suit, arguing that the Bush roadless rule violated the environmental impact analysis requirements of the National Environmental Policy Act and the interagency consultation requirements of the Endangered Species Act. A federal court in California agreed, holding that "the Forest Service failed adequately to consider the environmental and species impacts when it issued the State Petitions Rule, in violation of NEPA and ESA."[70] "Even if the revocation of the Roadless Rule's protections did not by itself trigger NEPA," wrote Judge Elizabeth D. Laporte, "the State Petitions Rule did more than merely reinstate the prior regime of management by individual forest plans.... [It] established a new regime in which management of roadless areas within the national forests would, for the first time, vary not just forest by forest but state by state."[71] She characterized Forest Service failure to engage in endangered species consultation as "arbitrary and capricious" and opined that "it would strain credulity to hold that the repeal of the protections in IRAs [inventoried roadless areas] would not have any effect...on the numerous species that make their homes in IRAs."[72] Judge Laporte reinstated the Clinton rule. The Bush administration appealed, and Wyoming went back to court in an unsuccessful attempt to enjoin enforcement of the Roadless Rule once again.[73] The administration continued to review state petitions, but the Clinton rule remained in effect in summer 2007.[74]

As a practical matter, the Bush administration bungled its roadless area policy, devoting six years to the repeal of the Clinton rule only to have it reinstated by a federal court. As of 2007, it had effectively run out of time. Bills have been introduced in Congress to establish the Clinton rule by law, but enactment is

impossible in a polarized political environment. Ultimate resolution of this issue, like that of R.S 2477, will depend upon the decisions of future presidents
or future Congresses, and—if they should fail—on future courts.

CONCLUSION

In politics—as in life—fear of loss is a stronger motivator than hope for
gain. Wilderness politics is tendentious in part because both sides fear losing the resources and opportunities they most cherish. Indeed, both sides
fear the loss of freedom. Environmentalists perceive the steady loss of actual
wilderness and fear for intact ecosystems, for biological diversity, and for the
freedom to pursue "outstanding opportunities for solitude or a primitive and
unconfined type of recreation."[75] Wilderness opponents observe the increase
in legal wilderness and fear losing the freedom to enjoy motorized recreation
or to carry on the traditions of ancestors who conquered a continent and
extracted a living from the land. Both sides are right. The decline in actual
wilderness and the increase in legal wilderness are on a collision course. The
time is not so far distant when the only actual wilderness will be the legally
preserved wilderness. Where that balance is finally struck will depend in significant part on future public policy choices, including decisions about R.S.
2477 and the Roadless Rule.

The history of wilderness preservation in America is a story of gradual policy change reflecting changing economic conditions and evolving public attitudes. As Americans have become wealthy and wilderness has become scarce,
the further sacrifice of wilderness to attain wealth has seemed increasingly
unwise. For more than a century, the impetus for wilderness preservation
has come primarily from urban Americans, and it has been resisted by those
for whom wilderness is still a fact of life. The former group is growing, and
the latter is in decline. If American politics were a simple matter of majority
rule, we would be preserving a lot more wilderness. But American democracy provides ample opportunities for influence by vocal minorities and local
majorities. The checks and balances imposed by the American Constitution
advantage the status quo by making any significant policy change difficult.

Under these political conditions, wilderness preservation is destined to
continue in fits and starts. Periods of progress, like that from 1964 through
1980, require more than mere majority support to succeed. They require
something approaching national consensus. Lacking that consensus, as we
apparently have since 1980, we will experience periods of consolidation or
retrograde movement.

Viewed on a scale of centuries, the clear trend is toward greater environmental damage and greater environmental concern, toward greater wilderness destruction and more aggressive wilderness preservation. Wilderness
was more appreciated in the twentieth century than in the nineteenth, and

it is nearly certain to be more appreciated still in the twenty-first century. Public policy will eventually follow public opinion, but it is an open question whether we will do enough—and soon enough—to preserve an enduring resource of wilderness for the American people.

NOTES

1 George Cameron Coggins, *Public Natural Resources Law* (New York: Clark Boardman Company, 1991), §2.04[1].
2 California v. Berglund, 483 F.Supp. 465 (E.D. Cal. 1980).
3 California v. Block, 690 Fed.2d 753, 768 (9th Cir. 1982).
.4 James A. Browning, John C. Hendee, and Joe W. Roggenbuck, *103 Wilderness Laws: Milestones and Management Direction in Wilderness Legislation, 1964–1987*, Tech. Rep. 51 (Moscow: University of Idaho College of Forestry, Wildlife, and Range Science, 1988), 54–69.
5 "Mohave National Preserve: Administrative History (Chapter 1)," April 5, 2004, Mohave National Preserve, http://www.nps.gov/archive/moja/adminhist/adhi1. htm (accessed July 19, 2007); and "Mohave National Preserve: Administrative History (Chapter 3)," April 5, 2004, Mohave National Preserve, http://www. nps.gov/archive/moja/adminhist/adhi3.htm (accessed July 19, 2007).
6 "Mohave National Preserve: Administrative History (Chapter 3)."
7 In 1990 California Senator Pete Wilson was elected governor. In January 1991 he appointed John Seymour to the Senate seat he had vacated. Frank Wheat, *California Desert Miracle* (San Diego: Sunbelt Publications, 1999), 230.
8 "Mohave National Preserve: Administrative History (Chapter 1)."
9 Wheat, *California Desert Miracle*, 242–43.
10 Ibid., 267–75.
11 "Mohave National Preserve: Administrative History (Chapter 1)."
12 Wheat, *California Desert Miracle*, 293.
13 Wheat, *California Desert Miracle*.
14 "Culture and Progress: The Yellowstone National Park," *Scribner's Monthly* 4, no. 1 (May 1872): 121.
15 Aldo Leopold, "The Last Stand of the Wilderness," *American Forests and Forest Life* 31 (1925): 600–01.
16 Paul S. Sutter, *Driven Wild: How the Fight Against Automobiles Launched the Modern Wilderness Movement* (Seattle: University of Washington Press, 2002).
17 Quoted in Mark W. T. Harvey, *Wilderness Forever: Howard Zahniser and the Path to the Wilderness Act* (Seattle: University of Washington Press, 2005), 59.
18 The Wilderness Act itself required review of roadless areas in national parks and national wildlife refuges. The Federal Land Policy and Management Act extended the requirement of roadless area review to BLM lands.
19 Mining Act of 1866, 14 Stat. 251, 39th Cong. 1st sess., chapter 262 (July 26, 1866), 253.

20 "Federal Land Policy and Management Act of 1976," Pub. L. 94-579, *Statutes at Large* 90 (1976): 2786.

21 Clearly R.S. 2477 is a federal law and within the jurisdiction of federal courts. Nevertheless, most highway claims have been adjudicated in state courts, and the federal agencies have historically been deferential.

22 Frederick N. Ferguson, deputy solicitor, Office of the Solicitor, Department of the Interior, "Standards to Be Applied in Determining Whether Highways Have Been Established Across Public Lands Under the Repealed Statute R.S. 2477 (43 U.S.C. § 932)," April 8, 1980, http://www.highway-robbery.org/documents/Ferguson_Letter_1980.pdf (accessed August 5, 2007).

23 Ibid., 4–5, 8.

24 Department of the Interior, "Departmental Policy on Section 8 of the Act of July 26, 1866, Revised Statute 2477 (Repealed), Grant of Right-of-Way for Public Highways (RS-2477)," December 7, 1988, http://www.rs2477roads.com/2hodel.htm (accessed August 5, 2007).

25 "Highway Robbery," Highway-Robbery.Org, August 7, 2007, http://www.highway-robbery.org/ (accessed August 11, 2007).

26 Tom Kenworthy, "In the West, Rugged Roads Lead to Controversy: Obscure Right-of-Way Law Being Used to Wrest Control Over Federal Wilderness Areas," *Washington Post*, June 21, 1992, Final Edition: A4.

27 U.S. House of Representatives, *Making Appropriations for the Department of the Interior and Related Agencies for the Fiscal Year Ending September 30, 1993, and for Other Purposes*, 102nd Cong., September 24, 1992, H. Rep. 901, 2.

28 Department of the Interior, *Report to Congress on R.S. 2477: The History and Management of R.S. 2477 Right-of-Way Claims on Federal and Other Lands* (1993), 56.

29 Department of the Interior, "Revised Statute 2477 Rights-of-Way," *Federal Register* 59 (August 1, 1994): 39216.

30 Senate Committee on Energy and Natural Resources, *To Recognize the Validity of Rights-of-Way Granted Under Section 2477 of the Revised Statutes, and for Other Purposes*, 104th Cong., May 9, 1996, S. Rep. 261.

31 Technically, the bill was reported by Alaska Senator Frank Murkowski's Energy and Natural Resources Committee, but its original content had been replaced with this more circumspect language: "No final rule or regulation of any agency of the Federal Government pertaining to the recognition, management, or validity of a right-of-way pursuant to Revised Statute 2477 (43 U.S.C. 932) shall take effect unless expressly authorized by an Act of Congress subsequent to the date of enactment of this Act." See Senate Committee on Energy and Natural Resources, *To Recognize the Validity of Rights-of-Way Granted Under Section 2477 of the Revised Statutes, and for Other Purposes*. Although the bill went no further, this language found its way into the 1997 Interior Department appropriations law.

32 "National Highway System Designation Act," Pub. L. 104-59, *Statutes at Large* 109 (November 28, 1995): 617–18.

33 Don Young, "Comptroller General Decision Letter B-277719," *Congressional Record* 143 (September 8, 1997): E1681.

34 "Omnibus Consolidated Appropriations Act," Pub. L. 104-208, *Statutes at Large* 110 (September 30, 1997): 3009–200, §108.

35 James Brooke, "Utah is Warming Up to Newest Monument," *New York Times*, October 13, 1997, Late Edition Final: A12.

36 Peter S. Canellos, "New Utah Preserve Ignites Emotions Anew Over Land Use," *Boston Globe*, March 2, 1997, City Edition, A: 1.

37 Neil A. Lewis, "House Tweaks Clinton Over Creation of National Monuments," *New York Times*, October 8, 1997, Late Edition Final: A16.

38 Southern Utah Wilderness Alliance v. Bureau of Land Management, 425 F.3d 735, 742-3 (10th Cir. 2005).

39 Southern Utah Wilderness Alliance v. Bureau of Land Management, 147 F. Supp. 2nd 1130 (D. Utah 2001).

40 Bruce Babbitt, Secretary of the Interior, *Interim Departmental Policy on Revised Statute 2477 Grant of Right-of-way for Public Highways; Revocation of December 7, 1988, Policy* (Washington, DC: Department of the Interior, 1997).

41 Bret C. Birdsong, "Road Rage and R.S. 2477: Judicial and Administrative Responsibility for Resolving Road Claims on Public Lands," *Hasting Law Journal* 56 (February 2005): 543.

42 The 2001 Senate was evenly divided, giving control to the Republicans by virtue of Vice President Dick Cheney's tie-breaking vote. In June, Republican Senator James Jeffords of Vermont defected, giving control to the Democratic Party. Republican control was reestablished after the 2002 elections. See Senate Historical Office, *Party Division in the Senate, 1789–Present*, 2007, http://www.senate.gov/pagelayout/history/one_item_and_teasers/partydiv.htm (accessed August 6, 2007).

43 Alison Suthers, "A Separate Peace? Utah's R.S. 2477 Memorandum of Understanding, Disclaimers of Interest, and the Future of R.S. 2477 Rights-of-Way in the West," *Journal of Land, Resources, and Environmental Law* 260 (2005): 112.

44 Southern Utah Wilderness Alliance v. Bureau of Land Management (10th Cir.), 768–69.

45 Ibid., 748.

46 Ibid., 757–58.

47 Ibid., 760.

48 Ibid., 765–66.

49 Office of the Secretary, *Departmental Implementation of Southern Utah Wilderness Alliance v. Bureau of Land Management* (Washington, DC: Department of the Interior, 2006), 4.

50 Michael P. Dombeck, Christopher A. Wood, and Jack Edward Williams, *From Conquest to Conservation: Our Public Lands Legacy* (Washington, DC: Island Press, 2003), 106–07.

51 Ibid., 107.

52 Ibid., 108.

53 William J. Clinton, *Presidential Memo on Protection of Forest Roadless Areas*. October 13, 1999, William J. Clinton Foundation, http://www.clintonfoundation.org/legacy/101399-presidential-memo-on-protection-of-forest-roadless-areas.htm (accessed August 15, 2007).

54 Dombeck, Wood, and Williams, *From Conquest to Conservation: Our Public Lands Legacy*, 111.

55 U.S. Forest Service, "Special Areas; Roadless Areas Conservation; Final Rule," *Federal Register* 66 (January 12, 2001): 3244. By law "major" administrative rules cannot become effective for at least sixty days, allowing Congress some opportunity to act legislatively if it should choose to do so (5 U.S.C. §801).

56 U.S. Forest Service, "Special Areas; Roadless Areas Conservation; Final Rule," 3244.

57 Ibid., 3245.

58 The State of Idaho filed a similar suit the following day.

59 Kootenai Tribe of Idaho v. Veneman, 313 F.3d 1094, 1104 (9th Cir. 2002).

60 Ibid., 1120.

61 Pamela Baldwin and Ross Gorte, *The National Forest System Roadless Areas Initiative*, Tech. Rep. RL30647 (Washington, DC: Congressional Research Service, 2006), 16.

62 Baldwin and Gorte, *The National Forest System Roadless Areas Initiative*, 18.

63 Kootenai Tribe of Idaho v. Veneman, 1126. On July 14, 2003, notwithstanding the decision of the Ninth Circuit, a federal district court judge in Wyoming permanently enjoined implementation of the Roadless Rule, citing violations of NEPA and of the Wilderness Act's prohibition of administrative creation of wilderness areas. Judge Clarence A. Brimmer characterized the process as "smelling of political prestidigitation" and designed "to give President Clinton lasting notoriety in the annals of environmentalism." Wyoming v. U.S. Department of Agriculture, 277 F. Supp. 2d 1197, 1232, 1239 (D. Wyo. 2003). The decision was vacated by the Tenth Circuit on July 11, 2005, because new regulations had been published by the Forest Service. Wyoming v. U.S. Department of Agriculture, 414 F. 3d 1207 (10th Cir. 2005).

65 Baldwin and Gorte, *The National Forest System Roadless Areas Initiative*, 24–25.

66 U.S. Forest Service, "National Forest System Land Management Planning," *Federal Register* 70 (January 5, 2005): 1023–61.

67 Baldwin and Gorte, *The National Forest System Roadless Areas Initiative*, 28.

68 U.S. Forest Service, "Special Areas; State Petitions for Inventoried Roadless Area Management; Roadless Area Conservation National Advisory Committee; Final Rule and Notice," *Federal Register* 70 (May 13, 2005): 25653.

69 Martin Nie, "Administrative Rulemaking and Public Lands Conflict: The Forest Service's Roadless Rule," *Natural Resources Journal* 44 (2004): 711, n.149.

70 Ross W. Gorte, Carol Hardy Vincent, Marc Humphries, and Kristina Alexander, *Federal Lands Managed by the Bureau of Land Management (BLM) and the Forest Service (FS): Issues for the 110th Congress*, Tech. Rep. RL33792 (Washington, DC: Congressional Research Service, 2007), 7-8.

71 California ex rel. Lockyer v. USDA, 459 F. Supp. 2d 874, 883 (N.D. Cal. 2006).

72 Ibid., 899.

73 Ibid., 911.

74 Ben Neary, "Judge Denies Wyoming's Request to Block Roadless Rule," *San Diego Union-Tribune*, June 8, 2007, http://www.signonsandiego.com/news/nation/20070608-1140-wst-roadlessrule.html (accessed July 6, 2007).

75 Gorte et al., *Federal Lands Managed by the Bureau of Land Management (BLM) and the Forest Service (FS): Issues for the 110th Congress*, 8.

76 "Wilderness Act," Pub. L. 88-577, *Statutes at Large* 78 (1964): 891, §2(c).

THE 1964 WILDERNESS ACT

APPENDIX **A**

Public Law 88-577

AN ACT

To establish a National Wilderness Preservation System for the permanent good of the whole people, and for other purposes.

Be it enacted by the Senate and House of Representatives of the United States of America in Congress assembled,

SHORT TITLE

Section 1. This act may be cited as the "Wilderness Act."

WILDERNESS SYSTEM ESTABLISHED STATEMENT OF POLICY

Sec. 2. (a) In order to assure that an increasing population, accompanied by expanding settlement and growing mechanization, does not occupy and modify all areas within the United States and its possessions, leaving no lands designated for preservation and protection in their natural condition, it is hereby declared to be the policy of the Congress to secure for the American people of present and future generations the benefits of an enduring resource of wilderness. For this purpose there is hereby established a National Wilderness Preservation System to be composed of federally owned areas designated by Congress as "wilderness areas," and these shall be administered for the use and enjoyment of the American people in such manner as will leave them unimpaired for future use and enjoyment as wilderness, and so as to provide for the protection of these areas, the preservation of their wilderness character, and for the gathering and dissemination of information regarding their use and enjoyment as wilderness; and no Federal lands shall be designated as "wilderness areas" except as provided for in this Act or by a subsequent Act.

(b) The inclusion of an area in the National Wilderness Preservation System notwithstanding, the area shall continue to be managed by the Department and agency having jurisdiciton thereover immediately before its inclusion in the National Wilderness Preservation System unless otherwise provided by Act of Congress. No appropriation shall be available for the payment of expenses or salaries for the administration of the National Wilderness Preservation System as a separate unit nor shall any appropriations be available for additional personnel stated as being required solely for the purpose of managing or administering areas solely because they are included within the National Wilderness Preservation System.

DEFINITION OF WILDERNESS

(c) A wilderness, in contrast with those areas where man and his own works dominate the landscape, is hereby recognized as an area where the earth and its community of life are untrammeled by man, where man himself is a visitor who does not remain. An area of wilderness is further defined to mean in this Act an area of undeveloped Federal land retaining its primeval character and influence, without permanent improvements or human habitation, which is protected and managed so as to preserve its natural conditions and which (1) generally appears to have been affected primarily by the forces of nature, with the imprint of man's work substantially unnoticeable; (2) has outstanding opportunities for solitude or a primitive and unconfined type of recreation; (3) has at least five thousand acres of land or is of sufficient size as to make practicable its preservation and use in an unimpaired condition; and (4) may also contain ecological, geological, or other features of scientific, educational, scenic, or historical value.

NATIONAL WILDERNESS PRESERVATION SYSTEM— EXTENT OF SYSTEM

Sec. 3. (a) All areas within the national forests classified at least 30 days before the effective date of this Act by the Secretary of Agriculture or the Chief of the Forest Service as "wilderness," "wild," or "canoe" are hereby designated as wilderness areas. The Secretary of Agriculture shall—

(1) Within one year after the effective date of this Act, file a map and a legal description of each wilderness area with the Interior and Insular Affairs Committees of the United States Senate and the House of Representatives, and such descriptions shall have the same force and effect as if included in this Act: *Provided, however,* That correction of clerical and typographical errors in such legal descriptions and maps may be made.

(2) Maintain, available to the public, records pertaining to said wilderness areas, including maps and legal descriptions, copies of regulations governing them, copies of public notices of, and reports submitted to Congress regarding pending additions, eliminations, or modifications. Maps, legal descriptions, and regulations pertaining to wilderness areas within their respective jurisdictions also shall be available to the public in the offices of regional foresters, national forest supervisors, and forest rangers.

(b) The Secretary of Agriculture shall, within ten years after the enactment of this Act, review, as to its suitability or nonsuitability for preservation as wilderness, each area in the national forests classified on the effective date of this Act by the Secretary of Agriculture or the Chief of the Forest Service as "primitive" and report his findings to the President. The President shall advise the United States Senate and House of Representatives of his recommendations with respect to the designation as "wilderness" or other reclassification of each area on which review has been completed, together with maps and a definition of Boundaries. Such advice shall be given with respect to not less than one-third of all the areas now classified as "primitive" within three years after enactment of this Act, not less than two-thirds within seven years after the enactment of this Act, and the remaining areas within ten years after the enactment of this Act. Each recommendation of the President for designation as "wilderness" shall become effective only if so provided by an Act of Congress. Areas classified as "primitive" on the effective date of this Act shall continue to be administered under the rules and regulations affecting such areas on the effective date of this Act until Congress has determined otherwise. Any such area may be increased in size by the President at the time he submits his recommendations to the Congress by not more than five thousand acres with not more than one thousand two hundred and eighty acres of such increase in any one compact unit; if it is proposed to increase the size of such an area by more than five thousand acres or by more than one thousand two hundred and eighty acres in any one compact unit the increase in size shall not become effective until acted upon by Congress. Nothing herein contained shall limit the President in proposing, as part of his recommendations to Congress, the alteration of existing boundaries of primitive areas or recommending the addition of any contiguous area of national forest lands predominantly of wilderness value. Notwithstanding any other provisions of this Act, the Secretary of Agriculture may complete his review and delete such area as may be necessary, but not to exceed seven thousand acres, from the southern tip of the Gore Range-Eagles Nest Primitive Area, Colorado, if the Secretary determines that such action is in the public interest.

(c) Within ten years after the effective date of this Act the Secretary of the Interior shall review every roadless area of five thousand contiguous acres or more in the national parks, monuments and other units of the national park system and every such area of, and every roadless island within, the national wildlife refuges and game ranges, under his jurisdiction on the effective date of this Act and shall report to the President his recommendation as to the suitability or nonsuitability of each such area or island for preservation as wilderness. The President shall advise the President of the Senate and the Speaker of the House of Representatives of his recommendation with respect to the designation as wilderness of each such area or island on which review has been completed, together with a map thereof and a definition of its boundaries. Such advice shall be given with respect to not less than one-third of the areas and islands to be reviewed under this subsection within three years after enactment of this Act, not less than two-thirds within seven years of enactment of this Act, and the remainder within ten years of enactment of this Act. A recommendation of the President for designation as wilderness shall become effective only if so provided by an Act of Congress. Nothing contained herein shall, by implication or otherwise, be construed to lessen the present statutory authority of the Secretary of the Interior with respect to the maintenance of roadless areas within units of the national park system.

(d) (1) The Secretary of Agriculture and the Secretary of the Interior shall, prior to submitting any recommendations to the President with respect to the suitability of any area for preservation as wilderness—

(A) give such public notice of the proposed action as they deem appropriate, including publication in the Federal Register and in a newspaper having general circulation in the area or areas in the vicinity of the affected lands;

(B) hold a public hearing or hearings at a location or locations convenient to the area affected. The hearings shall be announced through such means as the respective Secretaries involved deem appropriate, including notices in the Federal Register and in newspapers of general circulation in the area: *Provided*, That if the lands involved are located in more than one State, at least one hearing shall be held in each State in which a portion of the land lies;

(C) at least thirty days before the date of a hearing advise the Governor of each State and the governing board of each county, or in Alaska the borough, in which the lands are located, and Federal departments and agencies concerned, and invite such officials and Federal agencies to submit their views on the proposed action at the hearing or by no later than thirty days following the date of the hearing.

(e) Any modification or adjustment of boundaries of any wilderness area shall be recommended by the appropriate Secretary after public notice of such proposal and public hearing or hearings as provided in subsection (d) of this section. The proposed modification or adjustment shall then be recommended with map and description thereof to the President. The President shall advise the United States Senate and the House of Representatives of his recommendations with respect to such modification or adjustment and such recommendations shall become effective only in the same manner as provided for in subsections (b) and (c) of this section.

USE OF WILDERNESS AREAS

Sec.4. (a) The purposes of this Act are hereby to be within and supplemental to the purposes for which national forests and units of the national park and national wildlife refuge systems are established and administered and—

(1) Nothing in this Act shall be deemed to be in interference with the purpose for which national forests are established as set forth in the Act of June 4, 1897 (30 Stat. 11), and the Multiple-Use Sustained-Yield Act of June 12, 1960 (74 Stat. 215).

(2) Nothing in this Act shall modify the restrictions and provisions of the Shipstead-Nolan Act (Public Law 539, Seventy-first Congress, July 10, 1930; 46 Stat. 1020), the Thye-Blatnik Act (Public Law 733, Eightieth Congress, June 22, 1948; 62 Stat. 568), and the Humphrey-Thye-Blatnik-Andersen Act (Public Law 607, Eighty-fourth Congress, June 22, 1956; 70 Stat. 326), as applying to the Superior National Forest or the regulations of the Secretary of Agriculture.

(3) Nothing in this Act shall modify the statutory authority under which units of the national park system are created. Further, the designation of any area of any park, monument, or other unit of the national park system as a wilderness area pursuant to this Act shall in no manner lower the standards evolved for the use and preservation of such park, monument, or other unit of the national park system in accordance with the Act of August 25, 1916, the statutory authority under which the area was created, or any other Act of Congress which might pertain to or affect such area, including, but not limited to, the Act of June 8, 1906 (34 Stat. 225; 16 U.S.C. 432 et seq.); section 3(2) of the Federal Power Act (16 U.S.C. 796 (2)); and the Act of August 21, 1935 (49 Stat. 666; 16 U.S.C. 461 et seq.).

(b) Except as otherwise provided in this Act, each agency administering any area designated as wilderness shall be responsible for preserving the wilderness character of the area and shall so administer such area for such other purposes for which it may have been established as also to preserve its wilderness character. Except as otherwise provided in this Act, wilderness areas shall be devoted to the public purposes of recreational, scenic, scientific, educational, conservation, and historical use.

PROHIBITION OF CERTAIN USES

(c) Except as specifically provided for in this Act, and subject to existing private rights, there shall be no commercial enterprise and no permanent road within any wilderness area designated by this Act and, except as necessary to meet minimum requirements for the administration of the area for the purpose of this Act (including measures required in emergencies involving the health and safety of persons within the area), there shall be no temporary road, no use of motor vehicles, motorized equipment or motorboats, no landing of aircraft, no other form of mechanical transport, and no structure or installation within any such area.

SPECIAL PROVISIONS

(d) The following special provisions are hereby made:

(1) Within wilderness areas designated by this Act the use of aircraft or motorboats, where these uses have already become established, may be permitted to continue subject to such restrictions as the Secretary of Agriculture deems desirable. In addition, such measures may be taken as may be necessary in the control of fire, insects, and diseases, subject to such conditions as the Secretary deems desirable.

(2) Nothing in this Act shall prevent within national forest wilderness areas any activity, including prospecting, for the purpose of gathering information about mineral or other resources, if such activity is carried on in a manner compatible with the preservation of the wilderness environment. Furthermore, in accordance with such program as the Secretary of the Interior shall develop and conduct in consultation with the Secretary of Agriculture, such areas shall be surveyed on a planned, recurring basis consistent with the concept of wilderness preservation by the Geological Survey and the Bureau of Mines to determine the mineral values, if any, that may be present; and the results of such surveys shall be made available to the public and submitted to the President and Congress.

(3) Notwithstanding any other provisions of this Act, until midnight December 31, 1983, the United States mining laws and all laws pertaining to mineral leasing shall, to the same extent as applicable prior to the effective date of this Act, extend to those national forest lands designated by this Act as "wilderness areas"; subject, however, to such reasonable regulations governing ingress and egress as may be prescribed by the Secretary of Agriculture consistent with the use of the land for mineral location and development and exploration, drilling, and production, and use of land for transmission lines, waterlines, telephone lines, or facilities necessary in exploring, drilling, producing, mining, and processing operations, including where essential the use of mechanized ground or air equipment and restoration as

near as practicable of the surface of the land disturbed in performing prospecting, location, and, in oil and gas leasing, discovery work, exploration, drilling and production, as soon as they have served their purpose. Mining locations lying within the boundaries of said wilderness areas shall be held and used solely for mining or processing operations and uses reasonably incident thereto; and hereafter, subject to valid existing rights, all patents issued under the mining laws of the United States affecting national forest lands designated by this Act as wilderness areas shall convey title to the mineral deposits within the claim, together with the right to cut and use so much of the mature timber therefrom as may be needed in the extraction, removal, and beneficiation of the mineral deposits, if needed timber is not otherwise reasonably available, and if the timber is cut under sound principles of forest management as defined by the national forest rules and regulations, but each such patent shall reserve to the United States all title in or to the surface of the claim or the resources therefrom not reasonably required for carrying on mining or prospecting shall be allowed except as otherwise expressly provided in this Act: *Provided,* That unless hereafter specifically authorized, no patent within wilderness areas designated by this Act shall issue after December 31, 1983, except for the valid claims existing on or before December 31, 1983. Mining claims located after the effective date of this Act within the boundaries of wilderness areas designated by this Act shall create no rights in excess of those rights which may be patented under the provisions of this subsection. Mineral leases, permits and licenses covering lands within national forest wilderness areas designated by this Act shall contain such reasonable stipulations as may be prescribed by the Secretary of Agriculture for the protection of the wilderness character of the land consistent with the use of the land for the purposes for which they are leased, permitted, or licensed. Subject to valid rights then existing, effective January 1, 1984, the minerals in lands designated by this Act as wilderness areas are withdrawn from all forms of appropriation under the mining laws and from disposition under all laws pertaining to mineral leasing and all amendments thereto.

(4) Within wilderness areas in the national forests designated by this Act, (1) the President may, within a specific area and in accordance with such regulations as he may deem desirable, authorize prospecting for water resources, the establishment and maintenance of reservoirs, water-conservation works, power projects, transmission lines, and other facilities needed in the public interest, including the road construction and maintenance essential to development and use thereof, upon his determination that such use or uses in the specific area will better serve the interests of the United States and the people thereof than will its denial; and (2) the grazing of livestock, where established prior to the effective date of this Act, shall be permitted to continue subject to such reasonable regulations as are deemed necessary by the Secretary of Agriculture.

(5) Other provisions of this Act to the contrary notwithstanding, the management of the Boundary Waters Canoe Area, formerly designated as the Superior, Little Indian Sioux, and Caribou Roadless Areas, in the Superior National Forest, Minnesota, shall be in accordance with regulations established by the Secretary of Agriculture in accordance with the general purpose of maintaining, without unnecessary restrictions on other uses, including that of timber, the primitive character

of the area, particularly in the vicinity of lakes, streams, and portages: *Provided,* That nothing in this Act shall preclude the continuance within the area of any already established use of motorboats.

(6) Commercial services may be performed within the wilderness areas designated by this Act to the extent necessary for activities which are proper for realizing the recreational or other wilderness purposes of the areas.

(7) Nothing in this Act shall constitute an express or implied claim or denial on the part of the Federal Government as to exemption from State water laws.

(8) Nothing in this Act shall be construed as affecting the jurisdiction or responsibilities of the several States with respect to wildlife and fish in the national forests.

STATE AND PRIVATE LANDS WITHIN WILDERNESS AREAS

Sec.5. (a) In any case where State-owned or privately owned land is completely surrounded by national forest lands within areas designated by this Act as wilderness, such State or private owner shall be given such rights as may be necessary to assure adequate access to such State-owned or privately owned land by such state or private owner and their successors in interest, or the State-owned land or privately owned land shall be exchanged for federally owned land in the same State of approximately equal value under authorities available to the Secretary of Agriculture: *Provided, however,* That the United States shall not transfer to a State or private owner any mineral interests unless the State or private owner relinquishes or causes to be relinquished to the United States the mineral interest in the surrounded land.

(b) In any case where valid mining claims or other valid occupancies are wholly within a designated national forest wilderness area, the Secretary of Agriculture shall, by reasonable regulations consistent with the preservaton of the area as wilderness, permit ingress and egress to such surrounded areas by means which have been or are being customarily enjoyed with respect to other such areas similarly situated.

(c) Subject to the appropriation of funds by Congress, the Secretary of Agriculture is authorized to acquire privately owned land within the perimeter of any area designated by this Act as wilderness if (1) the owner concurs in such acquisition or (2) the acquisition is specifically authorized by Congress.

GIFTS, BEQUESTS, AND CONTRIBUTIONS

Sec. 6. (a) The Secretary of Agriculture may accept gifts or bequests of land within wilderness areas designated by this Act for preservation as wilderness. The Secretary of Agriculture may also accept gifts or bequests of land adjacent to wilderness areas designated by this Act for preservation as wilderness if he has given sixty days advance notice thereof to the President of the Senate and the Speaker of the House of Representatives. Land accepted by the Secretary of Agriculture under this section shall become part of the wilderness area involved. Regulations with regard to any such land may be in accordance with such agreements, consistent with the policy, as may be included in, and accepted with, such bequest.

(b) The Secretary of Agriculture or the Secretary of the Interior is authorized to accept private contributions and gifts to be used to further the purposes of this Act.

ANNUAL REPORTS

Sec.7. At the opening of each session of Congress, the Secretaries of Agriculture and Interior shall jointly report to the President for transmission to Congress on the status of the wilderness system, including a list and descriptions of the areas in the system, regulations in effect, and other pertinent information, together with any recommendations they may care to make.

Approved September 3, 1964.

THE ALASKA NATIVE CLAIMS SETTLEMENT ACT OF 1971, SECTION 17(d)

Public Law 92-203

(d) (1) Public Land Order Numbered 4582, 34 Federal Register 1025, as amended, is hereby revoked. For a period of ninety days after the date of enactment of this Act all unreserved public lands in Alaska are hereby withdrawn from all forms of appropriation under the public land laws, including the mining (except locations for metalliferous minerals) and the mineral leasing laws. During this period of time the Secretary shall review the public lands in Alaska and determine whether any portion of these lands should be withdrawn under authority provided for in existing law to insure that the public interest in these lands is properly protected. Any further withdrawal shall require an affirmative act by the Secretary under his existing authority, and the Secretary is authorized to classify or reclassify any lands so withdrawn and to open such lands to appropriation under the public land laws in accord with his classifications. Withdrawals pursuant to this paragraph shall not affect the authority of the Village Corporations, the Regional Corporations, and the State to make selections and obtain patents within the areas withdrawn pursuant to section 11.

(2) (A) The Secretary, acting under authority provided for in existing law, is directed to withdraw from all forms of appropriation under the public land laws, including the mining and mineral leasing laws, and from selection under the Alaska Statehood Act, and from selection by Regional Corporations pursuant to section 11, up to, but not to exceed, eighty million acres of unreserved public lands in the State of Alaska, including previously classified lands, which the Secretary deems are suitable for addition to or creation as units of the National Park, Forest, Wildlife Refuge, and Wild and Scenic Rivers Systems: *Provided,* That such withdrawals shall not affect the authority of the State and the Regional and Village Corporations to make selections and obtain patents within the areas withdrawn pursuant to section 11.

(B) Lands withdrawn pursuant to paragraph (A) hereof must be withdrawn within nine months of the date of enactment of this Act. All unreserved public lands not withdrawn under paragraph(A) or subsection 17(d) (1) shall be available for selection by the State and for appropriation under the public land laws.

(C) Every six months, for a period of two years from the date of enactment of this Act, the Secretary shall advise the Congress of the location, size and values of lands withdrawn pursuant to paragraph (A) and submit his recommendations with respect to such lands. Any lands withdrawn pursuant to paragraph (A) not recommended for addition to or creation as units of the National Park, Forest, Wildlife Refuge, and Wild and Scenic Rivers Systems at the end of the two years shall be available for selection by the State and the Regional Corporations, and for appropriation under the public land laws.

(D) Areas recommended by the Secretary pursuant to paragraph (C) shall remain withdrawn from any appropriation under the public land laws until such time as the Congress acts on the Secretary's recommendations, but not to exceed five years from the recommendation dates. The withdrawal of areas not so recommended shall terminate at the end of the two year period.

(E) Notwithstanding any other provision of this subsection, initial identification of lands desired to be selected by the State pursuant to the Alaska Statehood Act and by the Regional Corporations pursuant to section 12 of this Act may be made within any area withdrawn pursuant to this subsection (d), but such lands shall not be tentatively approved or patented so long as the withdrawals of such areas remain in effect: *Provided*, That selection of lands by Village corporations pursuant to section 12 of this Act shall not be affected by such withdrawals and such lands selected may be patented and such rights granted as authorized by this Act. In the event Congress enacts legislation setting aside any areas withdrawn under the provisions of this subsection which the Regional Corporations or the State desired to select, then other unreserved public lands shall be made available for alternative selection by the Regional Corporations and the State. Any time periods established by law for Regional Corporations or State selections are hereby extended to the extent that delays are caused by compliance with the provisions of this subsection (2).

(3) Any lands withdrawn under this section shall be subject to administration by the Secretary under applicable laws and regulations, and his authority to make contracts and to grant leases, permits, rights-of-way, or easements shall not be impaired by the withdrawal.

BIBLIOGRAPHY

The federal government produces an enormous documentary record as it goes about the business of policymaking. Following this paper trail has provided me most of the information for this study. Where the documentary record is less extensive, as it is for the earlier chapters, I have made relatively greater use of the newspapers and magazines of the era as well as the few relevant books about it. In preparing the later chapters, the evidence of the documentary record has been supplemented by interviews with participants in the policy process. Evidence of specific indebtedness is to be found in the acknowledgments, text, and notes of the various chapters. What follows is a selected bibliography of books that address wilderness issues, public lands policy, or the lives and times of individuals influential therein. Interested readers should also refer to the major conservation magazines, especially *American Forests, Audubon, Living Wilderness,* and the *Sierra Club Bulletin.*

Andrews, Russell P. *Wilderness Sanctuary.* Indianapolis: Bobbs-Merrill Co., 1953.

Ashworth, William. *Hell's Canyon.* New York: Hawthorn Books, 1977.

Baldwin, Donald N. *The Quiet Revolution.* Boulder, Colo.: Pruett Publishing Co., 1972.

Bowles, Samuel. *Across the Continent.* Springfield, Mass.: Samuel Bowles and Co., 1865.

Brooks, Paul. *The Pursuit of Wilderness.* Boston: Houghton Mifflin Co., 1971.

Brower, David, ed. *Wilderness: America's Living Heritage.* San Francisco: Sierra Club Books, 1961.

Brown, Tom. *Oil on Ice: Alaska Wilderness at the Crossroads.* San Francisco: Sierra Club Books, 1971

Bunnell, Lafayette H. *Discovery of the Yosemite.* Los Angeles: Gerlicher, 1911.

Burroughs, John, et al. *Harriman Alaska Expedition,* Volumes 1 and 2. 12 vols. New York: Doubleday Page Co., 1904.

Cameron, Jenks. *The Development of Governmental Forest Control in the U.S.* Baltimore: Johns Hopkins Press, 1928.

_____. *The National Park Service.* New York: D. Appleton and Co., 1922.

Catlin, George. *North American Indians.* 2 vols. Philadelphia: Leary, Stuart and Co., 1913.

Cavanaugh, Cam. *Saving the Great Swamp.* Frenchtown, N.J.: Columbia Publishing Co., 1978.

Chittenden, Hiram. *The Yellowstone National Park*. Cincinnati, Ohio: Robert Clarke Co., 1895.

_____. *The Yellowstone National Park*, 5th ed. Stanford: Stanford University Press, 1940.

Clawson, Marion. *The Federal Lands Since 1956*. Washington, D.C.: Resources for the Future, 1967.

_____. *The Land System of the United States*. Lincoln, Neb.: University of Nebraska Press, 1968.

_____, and Held, Bernell R. *The Federal Lands: Their Use and Management*. Baltimore: Johns Hopkins Press, 1951.

_____; Held, Bernell R.; and Stoddard, Charles H. *Land for the Future*. Baltimore: Johns Hopkins Press, 1960.

Clepper, Henry, ed. *Origins of American Conservation*. New York: Ronald Press Co., 1966.

Cooley, Richard A., and Wandesford-Smith, Geoffrey. *Congress and the Environment*. Seattle: University of Washington Press, 1970.

Council on Environmental Quality. *The Evolution of National Wildlife Law*. Washington, D.C.: Government Printing Office, 1977.

Coyle, David Cushman. *Conservation*. New Brunswick, N.J.: Rutgers University Press, 1957.

Cramton, Louis C. *Early History of Yellowstone National Park and Its Relation to National Park Policies*. Washington, D.C.: Government Printing Office, 1932.

Dana, Samuel Trask. *Forest and Range Policy*. New York: McGraw-Hill Book Co., 1956.

Dasmann, Ramond F. *No Further Retreat: The Fight to Save Florida*. New York: Macmillan Co., 1971.

Douglas, William O. *A Wilderness Bill of Rights*. Boston: Little, Brown, and Co., 1965.

Evans, Estwick. *A Pedestrious Tour of Four Thousand Miles*. Concord, N.H.: Joseph C. Spear, 1819.

Everhart, William C. *The National Park Service*. New York: Praeger Publishers, 1972.

Fenno, Richard F., Jr. *Congressmen in Committees*. Boston: Little, Brown and Co., 1973.

Foss, Phillip. *Politics and Grass: The Administration of Grazing on the Public Domain*. Seattle: University of Washington Press, 1960.

Frank, Bernard. *Our National Forests*. Norman, Okla.: University of Oklahoma Press, 1955.

Frome, Michael. *Battle for the Wilderness*. New York: Praeger Publishers, 1974.

_____. *The National Forests of America*. Waukesha, Wis.: Country Beautiful Corporation, 1968.

Gates, Paul W. *History of Public Land Law Development*. Washington, D.C.: Government Printing Office, 1968.

Gillette, Elizabeth R., ed. *Action for Wilderness*. San Francisco: Sierra Club Books, 1972.

Gilligan, James P. *The Development of Policy and Administration of Forest Service Primitive and Wilderness Areas in the Western United States*, 2 vols. Ph.D. diss., University of Michigan, 1954.

Greeley, William B. *Forests and Men*. Garden City, N.Y.: Doubleday and Co., 1951.

———. *Forest Policy*. New York: McGraw-Hill Book Co., 1953.

Gulick, Luther H. *American Forest Policy*. New York: Institute for Public Administration, 1951.

Hays, Samuel P. *Conservation and the Gospel of Efficiency*. Cambridge, Mass.: Harvard University Press, 1959.

Hendee, John C.; Stankey, George H.; and Lucas, Robert C. *Wilderness Management*. U.S. Forest Service: Miscellaneous Publication No. 1365, 1978.

Hibbard, Benjamin H. *History of the Public Land Policies*. New York: Macmillan Co., 1924.

Huth, Hans. *Nature and the American*. Berkeley: University of California Press, 1957.

Ise, John. *Our National Park Policy: A Critical History*. Baltimore: Johns Hopkins Press, 1961.

———. *United States Forest Policy*. New Haven: Yale University Press, 1920.

Johnson, Robert Underwood. *Remembered Yesterdays*. Boston: Little, Brown, and Co., 1923.

Jones, Holoway R. *John Muir and the Sierra Club*. San Francisco: Sierra Club Books, 1965.

Kaufman, Herbert. *The Forest Ranger*. Washington, D.C.: Resources for the Future, 1960.

Langford, Nathaniel Pitt. *The Discovery of Yellowstone Park, 1870, or Diary of the Washburn Expedition to the Yellowstone and Firehole Rivers in the Year 1870*. N. P. Langford, 1905.

———. *The Discovery of Yellowstone Park, 1870*, 2d ed. St. Paul, Minn.: J. E. Haynes, 1923.

Leopold, Aldo. *A Sand County Almanac*. New York: Oxford University Press, 1949.

Leydet, Francois. *The Last Redwoods*. San Francisco: Sierra Club Books, 1969.

Lund, Thomas A. *American Wildlife Law*. Berkeley, Calif.: University of California Press, 1980.

McCloskey, Maxine E., and Gilligan, James P., eds. *Wilderness and the Quality of Life*. San Francisco: Sierra Club Books, 1969.

McConnell, Grant. *The Decline of Agrarian Democracy*. Berkeley: University of California Press, 1953.

———. *Private Power and American Democracy*. New York: Alfred A. Knopf, 1966.

McGeary, M. Nelson. *Gifford Pinchot*. Princeton: Princeton University Press, 1960.

Maass, Arthur. *Muddy Waters: The Army Engineeers and the Nation's Rivers*. Cambridge: Harvard University Press, 1950.

Marsh, George P. *Man and Nature: or, Physical Geography as Modified by Human Action*. New York: Charles Scribner, 1864.

Marshall, Robert. *Alaska Wilderness, Exploring the Central Brooks Range*, 2d ed.

Berkeley: University of California Press, 1970.

Mason, Alpheus T. *Bureaucracy Convicts Itself: The Ballinger-Pinchot Controversy of 1910*. New York: The Viking Press, 1941.

Miller, Mike, and Wayburn, Peggy. *Alaska: The Great Land*. San Francisco: Sierra Club Books, 1974.

Muir, John. *The Yosemite*. New York: The Century Co., 1912.

Nash, Roderick. *Wilderness and the American Mind*. New Haven: Yale University Press, 1967.

————. *Wilderness and the American Mind*, rev. ed. New Haven: Yale University Press, 1973.

National Parks and Conservation Association. *Preserving Wilderness in Our National Parks*. Washington, D.C.: 1971.

Nature Conservancy. *Preserving Our Natural Heritage*, Volume 1. 2 vols. Washington, D.C.: Government Printing Office, 1976.

Nixon, Edgar B., ed. *Franklin D. Roosevelt and Conservation 1911-1945*. 2 vols. Hyde Park, N.Y.: Franklin D. Roosevelt Library, 1957.

Olson, Sigurd F. *The Singing Wilderness*. New York: Alfred A. Knopf, 1956.

Outdoor Recreation Resources Review Commission. *Study Report 3: Wilderness and Recreation—A Report on Resources, Values, and Problems*. Washington, D.C.: Government Printing Office, 1962.

Peffer, E. Louise. *The Closing of the Public Domain*. Stanford, Calif.: Stanford University Press, 1951.

Penick, James, Jr. *Progressive Politics and Conservation*. Chicago: University of Chicago Press, 1968.

Pinchot, Gifford. *Breaking New Ground*. New York: Harcourt, Brace, and Co., 1947.

Potter, David N. *People of Plenty*. Chicago: University of Chicago Press, 1954.

Public Land Law Review Commission. *One Third of the Nation's Land*. Washington, D.C.: Government Printing Office, 1970.

Puter, S. A. D. *Looters of the Public Domain*. Portland, Ore.: Portland Printing House, 1908.

Richardson, Elmo R. *The Politics of Conservation*. Berkeley: University of California Press, 1962.

Robbins, Roy M. *Our Landed Heritage: The Public Domain 1776-1936*. Princeton, N.J.: Princeton University Press, 1942.

Robinson, Glen O. *The Forest Service*. Baltimore: Johns Hopkins University Press, 1975.

Roueche, Berton. *What's Left—Reports on a Diminishing America*. Boston: Little, Brown and Co., 1968.

Russell, Carl P. *One Hundred Years in Yosemite*. Berkeley: University of California Press, 1947.

Sargent, Shirley. *Galen Clark: Yosemite Guardian*. San Francisco: Sierra Club Books, 1964.

Schwartz, William, ed. *Voices for the Wilderness*. New York: Ballantine Books, 1970.

Searle, R. Newell. *Saving the Quetico-Superior: A Land Set Apart*. St. Paul, Minn.: Minnesota Historical Society Press, 1977.

Selznick, Philip. *TVA and the Grass Roots: A Study in the Sociology of Formal Organization*. New York: Harper and Row, 1966.

Shankland, Robert. *Steve Mather of the National Parks*. New York: Alfred A. Knopf, 1951.

Shepard, Jack. *The Forest Killers—The Destruction of the American Wilderness*. New York: Weybright & Talley, 1975.

Sierra Club, North Star Chapter. *A Wilderness in Crisis—Boundary Waters Canoe Area*. Minneapolis: Sierra Club, 1970.

Smith, Frank Ellis. *The Politics of Conservation*. New York: Pantheon Books, 1966.

Stephenson, George M. *The Political History of the Public Lands from 1840 to 1862*. New York: Russell and Russell, 1967.

Stratton, Owen, and Sirotkin, Phillip. *The Echo Park Controversy*. Interuniversity Case Program #46. Indianapolis: Bobbs-Merrill Co., 1959.

Sutton, Ann. *Wilderness Areas of North America*. New York: Funk & Wagnalls, 1974.

Swain, Donald C. *Federal Conservation Policy, 1921-1933*. Berkeley: University of California Press, 1963.

Thoreau, Henry David. *Excursions*. Boston: Houghton, Mifflin Co., 1894.

Tilden, Freeman. *The National Parks*, rev. ed. New York: Alfred A. Knopf, 1968.

Udall, Stewart. *The Quiet Crisis*. New York: Avon, 1970.

VanHise, Charles R. *Conservation of our National Resources*. New York: Macmillan Co., 1910.

VanName, Willard G. *Vanishing Forest Reserves*. Boston: Gorham Press, 1929.

Watkins, T. H., and Watson, Charles S., Jr. *The Lands No One Knows*. San Francisco: Sierra Club Books, 1975.

Wolfe, Linnie Marsh, ed. *John of the Mountains: The Unpublished Journals of John Muir*. Boston: Houghton Mifflin Co., 1938.

———, ed. *Son of the Wilderness: The Life of John Muir*. New York: Alfred A. Knopf, 1945.

INDEX

Abourezk, James, 196-97, 202
Acadia National Park, 66
Adams, Ansel, 90, 250
Adirondacks, 26-27, 30-31
Agnew, Spiro T., 246
Agriculture: contribution of, to economy, 21, 23, 61, 63; on public lands, 106, 187
Agriculture, Department of. *See* Forest Service; National forests
Aiken, George, 188-92
Air Coordinating Committee, 89
Aircraft Owners and Pilots Association, 89
Air Transport Association, 89
Alaska, 85, 207-61; purchase of, 8, 207; State of, 211-12, 214, 218, 225, 233, 237, 246, 248, 250, 253
Alaska Center for the Environment, 224
Alaska Coalition, 221-22, 224, 230, 238, 240, 244-46, 248-50, 253, 255, 261
Alaska Conservation Society, 224
Alaska National Interest Lands Conservation Act, 116, 163, 197, 218-61, 267, 270
Alaska Native Claims Settlement Act (ANCSA), 211-18, 220, 226, 237, 251, 262 n.20
Alaska natives, 208-18, 261 n.8, 262 n.20; land claims of, 208-18, 238, 261 n.8, 262 n.20
Alaska Natives and the Land (Federal Field Committee), 212
Alaskan Federation of Natives (AFN), 209, 211-13
Alaskan Land Use Commission, 124
Alaska Wilderness Council, 220
Albright, Horace, 66, 74
Alderson, George, 188
Aleuts. *See* Alaska natives
Allott, Gordon L., 122, 124, 130, 142 n.162, 194

Almanac of American Politics, 183
Alpine Lakes Primitive Area, 152
American Academy of Political and Social Sciences, 67
American Alpine Club, 57 n.113
American Antiquities Act. *See* Antiquities Act
American Association for the Advancement of Science (AAAS), 29, 34, 69, 74
American Bar Association Journal, 208
American Civic Association, 45-46, 48-51, 57 n.113, 59 n.156, 66
American Farm Bureau Federation, 133
American Forestry, 70
American Forestry Association, 29-30, 36, 45, 56 n.113, 72, 101 n.131, 112
American Forestry Congress, 30, 34. *See also* American Forestry Association
American Legion, 78
American Mining Congress, 57 n.113, 131, 225
American National Cattlemen's Association, 57 n.113, 111, 113, 133
American Nature Association, 101 n.131
American Nature Study Society, 101 n.131
American Paper and Pulp Association, 29, 56 n.113, 142 n.149
American Petroleum Institute, 225
American Plywood Association, 163
American Pulpwood Association, 142 n.149
American Rivers Conservation Council, 224
Americans for Alaska, 249
Anderson, Clinton, 123-24, 126, 129, 139 n.92, 142 n.162, 194, 231
Anderson, John B., 238, 240-44, 248, 264 n.70
Andrus, Cecil D., 221, 233-36, 245, 249
Antiquities Act, 41, 233, 236, 244, 261, 267
Appalachian Mountain Club, 29, 41, 45, 224

National Parks and Recreation Act of 1978, 196-98, 204 n.18
National Parks Association, 66, 72, 85-86, 92, 101 n.131, 105-6, 137 n.29, 149, 221, 224
National Park Service: creation of, 48-51, 193; influence of, on Wilderness Act, 103, 106, 110-11, 117-19; rivalry with Forest Service, 65-76, 81-87, 94, 144. *See also* National monuments; National parks; Wilderness reviews
National Park Service Act, 50, 85, 146, 170, 267
National parkways, 100 n.121
National Petroleum Reserve. *See* Arctic National Wildlife Refuge
National Reclamation Association, 109-10, 133
National Recreation Areas, 97 n.48, 182-83, 194, 240
National Rifle Association (NRA), 215, 240
National Trails System, 194, 197-98
National Trails System Act, 176-78, 267
National Wild and Scenic Rivers System, 172-76, 182-83, 190, 194, 196-97, 214, 223, 230, 260, 267
National Wilderness Preservation Council, 107, 112, 116-19, 123, 138 n.55
National Wilderness Preservation System: additions to, 220, 234, 237, 246, 257-60, 263 n.39, 267, 270-71; creation of, 102-36, 170, 194; management of, 143-66, 194, 198, 202. *See also* Boundary Waters Canoe Area; Eagles Nest Wilderness Area; Eastern Wilderness Areas Act; Endangered American Wilderness Act; Federal Land Policy and Management Act; National forests; National monuments; National parks; National wildlife refuges; Primitive areas; Wilderness areas; Wilderness management; Wilderness reviews
National Wildlife Federation, 101 n.131, 105, 120, 191, 215, 224
National wildlife refuges: creation of, 40-42, 193, 214-16, 221, 223, 229-30, 249, 252, 260, 267; management of, 106-7, 110, 130, 146-51, 165-66, 186, 194, 213, 215-16
National Wool Growers Association, 29, 56 n.113
Natural Resources Council of America, 106
Natural Resources Defense Council, 224
Nature Conservancy, 101 n.131, 116, 235. *See also* Ecological Society of America
Nelson, A. Z., 113
Nelson, Gaylord, 244, 256, 264 n.85
Neuberger, Maurine, 123, 139 n.92
Neuberger, Richard, 105, 117-18, 122, 137 n.18, 138 n.58, 138 n.65
New York Board of Trade and Transportation, 30-31
New York Port Authority, 186
New York State Constitution, 31
New York State Park Commission, 30
New York Times, 30, 107, 180, 234
New York Zoological Society, 40
Neville, Philip, 200
Newlands Act, 41
Newsweek, 180
Newton, Walter H., 77-78
Niagara Falls, 26-27
Nitze, Paul H., 250
Nixon, Richard M., 162, 188, 210, 215, 219
Noble, John W., 34
Nolan, William I., 78-80
North Calaveras Grove, 25
North Cascades National Park, 196
Northern Pacific Railroad, 19, 28, 41, 184
North Slope Recreation and Transportation Corridor, 216
Northwest Mining Association, 57 n.113, 153
Northwest Territory, 7, 21

Oakes, John B., 234
Oberholtzer, Ernest C., 79, 82
Oberstar, James L., 201-2
O'Hara, Barratt, 108, 138 n.65
Oil, Chemical and Atomic Workers International Union, 224
Olmsted, Frederick Law, Jr., 49
Olmsted, Frederick Law, Sr., 25-26, 32
Olympic National Park, 82, 86-88
O'Mahoney, Joseph C., 121-22
One Third of the Nation's Land (Public Land Law Review Commission), 194
Oregon Compromise of 1846, 8
Oregon Trail, 198
Organic Act of 1884 (Alaska), 208
Organization of Petroleum Exporting Countries (OPEC), 238
Outdoor Recreation, Bureau of, 149, 177

Outdoor Recreation Resources Review
  Commission: creation of, 138 n.63; report
  of, 3, 118, 125-26, 129
Outward Bound, 145

Pacific Crest Trail, 176-78
Pacific Logging Congress, 57 n.113
Pacific Northwest Power Company, 182
Pacific Railway Act of 1862, 18-20, 62
Pacific Southwest Water Plan, 178, 180-81,
  204 n.23
Paine, Thomas, 80
Panic of 1837, 11
Pardee, George, 39
Patrons of Husbandry, 20
*Pedestrious Tour of Four Thousand Miles
  Through the Western States and Ter-
  ritories, A* (Estwick Evans), 13
Pelican Island National Wildlife Refuge, 40
Penfold, Joe, 189-90
Pentagon Papers, 246
Peterson, Russel W., 250
Pettigrew, Richard F., 35-36
Pfost, Gracie, 126-27, 134
Pickett Act, 40, 234
Pinchot, Gifford, 35-39, 45, 47, 49, 51,
  58 n.147, 66-67, 69, 115, 143
Pittinger, William A., 79
Platt National Park, 41
Pomeroy, Kenneth B., 112
Pool, Joe, 142 n.161
Pooler, Frank, 70
Population: of Alaska, 208; of United
  States, 23, 60-61, 110, 202
Potomac Heritage Trail, 177
Preemption, 9-11, 16 n.23, 22, 52 n.5
Preemption Act of 1841, 11, 16 n.23, 20,
  23, 34
*Preserving Wilderness in Our National
  Parks* (National Parks Association), 149
Primitive areas: in national forests, 74-76,
  79, 81-85, 87-88, 100 n.99, 107-8, 124,
  130, 132-33, 135, 140 n.114, 144, 151-55,
  162, 165-66, 172, 187, 227, 267, 271; in
  national parks, 149. *See also* L-20
  Regulation
Proxmire, William, 138 n.65, 139 n.92,
  264 n.85
Public domain: acquisition of, 7-9, 193;
  disposal of, 41, 271; management of, 7-8,
  22, 42, 124, 184, 193-95. *See also* Federal

Land Policy and Management Act; Land
  grants, federal
Public Land Law Review Commission
  (PLLRC), 133, 194, 263 n.61
Public Works Administration, 81
Purity policy, 145-46, 157-62, 187-92

Quebec Act of 1774, 7
Quetico Provincial Park, 198
Quetico-Superior Committee, 79-80, 89
Quetico-Superior Council, 79-80

Railroad industry, 19, 21, 23-24, 28, 31, 41,
  45, 61-62, 66, 184
Rainy Lake, 77, 98 n.61
Raker, John E., 47
Randolph, Jennings, 138 n.65, 139 n.92,
  252, 264 n.85
Raymond, I. W., 25-26, 28
Reagan, Ronald, 272, 274
REAL Alaska Coalition, 225, 237
Reclamation, Bureau of, 90-93, 178
Recreaton Resources of Federal Lands
  (National Conference on Outdoor
  Recreation), 73
Redwood National Park, 59 n.160, 186, 196
Reed, James A., 47-48, 222
Research reserves, 74
Reuss, Henry F., 107-8, 138 n.65
Right-of-Way Act of 1901, 44-45
Rio Grande River, 86
River of No Return Wilderness Area, 153-
  54, 270
Roadless Area Review and Evaluation:
  RARE I, 160-62, 188, 192; RARE II,
  161-64, 166, 260, 267
Roadless areas. *See* Boundary Waters
  Canoe Area; Primitive areas; Roadless
  Area Review and Evaluation; Wilderness
  areas
Robinson, Glen O., 145
Rockefeller, Laurence, 250
Rocky Mountain Club, 29
Rocky Mountain National Park, 66, 85
Romanticism, 13, 50
Roncalino, Teno, 197
Roosevelt, Eleanor, 121
Roosevelt, Franklin D., 79, 87, 91
Roosevelt, Theodore (Teddy), 39-41, 43,
  45, 58 n.141, 70, 86, 234